David Dilks was for more than 2(
History at the University of Leeds,
University of Hull. He previously w
Anthony Eden, Mr Harold Macmillar
associated with Churchill, and served ᴀꜱ ᴘresident of the International
Committee for the History of the Second World War from 1992 to
2000. He is the author of *Curzon in India*, *Neville Chamberlain* and *"The
Great Dominion": Winston Churchill in Canada 1900–1954*, and editor of
The Diaries of Sir Alexander Cadogan.

CHURCHILL

— AND —

COMPANY

ALLIES AND RIVALS

IN WAR AND PEACE

DAVID DILKS

I.B. TAURIS

LONDON · NEW YORK

New paperback edition published in 2015 by I.B. Tauris & Co. Ltd
www.ibtauris.com

Distributed worldwide by I.B. Tauris & Co Ltd
Registered office: 6 Salem Road, London W2 4BU

First published in hardback in 2012 by I.B. Tauris & Co. Ltd

Jacket image: Sir Winston Churchill, attending Bermuda Conference, 1953 (Photo by Leonard Mccombe/Time Life Pictures/Getty Images).

ISBN: 978 1 78076 967 7
eISBN: 978 0 85773 287 3

A full CIP record for this book is available from the British Library
A full CIP record is available from the Library of Congress

Library of Congress Catalog Card Number: available

Printed and bound by Page Bros, Norwich

Contents

Preface

On the evening of Friday, 23 February 1945, the Prime Minister listened in the Great Hall at Chequers as *The Mikado* was played on the gramophone. The sounds revived in his mind memories of the Victorian era, 'eighty years which will rank in our island history with the Antonine age'. Half a century earlier, in the glaring noonday of Bangalore, Lieutenant Churchill had devoured volume after volume of Gibbon's *Decline and Fall of the Roman Empire.* There he had read 'The reign of Antoninus is marked by the rare advantage of furnishing very few materials for history; which is indeed little more than the register of the crimes, follies, and misfortunes of mankind.' While Churchill's own times furnish by contrast such abundant material that it overbears our capacity to assimilate, they were certainly not wanting in crimes, follies and misfortunes. No one reflecting on the history of the twentieth century can doubt or escape the significance of despots and their dogmas or the murderous consequences of regimes made possible by the march of applied science. From Stalin to Hitler, Mao to Pol Pot, the tyrants bestride the pages.

This is a book about one of the heroes of the century, who worked within a political system and set of assumptions far removed from those of the dictators. Writing of Churchill with admiration, I have also tried to apply the critical scrutiny which he would have expected. My purpose has been to place him side by side with others, and where the context suggests it to put what he said and thought alongside their opinions and reactions. Both angles of view are indispensable if we are to form a faithful picture. None understood the perils of such an enterprise more acutely than the Chief of the Imperial General Staff, Alan Brooke. 'I wonder whether any historian of the future will ever be able to paint Winston in his true colours' he wrote in 1943 after days of high tension. 'It is a wonderful character – the most marvellous qualities and superhuman genius mixed with an astonishing lack of vision at times, and an impetuosity which if not guided must inevitably bring him into trouble time and again. ... He is quite the most difficult man to work with that I have ever struck, but I should not have missed the chance of working with him for anything on earth!'

The first section of this book attempts to portray the essence of Churchill's character and springs of action, and his many-sidedness as artist, writer, politician and colleague. How I wish I could advance a grander claim, to unveil an unknown Churchill! As to the main facts, however, we now know most of what can be learned, for he wrote more amply about himself than any other Prime Minister has done and is the subject of innumerable studies. I hope that readers will nonetheless find here some fresh perspectives. Most of the chapters which follow spring from unpublished papers given at conferences, or in three instances from lectures which after some hesitation I decided not to recast, despite the change of style between the sobriety of the written word and the flourishes of the spoken. It is perhaps a measure of the sustained interest in Churchill all over the world that one of these pieces was offered as a tribute to a colleague in Poland; one originated as an address given in France and another as a speech delivered in Toronto to a Society which commemorates Sir Winston's example; and Chapter 2 was composed in its first form for a conference consisting largely of visitors from the Commonwealth.

Though the essays are designed to be free-standing, all are intended to illuminate Churchill's activities among friends and enemies. Sometimes those categories are not easily separated; for a long while, Churchill thought of Stalin as a friend or at least a comrade-in-arms, and only with extreme reluctance did he come to look upon the new Czar of all the Russias as an enemy. He regarded Roosevelt with admiration and gratitude, whereas the balance of the evidence suggests that the President felt less warmly towards him, especially from 1943. Some of the chapters show Churchill as the dominant force in a variety of situations; others, like the one entitled 'Epic and Tragedy', reveal him and the War Cabinet in the grip of issues which they could influence only in a limited degree. The second chapter was written because outside the realm of the experts, the scale of the Commonwealth's exertions during World War II is too seldom appreciated. It reflects poorly upon us in this country that it should be so. The last chapter, unlike the others, does not delineate a particular crisis or chain of events. Its purpose is to draw attention to the influence of 'history' on statesmen and others, not least because no public man of the last century – with the possible exception of General de Gaulle – has combined on Churchill's scale, or with his effectiveness, the writing and the making of history. The unceasing references during our present economic troubles to the 'lessons of the 1930s' may perhaps give some point to such reflections. Never in the field of human argument can the name of a single thinker have been prayed in aid by so many politicians and commentators, or advanced in support of so many propositions quite incompatible. Keynes' own remark that practical men of affairs are often the slaves of some defunct economist has not lost its piquancy now that the defunct economist is Keynes himself.

Every part of the book illustrates the constant problems and occasional opportunities of working within severe constraints, the inevitable fate of this country in the middle of the twentieth century. As Churchill used to remark, the only thing worse than waging war with allies is to wage war without them. In that context his prolonged study of his ancestor the Duke of Marlborough paid a dividend which no one could have foreseen when he embarked on the enterprise in 1929.

France looms large, as in any study of Churchill it should. He loved the place for its history and associations, and could scarcely conceive of a Europe without the French army and French values. That said, the official France with which the British government had to deal between 1940 and 1945 was a different proposition from the France which Churchill cherished. 'I know there are many Frenchmen who do not like Great Britain', he said with some sadness. 'They have a perfect right to their opinion. Mais ce ne sont pas les Français que je recherche.' In old age, he did not feel called upon to deny with vigour the story that he had once described de Gaulle as resembling a female llama surprised in her bath. When every allowance is made, it remains a staggering fact that on the very morrow of victory, and victory by a hair's-breadth at that, the two countries could have come almost to the point of war in May 1945.

It was the month in which Churchill had asked the Chiefs of Staff to examine in deep secrecy the possibility of containing Russia by military force; a contingency described as 'unthinkable', but one which had become at least a possibility. That matters should have reached such a pass tells its own melancholy story. No such proposition could be contemplated without the active support of the United States, and relations with that country mattered more to Churchill than any other factor in the military and political conduct of the war. Until 1943 or even 1944, the weight of Britain's and the Commonwealth's contribution in all the main theatres had enabled the government in London to speak with a voice disproportionate to population, output of arms or financial resources. On Churchill's own admission, it was not until late in the war that he realized fully what a small country Britain is. This remark reveals a good deal about him.

Here, then, is Churchill in company: with Roosevelt and Stalin; Smuts, Menzies, Curtin, Mackenzie King, Fraser; de Gaulle and Bidault; Chamberlain, Eden, Attlee, Duff Cooper, Selborne, Amery; Mikolajczyk and Sikorski; Eisenhower, the Chiefs of Staff, Ismay, devoted Private Secretaries; and at long distance and in the twilight of his career, the unknown Russian leaders Malenkov and Khrushchev, with Molotov representing the old guard in a new guise. A few of that company may have disliked Churchill in his domineering or bullying moods; rather more believed his views outmoded; but all, or almost all, regarded him with awe.

I trust that the occasional use of 'WSC' as an alternative to 'Churchill' or 'the Prime Minister' will be tolerated, and that the Bibliography will provide some useful guidance to the vast literature now surrounding him.

Let me thank the kind friends who have given me advice, particularly Dr Peter Bell and Professors Simon Green, Roger Louis, George Peden, Sir Ian Kershaw and Nicholas Pronay. Like many another author, I owe a great deal to my wife's support and patience. The research and criticisms of our son Richard and the secretarial skills of Mrs Deborah Baboolal and Mrs Lorraine Trickett have proved invaluable. I am especially grateful to Dr Liz Evans for her aid over many years. Dr Lester Crook, Joanna Godfrey and others at I.B.Tauris have helped much. Not for the first time, I am indebted to Bruce Hunter and his colleagues at David Higham Associates.

David Dilks
Leeds, 1 January 2012

List of Illustrations

Colour images – four oil paintings by Winston Churchill

1   Marrakech, 1943

2   The Loup River, Alpes Maritimes, 1936

3   A landscape in Provence, c. 1947

4   Sailing boat in harbour at Antibes, 1930s

all © Churchill Heritage

Black and white images – personalities

5   Anthony Eden by Stoneman Walter, 1942.
© Imperial War Museums (HU 49409)

6   Winston Churchill and General Charles de Gaulle, 1944.
© Imperial War Museums (HU 60057)

7   General Dwight D. Eisenhower, Supreme Allied Commander, 1945.

8   Josef V. Stalin, 1945. Library of Congress Prints and Photographs
Division

9   Duff Cooper, later 1st Viscount Norwich, 1940.
© National Portrait Gallery

10 Stanislav Mikolajczyk standing in front of the Polish national
emblem, 1948. Photo by Nat Farbman/Time Life Pictures/
Getty Images

11 W.L. Mackenzie King, Prime Minister of Canada, 1942.

12 Jan Christian Smuts, 1934.

List of Abbreviations

C.-in-C.	Commander-in-Chief
CIGS	Chief of the Imperial General Staff
C.o.S.	Chiefs of Staff
EAC	European Advisory Commission
EDC	European Defence Community
FO	Foreign Office
HMG	His (or Her) Majesty's Government
M.P.	Member of Parliament
MP	Polish Section of SOE
NATO	North Atlantic Treaty Organisation
OC	Officer Commanding
SOE	Special Operations Executive
S. of S.	Secretary of State
UK	United Kingdom
UNO	United Nations Organisation
USA	United States of America
USSR	Union of Soviet Socialist Republics
WSC	Mr (later Sir) Winston Churchill

Codenames of Military Operations

Barbarossa	German attack on Russia, 1941
Husky	Allied assault on Sicily, 1943
Overlord	Allied invasion of Western Europe, 1944

List of Principal Characters

ALEXANDER   General Sir Harold, 1st Earl Alexander: C.-in-C., Middle East, 1942–3; Field-Marshal, 1944; Supreme Allied Commander, Mediterranean, 1944–5; Governor-General of Canada, 1946–52; Minister of Defence, 1952–4.

AMERY   Leopold: First Lord of the Admiralty, 1922–4; S. of S. for the Colonies, 1924–9, and for the Dominions, 1925–9; S. of S. for India and Burma, 1940–5.

ATTLEE   Clement, 1st Earl Attlee: Chancellor of the Duchy of Lancaster, 1930–1; Lord Privy Seal, 1940–2; Deputy Prime Minister, 1942–5; S. of S. for the Dominions, 1942–3; Lord President of the Council, 1943–5; Prime Minister, 1945–51.

AUCHINLECK   General Sir Claude: C.-in-C., Middle East, 1941–2; C.-in-C., India, 1943–7; Field-Marshal, 1946.

BALDWIN   Stanley, 1st Earl Baldwin: Chancellor of the Exchequer, 1922–3; Prime Minister, 1923–4, 1924–9; Lord President of the Council, 1931–5; Prime Minister, 1935–7.

BEAVERBROOK   Maxwell Aitken, 1st Baron Beaverbrook: newspaper proprietor; Minister for Aircraft Production, 1940–1; Minister of State, 1941; Minister of Supply, 1941–2; Lord Privy Seal, 1943–5.

BIDAULT   Georges: French statesman; Minister for Foreign Affairs 1944–5, 1947, 1953–4; Prime Minister, 1946, 1949–50, 1958.

BOR-KOMOROWSKI General Tadeusz: Polish soldier who led the uprising in Warsaw, 1944.

BROOKE General Sir Alan, 1st Viscount Alanbrooke: C.-in-C., Home Forces; CIGS, 1941–6; Chairman, Chiefs of Staff Committee, 1942–6; Field-Marshal, 1944.

CADOGAN Sir Alexander: British diplomat; Permanent Under-Secretary of the Foreign Office 1938–46; Permanent Representative at UNO, 1946–50.

CHAMBERLAIN Neville: Chancellor of the Exchequer, 1923; Minister of Health, 1924–9; Chancellor of the Exchequer, 1931–7; Prime Minister, 1937–40; Lord President of the Council, 1940.

CHERWELL Frederick Lindemann, 1st Viscount Cherwell: Churchill's scientific adviser from 1940; Paymaster-General, 1942–5 and 1951–3.

CHURCHILL Lady Randolph, née Jennie Jerome: daughter of Leonard Jerome of New York; mother of Winston (born 1874) and Jack Churchill (born 1880).

CHURCHILL Lord Randolph: younger son of the 7th Duke of Marlborough; father of Winston and Jack Churchill; S. of S. for India, 1885–6; Chancellor of the Exchequer, 1886.

CHURCHILL Winston Leonard Spencer: M.P., with short intervals, 1900–64; President of the Board of Trade, 1908–10; Home Secretary, 1910–11; First Lord of the Admiralty, 1911–15; Chancellor of the Duchy of Lancaster, 1915; Minister of Munitions, 1917–18; S. of S. for War and Air, 1918–21; S. of S. for the Colonies, 1921–2; Chancellor of the Exchequer, 1924–9; First Lord of the Admiralty, 1939–40; Prime Minister and Minister of Defence, 1940–5; Prime Minister, 1951–5, and Minister of Defence, 1951–2; Knight of the Garter, 1953; Nobel Prize for Literature, 1953.

List of Principal Characters

CHURCHILL   Mrs Winston, née Clementine Ogilvy Hozier, later
Baroness Spencer-Churchill: married Winston
Churchill, 1908; four children (3 daughters and 1
son, another daughter dying in infancy); Chairman,
Red Cross Aid to Russia Fund, 1941–6.

CLARK KERR   Sir Archibald, 1st Baron Inverchapel: British
Ambassador to China 1938–42; to Russia, 1942–6; to
the USA, 1946–8.

CLEMENCEAU   Georges: Prime Minister of France, 1906–9,
1917–20.

COLVILLE   J.R. ('Jock'), later Sir John: British diplomat;
Assistant Private Secretary to three Prime Ministers
(Chamberlain, Churchill, Attlee), 1939–41, 1943–5;
Private Secretary to Princess Elizabeth, 1947–9; Joint
Principal Private Secretary to Churchill, 1951–5.

COOPER   Duff, 1st Viscount Norwich: First Lord of the
Admiralty, 1937–8; Minister of Information, 1940–1;
Minister of State in the Far East, 1941–2; British
representative with the French Committee of
National Liberation, 1943–4; Ambassador to France,
1944–7.

CRANBORNE   Lord, later 5th Marquess of Salisbury: S. of S. for the
Dominions, 1940–2, 1943–5; Lord Privy Seal,
1942–3; Leader of the House of Lords, 1942–5,
1951–7.

CRIPPS   Sir Stafford: British Ambassador in Moscow,
1940–2; Lord Privy Seal and Leader of the House
of Commons, 1942; Minister of Aircraft Production,
1942–5; President of the Board of Trade, 1945–7;
Chancellor of the Exchequer, 1947–50.

CURTIN   John: Prime Minister of Australia, 1941–5 and
Minister of Defence, 1942–5.

de GAULLE   General Charles: leader of Free French forces
from 1940; President of the French Committee
of National Liberation, 1943–4; President of the

	Provisional Government of the French Republic, 1944–6; President of the Fifth Republic, 1958–69.
DILL	General Sir John, later Field-Marshal: Commander 1 Corps in France, 1939–40; Vice CIGS, April, 1940; CIGS, May 1940 to December 1941; Head of the British Service Mission at Washington, 1941–4.
EDEN	Anthony, 1st Earl of Avon: Foreign Secretary, 1935–8; S. of S. for the Dominions, 1939–40; S. of S. for War, 1940; Foreign Secretary, 1940–5; Leader of the House of Commons, 1942–5; Foreign Secretary, 1951–5; Prime Minister, 1955–7.
EISENHOWER	General Dwight D.: C.-in-C., Allied Forces, North Africa, 1942–4; Supreme Commander, Allied Expeditionary Force, Western Europe, 1944–5; Chief of Staff, US Army, 1945–8; Supreme Commander, NATO Forces Europe, 1950–2; President of the USA, 1953–61.
EVATT	Dr Herbert: Australian Minister of External Affairs, 1941–9; represented Australia at the War Cabinet in London, 1942, 1943.
FOCH	General Ferdinand: commanded Army Groups of the North during the battles of the Somme, 1916; in command of the Allied armies from March 1918; Marshal of France, August 1918.
FRASER	Peter: born in Scotland; Prime Minister of New Zealand, 1940–9.
GUBBINS	General Sir Colin: head of the British military mission to Poland, 1939, and of the military mission to Czech and Polish forces under French command, 1939–40; seconded to SOE, 1940; executive head of SOE (CD), 1943–6.
HALIFAX	Viscount, later 1st Earl: Viceroy of India, 1926–31; Lord Privy Seal, 1935–7; Lord President of the Council, 1937–8; Foreign Secretary, 1938–40; Ambassador in Washington, 1941–6.

HITLER

Adolf: founder of the National Socialist Party; Chancellor of the German Reich, 1933–45, and head of state from 1934; C.-in-C., German fighting forces from 1942; committed suicide, 1945.

ISMAY

General Sir Hastings ('Pug'), later 1st Baron Ismay: Deputy Secretary of the Committee of Imperial Defence, 1936–8, and Secretary, 1938–40; Deputy Secretary (Military) to the War Cabinet, Chief Staff Officer to Churchill as Minister of Defence, and a member of the C.o.S. Committee, 1940–5; S. of S. for Commonwealth Relations, 1951–2; Secretary-General of NATO, 1952–7.

KEYNES

John Maynard, 1st Baron Keynes: economist and public servant; author of *A Treatise on Money* (1930) and *General Theory of Employment, Interest and Money* (1936); served at the Treasury in both wars; the leading British delegate at the Bretton Woods Conference, 1944 and in the negotiations for an American loan to the UK, 1945–6.

KING

W.L. Mackenzie: leader of the Liberal party in Canada, 1919–48; Prime Minister (and S. of S. for External Affairs until 1946), 1921–6, 1926–30, 1935–48.

KHRUSHCHEV

Nikita: Russian politician; a member of the Politburo and the Praesidium of the Supreme Soviet; First Secretary of the Central Committee of the Communist Party of the USSR, September 1953; thereafter increasingly powerful; denounced Stalinism and 'the cult of personality', 1956; deposed 1964.

LINDEMANN

See Cherwell.

LLOYD GEORGE

David, 1st Earl Lloyd George: President of the Board of Trade, 1905–8; Chancellor of the Exchequer, 1908–15; Minister of Munitions, 1915–16; S. of S. for War, 1916; Prime Minister, 1916–22.

MACDONALD   Malcolm: S. of S. for the Dominions, 1935–8, 1938–9, and for the Colonies, 1938–40; High Commissioner in Canada, 1941–6.

MAISKY   Ivan M.: Russian Ambassador in London, 1932–43; Assistant People's Commissar for Foreign Affairs, 1943–6.

MALENKOV   Georgi: Russian politician; Deputy Prime Minister from 1946; for a time party leader after Stalin's death in March 1953; forced to resign as Prime Minister, February 1955; eventually despatched to Kazakhstan to manage a hydro-electric plant.

MENZIES   Robert, later Sir Robert: Prime Minister of Australia, 1939–41, 1949–66; succeeded WSC as Lord Warden of the Cinque Ports, 1965.

MIKOLAJCZYK   Stanislav: Vice-Chairman, Polish National Council, 1939–41; Deputy Prime Minister and Minister of the Interior (in the Polish government in exile) 1941–3; Prime Minister, 1943–4; Deputy Prime Minister (in Warsaw) 1945–7; afterwards lived in exile in the USA.

MOLOTOV   Vyacheslav: Russian politician; Commissar for Foreign Affairs, 1939–49, 1953–6; Ambassador to Outer Mongolia, 1957–60.

MONTGOMERY   General Sir Bernard, 1st Viscount Montgomery: in command of the 8th Army, August 1942; commander of 21st Army Group from 1943, and all Allied forces in the first phase of Operation Overlord, 1944; Field-Marshal, 1944; C.-in-C., British Forces of Occupation in Germany, 1945; CIGS, 1946–8.

MORAN   Charles Wilson, 1st Baron Moran: Royal Army Medical Corps from 1914 (Military Cross); Dean, St Mary's Hospital Medical School, 1920–45; Churchill's personal physician, 1940–65.

MOUNTBATTEN	Lord Louis, 1st Earl Mountbatten: Chief of Combined Operations, 1942–3; Supreme Allied Commander, South East Asia, 1943–6; Viceroy of India, 1947; First Sea Lord, 1955–9; Chief of the Defence Staff, 1959–65.
MUSSOLINI	Benito: President, Italian Council of Ministers; head of the government and Prime Minister, 1926–43; deposed, 1943; executed by partisans, 1945.
PEARSON	Lester B.: Canadian diplomat and politician; Ambassador to the USA, 1945–6; Under-Secretary, 1946–8, and S. of S., 1948–57, for External Affairs; Prime Minister, 1963–8.
PORTAL	Charles, 1st Viscount Portal: Marshal of the Royal Air Force; C.-in-C., Bomber Command, 1940; Chief of the Air Staff, 1940–6.
ROOSEVELT	Franklin Delano: Assistant Secretary of the Navy, 1913–20; Governor of the State of New York, 1929–33; President of the USA, 1933–45.
SELBORNE	3rd Earl of: Minister of Economic Warfare (with responsibility for SOE), 1942–5.
SMUTS	General Jan, later Field-Marshal: member of the Imperial War Cabinet in London, 1917–18; Prime Minister of South Africa, 1919–24; Minister of Justice, 1933–9; Prime Minister and Minister of External Affairs and Defence, 1939–48.
SPEARS	Sir Louis: British soldier and diplomat; WSC's personal representative with French government, 1940, and later with General de Gaulle; head of the British mission to Syria and Lebanon, 1942–4.
ST LAURENT	Louis: Canadian politician; S. of S. for External Affairs, 1946–8; Prime Minister, 1948–57.
STALIN	Josef V.: General Secretary, Central Committee of Communist Party of Soviet Union, 1922–53; Marshal of the Soviet Union, 1943; Generalissimo, 1945.

VYSHINSKI   Andrei: Russian State Prosecutor during the trials
              and purges of the 1930s; Vice-Commissar for Foreign
              Affairs, 1940–9; Foreign Minister, 1949–53; leader of
              the Soviet delegation to UNO, 1945–9, 1953–4.

WAVELL   General Sir Archibald, later Field-Marshal: C.-in-C.,
              Middle East, 1939–41; C.-in-C., S.W. Pacific,
              1941–3; Viceroy of India, 1943–7.

1

Churchill Up and Churchill Down

Politics and the Art of the Impossible

There are two Churchills: Churchill Up and Churchill Down.

(Lord Beaverbrook)

… not in the least like anyone that you or I have ever met.

(General Ismay)

In 1915, immediately after he had been forced to leave the Admiralty, Winston Churchill discovered painting; or as he looked upon the event, the Muse of Painting came to his rescue out of charity and chivalry. Still a member of the Cabinet, he found himself powerless to influence the course of events in the Near East. He had conceived of the operation at the Dardanelles as a means of bringing help to Russia, of outflanking the enemy; the campaign was to provide an alternative to the prospect of the troops' chewing barbed wire in France, as he put it to the Prime Minister, Asquith. Into this enterprise he had poured all his persuasive power, imagination, energy of mind and body. Thirsting for action, ardent for fame, impatient of difficulties, he had overborne many an objection and critic. Characteristically, for he was neither by nature a good listener nor always sensitive to the thoughts of those around him, he had failed to comprehend the developing fissure in his relations with the First Sea Lord, Admiral Fisher.

When Asquith decided the national situation was so serious that a coalition government must be formed, the Conservative leaders insisted upon Churchill's ejection from the Admiralty. They could point to the disasters of the campaign with which he above all other ministers was identified. Some of them detested him for apostasy. After all, he had entered Parliament as a Conservative, had transferred his allegiance to the Opposition and had soon been rewarded by office. He had attacked former Conservative colleagues with vehemence, ridiculed many of their policies, assailed their beliefs. It is unlikely that he ever realized how deeply these strokes had cut. What seemed to him, with his effervescence of spirit and fertility of language, a normal part of the rancour and asperity of politics caused profound offence to people differently brought up, more conventionally minded, less careless of others' reactions. Indeed, this same habit of almost brutal altercation occasioned the letter of 1942 from which the words at the head of this chapter are taken. Few knew the Prime Minister more intimately than General Ismay, who found his master a mass of contradictions, a child of nature:

> and he apparently sees no difference between harsh words spoken to a friend, and forgotten within the hour under the influence of friendly argument, and the same harsh words telegraphed to a friend thousands of miles away – with no opportunity for 'making it up' … I think I can lay claim to having been called every name under the sun during the last six months – except perhaps a coward; but I know perfectly well in the midst of these storms that they mean exactly nothing, and that before the sun goes down, I shall be summoned to an intimate and delightfully friendly talk – to 'make it up.'[1]

In that summer of 1915, Churchill had found himself condemned to remain a spectator, placed cruelly in the front seat, watching what seemed to him the casting away of great opportunities and the feeble execution of plans in which he heartily believed. The change left him gasping. 'Like a sea-beast fished up from the depths, or a diver too suddenly hoisted, my veins threatened to burst from the fall in pressure.'[2] Small wonder that he had been able to make a handsome living from pen and tongue; no other British Prime Minister of the twentieth century would have coined such phrases, and none possessed in like degree the capacity to ambush the unanticipated word.

Churchill did not boast about his painting. On the contrary, he would say 'I never had any lessons, you know.' Until 1915, he had not even visited a picture gallery. His friends and family noticed with wonder that while at the easel he remained silent. Unremitting in concentration, strict in the division of his time, accustomed to live by self-expression rather than self-denial, Churchill was always anxious to press into the day more than it could conveniently contain, and thus habitually unpunctual. The habit of taking a sleep in the afternoon and then working into the early hours enabled a good deal of his activity. It was remarked of Mr Gladstone, and would be equally well said of Churchill, that if the energy of an ordinary man equals one hundred, and that of an exceptional man two hundred, his was equal to at least a thousand.

His happy marriage and discovery of painting as a pastime – so says the one best placed to know[3] – did much to dispel Churchill's phases of despondency. Many of those who have written about him in recent times believe that he regularly showed the characteristics of a manic-depressive, and was oppressed by the 'black dog' to which he sometimes referred. This was certainly not the impression which Churchill normally created in his prime. On the contrary, those who saw him at close quarters during the most dire phases of both world wars found him buoyant, inspiring and high-spirited.

Churchill was an artist by instinct and practice. In his writings, speeches, private conversation, handling of meetings, reshaping of the house and gardens at Chartwell, he built up effects, mingled the homely and the grand, alternately bullied, cajoled and charmed. Painting provided another outlet for these instincts. 'One sees everything with a different eye; the shadow cast by a lampshade; by the telegraph posts on the road; all the things I have never noticed before I took up painting.'[4]

Even in his ardent youth as a soldier and war correspondent, Churchill's driving ambition was to enter Parliament and the world of high politics, across which his father had passed like some meteorite, burning brightly but briefly. As against a politician, a painter starts with one supreme advantage. Confronting a blank canvas, he is free to blend colours and create shapes as he pleases, limited only by imagination and technique. By contrast, the man of affairs must contend here with a lack of resources, there with colleagues whose opinions do not accord with his, and always with what another British Prime Minister termed 'the opposition of events'. Politics has often been described as the art of the possible, the management of the forces at play by opportune concession or a well-timed retreat on one front in order to secure an advance on another. That was altogether too tame a conception for Churchill's taste. Rather, he sought to make possible what other people had deemed impossible. Not infrequently, such enterprises went awry.

In November 1947, with the second war over, the Labour Party in power, the subcontinent of India just partitioned amidst carnage, Churchill was painting alone in his studio at Chartwell. Though he normally favoured landscapes, he decided to copy a portrait of his father. At this task he worked with intense absorption for perhaps an hour and a half, his mind 'freed from all other thoughts except the impressions of that loved and honoured face'. Suddenly he felt an odd sensation. He turned. An apparition had materialized, as vivid as the ghost of Hamlet's father on the battlements at Elsinore; for there, sitting in an armchair, was Lord Randolph Churchill, small and slim, twinkling of eye. His son was perhaps the most famous man in the world. They began to converse and a most revealing exchange it proved. At an early moment, when Winston Churchill said of painting 'I only do it for amusement', his father riposted with frankness 'Yes, I am sure you could never earn your living that way.' They talked of the monarchy, which the son described as being stronger than in the days of Queen Victoria; of racing; of Disraeli; and then, when Winston quoted from one of his father's speeches 'What a memory you have got! But you always had one. I remember Dr. Welldon telling me how you recited the twelve hundred lines of Macaulay without a single mistake.'

Informed that Britain had a Socialist government with a very large majority, Lord Randolph exclaimed 'Socialist! But I thought you said we still have a monarchy.' The son replied, no doubt with satisfaction, that the old republicanism of the later nineteenth century was as dead as mutton; the Labour men even attended parties at Buckingham Palace. 'Those who have very extreme principles wear sweaters.' Winston explained to his Papa that the Socialist ministers had nationalized the mines and railways and a few other services, paying full compensation, and described them as being, though stupid, quite respectable and increasingly bourgeois, not nearly so fierce as the old radicals, though of course wedded to economic fallacies.

Informed that the women now had votes, Lord Randolph remarked 'Good gracious!' 'It did not turn out as badly as I thought', the son conceded. Asked 'How do you get your living?' he replied 'I write books and articles for the press.' He might have added 'Papa, I must tell you that I have held your old office as Chancellor of the Exchequer; I have been Home Secretary and First Lord of the Admiralty; for more than five years I was Prime Minister; and now I am engaged upon a history of the war.' Deprived of this information, Lord Randolph merely rejoined 'Ah, a reporter. There is nothing discreditable in that.' A little while later, his son chanced to mention a government department which had been formed in the war. At this the father sat up with a startled air. 'War, do you say? Has there been a war?' He received the rejoinder 'We have had nothing else but wars since democracy took charge.' 'I was not going to talk politics with a boy like you ever', said Lord Randolph in severe style. 'Bottom of the school! Never passed any examinations, except into the Cavalry! ... You were very fond of playing soldiers, so I settled for the Army. I hope you had a successful military career.' 'I was a Major in the Yeomanry.' The figure in the armchair seemed unimpressed.

WSC's record of this encounter, which he entitled 'The Dream', possesses an abiding interest. When he says in respect of 1945 'All our enemies were beaten down. We even made them surrender unconditionally', his father retorts 'No one should be made to do that. Great people forget sufferings, but not humiliations'; and no counter-argument comes. When the father asks 'And India, is that all right? And Burma?' his son replies mournfully 'Alas! They have gone down the drain.' To Lord Randolph's question 'Is there still a Tsar?' Winston rejoins 'Yes, but he is not a Romanoff. It's another family. He is much more powerful, and much more despotic.'

Only at the end of this colloquy did the dapper figure learn with stupefaction not only that each of the two world wars had cost tens of millions of lives but that an even worse conflict might be looming, what the son described as a war of East against West, of liberal civilization against the Mongol hordes. At last Lord Randolph said 'As I listened to you unfolding these fearful facts you seemed to know a great deal about them. I never expected that you would develop so far and so fully. Of course you are too old now to think about such things, but when I hear you talk I really wonder you didn't go into politics. You might have done a lot to help. You might even have made a name for yourself.' He gave a benignant smile, struck a match to light his cigarette, and vanished.[5]

* * * * *

General de Gaulle tells us that he absorbed from his thoughtful and cultured father 'une certaine idée de la France'.[6] Winston Churchill, at least by the standards of later generations, had enjoyed only intermittent contact with his father and mother. He owed much to his faithful nurse Mrs Everest, a debt which he acknowledged handsomely at the time and ever afterwards. Rebellious and sometimes even mutinous by nature, intractable, hating much of his schooldays – a period which in later life he would call 'penal servitude' – he retained an admirable fealty to his parents. Moments of close contact with them, which seemed to a boy few and far between, were cherished and long remembered. Lord Randolph questioned him about the reign of King Charles I. What did Winston know about the Grand Remonstrance? 'I said that in the end the Parliament beat the King and cut his head off. This seemed to me the grandest remonstrance imaginable.' So spry a reply might have satisfied, we may think, even a demanding parent. However, it merely evoked censure: 'Here is a grave parliamentary question affecting the whole structure of our constitutional history, lying near the centre of the task you have been set, and you do not in the slightest degree appreciate the issues involved.'[7]

Lord Randolph too had an elephantine memory; in the son's case let us call it a Napoleonic memory, given his lifelong admiration for the Emperor. The father, a shrewd judge pointed out, had attained a high fame by his proficiency in the combined arts of parliamentary and democratic eloquence, attacking with equal facility and ferocity the Liberals and later the Conservatives. His manner and speeches alike alternated between extreme insolence and sweet reasonableness. Like Disraeli, he oscillated between the roles of adventurer and statesman:

> The fluidity of his principles and his love for bold experiments and dramatic conceptions might have landed him ultimately in any camp, or in none. But that his oratorical gifts … might have grown into a weapon of enormous efficacy and power in the State is no extravagant hypothesis.

Much of this might have been said with equal justice about the son. The same observer remarked that Winston Churchill was even then, in 1913, one of the few prominent speakers in the House of Commons who still cultivated the literary style. There he excelled in a form of speech in which structure, diction and form had been pressed into the service of an artistic whole. On the public platform he adopted a double style, for the exigencies of modern democracy seemed to require from its favourites a twofold gift, at one time the utterance of the statesman and at another the patter of the music-hall artist.[8]

Asked in 1929 the question 'Do you not think a great pen might do a greater life work than an eloquent voice and a political genius?' WSC pondered before answering,

> Perhaps what you say is true – though I'm not prepared to admit that I have either the one faculty or the other in any high degree. If I were to pronounce one way or the other I'd say I was much more at home with a pen than on the platform. To speak in public takes a great deal out of me. I never excelled as a platform speaker.[9]

In old age, musing a few days after a severe stroke in the summer of 1953, he reflected modestly,

> I am not an orator. An orator is spontaneous. The written word – ah, that's different. ... It was my ambition, all my life, to be master of the spoken word. That was my only ambition. Of course you learn a lot when you have spoken for fifty years, and as a result of my great experience I no longer fear that I shall say something in the House of Commons which will get me into a hole. In my youth I was always afraid of that. But that is only competent speaking. Oratory is repetition. Lloyd George and Bevan are carried away by their feelings. I'm not. I run short of something to say.[10]

Churchill records that his determined refusal to learn more than the bare minimum of Latin and Greek, a fact which detained him for some while in the lowest form at Harrow, brought an immense advantage. Because it was thought that the simpletons could tackle only English, he came under the guidance of a splendid teacher, Mr Somervell. Whereas he had always liked history at school, the textbooks had been of the dullest. But for the help of another respected master at Harrow, who convinced Churchill that mathematics was not a trackless bog of nonsense, he would not have entered (at the third attempt) the military college at Sandhurst, after which he could at last begin to develop the talents inadequately displayed at school. In this examination, he discovered with relief a question about

> these Cosines and Tangents in a highly square-rooted condition which must have been decisive upon the whole of my after life. It was a problem. But luckily I had seen its ugly face only a few days before and recognised it at first sight. I have not met any of these creatures since. ... I am very glad there are quite a number of people born with a gift and a liking for all of this; like great chess-players who play sixteen games at once blindfold and die quite soon of epilepsy. Serve them right!

To extend this quotation from *My Early Life*, the most beguiling of all Churchill's books, is a temptation too strong to resist:

> I had a feeling once about Mathematics, that I saw it all – Depth beyond depth was revealed to me – the Byss and the Abyss. I saw, as one might see the transit of Venus – or even the Lord Mayor's Show, a quantity passing through infinity and changing its sign from plus to minus. I saw exactly how it happened and why the tergiversation was inevitable: and how the one step involved all the others. It was like politics. But it was after dinner, and I let it go![11]

The interjection 'It was like politics' is characteristic – unexpected, wry, apt, quotable. Churchill's mastery over words seems to have been a natural, inherited faculty, married by Mr Somervell's teaching to a deep but unpedantic acquaintance with the sinews of the language.

> Thus I got into my bones the essential structure of the ordinary British sentence – which is a noble thing. And when in after years my schoolfellows who had won prizes and distinction for writing such beautiful Latin poetry and pithy Greek epigrams had to come down again to common English, to earn their living or make their way, I did not feel myself at any disadvantage.[12]

Even as a boy at Harrow, Churchill had dictated fluent essays for the benefit of a friend who found difficulty in composition, he requiting this service by doing Churchill's Latin translations. The possession of a wonderful memory, the capacity to assimilate whole pages or chapters almost at a glance, is not always an unalloyed blessing. Those who possess such a faculty sometimes become mere sponges, pressure upon which creates a flow of others' thoughts and wisdom. Nothing of the kind happened to WSC. His own inquisitive and turbulent nature saw to that. Though he once remarked 'After all, a man's Life must be nailed to a cross either of Thought or Action',[13] he made no such division of effort in his own career. Action there was aplenty from the very beginning; and thought of a kind which, especially after he had gone from Sandhurst to his first posting as a young officer, was untutored but had the merit of not springing from the need to pass an examination.

Churchill records that it was not until the autumn of 1896, near his 22nd birthday, that the desire for learning came upon him. Then serving as a subaltern in India, he asked his mother to send him books about history and philosophy and economics. Though possessing a wide vocabulary and a liking for the feel of words fitting and falling into their places like pennies in a slot, he realized his need of knowledge. The works of Gibbon and Macaulay, Malthus and Darwin, Plato and Aristotle, and of many another were flung into his mental firebox. His intellectual horizon was widened beyond measure, his style of writing permanently affected. 'It was a curious education. First because I approached it with an empty, hungry mind, and with fairly strong jaws; and what I got I bit; secondly because I had no one to tell me: "This is discredited".'[14] For the first time he began to envy the young cubs at university, but that mood did not last; later in life, he pitied undergraduates when he saw what frivolous lives many of them led in the midst of fleeting opportunity.

WSC even enquired about the prospects of entry to Oxford, but gathered with regret that proficiency in Latin and Greek was indispensable. In effect, he had set up his own university, and as for examinations, they were soon provided by the public, for his first book followed quickly. In those days, though many disapproved of the practice, officers were allowed to write dispatches for the newspapers. The rewards far outdistanced his pay in the army. At the beginning, he wrote of the events which he had witnessed: campaigns on the North-West Frontier of India; the re-conquest of the Sudan by Kitchener's forces and the battle of Omdurman, in which his life was probably saved by the fact that on account of a long-standing injury to his shoulder he had to use a pistol, not a sword; the Boer War, in which at the age of 25 he found himself the most highly paid newspaper correspondent in South Africa. While the large bulk of Churchill's prodigious literary output sprang from his own experience, first as a soldier or war correspondent and later as a minister in high office, all his weighty works contain more than personal reminiscence. That is true even from an early stage; his two books about the Sudan, for example, are based upon careful study of all the sources then available, and Churchill himself plays no significant part in the tale.

In his accounts of the great wars, no fewer than 12 volumes in all, Churchill insisted that he was not writing history. Rather, he was making a contribution to that history which would have to be established later, when passions had cooled, more documents had become available and perspectives had changed their shape. He was doing something which no one else could attempt, for he alone had spent a large part of World War I, and the whole of World War II, in high office. The former Prime Minister Lord Balfour, himself an author and philosopher of distinction, observed the process with amusement: 'At the moment I am immersed in Winston's brilliant Autobiography, disguised as a history of the universe.'[15]

Churchill's *Life* of his father remains a classic; sometimes partisan, to be sure, but carefully composed and based upon scrutiny of the evidence. In producing this biography, and at a time when he was starting to make his own mark in public affairs, he may have been moved only by a touching filial piety. Perhaps he was also anxious, as is suggested by those exchanges in the studio at Chartwell 40 years on, to show what he could do. Another Prime Minister of the past, Lord Rosebery, carried helpfulness to the point of penning a substantial memoir of Lord Randolph, which he suggested that Winston should incorporate in the book. Churchill resisted this offer – 'I had my own way of doing things, and the literary integrity of a work is capital' – not least because Rosebery's account had included the word 'scug', a term used at Eton College but considered by Churchill as 'derogatory and unsuited to a biography written by a son'.[16] Even when Rosebery explained that the term is harmless, the author stuck to his guns. It says much about him that he should have done so, and about Lord Rosebery that he should not have taken this disagreement amiss.

★ ★ ★ ★ ★

It was as General Ismay had discerned. Churchill fitted into no recognisable category. Intensely self-absorbed, which does not mean that he was indifferent to the interests of others, perhaps forced into such a cast of mind by the loneliness of his childhood and the lateness of his development, he possessed from early manhood a powerful belief in his own star, together with sufficient resources to employ a manservant, buy a bottle of champagne and another for a friend. Like his mother, of whom it was said that life for Lady Randolph did not begin on a basis of less than 40 pairs of shoes, he was often improvident; and like her, he not infrequently spent money before he had earned it. In sum, he lived from hand to mouth; or rather, as he used to express the point with a grin – for he dictated almost all his books and articles – from mouth to hand.

Izaak Walton sets it down that as no man is born an artist, so no man is born an angler. Certainly Winston Churchill was not born an orator. He had to learn the hard way. He would practise for hours in front of a mirror and commit whole texts to memory. Although he addressed great meetings with increasing facility in the boisterous General Election of 1900, at which he was returned to Parliament as a Conservative by a narrow majority in Manchester, it was a slow business. Having escaped in daring fashion from captivity in South Africa, he lectured with his lantern slides all over the British Isles before setting out for North America. So determined was he to establish himself and his finances that he did not even wait to take his seat in Parliament. After he had spoken at Ottawa, the *Evening Journal* there reported:

He has the manner and appearance of an athlete. He is clean shaven and his face is rather youthful looking … As a lecturer he is somewhat handicapped by a lisp. He does not indulge in the frills assumed by numerous lecturers. He evidently does not make any pretensions to oratory. He simply tells his story of the war in a chatty, conversational style. At times, however, when occasion offers he imparts a great deal of vigor to his delivery, giving an impression of that amplitude of energy and determination without which he could never have won the reputation he did in South Africa … Churchill has been ridiculed for his alleged egotism, and many who heard him last evening will agree that his critics were not without some justification. He has self-confidence and self-reliance, but more than that, he has evidently no mean opinion of Mr. Churchill.[17]

Though always ready of repartee, and sometimes devastating in swiftness of wit, Churchill seldom made an important speech, even in his prime, without a text. The fear of drying up haunted him. When he did speak impromptu, the effect could be overwhelming. Of his oration in 1943 to the soldiers of the victorious armies in the amphitheatre at Carthage, which General Marshall described as the finest he ever heard the Prime Minister make, Churchill remarks simply 'I have no idea what I said but the whole audience clapped and cheered as doubtless their predecessors of two thousand years ago had done as they watched gladiatorial combats.'[18] At the turn of the century, however, all that lay in the long future. At least in the early part of his life, he betrayed no signs of the melancholia said to afflict many of his family. On the contrary, he radiated a coiled energy, ate copiously, drank a good deal, smoked many a cigar, travelled without cease. His daughter, exercising the freedom permissible or even salutary within families, long afterwards described him as 'very much a young man in a hurry – and on the make – seeking to establish financial security as he embarked on his political career.'[19]

Those who think of Churchill as quintessentially British sometimes forget that he was half-American. Of his grandfather Leonard Jerome WSC once remarked 'A really remarkable man; he did exactly what he liked and he liked what he did.' Jerome, we learn, had illegitimate children. His wife, encountering one of her husband's mistresses, had said 'My dear, I understand what you feel. He is so irresistible.'[20] It was perhaps to this ancestry that Churchill owed the buccaneering strand in his nature and his fondness for gambling. He liked to describe himself as easily satisfied with the best of everything. Those ingredients of his character were not invariably in evidence, still less always dominant. Nevertheless, they were part of the 'mass of contradictions' which even so devoted a friend and supporter as Ismay detected. As for his mother, Churchill in middle age recalled with gratitude a description of a dark, lithe figure, radiant, translucent, intense, with a diamond star in her hair, who bore 'more of the panther than of the woman in her look, but with a cultivated intelligence unknown to the jungle. ... Her desire to please, her delight in life, and the genuine wish that all should share her joyous faith in it, made her the centre of a devoted circle.' Lady Randolph amidst all this retained her patriotic allegiance. When a horse bred in the USA won the Derby, her son remembered, she went about waving the American flag.[21]

Churchill had long intended to become a politician, and a metropolitan politician at that; not for him the patient creation of some great commercial enterprise or a high reputation in local government. Members of Parliament in those days received no pay. His distinction as a writer and increasing facility as a speaker provided the base for his career. He was by no means disposed to minimize this achievement. To his mother he wrote from Toronto on New Year's Day, 1901 'I hope my dearest Mama to be able to provide for myself in the future – at any rate until things are better with you. … I am vy proud of the fact that there is not one person in a million who at my age could have earned £10,000 without any capital in less than two years.'

The young man understood what he owed to the Jerome blood; for when he returned to England a few weeks later to embark on a political career that was to last more than 60 years, he sent his mother £300, which might equate in today's currency to £15,000. With the cheque went this note: 'In a certain sense it belongs to you; for I could never have earned it had you not transmitted to me the wit and energy which are necessary.'[22]

* * * * *

Churchill had a high respect for learned persons, provided they could defend their opinions against his assaults. He believed that the course of history had been determined more often than not by exceptional people and great events. He sought the company of Nature's princes, as they appeared to him: among the pioneers of irregular warfare, T.E. Lawrence with his 'noble features, his perfectly-chiselled lips and flashing eyes loaded with fire and comprehension'[23] and Orde Wingate; among painters Sir John Lavery, William Nicholson and Paul Maze; among the fighting men, Alexander and Portal. With politicians and statesmen, Churchill mingled at first on the easy terms secured by his parents' position and soon, to a far greater degree, by his own rapidity and readiness with words. Looking back after World War I had swept away so much, Churchill believed that the leading lights of British politics in the later nineteenth and early twentieth centuries, in the days when the future seemed secure, when society could move forward with sure confidence that much was well and all would be better, when the essential principles underlying the constitution were not challenged in any serious way, were men of towering stature. He described Lord

Rosebery, Arthur Balfour, John Morley and Joseph Chamberlain as the four most pleasing and brilliant figures to whom he had ever listened. Elsewhere, he adds Asquith and Lloyd George to this most select of companies. 'One did feel after a talk with these men that things were simpler and easier, and that Britain would be strong enough to come through all her troubles.'[24]

That these were figures of the highest intelligence needs not saying. Four of them held the office of Prime Minister. All in their different styles were orators, and three authors, of high distinction. All were older, most much older, than Churchill. From conversation with only one of his contemporaries did he derive such pleasure and profit: F.E. Smith, first Earl of Birkenhead. This conviction – that the people amongst whom he spent a good part of his later political life were of a lesser order than the giants of his youth and early manhood – was openly proclaimed. It explains a good deal about Churchill's relations with colleagues, and his detachment from the mainstream of British political life in the 1930s. L.S. Amery, deeply learned, experienced in the ways of government, whom Churchill had known since their days at Harrow, argued that the Victorians had been relatively small men making much fuss about relatively small issues. Churchill remained unconvinced. Politics, he said, were not what they had been. The level was lower.[25]

When that conversation took place, in the summer of 1929, Churchill was approaching his 55th birthday. He had been a public figure for 30 years, and a Member of Parliament, with one brief interval, since 1900. He had entered the Cabinet at the age of 33. He had left the Liberal Party after some 20 years, and in the Conservative administration which had just lost power held the office of Chancellor of the Exchequer for nearly 5 years. At the Treasury he had found himself less thoroughly at home than at the Admiralty or the War Office or the Colonial Office. And now here he was, bursting with energy, vastly experienced, the author of splendid books, saying that nothing in politics still interested him except attainment of the highest office; and of that he saw no sign. We must ask ourselves why.

★ ★ ★ ★ ★

After joining the Cabinet in 1908, Churchill had shown not only strong Radical sympathies in the abstract, but a determination to introduce useful, practical measures of social improvement. He became an ardent ally of the Chancellor of the Exchequer, Lloyd George, eleven years his senior and in many ways his mentor. In a strong campaign against increased spending upon the Royal Navy, the two of them irritated the Prime Minister, Asquith, who nevertheless admired Churchill's gifts and promoted him more than once. Those were early days, and much was forgiven on account of Churchill's competence and high spirits. Without doubt, he brought distinction to the government. One of his colleagues in the Liberal Cabinet of a few years later kept a diary. Here are some extracts from it:

At Cabinets of Monday and Tuesday we renewed discussion on the Mediterranean. Churchill was most abusive and insulting to McKenna [Home Secretary: Churchill's predecessor at the Admiralty]. He is really a spoilt child endowed by some chance with the brain of a genius. (17 July 1912)

Churchill is illmannered, boastful, unprincipled, without any redeeming qualities except his amazing ability and industry. I doubt his courage to desert during a victorious cruise, but he would, without hesitation, desert a sinking ship. (13 August 1912)

Very long Cabinet yesterday. We were favoured by addresses from Churchill on Education, Finance, Navy, Aviation and Electioneering and finally there was a general revolt summed up by the P.M. remarking that his views were pure 'cynicism defended by sophistry'. (24 June 1913)

The last three Cabinets have been tolerably peaceful, thanks to Churchill's absence. He has made up for it today by talking without cessation, interrupting everyone, even the P.M. and K. [Kitchener, S. of S. for War] and Ed. Grey [Foreign Secretary] on their own depts. (24 September 1914)

The Cabinet decided that the Admiralty must pay compensation, but Churchill would not consent to consider such cases jointly with the P.O. [Post Office] until I threatened to cut off all his own and the Fleet's postal or telegraphic communication. He behaved like an untruthful and spoilt schoolboy, which leavened by genius for speech is what he really is. (13 November 1914)

Churchill as always, in a hurry to be conspicuous ... Nervous, fretful, voluble, intolerably bumptious and conceited, he squanders our time and his own in increasing orations. These are interspersed with tags of Latin and French which are a source of unfailing amusement and contempt for the P.M. (23 March 1915)[26]

If such complaints came from a Tory estranged by Churchill's change of party, or from a Liberal rival, they might be dismissed as mere spurts of malice. They represent something more solid than that. Against them must be set Churchill's accomplishments as a Minister, most importantly the high state of readiness which the Royal Navy had reached by July 1914. Unlike some of his former Radical allies, Churchill never doubted either the justice of the Allied cause or the imperative need for Britain to enter the war. The surge of patriotic feeling, the scale of sacrifice, the feats of bravery, the size of the stakes, the diplomatic manoeuvrings, stratagems, tactics, the testing in practice of what had so often been rehearsed on paper or in discussion – all this absorbed every scrap of effort which even he could muster. He had been absorbed by warfare from childhood, first with his much-loved collections of toy soldiers, then in his career as a subaltern, through his active connection with the Oxfordshire Hussars, and in his speeches and books and articles. He had understood from its earliest days the importance of aviation, when machines were of the most primitive and fatal crashes frequent. After many flights, and on the point of taking his pilot's licence, he yielded with reluctance in the summer of 1914 to the entreaties of friends and the prickings of conscience, for he was already the father of two young children, Diana and Randolph, and Mrs Churchill was expecting another baby in a few months' time. In characteristic style he explained to her his decision to abandon flying, perhaps for ever:

This is a gift – so stupidly am I made – wh costs me more than anything wh cd be bought with money. So I am vy glad to lay it at your feet, because I know it will rejoice & relieve your heart.

Anyhow I can feel I know a good deal about this fascinating new art. I can manage a machine with ease in the air, even with high

winds, & only a little more practice in landings wd have enabled me
to go up with reasonable safety alone ...

You will give me some kisses and forgive me for past distresses –
I am sure. Though I had no need and perhaps no right to do it – it
was an important part of my life during the last 7 months, and I am
sure my nerve, my spirits & my virtue were all improved by it. But
at your expense my poor pussy cat! I am so sorry.[27]

When the war had lasted only a couple of months, Churchill took charge
of a rapidly deteriorating situation in Antwerp. He rallied the Belgian
ministers rather as he tried to sustain the French ministers in the still
more dire crisis of June 1940. If this was without question an act of
boldness and bravery, it was also one of irresponsibility; for WSC had in
effect abandoned his duties as First Lord, which had to be assumed for
some days by Asquith himself. That said, the extra few days of resistance
in Antwerp brought beneficial results for the Allies, for their control of
the Channel ports of France might otherwise have been lost.

WSC had already fought with eight regiments in three continents
(briefly in Cuba, and then lengthily in India and Africa); he longed to
command an army; and as the point was rendered by his friend and
coadjutor of later years Desmond Morton, Churchill 'readily asserted,
and I believe it to be true, that he adored physical danger, which gave
him a thrill almost of a sexual nature.'[28] The astonished Asquith in
London accordingly received a telegram saying that Churchill would be
willing to resign as First Lord of the Admiralty in order to command
the forces assigned to Antwerp, provided he were given the necessary
military rank and full powers. He felt sure that this arrangement would
afford 'the best prospects of a victorious result'. Not surprisingly, Asquith
found in this a real piece of tragi-comedy, and when Churchill's offer
to take command of the defences was communicated to the Cabinet
'it was received with a Homeric laugh.' Returning to London, the First
Lord waited upon the Prime Minister, and according to the latter's
account, having 'tasted blood' in these last days, he was beginning like
a tiger to raven for more. He begged that he might be relieved swiftly
of his post at the Admiralty and put in some sort of military command.
Great new armies were being raised at home. Were these glittering
commands to be entrusted to 'dug-out trash', 'mediocrities, who have
led a sheltered life mouldering in military routine'? For a quarter of an

hour Churchill poured forth what Asquith called a ceaseless cataract of invective and appeal:

> I much regretted there was no short-hand writer within hearing – as some of his unpremeditated phrases were quite priceless. He was, however, quite three parts serious, and declared that a political career was nothing to him in comparison with military glory.
>
> … He is a wonderful creature, with a curious dash of schoolboy simplicity … and what someone said of genius – 'a zigzag streak of lightning in the brain.'[29]

The defence of Antwerp had to be abandoned shortly afterwards. Violent criticisms were made of Churchill, most of them quite unfair. However, these voices represented more than a mere confederacy of dunces leagued against a man of genius. Even among his Liberal colleagues, the view spread widely that he was unreliable, self-promoting, too eager for his own glory, rash and impulsive. Within the Conservative Party there were many who believed such charges with the intensity often reserved for those who have defected. In the afterlight, WSC himself acknowledged it was lucky that his offer of resignation had been refused, and that on more general grounds he should never have gone to Antwerp, since 'Those who are charged with the direction of supreme affairs must sit on the mountain-tops of control; they must never descend into the valleys of direct physical and personal action.'[30]

On the eve of the war, Churchill had described himself as interested, geared up and happy. The implications were not lost upon him:

> Is it not horrible to be built like that? The preparations have a hideous fascination for me. I pray to God to forgive me for such fearful moods of levity – yet I wd do my best for peace, & nothing wd induce me wrongfully to strike the blow – I cannot feel that we in this island are in any serious degree responsible for the wave of madness wh. has swept the mind of Christendom.[31]

Six months later, when matters were about to be put to the test at the Dardanelles and Gallipoli, the First Lord of the Admiralty was discoursing after dinner. Suddenly he said 'I think a curse should rest on me because I love this war. I know it's smashing and shattering the lives of thousands every moment; and yet – I *can't* help it. I enjoy every second of it.'[32] Again, if this account came from an opponent or rival, it might be brushed away or at least heavily discounted. In fact it was recorded by Asquith's daughter Violet, than whom few admired his talents more fervently.

When Churchill left the government to fight in France, he carried with him convictions born of recent and most bitter experience. Three were of particular importance for his later career: first, it was delusive to pretend that in matters of war the Generals and Admirals must necessarily be right and the politicians wrong; secondly, that a minister who attempts to carry through a major military enterprise from a subordinate position runs risks which may be fatal not only to the enterprise but to his own career; lastly, that few political friendships survive the test of adversity. Dwelling in the trenches, surrounded by slime and rotting corpses and vermin, Churchill experienced intervals of calm after many years of ceaseless fighting, worry and excitement; he felt sometimes the longing for rest and peace, and even a desire to be quit of politics. The mood did not last. He does not seem to have feared death or injury. 'If my destiny has not already been accomplished, I shall be guarded surely', he told his wife; and from France again, a few months later 'Sometimes also I think I wd not mind stopping living vy much – I am so devoured by egoism that I wd like to have another soul in another world & meet you in another setting, & pay you all the love & honour of the gt romances.' [33]

Lloyd George, who replaced Asquith as Prime Minister, brought Churchill back into a government which was undoubtedly strengthened by his boldness, efficiency and parliamentary skills. A commission of enquiry had largely cleared WSC of blame for the disaster in the Dardanelles. Deeply mistrusted in many quarters on account of his involvement in Irish affairs before World War I, Churchill took a leading part in the negotiation of the Anglo-Irish Treaty of 1921. The old Liberal Party had already split; Lloyd George depended after the election of 1918 upon Conservative support; and Churchill sometimes found himself in a position of semi-detachment from the Prime Minister and other colleagues. That strains should arise in such circumstances is not surprising. Perfect harmony is not to be expected between fiercely ambitious men of aggressive personality. In the event, Lloyd George co-operated more readily with his senior Conservative colleagues than with his fellow-Liberal Churchill. Amongst their bones of contention one stood out above all others. It was partly a difference of practicalities, but also something more fundamental: a difference of philosophical, almost religious, significance. To Churchill, the new government of Russia and the creed of Bolshevism seemed an abomination; and what was worse, an abomination for export. Captain Anthony Eden, lately returned from brave service in the war, attended his first political meeting at Sunderland in 1919. There he heard Churchill say 'The ghost of the Russian bear comes padding across the immense field of snow.' The two of them had good cause to think again of that nightmare prospect when they were colleagues in harness together a quarter of a century later.

The Russians had made peace with Germany, with consequences which were nearly fatal to the West in 1918; the new regime repudiated the vast debts of the old, murdered the Czar and his family, extirpated its opponents, denounced the churches and indeed any creeds other than its own, proclaimed an intention to undermine other states and, since an immense field of snow lay not only to the west of Russia but to the south and east as well, to foment unrest and sedition in Asia. To WSC all this seemed not only 'foul baboonery' but pregnant with danger. He did his best to strangle Bolshevism at birth, and regretted that he had failed, whereas most of his colleagues judged these were enterprises too costly and uncertain to sustain. After all, Russia was an immense and remote country, with great potential for mischief. The Western Powers, narrowly the victors in 1918, were measuring the blood-tax and wondering how on earth to restore their finances; the United States had withdrawn promptly from international affairs by refusing to enter the League of Nations or ratify the Treaty of Versailles, which had been to no small degree shaped by the policies and philosophies of the President of the United States himself.

Thus Churchill's obsession with Russia and Bolshevism was regarded by many as proof of his instability or even his determination to break up the government. The Prime Minister, resolved to patch up terms with Russia if possible, came close to resignation. 'I told you', he wrote to the Chancellor of the Exchequer 'I thought Winston would be a real wrecker … I certainly could not go to [the Conference at] Genoa on Winston's terms. That means I must go altogether if they are insisted upon.' 'Tell me which way the little man [Lloyd George] is going', Churchill remarked at this time 'and I am off in the opposite direction.'[34]

However, it was not as a result of these deep and wide divisions over Russia that Lloyd George's government fell. Possessing the large bulk of the government's parliamentary strength, many in the Conservative Party had been anxious to break free from Lloyd George and Churchill. This the leading figures – Austen Chamberlain, Lord Birkenhead, Lord Balfour, Lord Curzon and others – had no consistent desire to do. They argued in essence that the dangers at home and overseas rose up so menacingly that only the Coalition could meet the situation. That they held such a belief, even though it entailed service under a Liberal Prime Minister who had but a few years before excoriated the Tories, is an index of their sincerity; for more than one of the leading Conservatives would have had a plausible claim to the post of Prime Minister if Lloyd George were forced to go.

The affairs of the Near East, combined with a deeper fear that Lloyd George's government was bent upon an aggressive foreign policy to be followed quickly by a general election, precipitated the collapse. For all their earlier disagreements, the Prime Minister and WSC were agreed that resurgent Turkey must be curbed by force of arms if need be. The Dardanelles and Gallipoli again! Telegrams went out to the Dominions recalling the heroic conduct of the Imperial forces a few years earlier. In hours of intense crisis, the matter was maladroitly handled in London. To the Prime Minister in Ottawa, Mackenzie King, it seemed that the whole business was chiefly an election manoeuvre by Lloyd George and his colleagues. While that view was in substance mistaken, it was certainly widespread. We find in King's diary 'It is a serious business having matters in [the] hand of man like Churchill – the fate of an empire! I am sure we have done right and aided the cause of peace by holding back.'[35]

The new Conservative government under Bonar Law eschewed the Near Eastern policies of its predecessor, took the view that Britain could not act as policeman of the world, rapidly held an election and won a comfortable majority. For the first time in more than 20 years, Churchill found himself without a seat in Parliament. By an amusing irony, he lost at Dundee to a Prohibitionist. Lloyd George and his Liberal followers were now much reduced in number; the Liberal Party was in any case deeply split between those who had followed Asquith after 1916 and those who had cleaved to Lloyd George; and many a harsh word had been spoken in the election campaign of November 1922. Churchill had long taken the view that moderate Conservatives and many Liberals were bound, by interest and duty alike, to work together, since the policies and beliefs they shared signified far more than their differences. The alternative to such a central grouping would be a Labour government under Ramsay MacDonald, a pacifist who had advocated a negotiated peace with Germany. Churchill disliked him and feared the consequences of socialism.

These were grounds upon which he might, if other things were equal, seek to rejoin the Conservatives. Such a step would have been almost inconceivable but for the long period of collaboration between Conservatives and Liberals during the years of coalition government from 1915 to 1922. It was one thing, however, for lifelong Conservatives to rejoin a full-fledged Conservative Cabinet. It was another matter for Churchill, whose attacks upon the Conservatives had lacked nothing in colour or vigour, not only before the war but after the dissolution of Lloyd George's government. Amongst other accoutrements of the old Liberalism Churchill wore the cloak of Free Trade long after the garment had been discarded by some and found threadbare by others. Here again, an extraordinary series of chances played their part in his early return to the Cabinet, something which no other leading Liberal, or ex-Liberal, achieved in the same fashion; and without that return to the centre of the government, it is unlikely that Churchill would have become Prime Minister.

At all events, his rapid rehabilitation was made possible by the fact that after Bonar Law was discovered to be mortally ill and replaced in 1923 by Stanley Baldwin, the latter decided that Britain's dire economic problems could be resolved only if it had a government authorized to introduce protective tariffs and stimulate Imperial development. Baldwin felt with justice that so momentous a change could not be introduced without a mandate. Accordingly a government with a solid parliamentary majority called an election within 12 months and lost it; hence the first Labour administration under MacDonald. Many leading Conservatives were still Free Traders, or something close to it, whereas Baldwin had been a convinced protectionist all his life and the same was true of a number of his colleagues, notably Austen Chamberlain and his half-brother Neville. It was judged, however, that defeat on this issue in 1923 had made it impossible to include any robust move away from Free Trade in the next Conservative manifesto. Had it been otherwise, Churchill could not have joined the government which followed the fall of MacDonald and the return of Baldwin to power in the autumn of 1924.

WSC had sought more than once to re-enter Parliament, standing as a Liberal in the election of 1923 and shortly afterwards as an Independent Anti-Socialist. In private, Baldwin had shown himself friendly to Churchill, who had been adopted as a 'Constitutionalist' for the seat in Essex which he thereafter represented for 40 years. It is a measure of Churchill's experience and ability, and doubtless of Baldwin's anxiety to separate him decisively from Lloyd George, that the Chancellorship of the Exchequer, generally accounted the second post in the government, fell to him when he had not even rejoined the Conservative Party; and it could not have turned out thus but for the fact that Neville Chamberlain, who had previously held the Chancellorship, refused it in favour of the Ministry of Health. Churchill himself was gratified and astonished at this preferment. 'Anyone can rat,' he is supposed to have said 'but I flatter myself that it takes a certain ingenuity to re-rat.'[36] Asquith, contemplating the row of ministers sitting opposite to him, described Churchill as an Everest among the sandhills. He exaggerated, but not to the point of absurdity; for Churchill had a glitter and glamour which his new colleagues had neither the capacity nor the desire to match. It was as if a bird of paradise had alighted in the rooks' parliament.

To be in charge of the nation's finances offered Churchill a very wide scope for intervention outside his own departmental concerns, a habit which had caused colleagues a good deal of anguish and friction over many years. Indeed, it offered more. Remaining a convinced believer in Free Trade, he refused to permit any but the most modest measures of safeguarding or protection. This was the main issue upon which he had left the Conservatives in 1904, and the leaders of that party in their turn were acutely conscious of the profound divisions in their ranks which had persisted ever since Joseph Chamberlain had first raised the banner. To those within and without the government who pointed out that many other nations did not espouse Free Trade, and that Britain had no weapons with which to retaliate, Churchill largely turned a deaf ear. Searching vigorously for economies, he squeezed the Royal Navy, Royal Air Force and Army hard. The First Lord, Baldwin's intimate friend W.C. Bridgeman, principled and tough, resisted as strongly as he could. At one point, it seemed that he and the entire Board of Admiralty would resign, so strongly did Churchill press them. A compromise was patched up with some difficulty. With the Prime Minister, Churchill rubbed along well enough. Living at 11 Downing Street, Churchill saw much of Baldwin and approved of his main purpose, to reduce industrial strife and bitterness between the classes. 'You know, Prime Minister,' remarked Churchill one day 'I don't exactly take you to be a Peter Simple.' 'Nor', Baldwin replied pithily, 'are you exactly Midshipman Easy.'[37]

With Neville Chamberlain Churchill collaborated amidst moments of creative tension, and to good effect; each was indispensable to the reform of local government, the extension of pensions and an elaborate scheme of de-rating. At an early stage of their association, Chamberlain recorded of the Chancellor:

> What a brilliant creature he is! But there is somehow a great gulf fixed between him and me which I don't think I shall ever cross. I like him. I like his humour and his vitality. I like his courage. …. But not for all the joys of Paradise would I be a member of his staff! Mercurial! A much abused word, but it is the literal description of his temperament.

This opinion varied somewhat, but not crucially, as the work of the government went on. The Permanent Secretary at the Treasury felt able to confide to Chamberlain, his former ministerial master, that Churchill behaved like an irresponsible child, ignored warnings and needed to be sat upon constantly, while Chamberlain reflected that the better he got to know the Chancellor, the less he thought of him; not because WSC seemed in the least villainous but because he was amoral, possessing courage, strong will and power of oratory but lacking judgement – a combination of qualities and deficiencies which made him 'a very dangerous man to have in the boat. But I don't see how he could be got out of it safely now.'[38]

Several further years of experience did not alter Chamberlain's view of Churchill's unreliability and what he called his 'furious advocacy of half-baked ideas'. For his part, and doubtless with no intention to cause permanent offence, Churchill had accused Chamberlain of pedantry and personal jealousy:

> Winston is a very interesting but a d -- d uncomfortable bed fellow. You never get a moment's rest and you never know at what point he'll break out. ... One doesn't often come across a real man of genius or, perhaps, appreciate him when one does. Winston is such a man and he has *les défauts de ses qualités*. To listen to him on the platform or in the House is sheer delight. The art of the arrangement, the unexpected turn, the mastery of sparkling humour and the torrent of picturesque adjectives combine to put his speeches in a class by themselves. ... In the consideration of affairs, his decisions are never founded on exact knowledge, nor on careful or prolonged consideration of the pros and cons.

This letter concludes: 'There is too deep a difference between our natures for me to feel at home with him or to regard him with affection.'[39] The sentiment was shared. Each was surprised and gratified when, under the hammer of Thor (as Churchill would have expressed it), they struck up an effective and confident partnership after September 1939.

Few in the Cabinet or the higher ranks of the Civil Service would have written a warmer testimonial than Chamberlain's and many a more damning one. The frustrations of L.S. Amery, his conviction that Churchill was essentially a politician rooted in the nineteenth century, unable to assimilate modern ideas, are amply documented in his memoirs and published diaries. Surveying the work of this Cabinet after its demise, Bridgeman characterized Churchill as

> The most indescribable & amazing character of all my colleagues. His fertile brain turned out ideas by the score on all subjects, very few of which bore the test of analysis, but that did not prevent the continuance of production. He laid eggs as rapidly as a partridge & if his nest was disturbed quickly started another, but the proportion of his eggs which came to maturity was small.

Very voluble in discussion, excitable, inconsistent as a colleague, a wonderful speaker and unrivalled coiner of phrases, WSC lived entirely in the present and took his colour from the particular office he happened to hold.[40] Bridgeman felt this with some fervour, for the Treasury under Churchill, in its pressure upon the Admiralty, had resorted to the arguments which before the war Churchill as First Lord had resisted with vigour and considerable success.

This is not to suggest that Churchill's stringency with the Service departments was based upon nothing more than a desire for economy, powerful as that desire was. He consistently and mistakenly dismissed the risk of a serious confrontation with Japan; and since Germany had virtually no navy, and Britain seemed unlikely to fight the United States, France or Italy, the case for steady building of new ships was undermined. The outlook in Europe appeared tranquil. Under Churchill's impetus, the Cabinet agreed that the Ten-Year Rule – that the British Empire would not be engaged in war with a first-class enemy for at least that time – should roll forward until countermanded. This had become the governing assumption of defence planning, and therefore of spending. It represented a fundamental error, indeed a misjudgement of the nature of international affairs.

Churchill and Birkenhead remained intimate friends and confidants until the latter's premature death in 1930. Bibulous, improvident, extravagant, intemperate of speech but much more moderate in policy, swift to seize a point, he had provided a kind of companionship, and not infrequently a restraint, which Churchill could find from no one else in the politics of those days. Later, the same need was partially met by the stimulus of Max Beaverbrook. Both appealed to the buccaneering element in Churchill's nature; his other colleagues looked drab and humdrum by comparison. Thus the Prime Minister would describe Birkenhead and Churchill cheerfully as 'our two banditti'; Churchill wrote well before leaving office in 1929 that he felt very independent of all his companions in the Cabinet; and Mrs Churchill told Birkenhead's widow 'Last night Winston wept for his friend. He said several times "I feel so lonely".'[41]

* * * * *

In the weighty sense of the word, Churchill was not 'worldly', as Lloyd George and Birkenhead were. He was a less good, or at any rate less cynical, judge of men and their motives than they. While he continued to seek forms of parliamentary or electoral accommodation with the Liberals, even he could scarcely re-re-rat. The economic problems with which he had grappled at the Treasury had proved intractable to a degree; Parliament, he thought, was far less well fitted to cope with them than with more strictly political issues. He did believe, however, that peace was securely established, and judged President Hoover entirely right to say that the prospects were better than they had been for 50 years. At least in respect of international affairs he could, so to speak, utter a public version of the Ten-Year Rule. Though disturbances might occur in barbarous parts of the world where the Russian Bolsheviks came into contact with other nations 'As far as the great civilized powers are concerned, I believe the foundations of peace are stronger now than they have ever been in our lifetime.'[42]

The Labour government which came to power at the end of May 1929, dependent as in 1924 upon Liberal support in the House of Commons, soon found itself in the grip of economic circumstances more dire than those with which its Conservative predecessors had grappled. Philip Snowden, who replaced Churchill at the Treasury, proclaimed stern financial doctrines. The senior officials of that great department greeted the Labour Chancellor with considerable enthusiasm. Churchill had never cared for their strict orthodoxy, any more than he cared for orthodoxy on most other subjects; but he had not felt able to confute with sufficient certainty the theories with which he was presented. In later years, he was to regret this profoundly. Economists, of whom the Treasury had only one at senior level, had not then established the authority which they possess today. As for Snowden, Toryism was to him a physical annoyance and militant Socialism – so Churchill impudently put it – a disease brought on by bad conditions or contagion, like rickets or mange. All British Chancellors of the Exchequer, he remarked ruefully, have yielded themselves to the compulsive intellectual atmosphere of the Treasury. But with the arrival of Snowden, the High Priest himself entered the sanctuary. 'The Treasury mind and the Snowden mind embraced each other with the fervour of two long-separated kindred lizards, and the reign of joy began. Unhappily a lot of things cropped up which were very tiresome.'[43]

British political parties are habitually coalitions, embracing a considerable range of views; that was certainly true of the Conservative Cabinet of the later 1920s. There was no other alignment into which Churchill could conveniently fit. To be sure, most of the Liberals still believed, though with a diminishing fervour, in Free Trade; but the Liberal Party was again propping up the Labour government, and Churchill regarded Socialism as an expensive delusion which if pursued seriously would ruin Britain's precarious position. The Conservatives were drawn increasingly to protection, tariffs and measures for the development of Imperial trade as the collapse of the international economy and banks moved to a frightening crescendo in the summer of 1931.

Before then, Churchill had parted company decisively with his recent colleagues. The immediate issue was not protection or Imperial Preference or food taxes, as it might easily have been; rather, plans to confer an increasing measure of self-government upon India. He played no significant part in the crisis which developed a few months later. The National Government, set up in August 1931 to save the pound under the Labour Prime Minister MacDonald, joined by leading Conservatives and some Liberals, he viewed with distaste. At the election a few weeks later, that government secured a majority unparalleled in British history; on such a scale, indeed, that the Labour Party was reduced to hardly more than 50 seats. MacDonald continued as Prime Minister, with Baldwin content to wield a good measure of power as Lord President; and in due course Neville Chamberlain became Chancellor of the Exchequer as successor to Snowden.

Until the summer of 1935, Churchill conducted a serious and weighty campaign against the government's proposals for India. He pointed with justice to the remarkable record of British administration there and elsewhere. He feared that many who had dwelt side by side peaceably for generations would fall upon each other with ferocity if Britain's controlling hand were withdrawn prematurely. These apprehensions were not confined to him, of course. A desire to avert them, and to preserve the political unity of the Indian sub-continent, pressed as insistently upon ministers as upon Churchill and his followers. Promises of political advance had long since been made to India. MacDonald and Baldwin alike felt that if India were to remain in a close association with Britain, the goal that they desired above all else, a further constitutional advance must be made. The complications were immense, and although many believed that Churchill's campaign was factitious, inspired by a desire to bring down a coalition government which he believed to have emasculated British politics, there is no reason to doubt the sincerity of his actions or the reality of his fears.

When the Government of India Act had passed into law in the summer of 1935, Churchill mended his fences with Baldwin, who had just assumed office for the last time as Prime Minister. To a large degree, the election in the autumn of that year was fought upon the issue of rearmament, as Churchill acknowledged at the time; and although he had criticized the government severely for some while past not only in respect of India but also for its tardiness in rebuilding Britain's air defences, he campaigned in support of the National Government. Shortly before the election, Churchill described Baldwin as a statesman 'who has gathered to himself a greater volume of confidence and goodwill than any public man I recollect in my long career'. When Baldwin thanked him, Churchill wrote

> What I said was no more than the truth; and I am vy glad that it is the truth: because things are in such a state that it is a blessing to have at the head of affairs a man whom people will rally round. But if your power is great, so also are yr burdens – and yr opportunities.[44]

The issue of Free Trade had by then ceased to matter as a source of division between Churchill and the Conservatives. Britain's adoption of tariffs in 1932, with a modest measure of preference for the Dominions and colonies, stilled a controversy which had convulsed British politics for the better part of 30 years. Churchill conceded that under the old system, whereby Britain and the colonies had persisted with Free Trade long after others had abandoned it, could not continue. The march of events and the state of the world had convinced him of the need for a fundamental change of outlook. Protection must be given a fair trial. 'What is the use of going on mumbling the politics of 20 years ago? Change comes. Old sayings, old circumstances, all are fads and pomps and must give way.' He had not failed to notice what his election address of 1931 calls 'almost prohibitive tariffs', chiefly imposed by the United States. Britain had kept the Free Trade flag flying, and her reward had been to see foreign tariffs raised higher and higher against her. 'Hitherto the Crown Colonies of Great Britain have been thrown open to the commerce of the whole world, as freely to foreigners as to ourselves. There has been no return of reciprocity. The time has come to put a girdle around the Empire estate.'[45]

Churchill had half-hoped to rejoin the Cabinet in 1935. Whether the Prime Minister could be expected to forget so quickly the long campaign that Churchill had just waged over India, which if successful must have brought the downfall of the previous administration, is open to debate. Churchill's qualifications were obvious; he alone had held the political headship of the three service departments, he would bring an immense accession of debating strength to the government, he still had boundless energy. Yet very few of the leading politicians wished to see him resume office in peacetime. That he would be a disruptive presence within the government could scarcely be doubted; he had made plain his poor opinion of many who would be his colleagues; he was erratic, apt to pursue momentary enthusiasms, drinking too much, in a word undependable. His inclusion in the Cabinet would be taken abroad, and most of all in Germany, as a sign that Britain regarded war as inevitable. These were powerful but not conclusive arguments. They were strongly reinforced during the Abdication crisis in the late autumn of 1936. Not for the first or last time, Churchill was harmed by his closeness to Beaverbrook. Both were friends of the King and consulted by him as the crisis developed. It was widely believed that Churchill was attempting to bring the government down. 'Winston did his best to cross us and at one moment had gorgeous visions of a clash between the Sovereign and his Cabinet, and the resignation of Ministers, general consternation and then in a flash of glory a champion stepping forth to defend his King in shining armour. I am told he had gone a long way in the formation of his Cabinet and in the plans for action when it was installed.' Thus Neville Chamberlain immediately after the King's abdication. 'I know my Winston', remarked Baldwin to Chamberlain. 'When he came to see me he looked like a cat that has been caught coming out of the dairy and thinks you haven't seen her but you had. When Lloyd George is out for mischief you can see the wash of his periscope but when Winston is trying to torpedo you, half his hull is out of the water.' This was not an unjust assessment. As WSC himself remarked in old age 'I am no good as a conspirator. I talk too much.'[46]

Churchill and Beaverbrook believed that the King's passion for Mrs Simpson, whom they called 'Cutie', marked no more than a temporary aberration. They suggested that the overstrained monarch should be declared too ill to undertake his royal duties for a while and the lady should leave the country. But then, as Churchill expressed it years later in recounting the story, 'Terrible things began to happen. Bricks were thrown through her dining room window, letters arrived threatening her with vitriol, angry slogans were written on the walls of neighbouring houses.' His Private Secretary Jock Colville, to whom this was said, enquired with incredulity '*You* didn't do things like that?' 'No,' Churchill replied. 'But Max did.' Colville duly asked Beaverbrook about it. 'Did you really throw bricks through the dining room window?' 'Perhaps some young man from the *Daily Express* did.' 'Do you think Winston was prepared to destroy his career entirely from personal loyalty to the King?' 'Yes, I think that was Churchill's motive. Would you like to know what mine was? I just thought it was all a lot of fun.'[47]

The senior members of the Cabinet had a good deal of most secret information, some of it coming from Beaverbrook himself. It is impossible to establish motives with any certainty. Perhaps Churchill may have had visions of bringing an end to Baldwin's regime, and even of forming a government. More probable is the simple explanation given by Beaverbrook. By instinct and habit a Cavalier to his fingers' ends, Churchill felt the strongest loyalty to the throne and its occupant. He remembered vividly the occasion a quarter of a century earlier when as Home Secretary he had taken part in the investiture of the King as Prince of Wales at Caernarvon Castle. He was accustomed to act upon his own impulses, and not to care unduly what the world might say. Certainly he paid a high price for a time. His motives being generally suspect, he was shouted down in the House of Commons, refused to flinch, found himself shunned in the smoking room afterwards. His faithful supporter Brendan Bracken, recalling the occasion years later, said 'I took Winston off to Lord North Street. He was miserable beyond belief; to be howled down in the House of Commons was a disgrace. But he kept saying to me he would never give in.'[48]

The whole episode confirmed many in the view that Churchill was a bad judge, unreliable, hostile to the government. It was alleged that he had been drunk when intervening in the House. Well-lubricated he doubtless was, but there was nothing unusual in that. He continued to consume into old age quantities of alcohol which would have rendered most younger men prostrate, and without much visible effect. The stand he had made on the King's behalf was undoubtedly an act of courage. It should be recorded that within a few months Churchill recognized that King George VI, for all his initial shyness and stammer, was far better fitted for the position than his more personable elder brother could ever have been. Of the latter, Churchill remarked simply 'Morning glory', remembering those flowers which flourish and fade within a forenoon.[49]

Churchill exaggerates somewhat to say that his political influence had fallen at this time to zero. The scale of German rearmament and the menacing attitude which Germany adopted towards her neighbours gave ever-increasing point to the warnings that he had uttered for years. The government's view of the essentials was less widely separated from his than many have assumed. In 1934, while MacDonald was still Prime Minister, the Cabinet had decided that Germany should replace Japan as the 'ultimate potential enemy', and that the British armed forces should be ready for war by 1939. These were not conclusions which could readily be discussed in public, and the dangers in the Mediterranean, the Middle East and Asia provided a background of constant anxiety as the crisis developed. In essence, WSC wished for swifter and heavier rearmament in the air than the government would concede and believed war with Germany likely, though not inevitable. He remained strangely detached from the Far Eastern aspects. After all, the Japanese attack upon China in 1931 and after had made the Ten-Year Rule obsolete and exposed the weakness of Britain's position. If it had been possible to eliminate, by withdrawal or treaty, the risk of war with Japan, the European position would have been transformed. At the time, and still more in *The Gathering Storm*, he simplified unduly the issues which ministers had to confront.

* * * * *

Churchill used to reflect afterwards that invisible wings had beaten over him in the 1930s. That he would enter the Cabinet if war broke out was generally expected and had been foreseen by Baldwin and Chamberlain. Though privy to many official secrets and enjoying privileged contact with ministers, Churchill did not hold office for a little over a decade. In that time he earned and spent hugely, not least in rebuilding Chartwell and its gardens. He managed to spend the money as fast as it came in, and sometimes faster. As soon as the monumental account of World War I was complete, he embarked upon the congenial task of restoring the repute of his ancestor John Churchill, first Duke of Marlborough. Whereas WSC's earlier books had all described the immediate or recent past, the exigencies of empire, military campaigns, the effect of personality in politics, Britain's machinery of government, his four hefty volumes on Marlborough marked a departure. Archives had to be investigated in several countries of Europe. Much of this work was done by research assistants. At Blenheim, however, he was able to read many papers hitherto unseen. He tramped over the battlefields. His admiration for the great Duke grew and grew. In the later stages of *Marlborough*, and in all his subsequent publications, Churchill had the indispensable help of F.W. Deakin, Fellow of Wadham College, Oxford, and later Warden of St Antony's, who once described himself candidly as one who had 'surrendered without terms long ago to the magic of the man.'

To write history in this fashion was not like painting, a diversion. Nor was it a way of making ready money, since he could earn more with less effort by dictating articles. Rather, it was a means of expressing a vision of men and events seen through what Deakin called 'the prism of a superb historical imagination'. Thus history was not a 'subject', like geography or physics; rather, it was to WSC 'the sum of things'.[50] Nor did he assume that history could be constructed solely from the papers which have come down to posterity. These often represent, he pointed out, 'a very small part of what took place, and to fill in the picture one has to visualise the daily life – the constant discussions between ministers, the friendly dinners, and many days when nothing happens worthy of record, but during which events were nevertheless proceeding.'[51] While Churchill did not claim that history is something which can simply be learned and then applied, he was convinced that those who cut themselves off from its study carry a heavy handicap in judging current and future events. It was his invariable practice to recommend the study of history to aspiring politicians and journalists, though he was not so sanguine as to expect any marked change of human conduct. 'Unteachable from infancy to tomb – There is the first & main characteristic of mankind',[52] he judged after brooding upon the events of 1914 and 1915; and his own account of 1945 he prefaced with the reproachful theme 'How the great democracies triumphed, and so were able to resume the follies which had so nearly cost them their life.' He once remarked that whereas in the civilized world we have largely succeeded in erasing the lion and the tiger from the human soul, we have not removed the donkey.[53]

Churchill's volumes on Marlborough contain much learning and many fine passages. As with most of his writings, they sometimes sound better than they read, a natural reflection of the fact that they were all dictated. That master of a more austere style, Evelyn Waugh, described Churchill's as 'sham Augustan' and found his effort to pin

33

the label 'liar' upon Macaulay's coat-tails too blatant. 'I was everywhere outraged by his partisanship & naïve assumption of superior virtue. It is a shifty barrister's case, not a work of literature.'[54] It was a good deal more than that, though it remains true that Churchill stretched many a point in the Duke's favour. What matters most is that for the better part of a decade the man who was soon to stand at the centre of Britain's war effort spent countless hours in the scrutiny of Marlborough's fortunes: Britain fighting a powerful enemy bent upon the domination of Europe; the supreme importance of naval power; all the trials of conducting a war in concert with allies; rivalries and jealousies among the politicians and the military; the supreme effort required for victory, the ease with which many of the fruits were thrown away, the small regard of Marlborough's countrymen for his memory. Here was an instance in which British and Allied strategy reflected in large degree the conceptions of one man. Churchill sensed the coming of another such struggle. As the chapters took shape, he would by an exercise of imagination identify himself with the personalities and the contours of each crisis. He would take memoranda and drafts from his research assistants, and transform them.

Detailed assessment of Marlborough's activities, not only as a strategist but as a man of state trying to create and cement an alliance, had an effect which Churchill could not have foreseen when he first turned to the records of the seventeenth and eighteenth centuries. Once the final volume on Marlborough was finished, he moved at once to the work eventually published as *A History of the English-speaking Peoples*. In the summer of 1939, when Deakin pointed out that there is no solid evidence for King Alfred's burning of the cakes, he was informed with 'energetic brutality and disarming kindliness' that myths have their historical importance at times of crisis: this myth symbolized British resistance to the invader, and was a source of inspiration to those dim and distant figures the Counts of the Saxon shore, striving to defend the island. 'I was duly chastened,' Deakin records in his good-humoured way 'and shortly afterwards, with inexorable historical logic, Churchill was to find himself the lineal and supreme successor of those Counts of the Saxon shore, and the leader of the most decisive British resistance in her history.'[55]

★ ★ ★ ★ ★

In common with almost every senior figure in British public life, Churchill had not looked to the creation of a continental army. He expected the French would furnish the bulk of the alliance's strength on land, at any rate in the first part of another great war. The conviction that France was superior to Germany on land has much to do with Churchill's belief that Britain and France should have gone to war with Germany in 1938. Once Hitler had seized the remnant of Czechoslovakia in March 1939, and thus in effect torn up the Munich agreement, the British and French governments responded with guarantees to Poland and other countries in South Eastern Europe, and Britain abandoned the tradition of centuries by introducing conscription in peacetime. In respect of policy, there was now little to prevent Churchill's return to the Cabinet. He possessed in abundance the qualities to which Mrs Churchill had pointed in May 1915, when begging the Prime Minister not to eject her husband from the Admiralty: the power, the imagination and the deadliness to fight Germany.[56]

Conversing privately with President Roosevelt in the summer of 1939, King George VI gained the impression that the President would not view favourably Churchill's succession to Chamberlain. The monarch himself seems to have held a more decided view, and said so to the Prime Minister of Canada, Mackenzie King, who was accompanying the royal party on its visit to the USA. The latter's diary records 'I agreed that it would be inviting disaster, simply challenging Germany.'[57] This entry appears to relate to the possibility that Churchill should become Prime Minister, and of that there was no realistic prospect in the summer of 1939. Chamberlain's view was the same as Mackenzie King's: that Churchill's inclusion in the Cabinet would be regarded by the dictators as an open challenge; and if there were even a faint possibility of easing the tension with them, the benefits of Churchill's presence would not justify the risk.

Once Germany invaded Poland, Churchill joined the War Cabinet, though for a day or two it was not clear that he would return to the Admiralty. Immediately before the war, British production of aircraft had overtaken Germany's; nevertheless, there were still large arrears to make up. As for the Royal Navy, Churchill himself observes that he now had at his disposal 'what was undoubtedly the finest-tempered instrument of naval war in the world' and says in terms that it would be unjust to Chamberlain's government and its service advisers to suggest that the navy had not been adequately prepared for a struggle with Germany, or with Germany and Italy.[58] He might with equal justice have added that thanks to the decisions taken under Baldwin and Chamberlain, Britain's spending upon defence was rapidly accelerating to figures previously unknown, and far larger than any achieved by the distinguished Liberal administration before 1914.

To raise and maintain a continental army in addition to these naval and air forces would evidently bring immense problems. Quite apart from the question of manpower, there was the matter of finance, because for some while Britain had been ordering warlike supplies without knowing how she would eventually pay for them. Churchill nevertheless favoured taking the risk; and after some hesitation, Chamberlain agreed that a force of 55 divisions should be raised. Immediately after the War Cabinet's meeting, he received a note from WSC: 'I hope you will not think it inappropriate from one serving under you, if I say that in twenty years of Cabinets I have never heard a more commanding summing-up upon a great question.'[59]

Regarding almost all the main issues of the war, Churchill found himself in harmony with Chamberlain and the other members of the War Cabinet. For example, they agreed that Italy should be kept neutral if humanly possible, that the Allies should not initiate the bombing of Germany, that even a few months' delay were invaluable as war production in the West mounted rapidly. Churchill chafed at the cumbrousness of the official machine, thirsted for offensive action at sea, at various times espoused policies which might have meant war with Russia or the locking-up of a large part of Britain's naval power in the Baltic, and caused many frictions and resentments in the Admiralty and with political colleagues. By March 1940, the First Lord was making it plain that he wished to be Minister of Defence, with substantial powers over the War Office and Air Ministry. The Prime Minister would not go so far, but did appoint him to be Chairman of the Military Coordination Committee. The experiment failed, amidst recriminations. Writing after the war, Churchill believed that the fault lay mainly with the inadequacies of the official machinery. The accounts reaching the Prime Minister, however, told a different tale, and one which was to be repeated endlessly over the next five years.

Churchill needed about eight hours' sleep a day, though he often contrived to manage with less for a while. He found, or at any rate persuaded himself, that he could extract a day and a half's work from every 24 hours by methods not available to those around him. As Chamberlain recorded in mid-April 1940:

> He goes to bed after lunch for a couple of hours or so, and holds conferences up to 1 in the morning, at which he goes into every detail, so I am informed, that could quite well be settled by subordinates. Officers and officials in his own and other departments are sent for and kept up until they are dropping with fatigue and Service Ministers are worn out in arguing with him. I say to myself that this is the price we have to pay for the asset that we have in his personality and popularity, but I do wish we could have the latter without the former.[60]

The situation became so difficult that even Churchill, whom no one ever accused of undue deference to the feelings of those around him, had to ask Chamberlain to preside. 'They'll take from you what they won't take from me.'

The two other Service ministers, at the Air Ministry and the War Office, said initially that they would sooner resign than concede the powers which Churchill sought; then everyone would know where responsibility resided. Chamberlain replied that if the new arrangements could not be made, he would himself resign and let Churchill be Prime Minister as well as Defence Minister; whereupon the two Secretaries of State said that this would be too great a disaster. They therefore acquiesced in the new proposals, which were accepted at once and gratefully by Churchill.[61] Beyond a general dissatisfaction, he was soon moved by episodes during the Norwegian campaign beginning in April 1940, when in important respects the War Office and Admiralty went their own ways. The system established in the last days of Chamberlain's premiership gave the First Lord a large additional measure of power. Of all ministers, he bore the greatest responsibility for what had been done in Norway. He defended himself and the government lustily in the debate of 7 and 8 May 1940. The government's majority fell to 81, more than ample in normal circumstances. Chamberlain said that he must nevertheless resign, since a national government, with Labour and Liberals brought in, was essential. Churchill urged him not to go, but found the Prime Minister 'neither convinced nor comforted'. The creditable fact is that Chamberlain and Churchill had formed a partnership of growing strength. Immediately upon returning from Buckingham Palace, where the King appointed him Prime Minister on the evening of 10 May, Churchill wrote to thank Chamberlain for his self-forgetting dignity and public spirit. He added what was no more than the bare truth 'To a very large extent I am in your hands – and I feel no fear of that.'[62]

* * * * *

In sum, the first eight months of the war had done nothing to calm the apprehensions, widespread among politicians, civil servants and serving officers, that Churchill was the Churchill of old: impulsive, sometimes bullying, self-centred. Would he not bring with him an entourage of undesirables? Would Whitehall have to endure a re-creation of Lloyd George's Garden Suburb, a rag-bag of irresponsible advisers who would create confusion to no good purpose? Would not rambling meetings, held at absurd hours, produce repeated changes of plan? Would the new Prime Minister overbear his advisers in the armed services to an unhealthy degree, or even overrule them in vital matters? All these fears were keenly felt. Some persisted, and it would be pointless to aver that all were groundless. Nonetheless, most were overborne in short order. The Labour and Liberal parties were willing to serve under Churchill, as they had not been under Chamberlain; the German invasion of the Low Countries, occurring in those very days, made the immediacy of the peril obvious to all; and for the following five years, party-political antagonisms faded into irrelevance, or occasionally became minor irritations. Many who had entertained the deepest doubts about Churchill's accession were converted by his comprehension of wide issues and capacity to drive the machine energetically.

He made no secret of the fact that he liked the post of Prime Minister far better than the other great offices he had held. Long convinced that much of history is decided by great men and women, and that everything turns upon great moments, he felt 'as if I were walking with destiny'. When he adds that 'all my past life had been but a preparation for this hour and for this trial', he was thinking of his life not only as a politician but of those years when he had been able to keep the wolf from the door with no weapon larger than the pen, the life of words and thoughts, research and reflection. Unlike Lloyd George in 1916, he had no obvious rival. Assailed by no doubts about the righteousness of the war, he was so constituted that he could issue, unflinching, orders which would bring death and sorrow to many. 'I thought I knew a good deal about it all, and I was sure I should not fail.'[63] Now he could 'discipline the bloody business at last. I had no feeling of personal inadequacy, or anything of that sort.' Forming a War Cabinet of five within an hour or two, he went to bed in the middle of the night. At breakfast the next morning he remarked to Mrs Churchill, 'There is only one man who can turn me out and that is Hitler.'[64]

* * * * *

It was said of Sir Henry Campbell-Bannerman, almost as if he had been a racehorse, that there never was such a change of form as between his time in opposition and his record as Prime Minister. The same was true of Churchill. The Churchill of the summer of 1940 was a different proposition from the Churchill of olden days or even of a few months before. He had never been a good intriguer; the ties of party had always sat lightly upon him. Both facts were suddenly advantageous in May 1940. Asked about the improved performance of another Prime Minister, Churchill replied characteristically 'Well, if you read Maeterlinck you will learn that if you feed a grub on royal jelly you may turn it into a queen bee.'[65] Suddenly he embodied Great Britain, and a great deal beyond its shores, as Clemenceau once personified France.

Throughout the 'phoney war', misnamed since the war at sea was waged with vigour from the outset, the War Cabinet had in general taken the view that delay worked to the Allies' advantage. Now all such arguments had been swept aside by the German onrush. Although WSC would have liked to keep Italy neutral, he saw no prospect that anything the Allies could offer would be so attractive to Mussolini as the prospect of a cheap victory at the German coat-tails. Here, then, was a contest to the death, where old inhibitions no longer had a place. Hearing a remark to the effect that South Africa's climate produced great men, Churchill bit hard on his cigar, thumped the table, and cried 'It isn't climate that makes great men. It's WAR!' In cadences of eloquence, he then described how the churning processes of conflict threw giants into places of high responsibility, amidst the affairs of pygmy man. [66]

Denying that he gave the people courage, Churchill remarked that it was he who had the luck to be called upon 'to give the roar.' Though few others would have thought of themselves as enjoying any kind of good luck at that time, there was one sense in which it was true, both for Churchill and for the many millions who looked to him. He was 'lucky' in the sense that he now held the post for which he was best fitted. He grew in stature, almost from day to day, to meet the new needs. 'The war has smelted out all the base metal that was in him', said Baldwin.[67]

It was ridiculous to think that France could be conquered by 120 tanks, WSC exclaimed to the Cabinet on 16 May; 'but it may be!' added the Permanent Under-Secretary of the Foreign Office.[68] With the collapse of the French armies went the main prop of Allied strategy in mainland Europe. Nor was it possible to look to the United States for any early relief. A couple of weeks earlier, Roosevelt had said that he thought Chamberlain and Churchill were the only two in the British government who really saw the magnitude of the problem ahead and that 'Churchill was tight most of the time'. At least this was one opinion shared by the President and Hitler, who used to call Churchill the 'whisky guzzler'.[69] Both were to find out, the President sooner than the Führer, that they had mistaken the man. Asked when it was all over which he would choose if he could relive one twelve-month, Churchill replied without hesitation, '1940 every time, every time.'[70] That was the time when words, thoughts and actions were fused. He had promised nothing but blood, toil, sweat and tears, without knowing how swiftly the crisis would come. He had to establish through words as well as deeds a mastery over the governmental machine, his ministerial colleagues, the House of Commons and the country. In a few months, he forged with them an alliance which survived bleak months of suffering and reverses.

Even though the pillars of the established world were crashing to ground around him, he devoted immense care to the composition of his speeches. The emotions upon which he drew, the sense of a climacteric when the forces of evil must be resisted to the last, the burning conviction that the British (in which definition he included the race dwelling around the globe) must so bear themselves that later generations would deem this their finest hour – all sprang unbidden from a lifetime's reading and experience. To find the right language was of supreme importance, if not always easy. On 28 May 1940, Belgium having just capitulated and the British and French armies being in dire straits, Churchill paced up and down the Cabinet Room in 10 Downing Street, rehearsing each new version:

> Meanwhile, the House ... must expect ... to hear ... bad news ... no ... the House ... should prepare itself ... for bad news ... no, not bad news ... bad tidings ... the House ... should prepare itself ... for bad tidings ... bad tidings ... hard tidings ... the House should prepare itself ... for hard tidings ... hard tidings ... heavy tidings ... for heavy tidings ... for hard and heavy tidings ... yes ... meanwhile the House ... should prepare itself ... for hard and heavy tidings ... yes, that is what I want to say.[71]

In face of this disaster, Churchill's mind turned at once to the offensive. How could small raiding forces cause the maximum of confusion and uncertainty in the countries which Germany had subjugated? Tanks and armoured fighting vehicles must be accommodated in flat-bottomed boats. Floating harbours must be built. A stream of minutes on such subjects flowed from the Prime Minister to General Ismay for consideration by the military staffs.

So much has been recorded about what Churchill did during the war that we may pause here to notice something which he did not do. When additional powers had been conferred upon him at the beginning of May 1940, he ordered General Ismay to create a high-powered central staff, to work immediately alongside Churchill himself. Ismay recalled Lloyd George and his Garden Suburb. The kind of staff which Churchill desired to establish was unnecessary and undesirable and would create immense confusion, Ismay contended; use of the existing machinery would serve far better. Telling this story with his habitual modesty, he remarks 'I was saved by the pressure of events.' In the crisis of the next few days, no one had time to worry about these questions of organization. Thus he continued to toil at 2 Richmond Terrace with his trusted colleagues around him, and made no attempt to recruit the Central Staff.[72] It has been generally acknowledged, not least by Churchill himself, that the efficient working of the Cabinet Secretariat was indispensable to the prosecution of the war. The division between its military and civil sides, instituted by Chamberlain in 1938, was retained. The double-banking of the Chiefs of Staff by Vice-Chiefs continued. Despite the pressure for a War Cabinet composed of members not responsible for big departments of state, Churchill moved steadily in the other direction, so that most of his colleagues had no time to indulge in exalted brooding. In the middle of the war, it was calculated that a member of the War Cabinet received each day reading matter as long as a novel, and this despite all attempts to curb the flow.

It was a war involving every agency of the state and every part of the population, fought all over the world. To prosecute such a war poses peculiar difficulties for a parliamentary democracy. If complete powers are ceded to the military men, how can the position of civilian ministers be maintained, the authority of Parliament and the judiciary upheld, even restricted liberties be preserved? To say that these tensions, immanent in the situation which Britain occupied, were resolved easily would be absurd. The most cursory reading of the biographies and diaries of the Chiefs of Staff and senior commanders – Alanbrooke, Wavell, Auchinleck, Cunningham, Portal, Pound – would dispel any such notion. Yet resolved the problems were. Churchill's great innovation lay not in the administrative machinery but in his determination to hold simultaneously the posts of Prime Minister and Minister of Defence. He did not preside over anything resembling the Ministry of Defence of post-war years. Indeed, the immense influence which he wielded in military matters, broadly defined, was exercised through General Ismay and his small staff in their accustomed places.

The balance of political strength within the government was immediately and sensibly altered; for the Secretaries of State for War and Air, and the First Lord of the Admiralty, members of the War Cabinet under Chamberlain, ceased to be so after 10 May. They were, however, members of the Defence Committee, where many of the more important decisions relating to the military conduct of the war were taken, especially between 1940 and 1942. Presiding there, Churchill was the dominant figure. He held all the powers which accrue to, and loyalties which focus upon, the Prime Minister. He was the indispensable man, Field-Marshal Smuts once remarked, because full of ideas. He had what Stalin called 'desperation', an untameable resolve to fight the war to a victorious finish no matter what the odds or the cost. To these formidable qualities we must add another that was indispensable: Churchill knew far more about warfare than any other minister. Attlee, leader of the Labour Party and Deputy Prime Minister from 1942, remarks that Churchill unlike Lloyd George had the military knowledge to tell the generals what was right.[73]

That was a view which few of them would have accepted and puts the point rather too high; for Churchill's knowledge was sometimes out of date, and he made some major misjudgements. It could scarcely have been otherwise. Like many others at high levels, not least in the armed services themselves, he did not grasp quickly the transformation wrought by the development of air power. He was apt to harass commanders in the field, often on the strength of those intercepted messages of the enemy which he insisted upon seeing in raw form. At the level of high tactics he did less well than in high strategy. All the same, this was a civilian justified in believing that he knew 'a good deal about it all', playing a part beyond the reach of a conventional politician.

He was at his best in deciding which issues mattered, concentrating his energies upon them, probing experts' advice in detail, nagging and pestering the departments. Though he has been quoted as saying that he thought it foolish to keep a daily diary, which would reflect the changes of opinion of the writer and when published make him appear indecisive or foolish,[74] his letters and minutes, and the records of meetings, are far fuller and more revealing than a diary. It is a sign of his self-confidence that he should insist upon setting down each decision on paper. He liked to do a good deal of his dictation from bed during the morning, and more into the early hours. Relays of secretaries stood ready. 'I shall require you to stay late, my dear', he greeted one of them; 'I am feeling very fertile tonight.'[75] He did his best to insist on concise submissions and pointed constantly to the importance of exactitude in language, a point which he illustrated by recounting the unfortunate consequences for the man who in giving instructions to his surgeon forgot the distinction between circumcision and castration.[76]

Within a few weeks of his becoming Prime Minister, Mrs Churchill wrote to him about reports which had come to her of his rough, sarcastic and overbearing manner. If it seems extraordinary that a wife should send such a letter after more than 30 years of marriage, we have to recall that Churchill habitually took more notice of what was submitted to him on paper than of what was said in conversation. 'I must confess that I have noticed a deterioration in your manner; & you are not as kind as you used to be.'[77] The people serving Churchill made every allowance for the burden he bore with a courage that extorted their wonder. Almost all were devoted to him. Otherwise, they could hardly have endured his swift changes of mood, unreasonableness, impossible demands. Even if these tempests endured rather longer than the psalmist's twinkling of an eye, they generally did not last. The process of order and counter-order took its toll. One of the private secretaries, who had served at the Admiralty before moving to No. 10, typed out a minute:

ACTION THIS DAY

Pray let six new offices be fitted out for my use, in Selfridge's, Lambeth Palace, Stanmore, Tooting Bec, the Palladium and Mile End Road. I will inform you at 6 each evening at which office I shall dine, work and sleep. Accommodation will be required for Mrs Churchill, two shorthand typists, three secretaries and Nelson. There should be shelter for all and a place for me to watch air raids from the roof. This should be completed by Monday. There is to be no hammering during office hours, that is between 7 a.m. and 3 a.m.

W.S.C.   31.10.40

All the senior staff, including Ismay, were convinced that this document was genuine.[78] It should be explained that Churchill loved fishes, birds, butterflies, animals (with a special fondness for pigs, because they treated human beings as equals) and cats most of all. Nelson was the black cat which, first at No. 10 and later in the Cabinet War Rooms, lived in intermittent harmony with the animal inherited from the Chamberlains, Munich Mouser. During a heavy air-raid one afternoon Churchill, clad in nothing but a silk vest after his sleep, was found on all fours addressing words of reproof to Nelson: 'You should be ashamed of yourself, with a name like yours, skulking under that chest of drawers while all those brave young men in the RAF are up there fighting gallantly to save their country.'[79] In the comparative safety of Chartwell resided the Marmalade Cat. One of the private secretaries took lunch alone there with Churchill on 3 June 1941; more exactly, there was another guest in the person of the cat, placed in a chair at the Prime Minister's right-hand side. In the intervals of composing, half under his breath, an important speech, then preparing arguments to use with Beaverbrook, then complaining about the conduct of military affairs in the Middle East, he cleaned the Marmalade Cat's eyes, offered some titbits of mutton and expressed his deep regret that cream was not available on account of wartime rationing. When this favourite of all his pets died during a week of grim news, Mrs Churchill, knowing how intensely her husband would be upset, insisted that he be not told until better tidings had come.[80]

* * * * *

In the main, Churchill relied upon the long-established organs of state. He did not have a circle, in the sense of a group which met and discussed matters with him regularly out of hours. There were those close to him like Brendan Bracken, who in due course became Minister of Information; Lord Beaverbrook, with whom from time to time he had violent rows, but with little effect upon their private friendship (Churchill is supposed to have said 'Some people take drugs; I take Max'); Desmond Morton, who in the first part of the war saw a great deal of Intelligence material on Churchill's behalf; and perhaps most important of all his close friend of many years Professor Lindemann, later Lord Cherwell. Under his aegis, plans and charts were presented to the Prime Minister so that he could grasp quickly the essentials of many complicated situations. Cherwell, himself a good hater, detested by some of those with whom he had to deal, was a scientist of high rank who could explain in layman's English the complicated technical questions upon which the outcome of the war might well depend. Not that WSC relied on him alone for such advice. One young man dealing with most secret scientific matters within the intelligence services, Dr R.V. Jones, later wrote of the Prime Minister: 'Alone among politicians he valued science and technology at something approaching their true worth, at least in military application, and he had early been briefed in nuclear energy for the future.'[81]

This aspect of Churchill's premiership has not always received the attention that it merits. He maintained direct and short links to the latest developments of science. As in the field of military strategy, some of the projects the Prime Minister pursued came to nothing. Some wasted energy and time when both commodities were in short supply, but in varied instances of the first importance Churchill's direct interest, springing from his wide-ranging curiosity, produced results which mattered; by way of example, the techniques for bending the beams, upon which the German air force was relying for its night bombing of Britain, a process in which the same Dr Jones played a leading part. The floating harbours which proved indispensable to the invasion of Normandy in 1944 owed a great deal to Churchill's insistence that planning and manufacture must begin early. It was a subject which had interested him for at least a quarter of a century. Now, in 1942, he gave directions in familiar style: 'Don't argue the matter. The difficulties will argue for themselves.'[82]

We cannot doubt that Churchill's determination to take a guiding hand in such matters derived largely from experience during World War I. His own self-confidence would anyhow have disinclined him to believe that experts would necessarily be in the right all the time, especially outside their own immediate sphere of competence. The same convictions account for many of his dealings as Prime Minister with fighting men. Nothing he had seen in World War I, or for that matter in the early part of World War II, had convinced him that the conduct of war might safely be left to the military; moreover, the politicians had to organize the civilian effort, find the money, convince Parliament. WSC was free to concentrate upon the strategy and diplomacy of the war, on a scale not approached by any prime minister since those days, because of the extraordinary circumstances. There was little parliamentary opposition; Mr Ernest Bevin, coming to politics directly from a lifetime of hard experience in the world of trade unions, and more generally the presence of the Labour leaders in the government, ensured collaboration on that front; the property of everyone was put at the disposal of the state; the normal constituency duties of an M.P. faded largely into irrelevance; and very large swathes of domestic and parliamentary business could be left to others: Chamberlain for the first few months until his illness, thereafter Sir John Anderson, Sir Kingsley Wood, Mr Attlee, Lord Woolton. This is not to say that Churchill took no interest in their proceedings. On the contrary, he practised a system whereby the departments were prodded up with vigour and in unexpected places, upon subjects ranging from the supply of cut flowers to the prompt payment of compensation for damage caused by air raids. The Minister of Food was instructed to look to the production of rabbits, for everything must be done to sustain the meagre meat ration. 'Almost all the food faddists I have ever known, nut-eaters and the like,' the Prime Minister informed him, 'have died prematurely after a long period of senile decay.' Churchill himself, who is recorded as consuming for a single breakfast two eggs, ham, chicken, coffee, toast, butter, marmalade, two oranges and a glass of juice, shook his head over the strange diets favoured by Lord Cherwell and Sir Stafford Cripps, whom he greeted thus when they chanced to arrive late: 'Well, gentlemen, if you have finished toying with your beetroot, we will get on with more important matters.' [83]

* * * * *

We can hardly state it too often: Britain did not stand alone in the summer of 1940. Every country of the Commonwealth and Empire fought from the beginning to the end. This was a fact of high military significance; it is hard to imagine, for example, that the position in the Middle East could have been held without the large contingents of troops from Australia, New Zealand and India. That response in communities across the continents moved Churchill also for its moral significance. Here was the British people with its mixture of decency and dauntlessness, scattered across the globe, uprisen against tyranny. Nor did he fear to enfold the Americans in this broad conception. Thus when speaking of the Japanese to Senate and Congress in Washington immediately after Pearl Harbour, he did not say 'What kind of people do they think we are?' but 'What kind of a people do they think we are?'

That Britain had sustained a military disaster alongside France was undeniable. Churchill's refusal to palliate those hard and heavy tidings had much to do with the bond which by mysterious means was sealed between him and many millions of people, in Britain and on wider shores, during that summer. He and the alliance had at least one stroke of good fortune in those days. The substantial land forces despatched to France even after Dunkirk were mainly retrieved, in a scramble and at the last minute, when they might easily have been lost. Though there was every reason to prepare against a German invasion of the British Isles, the fact was that it could succeed only if the Royal Navy lost command of the English Channel, or the Royal Air Force were defeated in the skies; or more probably only if both disasters occurred. To put ashore a force large enough to conquer Britain would have been a formidable undertaking at the best of times. Admittedly, no one knew whether the Luftwaffe could bomb London and other cities on such a scale as to render an orderly defence impossible. Nor could anyone tell with certainty whether bombing might so undermine morale that the British government would be compelled to sue for peace. Churchill did not believe either prospect likely. He took his stand on Britain's strength in those two arms of warfare. In fine, Britain could not be defeated by Germany and Italy unless she ran out of food, money or arms. The war was conducted in practice with a singular lack of concern about cost. Britain's overseas investments, especially those in the United States, were liquidated, often at lamentably low prices, in order to pay for arms; and later on, Lend-Lease came to the rescue. Starvation was another matter, and the losses of merchant shipping in the next two years mounted to so dreadful a total that stocks of some vital commodities were reduced to a few weeks' supply.

Chamberlain's mortal illness in the summer of 1940 put an end within months to a partnership which reflects well upon both men, and Churchill pondered before accepting the leadership of the Conservative Party. He asked himself first whether such a position was compatible with the headship of a coalition government supported by all parties. Incapable of considering any question apart from its historical context, he readily saw the advantages of being able to speak, in dealings with Labour and the Liberals, as leader of the party which had by far the biggest parliamentary battalions. But he had then to put to himself another more personal question, whether he was by temperament and conviction able to identify himself with the main historical conceptions of Toryism? Acknowledging that 'very varying opinions' were entertained about his public life of the last 40 years, he said that he had always faithfully served 'two public causes which I think stand supreme – the maintenance of the enduring greatness of Britain and her Empire and the historical continuity of our island life.' Alone among the nations of the world, the British had found the means of combining Empire and liberty, had reconciled democracy and tradition, had avoided over several centuries religious or political gulfs in their domestic life, had found the means of carrying forward the glories of the past through all the storms that had surged about.

This speech deserves our notice, for it is most revealing of the man. To the interplay and interweaving of past and present Churchill attributed what had been revealed to a wondering world in the ordeal of 1940, the unconquerable strength of a united nation; in that achievement all living parties, and indeed some dead ones like the Whigs, had borne their part. Party interests and party feelings must be sacrificed by all if the nation was to emerge victoriously from its perils, and the Conservative Party would not allow any other group to excel it in the sacrifice of such interests. In no other way 'can we save our lives and, what is far more precious than life, the grand human causes which we, in our generation, have the supreme honour to defend.'[84]

★ ★ ★ ★ ★

... a goodly personage, of heart courageous, politic in council, in adversity nothing abashed, in prosperity rather joyful than proud, in peace just and merciful, in war sharp and fierce ... (Sir Thomas More of King Edward IV)

Churchill's confidence that Britain would not be successfully invaded was a judgement of the first importance, vindicated in the event. It was a matter of balancing probabilities. A few miles across the Channel lay the unmistakable signs of preparation. If Britain and the Commonwealth – the United States being at best benevolently neutral and sometimes less – could not in any foreseeable future go back into Western Europe with large armies, what were they to do? First, they would stir up disaffection and organize sabotage. This appealed strongly to the Prime Minister's aggressive instincts and romantic conception of guerrilla warfare. In the event, the hope of setting Europe ablaze proved illusory, though once the Allied armies were manifestly on their way, four years later, it was a different matter. For a long time, WSC placed a strong faith in the bombing of occupied Europe, and especially of the German heartland. He explained to Parliament and people the reasons for this confidence. The price was horribly high, and the result for several years disproportionately small. Again, this outcome was easier to detect with hindsight than to predict.

At least the entry of Italy into the war in June 1940 afforded a welcome opportunity to indulge in raillery at the expense of Mussolini, to whom Churchill offered a safeguarded passage through the Straits of Gibraltar so that the Italian Navy could under the Duce's own command contest the mastery of the English Channel: 'There is a very general curiosity in the British Fleet to find out whether the Italians are up to the level they were at in the last war, or whether they have fallen off at all.'[85] If the Mediterranean had become a dangerous place for Allied shipping and aircraft, there was always the prospect of inflicting severe damage upon the Italian Navy. Italian land forces might be, and soon were, attacked with success in Abyssinia, Eritrea and Libya. The Middle East held essential supplies of oil. There were large interests at stake in Syria, Iraq, Palestine. The Suez Canal constituted the narrow throat of communication to the Indian and Pacific Oceans.

It was to this theatre that from August 1940, long before anyone could be confident that the threat of invasion had abated, the British government sent a large proportion of its armoured strength. The decision entailed a calculated and bold risk and originated with the CIGS, General Dill, and the Secretary of State for War, Eden. It was at first opposed by General Brooke, who was then C.-in-C. Home Forces and later to succeed Dill. The Prime Minister, once convinced, gave his indispensable support. Without that decision and a series of similar actions in 1941, the Middle Eastern position might well have been lost. Despite many reverses, this was the theatre from which heavy defeats were inflicted upon the Axis and to which large German forces were deflected. Eventually the armies advancing westwards from Egypt and Libya were able to join forces with those which had landed far to the west. Thus the whole of North Africa was at last cleared, and the way open for the invasion of Sicily and Italy, not to mention the fall of Mussolini and the armistice with Italy.

All that, however, lay far ahead and was achieved only after frustrations which caused Churchill puzzlement, anguish and anger. Two Commanders-in-Chief, Middle East, in the persons of Wavell and Auchinleck, were superseded. (We should notice that both went on to appointments of the highest importance within a short while. After deciding with reluctance that Auchinleck must be replaced in the Middle East, WSC said sorrowfully 'I felt as though I had just slain a noble stag.')[86] They were prominent among leading soldiers, another excellent example being provided by Dill, whose achievements and difficulties Churchill sometimes failed to appreciate fully. None of the three was adept in explaining himself persuasively or in the vigorous counter-arguments required to deal with the Prime Minister.

The British attack upon the French fleet in the summer of 1940, a decision for which WSC insisted upon assuming direct responsibility, had served to convince many people across the world that here was a country determined to battle on whatever the cost and a leader who would stop at little. It is credibly reported that Roosevelt was profoundly impressed. For a long while thereafter, it was mainly a matter of trying to avoid disaster in the many theatres where the British and Commonwealth forces were engaged: in the skies over Britain and increasingly over Europe; at sea in the Atlantic, home waters and the Mediterranean; and in all arms over the sprawling Middle Eastern theatre. Even in the Middle East, it took a very long time to concentrate sufficient forces to secure a decisive victory. Perhaps the Axis forces there might have been comprehensively defeated in 1941, but for the decision to send help to Greece. Churchill embarked upon that campaign with many misgivings, and only after being assured by Dill, Wavell and Eden that it was the right course to follow. There were all the moral arguments for coming to the defence of a small country; there was the important American factor, for the Greek enterprise had Roosevelt's strong support; there was the hope, which proved vain then and later, but to which Churchill was strongly attached, of bringing Turkey into the war or at least into a more helpful neutrality.

It need hardly be said that these complexities were much compounded in 1941, first by the German invasion of Russia and then by the Japanese attack upon the American fleet at Pearl Harbour and the British and Dutch territories in the Pacific. Even in the summer of 1940, Hitler had judged, mistakenly but plausibly, that Russia represented Britain's last hope, in other words that if Germany conquered the USSR, Britain would have no choice but to capitulate; and he was scarcely short of other arguments, including the conquest of living space and rich resources. It is a measure of Churchill's dominance that the text of his broadcast, delivered from Chequers on 22 June 1941, the day of the German invasion, had not been seen by the Foreign Secretary, let alone the War Cabinet. Refusing to resile from his many denunciations of Communism, Churchill nevertheless promised all aid that could be sent; which aid was more substantial than many accounts have allowed, much of it delivered at an appalling cost to the Arctic convoys.[87]

Neither at the time nor later did Churchill doubt that it was right to hold on in the Middle East, regardless of other dangers. Naturally, the British would much have preferred the entry of the United States into the war while Japan remained neutral. It is perfectly possible that the one event might have secured the other. Roosevelt judged that he could afford no such risk; and the United States Army, with which went its air force, was in a condition of grave weakness which the senior American officers did not conceal from their British counterparts when President and Prime Minister held the first of their wartime conferences in August 1941. Nor did the USA then have a coherent strategic policy.[88]

In his memoirs, Churchill confessed candidly that the Japanese menace occupied in his consciousness 'a sinister twilight'. However, he regarded it as a blessing that Japan's aggression had brought the United States wholeheartedly and unitedly into the war.[89] Immediately after Pearl Harbour, President Roosevelt concluded that there must be an Allied war council and that it should have its headquarters in Washington. The first decision Churchill accepted gladly and the latter with a good grace. He had displayed immense patience in wooing the President; he believed in the United States' good faith, even altruism; he and the President enjoyed each other's company. On the very night when he had asked 'What kind of a people do they think we are?', Churchill strained to open the window of his bedroom at the White House, and suddenly found himself short of breath with a dull pain over his heart. His doctor knew that these were signs of coronary insufficiency. 'You have been overdoing things', he said. Churchill's instantaneous reply speaks volumes. 'Now, Charles, you are not going to tell me to rest. I can't. I won't. Nobody else can do this job. I must.'[90]

His zeal did not diminish. He would sit up half the night in conversation or composing speeches and dictating telegrams. The entry of Japan into the war, the severe damage to the United States' fleet and the Japanese assault upon British and Dutch territories in South-East Asia created understandable fear and anger in Australia. The Australian Minister in Washington pressed his government's views hard upon Churchill, only to receive the reply 'You can't kick me round the room. I'm not kickable!'[91] At these meetings in Washington one of the crucial decisions of the war was taken, and one not necessarily to be expected from a power which had just suffered so severely in the Pacific: that the main purpose of Allied strategy should be to defeat Germany first, and then Japan. Military staffs on both sides might well have recommended that course anyway, but it was certainly aided by the masterly memoranda which Churchill had composed during the storm-beaten voyage to America. He felt confident from the start that the immense resources of the United States, once developed, would mean eventual victory.

It was not only a question of manufacturing capacity and manpower, but also of money. The different situations of the two countries brought into relief conflicting conceptions of modern warfare. Britain and her Allies needed dollars and supplies. At home, their economies had somehow to be controlled without high inflation. By contrast, the USA had both vast riches and a long way to go in rearmament. It does not simplify matters unduly to say that to the Americans, war became a function of production. Staggering quantities of tanks, aircraft and uniforms and all the other apparatus could be produced. Once that force could be brought to bear at the crucial points, the outcome of the war would be determined. To the British, accustomed to make do on a small margin of strength and severely stretched at many points, matters were more complicated. As Lord Moran put it 'It is as if Winston has a family of twelve children and there is not enough food for all of them – some of them must starve to death. He has to decide which';[92] or, as the Prime Minister would remark to the War Cabinet from time to time, 'Gentlemen, there are not enough teats on the old sow.'

* * * * *

After the fall of Singapore, which WSC himself characterized as the worst disaster and largest capitulation in British history, he said outright to a Secret Session of Parliament, 'The violence, fury, skill and might of Japan has far exceeded anything that we had been led to expect. … Neither of course were we prepared for the temporary eclipse and paralysis of the United States' sea-power in the Pacific.'[93] We need not wonder that in those few months after Pearl Harbour, Churchill sometimes felt low in spirits. As a consequence of the mild heart attack in Washington, he was not well. Public and Parliamentary criticism had to be met by a reconstruction of the government. Lord Beaverbrook, but recently appointed to a new position, insisted upon resignation and soon began a campaign in favour of support to Russia on a scale which neither Britain nor America could possibly manage at that stage. The Secretary of the Cabinet, agreeing with King George VI's Private Secretary that Beaverbrook was wholly evil, remarked that he had rarely in his life been so shocked as by the interview between Beaverbrook and Churchill when they parted company: 'They abused each other like a pair of fishwives.'[94] But their friendship survived apparently unscathed. Before long, Beaverbrook rejoined the government.

Though Churchill is reported as saying, in respect of fluctuations in his public standing, 'I'm like a bomber pilot. I go out night after night, and I know that one night I'll not return',[95] there is little sign that he entertained serious fears on that score, even in the troughs. Always insistent on seeing for himself, he realized from biting experience in World War I how readily those at the top lose contact with the fighting men. He showed a warm and practical sympathy with the privations endured by millions, went constantly to the places which had suffered the worst devastation and wept openly to see little Union Jacks hoisted amidst the wreckage. He understood instinctively the value of showmanship in the age of universal suffrage and can hardly be blamed for telling those who surrounded him in the bombed cities that he would let the enemy have the same treatment ten times over. Men and women who had lost their homes and livelihood were thrilled and heartened by his presence. At the end of a tour in London, the Prime Minister stood with his back to a large heap of rubble which had previously been a public building. Signalling for silence, he praised the public's fortitude and said that the ruin would make no difference to the nation's resolve to fight on until victory was gained. Nor was that the end of the matter, according to the information reaching the Minister of Health:

> He then raised one hand aloft with two fingers stuck up in his famous 'V' sign of Victory, turned his back on the audience, and with his other hand undid the front button of his trousers and relieved himself on the rubble. A multitude of people were convulsed with laughter and cheers.[96]

The well-calculated vulgarity of the V sign, his eccentricities of dress, the huge cigars, not to mention other manifestations, marked Churchill out from everyone else in public life, and from all the external characteristics thought to denote Britishness. If pressed, he might have described himself as half-American, half-cosmopolitan and wholly English. He owed a great deal to someone of a much more recognizable type, Attlee,[97] and to other colleagues of all political persuasions. After all, he was frequently abroad, sometimes for months. That the King's government was carried on during these absences says much for their loyalty and the excellence of the administrative machine. Despite the many tensions with the Chiefs of Staff and commanders in the field, the war effort was not stultified by blood-feuds between the fighting men and the civilians, a process of which Churchill had seen all too much during World War I. Nor in the event did he have any cause to fear intrigues to supplant him, however great the frustrations his colleagues sometimes felt and expressed. He knew well that his position depended upon combining the posts of Prime Minister and Minister of Defence and refused point-blank to consider any separation. His only conceivable Conservative rival, Anthony Eden, remarks that he grew to love Churchill,[98] and that emotion survived all tempests.

For men with big departments to run, the Prime Minister's hours of work were often infuriating and his demands inconsiderate. Pressed to attend yet another meeting late at night, Eden replied briskly 'I didn't sleep too well this afternoon.' By any normal standard, a vast amount of time was wasted under Churchill's unbusinesslike chairmanship. On the whole, his colleagues tolerated this situation with goodwill, not least because the Prime Minister could be relied upon to say something memorable. We may surmise that they realized his need of these rambling discussions, which provided a safety valve at times of intolerable pressure; and even when Churchill dismissed proposals or bullied his colleagues, a good deal of what they said sank in. Indeed, he would often after a few days produce as his own arguments which had been pressed upon him with no apparent success. He seldom took disagreements amiss or allowed them to interfere with private esteem. When he put to the War Cabinet a suggestion for a bold military stroke, Oliver Lyttelton dissented on the grounds that it would take two months to prepare. The infuriated Churchill said 'I have never heard in all my life a more idiotic suggestion advanced by a senior Minister of the Crown. Always an excuse for doing nothing.' There then raged for hours an argument which Attlee would probably have settled in 15 minutes. Others supported Lyttelton. At last the Prime Minister summed up: 'In short, we unanimously adopt the idiotic suggestion of the Minister of Production.'[99]

Such sallies enlivened every meeting or meal. When a member of the Cabinet remarked 'I'm afraid that I don't quite know where the Virgin Islands are', WSC rejoined 'Nor do I; but I do trust that they lie at a respectable distance from the Isle of Man.' Sometimes he would wax philosophical: 'Anger is a waste of energy. Steam which is used to blow off a safety valve would be better used to drive the engine.' And at other times he would reach by-ways of amusing inconsequence: 'Opinions differ. That is why we have check waistcoats.'[100] He needed, as every man at the summit of affairs does, to talk freely, without forethought or afterthought, among people who would not betray confidences; hence many unguarded expressions and many apparent contradictions. When we learn that on being told of the bombing of Rome the Prime Minister exclaimed 'Good. Have we hit the Pope? Have we made a hole in his tiara?',[101] we need not conclude that Churchill was hostile to organized religion. As a young man, he had become for a while strongly averse to the churches and their teaching, but then he found in his days of soldiering that he did not hesitate to ask for special protection when about to come under fire or to feel sincerely grateful when he arrived home safe.[102] He recognized to the full the importance of religious belief to those who had to go into battle against heavy odds, and to sorrowing families. He admired courageous people: in politics, those who faced unpopularity or loss of office for their convictions, in warfare those who met undaunted the most dangerous assignments, when despite murderous losses greater numbers pressed forward to fill the gaps so that 'Selection could be most strict where the task was forlorn. No units were so easy to recruit as those over whom Death ruled with daily attention.' When Mrs Churchill met by chance a submarine crew and greeted each member, the Petty Officer said to her 'Will you tell your husband that we dive for him?'[103]

Churchill venerated the House of Commons, a fact apparent to most Members. He had seen the undoing of administrations which lost their authority there and continued to take infinite pains over his orations, even at times of intense preoccupation. The faithful Ismay, finding the Prime Minister distressed at having to prepare such a speech, asked incautiously 'But why don't you tell them to go to hell?' Churchill, turning on him in a flash, retorted 'You should not say those things. I am the servant of the House.'[104] If the authority of the government was seriously challenged, he insisted that matters be put to the vote and did not refrain from landing hard blows. His former leader Lloyd George, uttering sharp criticisms in May 1941, received the retort 'It was the sort of speech with which, I imagine, the illustrious and venerable Marshal Pétain might well have enlivened the closing days of M. Reynaud's Cabinet'; and to the same critic's argument that the Prime Minister should be surrounded by people who would stand up to him and say 'No', he replied 'Has he no idea how strong the negative principle is in the constitution and working of the British war-making machine? The difficulty is not, I assure him, to have more brakes put on the wheels; the difficulty is to get more impetus and speed behind it.'[105]

Lloyd George was not the only one who believed that Churchill was showing all the qualities and failings which he had displayed during World War I. Nor were such voices heard only after the military reverses of 1941. The government had some persistent critics, and some well-informed ones. Sometimes they formed improbable liaisons, like that between Mr Emanuel Shinwell and Lord Winterton, known among their fellow-parliamentarians as 'Arsenic and Old Lace'. Occasional strictures from Mr Hore-Belisha were met by Churchill's tart reflections upon his pre-war record. The most eloquent of the opponents, Mr Aneurin Bevan, was also the most malignant. At last that doughty figure Miss Eleanor Rathbone, Member for the Combined English Universities and by no stretch of the imagination a Conservative, could repress no longer her indignation at what she called Bevan's virulent dislike of the Prime Minister: 'With what disgust and almost loathing we watch this kind of temperament, these cattish displays of feline malice.'[106]

It is true that the elaborate machinery of government provided many obstacles to action and equally true that many a time Churchill was restrained by reasoned objections from the Chiefs of Staff. If he did not override their collective opinion in matters of the first importance, he did press them hard and continuously. No single source testifies to this more eloquently than Brooke's diary. On several occasions the two of them came near to breaking point. But the fact that Brooke was chosen by Churchill to succeed Dill as CIGS in 1941, and was soon afterwards appointed chairman of the Chiefs of Staff Committee, reveals a good deal; for Brooke was notoriously quick-tempered, clipped in speech and fierce in argument. That Churchill should have wished to have such a man as his principal military adviser indicates at once a dislike of sycophants and a confidence in his ability to hold his own in detailed discussion of military questions. The Chief of the Air Staff, Portal, less explosive in speech than Brooke but equally tough, was much admired by Churchill. The First Sea Lord, Admiral Pound, had been ailing for some time and should have been replaced well before 1943. He was succeeded by Admiral Cunningham, a robust fighting sailor who was of the three Chiefs the least susceptible to Churchill's charm. They constituted a team of high quality and it was upon their alliance with Churchill that the British government, and by extension the Commonwealth, depended at conference after conference. Exasperated as they might be from to time, the Chiefs and their senior subordinates did not meddle in politics or challenge the control of the civilian enmeshed with all their great affairs.

It would have surprised them to learn that Churchill was far more patient than of old. Nonetheless, Mrs Churchill told the Prime Minister of Canada that it was indeed so. She explained how the writing of *Marlborough* had produced a real effect upon her husband's character; he had discovered that Marlborough's patience became the secret of his achievements. To the same interlocutor, Churchill said that he was quite a different man from the Churchill of earlier years. He confessed that he had made many mistakes in the First War and was making fewer in this one because of the earlier errors. 'Had learned a great deal ... Above all, he had learned to consider very carefully many matters and to be cautious.'[107]

* * * * *

Compelled to attend church frequently as a child, Churchill felt that he had built up so fine a credit in the Bank of Observance that he could draw confidently upon it for the rest of his life. For the first three years of the war he seemed able to call upon an equally ample reserve in respect of his health. His energy remained prodigious; he smoked and drank a great deal; he took scarcely any exercise and no holidays; he made constant exhausting journeys. At Cairo in November 1943, he said reflectively to his daughter:

> War is a game played with a smiling face, but do you think there is laughter in my heart? We travel in style and round us is great luxury and seeming security, but I never forget the man at the front, the bitter struggles, and the fact that men are dying in the air, on the land, and at sea.[108]

A short while afterwards, and now in his 70th year, he contracted pneumonia for the second time in nine months. His condition was thought so serious that Mrs Churchill was flown out hurriedly to be with him at Carthage; whence she reported as he recovered 'Has consented not to smoke and to drink only whisky and soda', and a few days later, as if she were dealing with a small child, 'Papa very refractory and naughty this morning ... All doing our best to persuade him that complete recovery depends on rest and compliance with regulations.'[109] After convalescing in Marrakech, he plunged back into business with vigour. Prudence would have dictated more rest, perhaps even an occasional free weekend. President Roosevelt recommended something of the kind. Such kindly meant exhortations had no greater effect than warnings from Lord Moran. A few days after the Allied armies crossed the Channel in June 1944, Churchill entertained King George VI at dinner. The conversation went on interminably. By a late hour, Field-Marshal Smuts and Mr Attlee were asleep. At one in the morning the Monarch enquired of his Prime Minister 'Well, aren't you going to bed tonight?' only to receive the reply 'No, Sir.'[110]

Churchill had always been apt to criticize the supposed timidity or misjudgements of commanders in the field. Brooke feared the effect upon ministers, who might be inclined to give the Prime Minister's condemnations greater weight than they deserved. On the night of 6 July, tired after a Parliamentary speech and having drunk too much, Churchill presided over a gathering at which he abused Montgomery. This was too much for the CIGS, who by his own account 'flared up' and according to Eden's 'exploded'. The committee was supposed to discuss the war in the Far East, a subject not reached until after midnight. WSC accused his colleagues of trying to corner him. Eden's diary calls this a 'really ghastly' meeting, and 'a deplorable evening'. He adds understandingly that it could not have happened a year earlier; all were marked by the iron of five years of war.[111]

Immediately before the second Quebec Conference, a few weeks later, Churchill was again ill. The voyage to Canada was blighted by disagreements and misunderstandings. He charged the Chiefs of Staff with framing up against him and opposing his wishes. So fraught did the situation become that even General Ismay tendered his resignation, which was instantly refused. So the ups and downs continued. At his best, Churchill could be affable and benign; at his worst, almost impossible to deal with. His grip on much of the Cabinet's business was declining perceptibly. The exhaustion felt even by the most resilient played its part, and was no doubt compounded by growing fears. Evidently Germany's defeat could not be far off, but with every passing day Britain's influence in the alliance declined. By 1944, in contrast to 1918, she was plainly a junior partner. The sad tale of British obligations to Poland, which could be honoured only with a considerable degree of Russian goodwill, illustrates the tensions. If the harshness of Churchill's language to the Polish leaders does him little credit, it remains true that he and Eden made a faithful but doomed effort to secure a decent future for Poland.

Colleagues would complain that Churchill was unyielding or irrational when his emotions or convictions were strongly engaged. One issue of the first order, India, illustrates the problem vividly. The India Office was held throughout Churchill's wartime Premiership by L.S. Amery. The two were long acquainted, from the days when Churchill had incautiously thrown Amery into the swimming pool at Harrow. Learned, imaginative, fearless, tireless, not afraid to stand up to the Prime Minister, Amery endured many rebuffs. Their relations had been soured by episodes in the summer of 1940, which Churchill's memory did not readily forgive. India was a subject upon which the Prime Minister held vehement views. Whereas Amery believed that the promise of genuine constitutional advance, culminating in a Dominion status which would carry the right to secede, must provide the right line of British policy, Churchill wished to do as little as possible in that direction, at least while the war lasted. He realized the importance of India's war-effort and dreaded the day when British control of India would release ancestral hatreds with horrible consequences. He regarded Gandhi as a sanctimonious fraud.

In some of these judgements he and Amery were not far apart. As to the means of meeting the immediate situation to best advantage, they differed time and again. There was a great deal at stake: India's position in the post-war Commonwealth or outside it, internal security, the Crown's obligations, touching British honour, to the Princely States, immensely complicated issues of administration and much else. The Japanese conquests in Burma raised the prospect of invasion and perhaps of upheavals so great as to paralyse India. 'Quit India,' said Gandhi and many of his followers. Luckily for the Allied war effort, and for India itself, there was no risk that such advice would be followed by the governments in New Delhi or London, though Churchill did record immediately after Pearl Harbour: 'Personally I would rather accord India independence than that we should have to keep an army there to hold down the fighting races for the benefit of the Hindu priesthood and caucus.'[112]

This was one of the fantasies against which the Secretary of State for India battled a couple of months later during two hours of fruitless discussion at the India Committee under Churchill's chairmanship. Amery recorded sadly:

What really killed the whole discussion was Winston's complete inability to grasp even the most elementary points of the discussion. After one had spent ages explaining the effect of enabling a province to stand out he still harped back to the iniquity of any body on which there was a Congress majority, as if majority mattered in such a case. He seems quite incapable of listening or taking in even the simplest point but goes off at a tangent on a word and then rambles on inconsecutively ... Certainly a complete outsider coming to that meeting knowing nothing of his reputation would have thought him an amusing but quite gaga old gentleman who could not understand what people were talking about. Coming out Cripps told me that he had been nearly as bad at a meeting earlier in the day and I went away seriously disquieted.[113]

Not by coincidence perhaps, this occurred at a time when Churchill was in unusually low health and spirits. Alas, matters did not improve much. The same diarist recorded after a meeting in late July 1942 that

In Cabinet, Winston let himself go with a flood of almost childish out of date objections to the poor much harassed British soldier having to face the extra humiliation of being ordered about by a brown man etc., ... We fought tooth and nail for half an hour or more and I could not help telling him that on this question he was just a mass of out of date prejudice.

A little later, Churchill exclaimed to Amery 'I hate Indians. They are a beastly people with a beastly religion.'[114] By 'Indians' he meant of course Hindus, about whom he made equally disobliging remarks on other occasions. Like much of Churchill's unguarded talk, this should not be taken too literally. Deeply proud of the work which the British had done in India, he pointed out that no great population in the world had been so effectively protected from the horrors of the war as the peoples of the sub-continent.[115] He chafed at the staggering increase in British debt to India; this was one of the substantial subjects upon which he and Amery disputed regularly. Against his fulminations about pullulating and multiplying Hindus, which naturally attract scandalized commentary, we should place more far-sighted observations. The King's Private Secretary happened to record a conversation in which Churchill told Sir

R. Mudaliar, India's representative at the War Cabinet and Pacific War Council, that things must change. The old notion that the Indian was in any way inferior to the white man must go. 'We must all be pals together. I want to see a great shining India, of which we can be as proud as we are of a great Canada or a great Australia.'[116]

Amery noted after a row in which the Prime Minister had accused him of inciting the Viceroy against the Cabinet in London:

> It is an awful thing dealing with a man like Winston who is at the same moment dictatorial, eloquent and muddle-headed. I am not sure that I ever got into his mind that India pays for the whole of her defence including the British forces in India … none of them [the members of the War Cabinet] ever really have the courage to stand up to Winston and tell him when he is making a fool of himself. Winston cannot see beyond such phrases as 'Are we to incur hundreds of millions of debt for defending India in order to be kicked out by the Indians afterwards? This may be an ill-contrived world but not so ill-contrived as all that.' But we are getting out of India far more than was ever thought possible …[117]

After many hesitations, WSC had taken the extraordinary step of appointing a soldier, in the person of Wavell, as Viceroy of India. He seems to have regretted it quickly, and on a number of occasions treated Wavell badly. Vehement as the Prime Minister's quarrels with Amery had been at earlier stages, they became still more inflamed in the last year of the war. Churchill's extreme tiredness no doubt played its part. At the Cabinet on 4 August 1944, in what Amery's diary describes as 'a state of great exultation', Churchill averred that after the war he was going to go back on all the shameful story of the last 20 years of surrender; there would be no obligation to carry out promises made at a time of difficulty and anyway not taken up by the Indians. It might be necessary to get rid of wretched sentimentalists like the Viceroy and most of the present British officials, who had become more Indian than the Indians. What was all Amery's professed patriotism worth if he did not stand up for his own countrymen against Indian money-lenders? Evidently it was not only upon the Prime Minister that five years of war had laid their mark, for Amery retorted that he could not see much difference between Churchill's outlook and Hitler's.

This, we read without surprise, annoyed the Prime Minister mightily. Amery's account continues: 'I am by no means sure whether on this subject of India he is really quite sane – there is no relation between his manner, physical and intellectual, on this theme and the equability and dominant good sense he displays on issues directly affecting the conduct of the war.'

There followed a tirade from the Prime Minister against the worthlessness of the Indian army. This was too much for Amery, who says that he went for the Prime Minister hammer and tongs. 'I think the Cabinet enjoyed the fun, partly shocked and partly delighted that Winston should be spoken to in straight terms.'[118] Worse was to come. Early in November 1944, the two men had a quarrel of heroic proportions at the Cabinet. Even by his own account, Amery exploded violently and told the Prime Minister to stop talking damned nonsense. Churchill said 'Have you recovered your temper, or would you like to withdraw? I'm not going to sit here and be insulted by you.' As the meeting ended, Amery told Churchill that he was sorry if he had used strong language but wished that the Prime Minister would find time to talk to him about these matters and find out how they really stood. 'It is terrible to think that in nearly five years, apart from incidental talks about appointments etc. he has never once discussed either the Indian situation generally or this sterling balance question with me, but has only indulged in wild and indeed hardly sane tirades in Cabinet ...'[119]

Other ministers fared better. Nevertheless, the position at the heart of the government had become deeply unsatisfactory to many of them. Hours were wasted over small points of business. As the Permanent Under-Secretary of the Foreign Office recorded 'The old P.M. is failing', and again after a discussion at the Cabinet on the next day 'Too awful. P.M. rambled on till 7 stating with vehemence opinions based on no ascertained facts.' The Foreign Secretary himself, near the end of his tether, asked if the Cabinet had confidence in him, reflected that when any new hare was raised Churchill could not resist chasing it across many fields, and at another meeting of the War Cabinet in January 1945, made a scene: 'What's the good of a Foreign Secretary who isn't even trusted to draft a telegram?' He said that he was fed up and would resign, but calmed down.[120] By the second half of January 1945, the position had become so bad that the Deputy Prime Minister himself felt moved to protest. Inexpertly typing his letter so that no secretary should see it, Attlee complained of Churchill's rambling monologues, lack of respect for his colleagues' views, failure to read Cabinet papers. 'I consider the present position inimical to the successful performance of the tasks imposed upon us as a Government and injurious to the war effort.' WSC was at first furious. However, Mrs Churchill believed Attlee to be right, and even Lord Beaverbrook judged it a very good letter, though it was a main part of Attlee's purpose to deplore the influence exercised by Beaverbrook himself. Churchill replied tersely to Attlee: 'You may be sure I shall always endeavour to profit by your counsels.'[121] Perhaps he intended this, but it made little difference. Memoranda still went unread and chaotic discussions in the Cabinet unchecked. Churchill himself confesses that by the spring of 1945 he was physically so feeble that after meetings of the Cabinet in its underground quarters, he had to be carried upstairs in a chair by the Marines. He kept worse hours than ever and doubted if he had the strength to carry on.[122]

The conclusion is inescapable that even Churchill's constitution could not bear such a load. Vast problems loomed: the growing dissensions within the alliance, fears about Russian intentions and power, Britain's mountainous debts, the prospect of an early general election and of a long war against Japan. With an astonishing resilience, Churchill would rally for great occasions or opportunities. He had suppressed his doubts and done his best to reach agreements with Stalin; against open American disapproval, the British government had intervened decisively in Greece; he had tried repeatedly to prevent undue weakening of the armies in Italy, and had thought that the landings in the south of France a waste of resources, upon both of which points there is a strong case to be made for his view; he wished the Allied armies to meet the Russians as far east as possible in Europe, and not to retreat until Stalin's intentions were clearer.

When victory in Europe was at last secured, the Foreign Secretary found himself in distant San Francisco, playing a leading part as the foundations of the United Nations Organisation were laid. He had the gift of saying much in a few words. Although he had borne the brunt of many sharp arguments with Churchill, he knew where the main credit lay and hated not to be with him at this moment of triumph. 'All my thoughts are with you on this day which is so essentially your day. It is you who have led, uplifted and inspired us through the worst days. Without you this day could not have been.' Churchill replied 'Throughout you have been my mainstay.' [123]

* * * * *

That the war with Japan would end so swiftly could not be known to Churchill or anyone else in the spring of 1945. The atomic project was shrouded in deep secrecy and none could tell whether or when an atomic bomb would be tested successfully. Allied plans looked to a campaign of a further 12 or 18 months. The cost to Britain was estimated at £1,000 million or more. It was expected that as the first waves of troops came home from Europe, new armies and fleets would be moved to the Pacific. These expectations, unfulfilled in the event, affected Churchill's conduct deeply and had their bearing upon affairs in Europe as the Russian attitude became more menacing. How could it be possible to withdraw so many troops and fight a major war at the other end of the world? Churchill's hope that the coalition government might be prolonged until the end of the war against Japan was for a while shared by a number of the Labour leaders, including Attlee. We, who know that the war against Japan ended within a few weeks, must remind ourselves that those who were negotiating on these lines in 1945 believed they were discussing an extension of perhaps two years. Signs of Labour restiveness had been apparent for months. The estrangement was exacerbated by a profound distrust – not unshared by many Conservatives – of Beaverbrook, Bracken and the influence they were supposed to carry with the Prime Minister.

There is also a domestic context in which the Japanese factor counted heavily. Churchill is often accused of having no interest in the plans for social betterment after the war. Though he concentrated hour by hour upon military matters and those areas of high policy where strategic and diplomatic considerations could not be separated, he had a strong sympathy with many of the projects worked out patiently during the war by ministers of all parties. In a broadcast of 1943, for example, he proclaimed the attractions of a four-year plan. It would embrace a system of unified, compulsory and national insurance 'for all classes for all purposes from the cradle to the grave.' The country could not afford idle people, at the top or the bottom. 'Unemployables, rich or poor, will have to be toned up. ... we cannot have a band of drones in our midst, whether they come from the ancient aristocracy or the modern plutocracy or the ordinary type of pub-crawler.' The country must grow more of its own food. On broad and solid foundations, a National Health Service must be established. Larger families must be encouraged, for on existing trends a smaller working and fighting population would have to support a rapidly increasing cohort of the elderly. There must be a great improvement in public education.[124] Nothing could be easier than to promise large benefits at an early date. Without question Churchill remembered what happened to 'homes fit for heroes' and other plans insufficiently prepared 25 years before. When he still hoped that they would continue in harness together, Churchill wrote to Attlee 'we should do our utmost to implement the proposals for social security and full employment contained in the White Papers which we have laid before Parliament.' Indeed, it transpired at a later stage that these words had been drafted by Attlee himself. In the event, the Labour and Liberal parties withdrew from the government, and the wartime coalition came to an abrupt end in May 1945. In tears, the Prime Minister addressed the departing ministers. 'The light of history will shine on all your helmets.'[125]

Churchill's friend and collaborator of many years, Desmond Morton, once remarked in an unconscious echo of Ismay 'I myself have never known nor conceived such a mass of contradictions as Winston.'[126] Almost overnight, those contradictions became startlingly apparent in June 1945. Fatigued, fearful about Russia, far from certain about the intentions of the United States, daily reminded of Britain's dreadful economic position, Churchill stepped down from his lofty position as leader of a national administration and become again the swashbuckling party politician of old. He dreaded the introduction of anything like full-blooded Socialism, deplored the proposal that the major industries should be nationalized, regarded as ludicrous the notion that a nation could vote itself into prosperity. Advances in insurance and health services were quite another matter. The temptations of making large promises without knowing where the money was coming from were obvious; and it is to Churchill's credit that he should have resisted them at a time when the country was expecting to spend unimaginable amounts on the campaign in the Far East and would inevitably end the war financially dependent upon the United States.

That said, he would have done far better to emphasize what was easily lost to sight, the fact that the new Parliament would assemble with a mass of social legislation broadly agreed between the parties. Despite all the constraints, it would not have been difficult to strike a positive and constructive note, with telling examples. As it was, Churchill concentrated in his first broadcast upon the perils of a Socialist system and declared roundly that it could be established only with a political police. Of course, when he talked in this theoretical way about Socialist systems, he had in mind the grim example of Russia. Disregarding his wife's plea, he remarked that a Socialist government conducting the entire life and industry of the country would have to fall back 'on some form of Gestapo no doubt very humanely directed in the first instance'.[127] It chanced that Anthony Eden was confined to his house by illness at this time. A little while later, Churchill deplored that fact and said that as a result he had no one to consult; had Eden been at his side he would not have made mistakes in broadcasts. This, Eden's diary remarks, 'is not true though very generous, because each must say what he thinks. But we agreed that there was anyway a strong leftward undertow.'

Most people, including some of the Labour leaders, seem to have expected a Conservative victory. Touring the country, Churchill was received with enthusiasm and was encouraged, as well as moved, by that fact. Eden surmises that the people were in truth only saying 'Thank you. You have led us superbly. We shall always be grateful to you.' The Prime Minister could not be expected to sense that there was also something valedictory in this message. 'He would not have been Winston Churchill if he had.'[128]

It is a sure mark of Churchill's exhaustion that after the election campaign, but before the results were known, he went for a week's holiday to France and there paid scant attention to telegrams and the affairs of the world. In the whole of the war, he had painted only one picture, at Marrakech, which he gave to President Roosevelt. Now, as of old, he began at once to tackle landscapes again and found that with palette spread and brush in hand it was easy to drive away intrusive thoughts. After this brief taste of his pre-war life, he flew directly to the Potsdam Conference, returning thence to London for the results of the election. It soon became clear that the Conservatives would be defeated. Captain Pim, who had looked after Churchill's famous map room, read out some of the figures. The Prime Minister, immersed in his bath, said simply 'This may well be a landslide and they have a perfect right to kick us out. That is what we have been fighting for. Hand me my towel.'[129]

★ ★ ★ ★ ★

Amongst Churchill's qualities we must place high his capacity to speak compellingly and to uplift. He would have been amused to read that a survivor of the Battle of Britain, reminded of 'Never in the field of human conflict was so much owed by so many to so few', said jauntily in the summer of 2010 'We thought he was referring to our mess bills.' His close relations with Roosevelt and the American military, despite vicissitudes; his firm resistance to the belief that the so-called Second Front, in the shape of a full assault on mainland Europe, could be undertaken with success in 1942 or 1943; the determination to reinforce the Middle East and mount the campaigns in North Africa and the Mediterranean; his courage in visiting Stalin in August 1942, and repeated attempts to make tolerable terms with Russia; his sustained support for the Intelligence services; the unity of the government at home; his insistence that even after all the horrors, Germany must find an honoured place in the European family when she had been thoroughly purged of Nazism – all this and much more can properly be entered on the credit side of the ledger. The stormy relations with de Gaulle ('I, of course, am exceedingly pro-French; unfortunately the French are exceedingly pro-voking');[130] insufficient understanding of the Japanese threat; the later stages of the campaign in Italy; the inability to prevent the landings in the south of France in August 1944; the lack of a coherent policy towards India; susceptibility to Stalin's blend of brusqueness and blandishment; an impulse to interfere unduly with commanders in the field; an undue fondness for side-shows – these aspects may be judged more critically, though at least some of them derive from the last part of the war when Britain's influence in Allied councils was declining. Churchill has been unjustly criticized for his belief in the summit meetings. There being no political equivalent of the Combined Chiefs of Staff, the conferences with Roosevelt and Stalin and their coadjutors provided the only effective means by which much business could be settled, not least because the machinery of administration in the USA was often ill co-ordinated,[131] while the Russian government depended on Stalin and one or two others. As WSC was well aware, his own knowledge of military issues, and formidable powers of exposition and persuasion, often enabled him to secure the decisions he sought, or something near to them.

Field-Marshal Dill rendered services beyond price as Britain's chief military representative in Washington from 1941 and died in harness, so deeply esteemed by his American colleagues that he is the only British citizen buried in Arlington Cemetery. A few weeks before his death towards the end of 1944, Dill told the Prime Minister of Canada that he thought Churchill had enjoyed the war, to which Mackenzie King replied that 'it was clear it was the very breath of life to him'. Dill also remarked that while Churchill was loyal to his friends, he had 'distinctly two sides to his nature – one which could be quite ruthless and harsh.'[132] There was truth in that view, which would have been echoed by many of those close to Churchill. When it was all over, General Ismay confessed he had often felt that he ought somehow to save the Chiefs of Staff from more of the unnecessary, aggravating and sometimes humiliating burdens

> that were thrust upon their already overloaded shoulders. But I found that if I tried to apply the brake too hard and too often, I merely made matters worse. The trouble was that our beloved Chief regarded any disagreement with his views as a *personal* affront; he never understood that if you [Brooke] – and I in a more lowly field – had started saying we agreed with him when in fact we didn't, we would have been of no more use to him.

Nevertheless, though we might well expect that his professional instincts as a soldier would lead him to the opposite conclusion, Ismay also judged that Churchill 'in his grasp of the broad sweep of strategy ... stood head and shoulders above his professional advisers.'[133]

* * * * *

A few days after Lord Randolph had manifested himself in the studio at Chartwell, WSC said that he wished certain people could have been alive to see the last years of the war; his father and mother, and his cousin the Duke of Marlborough, with whom he had stayed for months at Blenheim. Among politicians, he named only two: F.E. Smith and Arthur Balfour.[134] Wounded but determined to fight on, Churchill led the Opposition rather as Balfour had done after another landslide, that of 1906. As usual, the peculiarities of the British electoral system had produced a somewhat distorted result, for Labour, with some 12 million votes, now held 393 seats, and the Conservatives, with about 10 million, had but 213. When WSC's colleagues intimated that he might retire, he answered that he had always preferred to stay in the pub until closing time and reflected that, like his ancestor the great Duke, he had been defeated in the end not by battle but by politics at home. To his daughter Sarah he remarked philosophically, as they took a holiday in Italy, 'Every day I stay here without news, without worry, I realise more and more that it may very well be what your mother said, a blessing in disguise. The war is over, it is won and they have lifted the hideous aftermath from my shoulders. I am what I never thought I would be until I reached my grave, sans soucis and sans regrets.'[135] Slowly he regained poise and energy, painting many a picture. He delivered speeches which resonated in every part of the world; the one given at Fulton, Missouri, early in 1946, spelt out in sober terms the painful realities, far removed from the hopes which Churchill himself had entertained 12 months before at Yalta. He encouraged the rebuilding of Europe and the burying of enmities there, and embarked promptly upon the writing of six volumes about the war, their backbone provided by the memoranda, minutes and telegrams by which he had conducted business. These amounted, it was discovered, to about 1 million words. Even with the help of the team he assembled, depending heavily upon Bill Deakin, the effort required to convert all this into a coherent story was formidable.

Whatever the failings of Churchill's account, the reader finds in it not only a deep quarry of documentary material but a capacity to delineate complicated issues in clear terms, an ability to convey the atmosphere of crisis in which momentous decisions had to be taken, many penetrating insights into the characters of those with whom he consorted. It is often charged that Churchill lacked interest in the people around him, and did not care to enquire about them. That is undoubtedly true in some instances, but the notion that he was incapable of such insights cannot for a moment survive the reading of his books about the two wars, or of *Great Contemporaries*. The study of history and the making of history, in short, were twined together in Churchill; the man who had made history then wrote about it, but what he had done was itself informed not only by his historical imagination but by study and reflection. Hence the remark to Mackenzie King that his policies during the second war were conditioned by mistakes which he had made during the first.

The Labour government pressed ahead with the extensions to the welfare state, many of which amounted to consolidation and expansion of what had been done piecemeal in the previous 40 years; it embarked upon a large and expensive programme of nationalization; and it soon found that many of the financial assumptions were unduly optimistic. Churchill had pointed out in August 1945 that the swift ending of the Japanese war constituted a 'wonderful windfall'.[136] But the abrupt cancellation of Lend-Lease, the rapid exhaustion of the large loans secured in 1946 from the United States and Canada, the devaluation of the pound, the threatening external circumstances, which caused the government to reintroduce conscription and embark upon heavy rearmament, all undermined the high hopes of 1945. At the election of 1950, less than five years after that glad morning, Labour's huge majority was reduced to ten. Attlee continued as Prime Minister until another election in the autumn of 1951. Though Churchill and the Conservatives then scraped home with a small majority of seats, they had actually received fewer votes than Labour.

Of that fact the new Prime Minister was well aware. The sheer scale of the dangers abroad and at home oppressed him. The economic position was parlous to a degree. Indeed, one of his first acts was to reduce the rearmament programme left by the Labour government, because it was beyond the country's capacity to finance. Severe rationing still prevailed. The frontiers of the state had advanced mightily, and to Churchill's mind dangerously, as a consequence of the war and the Labour government's predilection for planning and controls. These must be reduced as rapidly as possible, he argued. The main acts of nationalization must be accepted, however reluctantly. Above all, the country could not survive without a release of energy and enterprise. 'The production of new wealth must precede common wealth, otherwise there will only be common poverty.'[137] The votes cast in the election had shown, Churchill reflected, that the country was evenly divided, and at a time when common effort was needed, too many seemed bent upon warfare with each other. All this was far removed from the days of wartime, when apart from a few dissidents Parliament could be relied upon for support and all the main parties were represented in the government.

Churchill had recovered swiftly from a mild stroke in 1949. In February 1952, soon after he took office for the last time as Prime Minister, he suffered a failure of circulation and for a little while could not find the words he wanted. This happened after he had paid a taxing visit to Washington and Ottawa – acutely conscious of Britain's position as junior partner and proportionately grateful to President Truman for allowing the two of them to talk as equals – and the early death of the King, which had affected him profoundly. 'You'll have to pull out', Lord Moran said to his patient, 'or arrange things so that the strain is less.' At least Churchill listened attentively before replying, 'I keep having to make important decisions, terrible decisions. It never stops. It is worse than the war.'[138]

Recovering quickly from this spasm, Churchill brushed aside suggestions that he should retire or even sit in the House of Lords while remaining Prime Minister. He kept the Cabinet small, and allowed a wide latitude to its members. At the senior level they were mainly people of exceptional ability: Butler, Eden, Macmillan, Lyttelton, Cherwell, Lennox-Boyd, Monckton. Remembering the part which the trade unions had played in the war effort, Churchill insisted that everything should be done to work in harmony with them and his private relations with many of the trade union leaders were friendly, almost affectionate. Though Britain was on the breadline when the government took office, the economic position improved markedly over the next two or three years. Churchill liked to be surrounded by people whom he knew and trusted from the war. Field-Marshal Alexander, who seemed to personify the best of soldiering in the old days, when there was still a place for chivalry and respect, assumed with reluctance the office of Minister of Defence. During discussion at the Cabinet of a tangled problem of domestic politics, Churchill asked Alexander for his opinion. 'Well, Prime Minister, I'm a soldier and I don't know much about politics; but I feel we should do whatever is decent, fair, right and honourable.' A long silence ensued among the politicians. Then the Prime Minister spoke: 'Never in my long experience have I heard so outrageous a doctrine propounded by a Minister of the Crown.'[139]

Plainly, Churchill was not the man he had been in the war. Although on his return to No. 10 the messengers presented him with the slips marked 'ACTION THIS DAY', carefully preserved from 1945, they were never used again. The Prime Minister was widely regarded, far beyond the bounds of his own party, as the man who had symbolized resistance to tyranny. People who had at first criticized what he said at Fulton had long since accepted his analysis and indeed gone beyond it. The leading members of the Labour Party had mainly served in the wartime coalition; and others who wished to picture Churchill as reckless or warmongering found a good deal of the wind taken out of their sails by the revelation that Attlee and a handful of senior ministers had in deep secrecy caused the manufacture of a British atomic bomb. That such a step should be even contemplated, let alone financed and carried through, by a Labour government tells its own story. The hideous prospect of nuclear warfare dominated Churchill's thought during this last spell in power. Everything depended upon the willingness of the United States to defend Western Europe. General Ismay had been brought into the government from retirement. The Prime Minister pressed him vigorously to take up the office of Secretary-General of NATO. Though in no doubt about the importance of the post, Ismay acquiesced with reluctance, saying how much he regretted leaving his home in Worcestershire and his beloved herd of Jersey cows. The Prime Minister, not at all abashed, retorted 'Quite easy. Milk the cows in the morning, fly to Paris and milk the Americans in the evening.'[140]

WSC remained in old age a master of the unheralded and penetrating remark. 'Do you realize that from the time the Romans left Britain until the arrival of the American heiresses, this country was completely without central heating?' 'This Treasury paper, by its very weight, defends itself against the risk of being read.' 'The head cannot take in more than the seat can endure', he observed in respect of post-prandial oratory; at a meeting to consider an election manifesto, when several elderly gentlemen had left the room in succession, 'Let us adjourn for five minutes; an empty bladder is the indispensable prelude to a fruitful discussion'; to one of his horses, about to run in the Gold Cup at Ascot, 'If you win this race, you will spend your life surrounded by delicious mares' and then, after a pause, 'If you don't, you will become a gelding.'[141]

Churchill said to the Chiefs of Staff in 1952, concerning naval command in the Atlantic, a matter which had nearly proved deadly in war and might prove so again, 'I would have liked to agree with you ... but I cannot give up my convictions. If I had I should not be here.'[142] Churchill's convictions in the new state of international affairs proved different from those which many expected. Had he not condemned Baldwin and

Chamberlain for appeasement? Was not the folly of appeasement the principal lesson which readers must take from *The Gathering Storm*? Could not he of all men be relied upon to stand four-square against another horrible tyranny? That the United States and Britain should be strongly armed was not in dispute. Nevertheless, the new weapons were of a destructive power undreamed of even a few years before.

To a large extent, he went his own way. Eden being seriously ill, the Prime Minister took charge of the Foreign Office in the spring of 1953. With Roosevelt long gone, Stalin recently dead, a new and untried President in Washington, the Prime Minister in London perhaps saw the opportunity to do something which no one else could do, something constructive, a resumption of the role he had played in the war. The speech he delivered in Parliament on 11 May 1953 reverberated everywhere. Churchill had been saying for years that he believed there should be a summit meeting between the Americans, the Russians and the British. In the previous year, a microphone had by accident been left switched on at Churchill's table during a banquet in Ottawa. Delighted journalists heard him remark to the Prime Minister of Canada 'The Almighty works in a mysterious way, his wonders to perform. He has used His servant Stalin to make the closest association ever dreamed of to unite the nations of the West.'[143] Now something might perhaps be made of the new situation. In respect of the Russians, he used to say 'A bear in the forest is a matter of legitimate speculation; a bear in the zoo is an object of public curiosity; a bear in your wife's bed causes the gravest concern.'[144] The facts of the situation, Churchill insisted, were such that terms could not be dictated to Russia. Some friendly alternative had to be presented. But surely that course would mean consorting with evil and conceding points of principle? This was very much the argument advanced by the government of the United States, in an ironic reversal of the positions of 1945.

'Appeasement', it turned out, is a less straightforward matter than it looks. One man's truckling to a dictator is another man's wise recognition of facts. One man's scuttle is another man's sage measurement of the rising tide of nationalism. Some almost comic contortions resulted. Churchill, Eden and Macmillan, successive Conservative Prime Ministers, all owed a good deal of their political position to their opposition to 'appeasement'. Immediately after Churchill's speech of 11 May, Macmillan recorded in his diary 'Will Central and Eastern Europe be "sold out" out in a super-Munich? .... I shall *not* stay if we are now to seek "appeasement" and call it Peace.'[145] Eden himself never ceased to deplore that speech, but on the occasion of the conference at Geneva in 1954, where large concessions were inevitably made to Communist aggression, *Punch* produced a caricature of Eden which made him look remarkably like Chamberlain. Arguing vigorously in favour of an early meeting with Malenkov, WSC even exclaimed to senior Conservative colleagues 'Now I begin to understand what Chamberlain felt like.' Assenting with reluctance to Eden's pressing desire to make terms with Egypt, remove British troops from the Suez Canal and leave the Sudan, WSC remarked that he had not previously realized that Munich is situated on the Nile.[146]

Churchill could still deliver fine orations, and excelled in terse and funny replies to Prime Minister's Questions. This mastery reconciled to his continuance in office many in the Conservative Party who would otherwise have liked to see him go, and although colleagues in the Cabinet would grumble from time to time about the Prime Minister's habits or increasing slowness and deafness, no one cared to challenge him openly. This was particularly so of Eden, his designated successor.

We may suspect, but cannot know, what fate would have awaited Churchill's initiatives had be not been struck down in the midsummer of 1953. Someone less determined, less self-absorbed, more receptive to wise advice would long since have heeded the warning signs. Churchill was not so constituted. He had to be taken as a whole. 'You were a rich man once, physically', said his doctor, 'but you've gone through a fortune.'[147] Churchill and his wife faced the new situation with dignity. 'His courage is only matched by an astounding humility which has come over him, and Lady C. is no less heroic.'[148] Thus his Private Secretary, Jock Colville. The Prime Minister's speech was indistinct and his movement severely affected; it seemed quite possible that he would die within a day or two. In the event he recovered by slow steps. He became more sweet-tempered and serene, adjectives which no one close to him would have used in the war. Nonetheless, he had no desire to retire if it could be helped, and the possibility of some easement between the great powers preoccupied him. As the date of his departure was repeatedly postponed, a number of his leading colleagues lost patience and ascribed the delays to a selfish desire to prolong his stay in office. There they did him less than justice. All the evidence suggests that he wished to stay in the hope that the three powers would meet or, if America refused, that he could himself and measure Stalin's successors.

During the months of recuperation, Churchill repaired some of the gaps in his formal education, discovered that he liked Trollope, was arrested by *Jane Eyre*, powerfully impressed by *Wuthering Heights* (after seeing a harrowing filmed version of which he remarked merely 'What terrible weather they have in Yorkshire!'), and gurgled with amusement over *Candide*.[149]

WSC's authority in the House of Commons, his palpable desire to treat the place less as a cockpit than as a council of the nation, helped him to remain in office. The discovery early in 1954 that the United States had already manufactured and tested the hydrogen bomb may well have contributed to the delay in Churchill's retirement, for in his heart of hearts he doubtless thought himself better fitted than any other minister to cope with the revolutionary changes of strategy and outlook which would be required. His astonishing memory remained but little impaired. The same is true of his resolve. The more strongly he was pressed by colleagues to declare the hour of his going, the more determined did he become to resist the process. His eccentricities did not diminish. We may be confident that Mr Attlee or Mr Baldwin, to make no mention of Mr Gladstone, would not have conducted the government's affairs with a budgerigar flying round the room, pecking at Cabinet papers, occasionally taking nips from the whisky-and-soda at the Prime Minister's bedside and settling upon the domed head of the Chancellor of the Exchequer with the inevitable consequences. To later meetings Mr Butler came armed with a silk handkerchief, with which he would mop up occasionally while murmuring 'The things I do for England …' Another visitor, summoned to talk over some business concerning the BBC, recorded his mild surprise that the budgerigar did not contribute to the discussion. Nor is it likely that any other Prime Minister, having installed tanks full of exotic fish at Chequers, would address a black guppy thus: 'Darling, I do love you. I would make love to you if I only knew how.'[150]

On the occasion of Churchill's 80th birthday in November 1954, admiration and affection were expressed in many lands. He was touched, perhaps a little surprised. Efforts to hold a summit meeting with the Russians having failed for the moment, he resigned in April 1955, and left public life for good. His successor Anthony Eden was able within a few weeks to call a general election, win a largely increased majority and hold the meeting with the Russians about which everyone had been so apprehensive. Although Churchill's tenure of office from 1951 to 1955 is sometimes regarded as an appendix at best or a sad declension at worst, his last administration had solid achievements to its credit and stands well by comparison with many which have held office since then. Churchill once reflected that 'To hold the leadership of a party or nation with dignity and authority requires that the leader's quality and message meet not only the need but the mood of both.'[151]

Need and mood alike varied to a startling degree between Churchill's two periods of office as Prime Minister. In the first phase, he had met the mood wonderfully well and the need in a fashion which no other figure in British public life could have matched. In the second, he had adapted himself with skill and flexibility to his country's reduced circumstances.

During the first months of retirement, he went downhill rapidly, as commonly happens when a man finds he has neither the stimulus nor the duties of high office. 'I only want to be myself again', he said pathetically.[152] He had drawn too freely, however, upon his credit in the bank of health. For a few years more, he painted; he found solace in long holidays in the South of France; having been accustomed to sing music hall songs and admire military bands, he discovered a taste for music, including Sibelius and Brahms. Like the embers of a great fire in some banquet hall deserted, he would occasionally sparkle. More often, depressed by the fall in Britain's standing, he lapsed into moods of melancholy. 'I have worked very hard all my life', he said, 'and I have achieved a great deal – in the end to achieve nothing.' This last word was uttered with sombre emphasis.[153]

Two generations later, we are entitled to reach a different verdict. 'Through him the gale of life blew high.' The child of nature had proved himself a force of nature, and one in whose example we may find inspiration and reassurance.

2

Great Britain, the Commonwealth and the Wider World, 1939–45

What was the nature of the miracle, Mr Churchill mused in the House of Commons in the fifth year of the war, that had called men from the uttermost ends of the earth, some riding 20 days before they could reach recruiting centres, some sailing 14,000 miles across the seas before they gained the battlefield, and had made governments as proud and sovereign as any that ever existed cast aside their fears and set themselves up to aid the good cause? He could find no sufficient answer in material advantage or calculation of self-interest. Important factors those might be, but not to be placed ahead of deeper and more mysterious influences

> which cause human beings to do the most incalculable, improvident, and, from the narrow point of view, profitless things. It is our union in freedom and for the sake of our way of living which is the great fact, reinforced by tradition and sentiment, and it does not depend upon anything that could ever be written down in any account kept in some large volume.[1]

Well before Christmas 1939, Canada's High Commissioner in London, Vincent Massey, and the Secretary of State for the Dominions, Anthony Eden, had travelled to Scotland to greet the first volunteers from Canada. As each of the troopships passed, the crews of the Home Fleet cheered and the Canadians replied lustily while the band of HMS *Warspite* played 'O Canada'. When contingents from Australia and New Zealand arrived in the Middle East, the same minister went to greet them at Suez, remembering the times from World War I when his own regiment had stood alongside the New Zealanders at the battle of the Somme and the Australians at Villers-Bretonneux. As he puts it tersely, 'No tougher fighting neighbours could be dreamed of.' During a foray in the desert, where he inspected one of the Indian brigades soon to win so fine a reputation, his plane landed to refuel at a remote spot where only two other aircraft were to be found. One pilot turned out to be a Scot and the other a South African. Asking himself what had moved men from all the Dominions to leave their homes and offer man's proudest gift, service as a volunteer, Eden judged it something beyond sentiment and kinship; they had come because as one of the pilots remarked in the simplest but most expressive terms, 'It seems there is a job of work to be done.' Just so, remarked Eden in recounting all this to a British audience in February 1940, when the German war machine seemed quiescent except at sea, when Italy was still neutral and in brief spells even benevolently so, when Japan glowered only as a distant menace:

> Though separated by thousands of miles of ocean, these men, who might very well have been excused had they failed to appreciate the extent of the peril that pressed in the first instance upon us, saw clearly from the first. They understood the issue, and it is this clear perception, the vision of the men beyond the seas who see truly, that should give us courage now.[2]

A few months later, with the position transformed, France collapsing and Britain in danger of invasion, the smallest and remotest Dominion despatched a telegram to London. If the British decided to fight on, it said, the government in Wellington would pledge its support to the end, and any decision taken in these most difficult circumstances would be understood and accepted. Churchill replied in the early hours of 16 June: 'I am deeply touched by your message, which is only in keeping with all that the Mother Country has ever received in peace or war from New Zealand.' The Australian government sent similar tidings and received a like reply.[3]

The combined populations of the Dominions amounted to hardly more than 30 million people; some 7 million in Australia, 11.5 million in Canada, 11 million in South Africa, 1.5 million in New Zealand. The population of the United Kingdom stood at about 47 million, and of India at 370 million. Even now, when figures have been repeatedly refined, it is not altogether easy to arrive at accurate estimates of the human cost of the war. Churchill prefaced his account with a table showing that on land Britain and the Commonwealth consistently had more divisions than the USA in fighting contact with the enemy until the summer of 1944, not only Africa and Europe but also in Asia. The Commonwealth sustained a total of some 412,000 deaths, to which had to be added 60,000 civilians killed in air raids on the United Kingdom, and losses in the Merchant Navy and the fishing fleet of some 30,000. Against that, the United States had suffered 322,000 deaths.[4]

In respect of numbers mobilized for fighting, comparisons are not always reliable because definitions vary. In the case of Great Britain that total lay somewhere between 5 and 6 million, and in the Dominions proper perhaps 2.5 million; if India, constitutionally less than a Dominion but in every sense much more than a colony, is added to the equation, the overseas Commonwealth's contribution comes to at least 5 million. The sea and air forces of the Commonwealth and Britain accounted for most of the German and Italian submarines destroyed in each theatre of war and for the sinking or partial ruin of all the German battleships, cruisers and destroyers, not to mention the Italian fleet. Not until 1944 did the United States' air forces cast more bombs on the enemy than did the British and Commonwealth forces. In respect of shipping, British losses were greater than those of the United States and all other nations outside enemy control added together.[5]

Under the heading 'Casualties', which includes those taken as prisoners of war, the United Kingdom had about 755,000 and Canada over 100,000; in each of those instances, the total of casualties was about three times as great as the number killed. The ratios were different for Australia, New Zealand, South Africa, India and the colonies; for example, Australia lost some 23,365 killed but had 95,561 casualties, including the prisoners of war, and for New Zealand the ratio was much the same. In other words, there were about four times as many casualties as were killed. However, South Africa had six times as many, at 179,935. Casualties from the colonies, at 36,172, were nearly six times the total killed. The grim tally of British and Commonwealth casualties amounts to 1,246,000.[6]

In Britain, as in the Dominions, expansion of the armed forces was an untidy business, necessarily so in powers which had begun to prepare late for war. Because the danger was proximate to Britain, and she had a large population and industrial capacity, the process started earlier in this country. Broadly speaking, in Britain the purpose was to regain former strength in the Army and Royal Navy and to build upon a growing strength in the Royal Air Force. With important qualifications, something of the same was true in India. In the four Dominions, however, the war brought effects going far beyond that. Canada, for example, was converted into a major industrial power. Undreamed-of enlargement was hurriedly embarked upon and had then to be adjusted to the realities of politics or supply; very often to the supply of that commodity which could not be immediately manufactured by modern methods, manpower. To measure war expenditures as a percentage of national income is a process almost as perilous as the calculation of casualties. Roughly speaking, Britain was spending 50 per cent of her national income on direct war expenditure by the end of 1940, and about 54 per cent by the end of 1941, a figure which remained more or less level for the rest of the war. The United States' expenditure reached a peak of some 47 per cent in 1943, and thereafter declined to about 44 per cent; New Zealand's figure stood briefly on the same level as that of the United Kingdom, and then reduced to something below 50 per cent; that of Canada was a little less; and the war expenditures of the USSR – although the structures there were so different that comparisons must be treated with caution – having reached about 47 per cent of national income by the end of 1942, went down to about 44 per cent by the latter stages.[7]

Even now, when we have had two generations in which to assimilate the facts, the scale of the effort is startling. Whereas the strength of the Canadian armed forces in 1939 stood at 10,800 men, by 1945 over 1,000,000 had served. The Australian total was scarcely less. New Zealand's armed forces rose at their peak to a strength of 157,000, which represented one in ten of the population. The Royal Canadian Navy attained in a short time a strength of 50,000 men and by 1942 had in commission some 500 ships, chiefly used on escort duty for shipping in the Atlantic.[8] In the last year before the war, Australian expenditure on defence had stood at £14 million; within two years it had reached £200 million. The Royal Australian Navy had been placed at the disposal of the Admiralty from September 1939; by 1941, it had an eight-inch cruiser and four destroyers in the Mediterranean, and two sloops in the Red Sea. Of the male population of Australia between the ages of 14 and

64, rather more than a quarter served in the Armed Forces, some 15 per cent in munitions and war factories, and over 30 per cent in other essential activities. The total amounted to 71.5 per cent, a figure wholly remarkable in a country of such vast size with a scattered populace.

India's contribution to the war effort, which for political reasons it was for years almost indelicate to mention, equates in round numbers to that of the whole overseas Empire and Commonwealth put together. She raised a military force of about 2.5 million men. Indian troops fought in Malaya, Burma, East Africa, North Africa, Tunisia, the Middle East, Sicily, Italy and in smaller numbers in Greece and Indo-China. Of the 27 VCs won in Burma, no fewer than 20 marked the valour of members of the Indian Army. The 14th Army in Burma became the largest force in the world operating as a single unit, with 1 million men, of whom 700,000 were Indian.[9] Itself as big as Western Europe, India had become a vast base, from which the armies and air forces moved east and west. The country supplied unimaginable quantities of war material and food, and all this was achieved where conscription would have been out of the question. Nor was it introduced in New Zealand or Australia until mid-way through the war; it would have been unthinkable at any stage in South Africa; and the prospect of conscription for military service abroad, fiercely opposed in Quebec, strongly pressed by many in the English-speaking parts of Canada, loomed larger there than any other political question of the war. All this makes the scale of mobilization and sacrifice the more astonishing. (Let us note in parenthesis that Eire, for effective purposes no longer a member of the Commonwealth, retained a strict neutrality throughout. For their inability to use the Southern Irish ports and airfields the Allies paid a heavy forfeit in the battle of the Atlantic. At least we should recognize with gratitude that many Irish citizens managed to enlist by a variety of means; stocks of clothing were held at Holyhead and other ports so that Irish servicemen going home on leave could appear there as civilians and then change back into uniform when they returned to the United Kingdom. Some of them were court-martialled when they eventually went back to Ireland.)

The Dominions and India were compelled to weigh, indeed often to suffer harshly from, factors far outside their normal calculations. Having committed forces to the United Kingdom or the Allied armies in North Africa or the convoys in the Atlantic, they confronted deep anxieties at home. Ottawa had to be told that demands elsewhere prevented

Britain from deploying any substantial part of the Royal Navy off the shores of Canada, or releasing more of Canada's own ships. Australia and New Zealand had to face imminent perils from Japan, with their troops committed far away; when the enemy sank every ship in Darwin harbour, the point could scarcely be missed. Little wonder that anxious and angry exchanges occurred; that from the other side of the world the Prime Minister and the War Cabinet in London appeared to misread the dangers in the Pacific; or that, seen from Britain, Australian politicians seemed not to understand the significance of what was happening in the Middle East. The claims of the campaigns in Greece, Crete or Iraq, the Western Desert or Sicily or Italy, the constant anxieties about the loss of shipping, became daily preoccupations, in a style never before known, in Wellington and Ottawa, Canberra and Pretoria, Delhi and Colombo.

For a time in 1940, after the fall of France, Canadian troops provided the main organized military force in Britain; Canadian troops were captured in Hong Kong at the end of 1941; the sad tale of the raid on Dieppe, in which the bulk of the casualties were Canadian, needs no retelling; Canadian troops landed with the first wave in Sicily in 1943, fought long in Italy and were heavily engaged in France from D-Day. Australian formations played a large part in battles in the Western Desert, suffered badly in Greece and Crete, were besieged in Tobruk and engaged in Syria; a large Australian force was lost when Singapore fell; an Australian division remained during 1942 in the Middle East and took part in the Battle of El Alamein. A New Zealand Division fought in Greece and Crete, in the Western Desert, and thereafter in the campaign which ended with expulsion of the Axis from Tunisia in 1943; the same formation served in Italy and is judged to have endured more hard pounding during the war than any other single division.

* * * * *

The Dominions had joined the struggle with varying degrees of enthusiasm. Australia and New Zealand stated from the first that if Britain was at war, so also were they; though Canada's attitude was not in doubt at the last, the declaration was delayed for a week until Parliament in Ottawa had made its own decision; only the fall of the government and Smuts' ability to form an administration enabled South Africa to complete the quartet, though her forces serving outside the Union were confined for a long period to Africa. Like other Commonwealth troops, they were placed under the command of the Commander-in-Chief, Middle East. In practice, Smuts was closely consulted about their use and a great deal else. The Dominions put their forces under British, and in the later stages sometimes American, command, but on terms like those applying to the British Expeditionary Force in France in the first winter of the war, so that (say) the senior Australian officer in the Middle East could forbid the use of troops under his authority if he did not agree with the plans and dispositions of the British Commander in that theatre. At different stages and places, these rules occasionally produced frictions and worse; but in relation to the scale on which the Commonwealth forces operated, those disagreements were few and no doubt minimized by the knowledge that the rules existed.

Such disputes were in any event less important than those between governments, of which the most significant was the insistence of the Australian government upon the return of most of its troops from the Middle East and North Africa during 1942. Again, these clashes have to be measured against the scale of events; and we ought not to allow the inevitable and often justified complaints about failures of consultation, inadequacy of equipment, primacy accorded to another theatre, to obscure the essence. If the Australian government decided that its forces must be withdrawn to what the British knew as the Far East but Menzies called the Near North, most of the New Zealand troops remained in North Africa and the Mediterranean; the Canadian armies, after years of training and thirsting for action, proved themselves valiantly in many an operation from Sicily onwards; Smuts was able to ensure that the South Africans played a substantial role in the campaigns of 1944 and 1945.

After 1941, the British and American high commands built up the best-articulated system of military operations ever practised between allies. Measured over the six-year span of the war, the effort of the Dominions and the Empire was more than comparable with that put forth by the USA. Hence, as Churchill used to remark, the fact that until 1944 the British and their immediate allies could always speak on terms of equality or better to the United States,[10] but with the profound difference that the USA held huge reserves of manpower, was invulnerable to direct attack, and could act not only as the arsenal but also as the banking-house of victory. In relation to her risks, the USA was worse prepared in 1941 than Britain had been in 1939. Although Britain and the Commonwealth might have avoided defeat at the hands of Germany and Italy, even had the United States remained benevolently neutral, the same assertion can hardly be made in respect of the campaigns in the Pacific. It was not only the immense potential strength of the United States that mattered; her entry into the war brought a confidence not shattered even by the disasters of 1942 that in the end an alliance of such strength, even if Germany should triumph against Russia, would prove victorious. Thus Churchill's recollection of his emotions on learning what had happened at Pearl Harbour: 'So we had won after all!'[11]

Lend-lease enabled the Allies to wage war with greater strength than they could muster from their own resources. The size of the Commonwealth's contribution in almost every campaign enabled the British to do likewise; for sharp as the disagreements might be from time to time, the Dominions seldom pressed those quarrels to the point of outright opposition. They were independent not only of Britain but of each other. The forces moving Mackenzie King, Smuts, Fraser, Menzies and Curtin varied with their own temperaments and the geographical and political positions of their countries. Even when the same pressures might have been expected to produce similar results, as in the cases of Australia and New Zealand, they often did not. Perhaps it seems mischievous to point out that the British did not enjoy Dominion status; at any rate they, geographically isolated from the rest of the Empire, with responsibilities all over the world and an eye to the future of Europe as well as distant places, had to take account of a complicated blend of factors and circumstances. That was particularly true of relations with the United States.

Nor must we concentrate entirely upon the exertions of the Dominions and India. Many men and women from the Colonial Empire enlisted and fought with conspicuous bravery. Of the 6,520 men who left Southern Rhodesia to fight outside their own country, more than 700 received decorations for service in Abyssinia, the West African Frontier Force, Somaliland and the Middle East. Troops from West Africa served in Burma, and from other parts of Africa in Eritrea, Abyssinia and Somaliland. These are given only as examples at random. Every part of the Commonwealth, but especially Canada, Australia, New Zealand and India, supplied immense quantities of food as well as munitions to forces fighting all over the world and to the beleaguered British Isles; without that effort it would have been impossible to maintain the meagre rations of wartime Britain. If we measure by another yardstick, of the 487 squadrons under the command of the Royal Air Force in the summer of 1944, 100 came from the Dominions.[12] The Typhoon force of the Second Tactical Air Force consisted of 20 squadrons with about 450 pilots. During the battles of that summer, 151 were killed in action and a further 120 crash-landed or bailed out, 38 becoming prisoners of war. These losses were in proportion as large as those sustained by the RAF in the Battle of Britain. Of the 151 pilots killed, 78 were British, 41 Canadians, 3 Americans serving with the Royal Canadian Air Force, 8 Australians, 6 New Zealanders, 5 Rhodesians, 4 South Africans and 2 Belgians; with one each from India, Ceylon, France and Norway.[13]

It is glibly said that whilst fighting a war to save the Empire, the British ensured that they lost it. That is too simple by half; the war fought in 1939 was not occasioned by a direct threat to the overseas Empire, since Germany had no means of effective attack upon any part of it. This was the dilemma which had preoccupied ministers before the war, and none more than Chamberlain. If Britain found herself at war with Japan, an event which nearly occurred in the summer of 1939, she could fight only by placing the bulk of the Royal Navy in the Indian Ocean and the Pacific. If she did so, she would have little practical help, at least in the earlier stages, from the Dominions whose own defences were painfully thin. Moreover, war in the Far East must increase the risks with Italy and even more with Germany. Conversely, if Britain went to war with Germany, the temptations to Italy and Japan would be the stronger; which is in essence what happened in 1940 and 1941. It was the maintenance of three front-rank fighting forces for six years, in campaigns waged from one side of the globe to the other, that broke Britain as a great power in her own right; and it was the scale and solidity of support from overseas which for a time made it possible to conceive of the Commonwealth as a power dwelling on level terms with the USA on the one side and the USSR on the other.

As for the argument that the war need not have been fought, or could have been brought to an end by agreement with Germany, we have yet to uncover the ingredients of a bargain which would have left a tolerable peace, hard enough in any circumstances to conceive with Hitler in power; similarly, to persuade ourselves that if Germany were left alone or even encouraged to attack Russia and then defeated her, invincible might would not have been turned against Britain and her natural partners within and without the Empire. In short, we have to believe that Hitler would have had the intention and incentive to keep whatever bargain he had made. That is not to deny that the war might have been shortened, though even there the evidence is far from conclusive, or that such an abbreviation would have been a benefit of the first order to the Commonwealth.

We have also to ponder the nature of the relations between individual Dominions and Great Britain, for the texture and fabric differed in each case. The factors to be weighed in a crucial question between Britain and India were quite different from those between Britain and Canada, or Britain and South Africa. We must study the relations of the Dominions with each other, for their histories, policies and expectations differed; let us compare, for example, South Africa and New Zealand, or Australia and Canada. After the painful birth-pangs of the Empire Air Training Scheme, which blossomed so bountifully that it produced 125,000 aircrew in Canada alone and substantial numbers elsewhere, making a contribution to victory which Eden rightly calls capital, the British High Commissioner in Ottawa wrote to London in December 1939:

> I foresee the future course of events in the guise of the United Kingdom driving a team of the three other Dominions concerned to which the structure of the training scheme itself is hitched. I have little doubt that this somewhat unwieldy equipage will reach its appointed destination. I would only say that the driver must not be surprised, or take it unduly amiss, if one of the team from time to time turns round to argue on the subject of the road to take, the speed to be used, or even the advisability or possibility of proceeding further at all.
>
> Upon reflection I realise that the foregoing merely represents, in the form of a parable, the abiding problem of intra-Imperial relations.[14]

There is another context in which Canada's role deserves particular attention, that of war finance. Canada was the only Commonwealth country not included in the Sterling Area, which did however embrace Egypt, Palestine and Iraq. The Crown Colonies had lent Britain for the war the whole of their currency reserves. British liabilities increased in an alarming way; those to Canada were by the end of 1941 growing by some £250 million a year. In the first phase, Britain had paid for her imports from Canada by selling gold and securities, and then by borrowing. In the spring of 1942, the Canadian government made an outright gift of $1,000 million. That met Britain's needs, many of which she was incurring on behalf of other powers, for about 12 months. In the spring of 1943, Parliament in Canada made available a further $1,000 million to enable Britain and the Allies to obtain war supplies from her free of charge; and when in turn that second bounty was used up, Canada provided a further $2,000 million to cover war expenditure. The cost to Canada was more than three times per head the cost of lend-lease to the citizens of the United States. The official historians say with justice 'The needs of war had been met from beginning to end without hesitation or stint.'[15]

It would be graceless not to record such generosity, and the more so because relations between the British and Mackenzie King's government were sometimes troubled. The High Commissioner in Ottawa from 1941, Malcolm MacDonald, knew King closely, took care not to offend his susceptibilities and was rewarded with many confidences from that solitary, shrewd, calculating Prime Minister. King realized that if the question of conscription became acute while he was away at an Imperial Conference, there might be those who would force the issue in his absence. That would almost certainly mean a split in the Cabinet and perhaps the resignation of its French-Canadian members. Moreover, he averred that the system of consultation between the United Kingdom and the Dominion governments was working excellently and that the whole world could see for itself the unity of the Commonwealth in action.[16] It is true that there had been some disagreeable frictions; for example, the USA-Canadian Defence Board constituted an agreement between a foreign country and a Dominion for the defence of North America, made without consulting London. Roosevelt declared that the USA would offer to South American countries the use of the bases which the British had leased to America free of rent; but those bases were withheld from the British, to whom the territories belonged. However, all this occurred while the Lend-Lease Bill was making its way through Congress, and the British had learned in a hard school how to bite their tongues.

In the end, Mackenzie King did pay a brief visit to England in 1941 and received a somewhat mixed reception from the Canadian troops. Churchill remarked understandingly that the men were fed up with drill and discipline instead of fighting. 'Besides, there is Party feeling in Canada and the Government is organized on a Party basis. This cannot he helped.' As for conscription, he did not press the issue. After all, the war was turning out to be strangely different from the last, for in two years' struggle with the greatest military power, armed with the most deadly weapons, barely 100,000 people from Britain and the Commonwealth had been killed, of whom nearly half were civilians. It would be hard to argue an immediate necessity for conscription in Canada in such circumstances.[17] Mackenzie King gave on his return an account of the British martyrdom of daily anxiety and prolonged weariness, and said that he marvelled at the fidelity, ability and resilience with which ministers carried on their duties in London. He repeated that it would be difficult or impossible to improve upon the system of Commonwealth consultation already in force.[18]

★ ★ ★ ★ ★

The widening of the war to embrace the Mediterranean, the Middle East and North Africa, and then the Pacific from the end of 1941, altered the scope of the struggle: in the first instance because Commonwealth forces were heavily engaged, as they had not been in the first nine months; and then because Japan's belligerency threatened the Indian sub-continent, Ceylon, South-East Asia and Australasia, brought the United States into the war and thus changed the balance of power decisively. In 1940, Churchill had not believed that Japan would declare war unless Germany mounted a successful invasion of Britain; once the Japanese had seen that Germany had failed or dared not try, he looked for easier times in the Pacific. If that prognosis proved inaccurate, he guessed that an attack on Singapore was unlikely; and if that prediction too were wrong, Singapore ought to stand a long siege. Here, it is scarcely necessary to say, were major strategic miscalculations. Even if Japan did enter the war, Churchill and his colleagues did not wish to move the Mediterranean fleet to the Indian Ocean or to relieve Singapore unless such a step were found vital to the safety of Australia and New Zealand, because such a transference would entail the loss of the Middle East and all prospect of beating Italy in the Mediterranean would be gone. He judged an invasion of Australia or New Zealand by a considerable Japanese army most unlikely, and adhered to that view throughout. If such an invasion occurred, however, he had – so he told the Prime Ministers of those two Dominions in the summer of 1940 – 'the explicit authority of [the] Cabinet to assure you that we should then cut our losses in the Mediterranean and proceed to your aid, sacrificing every interest except only the defence and feeding of this Island on which all depends.'[19]

When Menzies telegraphed from Canberra about the Dakar expedition a few weeks later, telling Churchill that the absence of reliable information from Britain had frequently proved humiliating and that clear-cut victory in the Middle East was essential, his opposite number in London retorted that he could guarantee nothing of the kind ('I think the only certainty is that we have very bad times indeed to go through before we emerge from the mortal perils by which we are surrounded'). Thereupon Menzies repeated that Australian anxiety about the Middle East was not only intelligible but acute:

> Please, my dear Prime Minister, do not interpret the anxieties arising from these facts as either fearful, selfish or unduly wrong-headed. And above all, please understand that whatever interrogative or even critical telegrams I may send to you in secret, Australia knows courage when it sees it and will follow you to a finish, as to the best of my abilities I certainly shall.[20]

From Wellington, the Prime Minister pointed out that New Zealand had at the end of 1940 no aircraft to deal with attacks from the sea or protect shipping. He pressed for the long-range bombers which New Zealand lacked only because she had allowed the Hudsons originally destined for her to be retained by the United Kingdom instead. The Dominion possessed not a single aircraft suitable for reconnaissance or attack against a raider at any substantial distance from her shores; he anticipated grave difficulty in explaining the situation to Parliament. Awaiting the result of battles in Libya, WSC hesitated, and asked Fraser to understand the supreme importance of the Middle East, where the armies represented the whole Empire. If Italy could be broken, Japan – or so the Prime Minister thought – would become very cautious. 'Thus all hangs together and I hope you will have good confidence in us ... We will certainly send you some Hudsons for action against raiders but I know you would not wish to take more from the North Western approaches to Great Britain than is absolutely necessary in these next few months.'[21]

Even when full allowance is made for the fog of war and the heat of battle, there was substance in the complaints frequently made during 1940 that the Dominions were not kept as fully informed as they needed to be. The Secretary of State for Dominion Affairs, Lord Cranborne, pointed out the advantages of telling the Prime Ministers as much as possible, which greatly aided practical co-operation and helped them to frame their own policy and its presentation. Churchill feared the military risks of scattering deadly and secret information.[22] In general, the system relied upon the transmission of telegrams to the High Commissioner in each Dominion, or London, who took messages only to the Prime Minister. Sometimes, and especially during prickly dialectics with Australia, Churchill would communicate directly with his counterpart.

Those clashes of opinion, born of defeat in the field and bearing out all too painfully Churchill's prediction of 'very bad times indeed to go through', and of the knowledge that Australia was threatened while so many of her forces were serving far away, were the most serious which arose between Britain and any Commonwealth country during the war. They have been extensively chronicled: the expulsions from Greece and Crete; the contrast with what Churchill called the grandeur of the New Zealand government's attitude; Menzies' conviction that the War Cabinet should consist of five or six ministers without departmental responsibilities and his own desire to take a leading role in London; the insistence of the Australians upon the removal of their forces from Tobruk; the distress of the Commander-in-Chief in the Middle East, Auchinleck, who at first wished to resign. As Churchill telegraphed,

I was astounded at [the] Australian Government's decision, being sure it would be repudiated by Australia if that could be made known. Allowances must be made for a Government with a majority only of one faced by a bitter Opposition parts of which at least are isolationist in outlook.

It is imperative that no public dispute should arise between Great Britain and Australia. All personal feelings must therefore be subordinated to appearance of unity.[23]

His further pleas to Canberra produced no effect. Critical comments from America and elsewhere about large forces retained inactive in the

United Kingdom caused Churchill to explain that the main problem was the shortage of troop-carrying tonnage. That, not the safety of the United Kingdom, was now the limiting factor. And while it was obvious that the events of December 1941 greatly increased Japanese power in the Pacific, the Prime Minister still did not feel that there was any early danger of the fall of Singapore.[24]

Some months before, meeting the President off Newfoundland, Churchill had remarked to American colleagues that he would rather have an American declaration of war at once and no supplies for six months than double the supplies and no declaration. Roosevelt, to whom this was repeated, thought it a hard saying. He remarked to Churchill in private, 'I shall never declare war; I shall make war. If I were to ask Congress to declare war they might argue about it for three months.'[25] Significant as American aid had been, on the material plane and as an encouragement to morale, it was not that which had enabled the Commonwealth to survive the first two years and three months of the war. Nor, it was clear, would salvation come promptly from a power poorly armed for land and air warfare, and one which had just suffered so heavily at Pearl Harbour. There followed with the USA a process whereby an elaborate but effective system was created for the sharing of military command and for the ordering and co-ordination of supplies, built up on a basis which increasingly allowed the British far less latitude than they enjoyed in their relations with the Dominions. Churchill used to say that no lover ever studied the whims of his mistress as carefully as he studied Roosevelt's. As for American views of the Empire and its arrangements, the pressure for the reduction or abolition of Imperial Preference could be felt at stages during the war, and the British made the necessary safeguards on paper; the Prime Minister took care that the Atlantic Charter – the high-sounding declaration signed by the President and himself in August 1941, which pointed to 'the right of all peoples to choose the form of government under which they will live' – should have no immediate relevance to colonial territories; and occasional interventions, like the suggestion that Britain should cede Hong Kong to China, or Roosevelt's discussion of the Indian problem with Churchill 'on the usual American lines' immediately after Pearl Harbour, made little difference. The President never raised the issue in conversation again, so vehemently did his companion react. As Churchill observed in *The Hinge of Fate*, states with no overseas possessions are capable of rising to moods of great elevation and detachment about the affairs of those that have; just as, he added pointedly, 'In countries where there is only one race broad and lofty views are taken of the colour question.'

In respect of Roosevelt's suggestions about India, WSC permits himself one of his few direct criticisms of the President. A principal reason for the despatch of the Cripps mission in March 1942 lay in the American attitude; when the mission failed, as was probable from the beginning, Roosevelt told Churchill that in the United States the deadlock was almost universally believed to derive from the British government's unwillingness to concede the right of self-government to India. The President proposed a solution upon which Churchill comments crisply 'I was thankful that events had already made such an act of madness impossible.' He also remarks that had he not enjoyed the support of all his leading colleagues who had studied Indian issues he would not have hesitated to lay down his burden, 'which at times seemed more than a man could bear'. To Roosevelt he telegraphed, 'Anything like a serious difference between you and me would break my heart, and would surely deeply injure both our countries at the height of this terrible struggle.'[26]

* * * * *

Not by coincidence the military disasters of 1942 brought with them wounding exchanges between Canberra and London, and at home stern criticism of Churchill's style of government. This was the only phase of the war in which he appeared to have, on a superficial view, serious rivals; but there was in reality no prospect that Churchill would be supplanted by Sir Stafford Cripps, still less by Mr Menzies. London was constantly pressed to find scarce resources for vulnerable places. The Prime Ministers of the Dominions, with local or regional anxieties, would send urgent pleas. This was most true of Australia and New Zealand in respect of the Pacific, east and west; and to a lesser degree of South Africa, though few could have been more understanding of Churchill's difficulties or comprehending of the broad issues than Smuts.

The British High Commissioner in South Africa Lord Harlech, himself a former Secretary of State for the Colonies, reported Smuts towards the end of 1941 to be extraordinarily well and vigorous; carrying the burdens of state with a lion's heart, head and shoulders above all his Cabinet colleagues, full of faith and a philosophic detachment which scorned the personal and political quarrels rampant in South Africa, not only Prime Minister but Minister for External Affairs, Minister of Defence and Commander-in-Chief of all the South African forces.[27] Smuts had a range of experience, political and military, which no other figure in the overseas Commonwealth could approach. He had shown valour in the field, as had many of those to whom Churchill was close; courageously he had accepted defeat after the Boer War and then worked fruitfully with his old enemies; he had been a member of the Imperial War Cabinet in Lloyd George's time, and knew much about warfare; he possessed a wide view of the world; his views often coincided with those of Churchill, but in some matters of importance did not; the two conversed with freedom. Eden says that the partnership was incomparable, though the personalities could scarcely have differed more, the one with his neat philosophic mind and the other so 'rammed with life'. Churchill once reflected that Smuts was as he imagined Socrates might have been. The Prime Minister of South Africa stood high in Churchill's list of those with whom it was agreeable to dine. More apt than Churchill to brood even in the middle of the war about its sequel, he once told Eden that he realized the Foreign Secretary's position was very difficult 'because W's mind had a stop in it at the end of the war and he, Smuts, quite understood that I must have a foreign policy on which to work with Allies here, with Americans and Russians.'[28]

The British High Commissioner in Wellington wrote that the sinking of the *Prince of Wales* and *Repulse* in February 1942, coming on top of the disaster at Pearl Harbour, and the fact that the cities of New Zealand were exposed to the risk of raids by Japanese cruisers, caused the man in the street for the first time to feel the war in the pit of his stomach. Yet nowhere had he heard criticism of the policy of sending so many of the able-bodied men out of the country, or any suggestion of bringing back New Zealand's forces fighting overseas.[29] That is an startling fact, and that it should have been sustained through swelling perils is more startling still. In the end, the conviction of WSC and the War Cabinet that Japan could not mount a successful invasion of Australasia was borne out by events; other beliefs, especially those relating to Singapore, were not. The latter fact was certain and immediate, the other opinion contingent and not always convincing.

We may take the events of a single week in the second half of January 1942 to illuminate issues then known only to a small circle and in recent times so much discussed that other and still more important matters are easily lost to view. The issues, themselves representing but a fragment of the War Cabinet's business, were these: Smuts' view of military and Indian matters; Australian fears for the future of Singapore; the means of co-operation with Dominion governments; representation of the Dominions in the War Cabinet; the future of Imperial Preference and negotiations with the United States over Lend-Lease; the prospect that events in the Pacific would cause Australia and New Zealand to draw closer to the United States; and distressing reports from the British High Commissioner in Canberra.

Like Churchill, Smuts judged that even with Japan now rampant, reinforcements should be sent to the Middle East. From Pretoria, he asked that WSC should consider a more favourable response to India's political aspirations, since Dominion status would have to follow the war as a certainty:

> Why not deal with India in the same generous large spirit in which you have dealt with Russia? The case seems to me unanswerable and we should use all our resources to secure agreement between the religious communities of India and thus win the goodwill of India not only for the war effort but also for the troublous years thereafter. India is more important to us than China and generosity now is [the] only wise policy with her.[30]

Cripps, when he set off for India a couple of months later, bore with him a British undertaking to grant full independence to India after the war, if it should be demanded by a Constituent Assembly. But that is to anticipate. It was the onrush of the Japanese forces which gave urgency to the issues in India. The new Prime Minister of Australia, Curtin, pointed out on 24 January 1942 that any evacuation of Singapore would be regarded as an inexcusable betrayal, which was a point easily met because the War Cabinet had abandoned any such intention, and that Singapore was a central fortress in the system of Imperial and local defence. In Australia it had been understood that the base would be made impregnable or at any rate capable of holding out for a prolonged period until after the arrival of the main fleet.[31] It is hard not to sympathize with the sense of incipient disaster.

During his visit to Washington three weeks earlier, Churchill had agreed to establish a Far Eastern War Council, in which Australia and New Zealand as well as The Netherlands would be represented at Cabinet level under his own chairmanship. That fact went some way to fulfil the substantial demands which Australia had been putting forward, but as the Secretary of State for the Dominions pointed out, failed to satisfy her requirements in two ways: first, the Australian government had argued that consultation at ministerial level would prove inadequate unless a Dominion government received information and could make its views known while plans were still being formulated; secondly, the work of the Far Eastern War Council would be limited to that theatre.[32] It was largely to meet Australian wishes that the Pacific Council in Washington was also established, carrying a message for the future which the British did not miss. The right of Australia to be heard at the War Cabinet in the formulation and direction of policy was conceded in those matters which were of central concern to Australia, but not for the rest of the proceedings.

What the Secretary of State, Lord Cranborne – himself knowledgeable about foreign and Commonwealth affairs, disinterested, industrious, no uncritical admirer of Churchill and not afraid to address pointed minutes to him – called 'the agitation' had been confined almost entirely to Australia and, as he openly admitted, to 'certain sections of opinion in this country.' He advised that it would be a momentous mistake for the British to underestimate the strength of feeling in Australia, evidence of which was arriving from all quarters. Cranborne observed almost matter-of-factly that the process was being fuelled by the Australian government itself and particularly by Dr Evatt. The British High Commissioner in Canberra, himself a former minister in London, put the point even more bluntly: the Australian government, he wrote, was ignoring the spirit of Imperial partnership, propagating a nationalist outlook and abusing the United Kingdom authorities, including the administration in London. He was clear that this campaign was inspired and conducted by ministers; the government had done nothing to dissociate itself from the process, though Sir Ronald Cross did not suspect Curtin of taking an active part. The High Commissioner remarked that should Australia suffer acutely in the coming struggle, the permanent weakening of Australian ties with Britain might well result.

These were some of the grounds upon which Cranborne argued that the problems must be tackled forthwith and radically. Hence the decision about the attendance of an Australian representative at the War Cabinet, and the condition that he should be authorized to take decisions on behalf of the Australian government, without reference to Canberrra, in those instances where a conclusion had to be reached at once. Cranborne rightly judged that this was a question not merely of machinery but even more of status, and that to concede such rights to Australia would mean doing likewise for the other Dominions.[33]

The offer was accordingly made. Canada and South Africa declined; New Zealand availed herself of the right to be represented at the War Cabinet, but more sparingly than Australia. When the High Commissioner in Canberra suggested that if present tendencies continued, Britain should counter with an unaccommodating attitude to Australia in financial and economic matters, Cranborne pronounced immediately against anything of the kind, which would 'merely exasperate the Australian Government and give further stimulus to their tendency to look to the United States for help.'[34] In respect of Imperial Preference, it was quite possible to put an acceptable interpretation upon the American wish for the 'elimination of all forms of discriminatory treatment in international commerce', namely that the Commonwealth would be committed to modifications only in return for compensating advantages; but there was little doubt that the Dominions would look askance on any response which might prejudice the prospects of future collaboration with the USA. As Cranborne remarked in those tremulous days just before the fall of Singapore, 'The general war situation, and the increased dependence of Australia and New Zealand in particular upon immediate [American] co-operation in the Pacific, are likely to strengthen Australia certainly and possibly also New Zealand in this attitude.'[35]

The garrison of Singapore consisted largely of soldiers from the overseas Commonwealth. At the surrender on 15 February 1942, some 32,000 Indian troops, 16,000 British and 14,000 Australians were taken prisoner. More than half died before the end of the war. While the War Cabinet had wished to divert a large Australian force for the defence of Burma, Curtin and his colleagues insisted that the troops return forthwith to Australia because of the Japanese threat from New Guinea. Again angry messages passed to and fro, some of them so secret that they were seen neither by the British High Commissioner in Canberra nor by the Australian High Commissioner in London.[36] With Malaya and Burma in Japanese hands, would Calcutta be bombed or Bengal invaded? If forces were taken from Ceylon, would that country fall, an event which Churchill believed would 'cripple our whole war effort in the Middle East as well as India'?[37] In the Bay of Bengal during that spring, the Allies had no effective naval force, largely because they could offer no powerful air support. In other words, the situation in Asia was demonstrating what had already become apparent elsewhere, that sea power by itself, even if exercised by the greatest ships from secure bases, could not prevail against naval strength strongly reinforced from the air. During his abortive mission in March and April 1942, Cripps reviewed the prospects with Wavell and the Viceroy, and reported the air and naval situation to be 'disastrously dangerous ... We have so little in India that it is impossible to see how it can be held once the Japanese have unlimited access for aircraft carriers to all and any points around its coast.'[38] The military commanders telegraphed in similar terms. The Deputy Prime Minister in London, Attlee, who had just become Secretary of State for the Dominions, wished to give priority to India at the expense of a less intensive attack by the bombers upon Germany. Churchill, mindful of the fate which had awaited some of the aircraft belatedly deployed to Singapore, replied 'Everybody would like to send Bomber Command to India and the Middle East. However it is not possible to make any decisive change. It is no use flying out squadrons which sit helpless and useless when they arrive.' He pointed out another consideration which loomed continuously, that the brunt of the battle on land was falling upon Russia, where the outcome was by no means certain:

> We have built up a great plant for bombing Germany which is the only way in our power of helping Russia. From every side people want to break it up. One has to be sure that we do not ruin our punch here without getting any proportionate advantage elsewhere.[39]

These examples provide some measure of the risks which were being run now that this war, unlike the first, had become a truly world-wide affair. The importance of defending India needed no emphasis. Wavell was amply entitled to point out that the forces within the sub-continent were quite inadequate to cope with a serious invasion. There were also the political aspects. After all, India had sent her troops, as soon as they were sufficiently equipped and trained and often before, to fight elsewhere. There were at that moment in the spring of 1942 the equivalent of some seven Indian divisions in the Middle East, a much larger and better-trained force than was available in the sub-continent itself.[40]

* * * * *

When Churchill received at Washington in June 1942 the news of the fall of Tobruk and the surrender of some 30,000 men, he could not believe it and had to enquire of London by telephone. Never, the Prime Minister remarked afterwards, had an Englishman been placed in so unfortunate a position since Burgoyne surrendered at Saratoga. The event seemed to verge on disgrace.[41] Neither Roosevelt nor Harry Hopkins spoke a word of reproach. 'What can we do to help?' asked the President. Churchill replied, 'Give us as many Sherman tanks as you can spare, and ship them to the Middle East as quickly as possible.'[42] This was done directly. As it chanced, a South African division had largely formed the garrison left to hold Tobruk. Smuts, recorded the British High Commissioner in Pretoria, took the blow with his usual amazing calmness, bravery and detachment. He made an immediate appeal for 7,000 European recruits for the South African fighting forces under the slogan 'Avenge Tobruk'. The event appears to have had in South Africa an effect somewhat akin to that produced in Australia and New Zealand by Pearl Harbour and its sequels. Realization suddenly came that a period of austerity was imminent, with what the High Commissioner called a long overdue awakening of war-mindedness. The debate in London on a motion of censure in the House of Commons had been followed with some anxiety. In South Africa, it was generally thought unfortunate that Churchill had been with the CIGS in the USA at such an uncertain moment in the fate of the Middle Eastern campaign. Lord Beaverbrook's advocacy of a second front in Western Europe, at the expense of the more vital existing second front from Libya to the Persian Gulf, was mistrusted; and it was felt that the holding of the eastern Mediterranean, Syria, Iraq and Iran was of far greater importance to Russia, and to the general strategic plan of the war, than any alternative venture could be. Australia's savage political criticism of Great Britain had been ill received, whereas admiration was felt for the heroic performance of the New Zealanders in Libya. As for Smuts:

> Everything is submerged in his burning faith in the ultimate triumph of good over evil, and his profound belief in the moral rightness of the Allied cause. He is, I fear, a lonely figure even among his supporters; while his very spiritual and intellectual eminence is the more exasperating to his enemies. It is essential at times like these to bear in mind that the majority of Afrikaans-speaking South Africans (of Dutch, German and Huguenot stock) are consumed with a passionate, emotional dislike of any connection with the British Commonwealth, by an all-dominating negrophobia, and by the ideal of narrow isolationism under the dominance of their fundamentalist and reactionary Predikants. The analogy with Southern Ireland is all too complete. General Smuts is regarded by his opponents as guilty of the three greatest sins (1) theological heresy (2) cosmopolitanism (3) Liberalism.[43]

It was Smuts who joined Churchill in Cairo a few weeks later for the painful decisions which resulted in the supersession of Auchinleck, and he who approved wholeheartedly the Prime Minster's handling of the encounter with Stalin in Moscow, when it was necessary to break the news that there would be no second front in 1942 (or more accurately no fourth front, in view of the wars already raging in the Middle East and the Far East) and to bear, with such equanimity as WSC could muster, Stalin's crude taunts about British cowardice.

At this point the contest had run half its course. Thenceforward, the military balance slowly tilted, and with that process most sharp antagonisms within the Commonwealth concerning the conduct of war diminished. It is true that the withdrawal of Australian troops from the Mediterranean and Middle East placed New Zealand in a quandary, as did repeated requests by the United States for additional New Zealand troops in the Pacific. The government of Australia had allowed substantial forces to remain in the Middle East and Ceylon but once the tide had turned decisively in the Middle East, it was no longer possible to resist Australian demands for withdrawal. On one of the telegrams Churchill noted sorrowfully, 'We shall have to let them go. But shipping cannot be unduly deranged.'[44]

The New Zealanders were commanded by General Freyberg, VC, born in London but brought up in Wellington, an officer of legendary dash and courage. When he was introduced in hospital to Queen Mary, after the battle of the Somme, as a soldier who had been wounded in 20 places, Her Majesty is said to have remarked memorably 'I didn't know that a man *had* that many places.' No one understood better than Freyberg how to interpret his country of adoption to his country of birth. On General Montgomery's observing that the New Zealand Division did not seem to have been taught to salute, he received the cheerful reply 'That's all right, Monty. If you wave to them, they'll wave back.' Remembering the mythical creature thought able to survive fire, WSC hailed Freyberg as 'the salamander of the British Empire'. By the late autumn of 1942, the New Zealand Division had suffered 18,500 killed, wounded or captured out of a total of 43,500 sent to the Middle East. Churchill pointed out to Fraser in Wellington that if the return of the Division had to follow that of the Australians, there would be a further heavy drain upon shipping. Parliament in New Zealand decided in secret session and without a dissenting voice not to recall the troops for the moment. Well might Churchill express profound gratitude: 'I am sure the President of the United States will share our feelings here of admiration for New Zealand and all that she stands for.'[45] It is reliably reported that in his enthusiasm WSC referred to the Prime Minister of New Zealand as 'that dear old man', forgetting for the moment that Mr Fraser was ten years younger than himself. Under the military arrangements in the south-west Pacific area, Australia had surrendered part of her sovereignty and assigned all her competent forces to the Allied Commander. It is easy to forget the proportions; the land forces in that theatre at the end of November 1942 comprised ten Australian and two American divisions.[46] Fraser pointed out, as Curtin was to do on more than one occasion, that for the preservation of British influence in the Pacific, it would be most inexpedient if active operations there were conducted by the USA without British collaboration.[47]

This was a message to which the British government was sensitive. When he met representatives of the Dominions in May 1943 at Washington, and in the White House of all places, Churchill drew attention to two important principles which he asked everyone working in Washington to bear in mind: the development of the fraternal association between the Commonwealth and the United States, and the fostering of the conscious identity of the Commonwealth itself. The only other Prime Minister there was Mackenzie King, who said in the presence of Roosevelt that the fact that all the Dominions had with one accord entered the war at the beginning was something that none would forget. Considering the USA's long neutrality and King's habitual caution, this was a remark of some note. Even Dr Evatt, whose relations with the British (and plenty of others) were not invariably easy, had the grace to volunteer that the improvement in the situation was attributed in Australia largely to Churchill's exertions, while the Indian representative, Sir Shankar Bajpai, remarked that many in his country were beginning to realize the great value of remaining within the Commonwealth, which had so nobly sustained the cause of liberty and which held out such hopes for progress in peace. None of the governments represented raised any serious question about the control of operations by the Combined Chiefs of Staff, by whose decisions, said Mackenzie King, the Canadian government was perfectly prepared to abide.[48]

As the Russians held and then repelled the German invasion, and the Americans increased their forces and production, the Dominions and the British had to ask themselves how they would relate to the wider world both in preparation for the peace-making and after the collapse of the German, Italian and Japanese empires. Successive Secretaries of State, Cranborne and Attlee, urged repeatedly that the Dominions must have the opportunity to pull their full weight in considering the postwar settlement. From Britain's point of view, what was most desirable was support and recognition of her predominant position in many of the issues, and that was far more likely to be secured if the Dominions were consulted early and serious account taken of their opinions. Attlee viewed the future of Germany and the post-war arrangements in Europe as vital to the Commonwealth and Empire because they involved the issue of peace or war again in the next generation; he was sure that Britain should consult the Dominions before she turned to her other major allies or reached her own conclusions.[49] In the event, a proposal for a meeting of the Dominion Prime Ministers in London had to be put back.[50] After elections in three of the four Dominions during 1943, Smuts' position was vastly reinforced by an overwhelming victory; the same was true of Curtin and his Labour government in Australia, and the Labour administration in New Zealand was returned with a slightly reduced majority in September.

If Mackenzie King were to be taken literally, a general election might also have occurred in Canada. He felt distressed because insufficient attention had been paid to the Canadian troops' role in the invasion of Sicily, and made a damaging statement. Casting around for an explanation, Malcolm MacDonald remarked that although Canadian ministers appreciated the vast amount of information sent from London and the conscientious way in which Canada had been consulted on almost every question, there had been important exceptions and on those occasions 'Ministers here felt that Canada was being treated as though she were a Colony rather than a Dominion, and they have resented this.' King's statement, MacDonald reported, had produced a deplorable effect throughout Canada, where everyone had gained the impression that when Canadian troops were at last going into action on a considerable scale, the government in London had tried to prevent the facts from reaching the public, though it was believed the American authorities had been well disposed. Against the High Commissioner's sentence 'I fear the evil effects of this deplorable incident will last for many years', WSC merely endorsed 'Rubbish'. However, he did not hesitate to tell King that his remarks, seeming to suggest that Canada had received better treatment from the Americans than from the British, had made painful reading. It had been necessary to give great prominence to the role of the United States, though the British and Commonwealth forces had by far the larger share in the invasion of Sicily, and the newspapers in London were full of the exploits of the Canadian Division:

I am sure you will realise how difficult it is to keep all these things straight especially when so much else is going forward, and I know you will believe that my most earnest desire is to give the utmost satisfaction to you and to your troops on whose dramatic entry into this successful battle I offer you and your colleagues my sincere congratulations.

Please always if possible let me know if anything causes trouble, as I am always most desirous of meeting your wishes and making all go well.[51]

At one stage, King said that if any statement reflecting on the truth of his own remarks were made by Churchill, Parliament in Ottawa would be dissolved and he would appeal to the country, fighting the election not only on this incident but appealing against the treatment of Canada by the British government on many occasions in the previous two years. He strode angrily up and down. MacDonald, well used to the Prime Minister's vagaries of mood, contested this reading of the facts. They argued the whole evening. Next morning, the Prime Minster of Canada was less angry, though the two of them went over the case afresh. When they met that afternoon, the crisis had passed. MacDonald, himself a skilful upholder of his own country's interests and a perceptive interpreter of Canadian feelings, felt sure that the threat had merely been an unconsidered explosion of pent-up feelings; but those sentiments were widespread amongst ministers, public servants and informed citizens all over Canada, and must be taken to heart.[52]

A few weeks later, Churchill and Sir John Anderson (Lord President of the Council) met the War Committee of the Canadian Cabinet at Quebec. This was the first occasion upon which the two bodies had taken counsel together. Once more Mackenzie King and the Minister for National Defence said that while Canada did not demand any equal voice in determining the high strategy of the war, the Canadian public were increasingly concerned that there should be adequate recognition of their substantial contribution. Mr King made a discreet reference to occasional serious difficulties when decisions taken jointly by the USA and the UK had been announced without the opportunity for Canadian comment.[53]

Returning to the Dominions Office later in 1943, Lord Cranborne told the Australian High Commissioner that he had been impressed with the improvement in relations as compared with 1941 and promised to keep Stanley Bruce informed of the course of events at the Foreign Ministers' conference in Moscow. With some justice, the High Commissioner remarked that he had an obligation to his own Prime Minister to ensure that in respect of major issues Australia would have the opportunity to express her view before decisions were taken. Apparently Bruce's colleagues in Australia imagined that he was regularly attending the meetings of the War Cabinet, and for the sake of harmony Bruce had done nothing to correct them. WSC declined to give way and Bruce did concede that while the arrangement for an Australian accredited representative had not worked on the lines foreseen, the main purpose was to a great extent being achieved.[54]

Nevertheless, the decisions by then being taken affected far more than the conduct of the war in its last phase. We have only to think of the discussions late in 1943 between Stalin, Roosevelt and Churchill at Tehran where, Churchill said, he realized for the first time

> what a very *small* country this is. On one hand the big Russian bear with its paws outstretched – on the other the great American Elephant – and between them the poor little British donkey – who is the only one that knows the right way home.[55]

How were Britain and the Dominions, with a combined population of 80 million, to hold their own with the United States at 130 million or the USSR with 150 million? The answer looked obvious enough in theory: only if the Commonwealth could act as one in major questions of foreign policy. For all that may be written now about frictions and disunity, it was the extraordinary degree of cohesion achieved during the war which made such a conception possible. It was shared by politicians of differing hues. Attlee, for example, took it to be a fundamental assumption that whatever international organization might be established after the war 'it will be our aim to maintain the British Commonwealth as an international entity recognized as such by foreign countries, in particular by the United States and the Soviet Union.' He acknowledged the complexities. Each of the Dominions must rank in the world as an independent nation. The days were long past when Britain could represent the entire Commonwealth. Other states would not agree to separate representation of each Dominion on the main international bodies. Nor was it likely that the Dominions would agree that one of them should be the representative; as Attlee expressed the point, the Dominions were more jealous of each other than they were of the United Kingdom. In almost any subject likely to come before an international body, Britain would have more at stake than any one of the Dominions and public opinion would be unlikely to agree that Britain's interest should be represented by another country, even a Dominion.[56] What of major commercial questions, where each Dominion would certainly desire its own voice? And if the new international organization were to have a largely regional basis, as Churchill repeatedly proposed, where would Canada be left? The prospect of lying entirely within the American sphere was by no means agreeable and the Canadian government would have no time for an international system based on bodies composed of a few great powers.[57] While there might be certain tendencies common to the self-governing Dominions, there was no such thing as a 'Dominion point of view', for each had its own characteristics and problems and each would increasingly assert its national identity.[58]

In point of collaboration and the sharing of information, such issues were tackled thoroughly and effectively between Britain and the Dominions. A great deal of most secret information went to each Prime Minister. Experience showed the system to be secure;[59] the Foreign Office and the Dominions Office, relations between which did not always run smoothly, exerted themselves. All manner of ideas received serious attention: a Commonwealth-wide Cabinet, a unified Commonwealth Defence Service, a Commonwealth Economic Board; more practically, Dominion representation in the United Kingdom Cabinet for questions of foreign policy, exchanges of officials between foreign services of the Commonwealth, amalgamation of the Foreign Office and the Dominions Office, better co-ordination of publicity, and much else in the same vein.[60]

When the British Ambassador in Washington, Lord Halifax, spoke in Toronto on 24 January 1944, to the effect that the members of the Commonwealth should for the general good act together in international affairs after the war, he was saying something which had been said not only by British ministers but also by Smuts and Curtin. Mackenzie King, at first furiously angry, remarked that Halifax' speech looked to him 'like part of a deliberate design by the United Kingdom Government and some Dominion statesmen to revive an Imperialism which left the Dominions something less than national sovereignty.' 'I did my best to disabuse him of this idea' telegraphed MacDonald. Halifax must have known, King argued, that the speech would be used by political opponents, a view which, as it transpired, Churchill largely shared. It is plausible that King made the most of the opportunity. MacDonald remarked that he had been put quite unwarrantably into one of his worst moods and had as usual on such occasions talked of going to the country and fighting a General Election. 'He is, of course, looking for a slogan which will win him the next Election and one which resisted "reactionary Imperialism" would undoubtedly help to do the trick.' King declared himself to be entirely in favour of close consultation and effective co-ordination of policy on all matters of common concern in the Commonwealth. Of the system under which all the main questions were discussed fully in the Cabinets of the Dominions and Britain, and views were exchanged promptly, he asked – in language which must have been read with a certain sense of irony by some of those in the inner circle – 'What more effective means could possibly be found of obtaining a consensus of view, an approach towards common policy and a co-ordination of policies?' In sum, King disagreed with the contention that the United Kingdom must have the constant support of the Dominions if it were to preserve some balance with the USSR and the USA. Referring to Halifax and Smuts, King said 'With what is implied in argument by both these eminent public men I am unable to agree. What we must strive for is close co-operation among those great states themselves and all other like-minded countries.'[61]

The reactions in Canada were considerable and spilled over into negotiations about the control of Canadian forces. Mackenzie King intervened vigorously; Malcolm MacDonald exercised his emollient influence; and the matter was resolved. MacDonald felt confident that in wider issues Canadian co-operation with Britain and the rest of the Commonwealth was assured provided that the British did not create too many difficulties by saying or doing things which upset French-Canadian opinion or which appeared to suggest an infringement of national sovereignty, or that the British would wish Canada to side with them in a process of 'ganging up' against the United States.[62] As he pointed out on another occasion, steps towards a formal Imperial unity might be regarded in the USA as a deliberate move to counter American strength in world affairs and neither in Australia nor in New Zealand was there a parallel to that factor, or to the French Canadian one. About 20 per cent of the people of Canada were French Canadians, and more than a further 20 per cent were not of British stock. Moreover, Canada with her 11 million stood alongside a power with 12 times that population. To the question 'What would be the attitude of the Canadians to a plea for closer Imperial co-operation in general and for a new and formal Imperial machinery to achieve it?' MacDonald could answer succinctly: 'They are in favour of the former and opposed to the latter.'[63]

Commonwealth Prime Ministers had not met since 1937. Careful preparations were made for their gathering of May 1944. Ernest Bevin, then Minister of Labour but soon to be Foreign Secretary, favoured the division of the Empire into zones for defensive purposes, and said that like Smuts and Halifax he was most anxious to ensure that the Commonwealth should act wherever possible as a unit. We must take as a measure of the optimism of the times Bevin's view that Europe within a few years would probably not present the same difficult problems as hitherto.[64] The acknowledged fact that Commonwealth consultation had improved markedly and the co-operation between the various Commonwealth missions in Washington[65] did much to strengthen the hand of those like Mackenzie King who wished to rely on that system. The British knew in advance that Curtin's suggestions – which included the creation of a standing sub-committee of the Committee of Imperial Defence, and the establishment of a joint permanent secretariat of the Imperial Conference itself – would not be acceptable to Canada, and Cranborne cast about for less formal instruments.[66] King's position, quite apart from its intrinsic merits, had all the strength which accrues to a leading power in any organization where unanimity is essential. He argued that Britain's most faithful allies in two wars had been the countries of the Commonwealth, a fact that could scarcely be overlooked by any nation which might wish to attack her. By contrast, a formal unity of policy might bind the Commonwealth countries together in such a way that differences would be magnified and disputes advertised. The prestige of the Commonwealth had never stood higher and was

> based upon a belief that in the British Commonwealth there has been evolved a unique alliance of a particularly tough and enduring kind whose members act together, unlike so many allies bound by explicit treaties, not because they are compelled to act together, but because they have the will to act together.[67]

In practice, most of the suggestions of Curtin and Fraser, who went even further, were quietly shelved. Nonetheless, Curtin who had gone to Britain tired and depressed, anxious because he believed that Churchill did not hold a good opinion of him, returned to Australia with his self-confidence much increased. He had found relations with the other Prime Ministers excellent, believed with good reason that he had struck up a genuine friendship with Churchill and had been impressed by the minute ration of butter and sugar in his hotel.[68] It was he who had pointed out at the conference that from a population of 7 million, no larger than that of London or New York, 870,000 men had thus far enlisted in the Australian forces and over half a million had volunteered to serve anywhere in the world. The proportions in New Zealand were not far different. Churchill assured both Prime Ministers that the British people were prepared to make sacrifices to ensure the permanent defeat of the Japanese peril, because 'It should never be said that we were willing to accept the help of others in our own extremity, but were unprepared to take our share in the troubles of others.'[69]

The three Vice-Chiefs of Staff had argued strongly for Commonwealth cohesion in defence after the war, because the United Nations must depend on the whole-hearted co-operation of the principal member states and their willingness to use force to prevent aggression; alternatively, if a world-wide system broke down, a united Commonwealth would be essential for the security of Britain and the Dominions.[70] At this point, 12 months before the end of the war with Germany, the future shape of international organization remained obscure. For the present and immediate future, the conference marked a high tide of approval and praise from all the Dominions for the way in which Britain's policy had been conducted. As Eden's diary notes,[71] the Dominion Prime Ministers displayed a vigorous and active approval, and the occasion stood in marked contrast with that of 1937, when he had also been Foreign Secretary. His review dealt with Russia, where he said that he could not tell whether she would work with other nations and accept the rules of conduct without which international collaboration would be impossible; the USA, where the picture was infinitely happier; Poland and Central Europe; every aspect of the Mediterranean situation from Italy to Portugal and France to Turkey; Northern Europe; China; Hong Kong and the Middle East. The Prime Ministers of New Zealand and Australia expressed their confidence in the policy which the British government had followed and was proposing. Mackenzie King, the turbulence of a few months earlier apparently forgotten, said that

> When he considered that United Kingdom Ministers had been dealing with two vast conflicts – the war between nations and the war between classes – he felt that situation after situation had been met marvellously and the way in which they had been handled commanded the strongest possible admiration. In saying that he felt that he spoke from the heart of the people of Canada.

The Indian representative, Sir Firoz Khan Noon, who took care to point out that he received his instructions from the government of India and not from London, explained why he hoped the foreign policy of the Commonwealth would remain in British hands:

> For the moment we may well be pleased with the peace and contentment which prevails among the non-European people under the British flag in full realisation of the fact that they can develop to their full political stature inside the British Commonwealth of Nations and that in our foreign policy we stand unitedly behind the Foreign Secretary, and are well pleased with what he has already achieved for us.

Even with some discount for official courtesies, the records of these meetings are impressive. When it came to Smuts, he said simply that he had no fault to find. South Africa had been kept so amply informed at every stage that the material was sometimes difficult to cope with on account of its very fullness. He too paid tribute to Eden for the way in which what he described as the foreign policy not only of the United Kingdom but of the Commonwealth had been conducted during the war:

> The Empire had been faced with grave decisions and terrible crises. He could not remember over the whole period of nearly five years when foreign policy as conducted here from London had not been such as they in other parts of the Empire, and especially in South Africa, could follow.[72]

In respect of the military operations, Churchill gave candid accounts and doubtless heard with pleasure Mackenzie King's repeated tributes to his wisdom in putting off until 1944 the invasion of Western Europe, despite all the pressures; he described the deep suspicions of the Americans, who thought he entertained designs to drag them into the Balkans; he remarked that the arrival of the Eighth Army in Tunisia had given the Commonwealth the numerical superiority and thus the dominant voice and 'had enabled us to lead the Americans along into Sicily and Italy.' When Smuts observed that if he had had a free choice, perhaps he would have hesitated to approve the switch of the main effort from the Mediterranean to north-west Europe, Churchill rejoined in terms which left no doubt that the American voice had been predominant in that decision, or that he was wholly committed to Overlord. In respect of the great unknown factor which loured over these discussions, Churchill said that he was confident the spirit of freedom in the world would face up to the brutish regimentation of Communism. He dreamed of a united states of Europe of which Britain and Russia would be the outside pillars, with the British Empire woven into the world organization and a fraternal association of the English-speaking peoples. To the question 'Would Russia make for power and world dominance at once?', he said that he hoped and believed not. Indeed, he refused entirely to consider the possibility of a confrontation between Russia and the English-speaking peoples, while acknowledging that a country with a huge population and the most rigid control would at the end of the war be freed from the two menaces which had confronted it in history, Germany and Japan. Nevertheless, he believed that the USA and the Commonwealth, including India and the Colonies 'in their various stages of development', might well be a force which could work in harmony with Russia.[73]

A little less than 12 months later, the Prime Minister was to address another gathering of Dominion statesmen, but in more sombre tones. By then, the American role in the alliance had grown by leaps and bounds; the defeat of Germany was clearly a matter of weeks, though a long campaign against Japan seemed likely to follow; the South African forces had moved beyond the confines of the continent; it had proved politically impossible to send South African squadrons to India; the US and British governments had disagreed openly about Greece. The more firmly Russia got into the saddle now, Smuts told Churchill in the autumn of 1944, the further she would ride in future. While a world organization was necessary, it was no less essential that the Commonwealth should emerge as strong as possible from this ordeal and thus 'make us an equal partner in every sense for the other Big Two.'[74] Curtin told Churchill of the extreme importance of flying the Union Jack in the impending operations in the Pacific;[75] and Keynes pointed out that the British were bearing a wholly disproportionate share of the financial burden of the war.[76] London had agreed to take all the bacon, beef and eggs which Canada could export. In Australia the meat ration was cut by 12.5 per cent on the grounds that it would be unthinkable to reduce exports to Britain, since the courage of the British people, civilians as well as servicemen, had established the justness of their claim to share Australian food. The Canadian forces were deeply engaged in Northern and Western Europe and the Australians in fierce encounters with the Japanese from Borneo to Bougainville Island;

the Second New Zealand Division was fighting valiantly in Italy, as was a South African Division; Indian forces were engaged in the Mediterranean and Burma; the government of Newfoundland was able to announce a surplus for the fifth consecutive year. This fact must have made the British ministers' eyes grow round with wonder as they contemplated the soaring scale of the 'sterling balances', the sums standing to the credit in London of Egypt, India and other countries.[77]

When Fraser sent from New Zealand some critical comments about the outcome of the Yalta conference, Churchill observed that Britain and the Commonwealth were very much weaker than Russia and America and thus not in a position to give 'clear, cool, far-seeing altruistic directions to the world. We have to do the best we can. We cannot go further in helping Poland than the United States is willing or can be persuaded to go...'. He conceded that the proof of the pudding lay in the eating and said that he had good hopes that Russia, or at any rate Stalin, desired to work in harmony with the Western democracies. The alternative, he added revealingly, would be despair about the long-term future of the world.[78] Having adopted this line of argument, which is irreconcilable with the notion that he had no illusions about Russia and was compelled to give ground because the American government had many, the Prime Minister found himself driven to say to representatives of the Commonwealth in early April 1945 that since Yalta, the atmosphere with Russia had changed beyond recognition. He conceded that he had gone bail in Parliament for the good faith of Russia, and deeply regretted the change that had occurred. All the same, when the Prime Ministers of New Zealand and South Africa, the Deputy Prime Minister of Australia and the High Commissioner for Canada discussed the prospects, Churchill said that he thought they were not far away from achieving two grand objectives: to ensure that the United States became a member of the future world organization and to draw Russia from seclusion into the genial sunlight of the comity of nations. In respect of immediate policy, there were few differences. The Deputy Prime Minister of Australia, Mr Forde, paid a warm tribute to the handling of matters during the war, and Churchill to the Commonwealth.[79]

The Dominion governments went on from London to play leading roles in the conference at San Francisco. They demonstrated their independence, to any with eyes to see, by opposing British policy on several points of substance. Although the issues differed, this was true of

Australia's delegation under Dr Evatt, New Zealand's under Fraser and Canada's under Mackenzie King. The questions ranged from the veto of great powers to aspects of trusteeship, and from Argentina to regional groupings. As Eden reported cheerfully to Churchill at the end of April:

> We are a pretty good Empire party here. Smuts has been most helpful at every point. We [the delegates] are giving him the Chairmanship of the most important commission [on the General Assembly]. Mackenzie King has intermittent colds in head and feet, brought on by the imminence of his general election, but on the whole he is in good heart and very helpful. Evatt and Fraser are making clear to the Americans and all concerned that we do not control their votes …[80]

Even at San Francisco, to which Molotov and the Russian delegation had come at the last minute and at which they had to admit that the Polish leaders taken to Moscow had in effect been kidnapped and put on trial, hopeful assumptions were breaking down upon hard facts. Smuts' forebodings made him telegraph in mid-May that 'Russia must be made to realise without delay what she is up against before she commits herself to a policy which may mean her ruin and Stalin following the fate of Hitler.'[81] That was not far from the view which Churchill had latterly urged upon the dying Roosevelt, and now pressed again with little greater success upon the new President.

From this distance of time, we cannot fail to be conscious of expectations belied and heroic sacrifices made for advantages which proved evanescent, and of the fact that the Commonwealth as a third force in world affairs could not be long sustained in the face of Russian and American might, the exhaustion and bankruptcy of Britain, the new forces apparent with the emergence of India and Pakistan as independent republics. In some of the colonial territories, the reputation of the Empire for invincibility had collapsed; everywhere, the forces unleashed during the war undermined the legitimacy of Empire.

We readily see now that during the war the Commonwealth and Empire reached a pitch of endeavour, and cohesion in military and political affairs alike, which it could never again attain. Even if the efforts of the Dominions, India and the Colonies had proved to be something marginal, such an example of co-operation would have been remarkable;

but what was achieved was far from marginal. It is not fanciful to say that the contribution of the overseas Commonwealth was indispensable to survival between 1939 and 1942, and to the regaining of the lost ground after that. To defeat Germany, Italy and Japan was necessary for the restoration of freedom. That triumph should have been followed by tragedy in the shape of the confrontation with Soviet Russia caused many to lament that the war had been fought in vain. But the collapse of the Russian empire in recent years, the fulfilment of Churchill's prophecy that in the end the tyranny would not prevail against deeper-running currents, lends a fresh perspective. A later generation has no cause to quarrel with a judgement expressed by Smuts during a meeting with fellow Prime Ministers at the subterranean offices of the War Cabinet on the first day of May 1944:

> It was a wonderful feat to have weathered the storm for four and a half years, during two of which we had stood alone. How the British Commonwealth, with its comparatively slender resources, had fought Germany and Italy at a time when Russia was bound by treaty to the enemy, and when Europe was overrun, would stand out in history as one of the most remarkable achievements ever known.[82]

3

An Affair of the Heart

Churchill and France

It was not only General de Gaulle who possessed, and was possessed by, 'une certaine idée de la France'. To Winston Churchill, France was a country which he had visited from his boyhood and a place of glorious martial tradition. France had nurtured the most heroic of all European legends, that of Joan of Arc, of whom he once wrote 'I think she is the winner in the whole of French history. The leading women of those days were more remarkable and forceful than the men';[1] it was the state which in an outburst of ardour had changed the fate of the world under the impetus of Napoleon, in homage to whom he repeated the saying 'That was the most beautiful countenance from which genius ever looked upon mankind';[2] it was the French who had borne the brunt, especially in the first two years of the Great War, and had thus done much to preserve the security of Great Britain and save the world. France harboured a civilization of infinite richness and variety. It was the land of sunshine and champagne.

In large questions of foreign policy, Churchill liked to adhere to a few simple principles. Paramount from 1940 was the importance of close relations with America; he was a consistent supporter of a national home for the Jews and thus of Israel; he believed in the benefits of British rule in Africa and Asia. Not that he adopted attitudes towards the United States or Israel uncritically or without regard to circumstances; nor did his tactics and strategy lack subtlety. All the same, he had strongly entrenched attitudes, from which he seldom deviated for long; and amongst them was an enduring love of France.

Ejected from office and abandoned by most of his colleagues, Churchill went to fight there in November 1915. Disgusted with politics, he wrote to his wife from the battlefield:

> I have lost all interest in the outer world and no longer worry about it or its stupid newspapers. … Filth and rubbish everywhere, graves built into the defences and scattered about promiscuously, feet and clothing breaking through the soil, water and muck on all sides; and about this scene in the dazzling moonlight troops of enormous rats creep and glide, to the unceasing accompaniment of rifle and machine guns … Amid these surroundings, aided by wet and cold, and every minor discomfort, I have found happiness and content such as I have not known for many months.[3]

In those same weeks, Churchill remarked to one of his military companions 'I am never going to have anything more to do with politics or politicians. When this war is over I shall confine myself entirely to writing and painting.'[4] But that was said in a mood of deep disillusion and his appetite for the affairs of state returned. Recalled to high office, he found himself as Minister of Munitions thrown into constant collaboration with the French. He accompanied Clemenceau to the front at the end of March 1918, when the issue of the war trembled in the balance. Clemenceau, then aged 76, insisted upon witnessing the battle at close quarters and was with difficulty persuaded to leave what he called 'un moment délicieux'.[5] Marshal Foch demanded enormous sacrifices from the British armies during 1918, and himself passed through a grim ordeal. Knowing the outcome, we may easily forget the high tension: how nearly the battle was lost in that summer; the incursion of the German armies through the centre of the French line and the virtual destruction of four or five British divisions mutilated in earlier encounters; the aggravation of the stresses between the British and French High Commands; Clemenceau's fearlessness in upholding the authority of Foch, whose resistance to the German offensive at the end of the second week in July was described as one of the greatest deeds of war and examples of fortitude of soul which history has recorded.[6]

Those were Churchill's words. In Paris when the German armies stood less than 50 miles away, he did not forget that France had lost nearly 1.5 million dead, far more than the entire British Empire. Driven by the cataclysm to reflect upon the relationship between Foch and Clemenceau, he discerned in it something far beyond the personal. To the British, the strain of violent civil conflict in France was incomprehensible. The cruelties and excesses of the Commune in Paris of 1871 Churchill regarded as standing in a lineal succession from the revolutions of 1789 and 1848; writing near the end of his life, in 1958, he remarked that 'the Commune left scars on the French body politic that are visible to this day'.[7] He pondered upon the intensity and intricacy of French politics, reaching their extreme in the 1880s and 1890s. The fierce and poisonous life of the French Chamber in those days, marked by a succession of outrages, forgeries, murders and intrigues, Churchill observed mischievously, found a modern parallel only in the underworld of Chicago but with the difference that the actors were men of the highest ability, of learning and eloquence, of repute and power. 'It was a terrible society, grimly polished, loaded with explosives, trellised with live electric wires.' In the last quarter of the nineteenth century, at least four major scandals had convulsed France, a country riven by memories of revolution and divided into unforgiving factions of Royalists, Bonapartists, Republicans and Socialists, a state newly defeated in the field where nothing was secure or unchallenged.[8] He wrote with sympathy of Foch, as a young volunteer lieutenant the helpless witness of his country's defeat by Prussia in 1870, fitted to feel alike France's agony and his own impotence. Thereafter, Foch had embodied the spirit of *revanche* which, Churchill judged, is ill-translated as 'revenge' because in the emotion of *revanche* there was no zest of spite or cruelty and no greed for material gain or personal splendour; instead, a life-long wish to see the France which had been levelled in the dust restored to her honourable position.[9]

As for Clemenceau, he embodied France, and insofar as any single human being, miraculously magnified, can ever be a nation, indeed he was France; an apparition of the French Revolution at what Churchill calls its sublime moment, before it was overtaken by the Terror, representing the French people risen against tyrants, whether of the mind or the soul or the body, whether foreign or domestic, whether invaders or defeatists, against all of whom Clemenceau waged inexorable war. Thus he personified one France, and Foch another; ancient, graceful and cultured, the France of Versailles and Joan of Arc, a submerged national identity. It was the combination of the two, Clemenceau and Foch, embracing that ancient and modern history, which during 1918 brought into the service of the

French people – and, we may add almost a century later, of a much wider community and cause – what Churchill characteristically terms 'all the glories and the vital essences of Gaul.'

Between Foch and Clemenceau flowed the river of blood represented by the Revolution, and between them towered also the barriers which Christianity raises against agnosticism. All the same, when the two of them contemplated the inscription upon the golden statue of Joan of Arc – 'la pitié qu'elle avait pour le royaume de France' – and saw the gleaming, uplifted sword of the Maid, their hearts had beaten as one. Churchill explains in his essay on Clemenceau that the French had a dual – that is, divided – nature in a degree not possessed by any other great people, and with no parallel in Great Britain or the United States or even Germany,

> an unending struggle which goes on continually, not only in every successive Parliament, but in every street and village of France, and in the bosom of almost every Frenchman. Only when France is in mortal peril does the struggle have a truce. The comradeship of Foch and Clemenceau illustrates as in a cameo the history of France.[10]

After the war, the political and military position of France was to all outward appearances secure. So long as the Treaty of Versailles was enforced, even imperfectly, France could not be invaded again by Germany. For the moment, neither Britain nor France had immediate need of the other. Disagreements abounded. The British had no sympathy with any policy of crushing Germany. When the President of the Republic, M. Doumergue, spoke earnestly of the common interests and essential unity between Britain and France, Churchill described the harm done by Poincaré's manner and language, which had chilled the sentiments of some of the warmest friends of France, amongst them Churchill himself. Reviewing possible dangers in Asia or Africa, WSC (by then Chancellor of the Exchequer) remarked that none compared with the awful risk which would be run if the age-long quarrel between France and Germany led to Britain's being involved again in a European war. He repeated what he had often said in public, and was to say with still greater force after 1945, that the real guarantee against a renewal of war would lie in agreement between England, France and Germany. That alone would give the security which everyone sought. When Doumergue replied that a close understanding between Britain and France was the indispensable preliminary, Churchill observed pointedly that for Britain the risks attaching to an effective arrangement with Germany would be far less than those of assuming a defensive relationship with France so long as the fundamental antagonisms between France and Germany continued unappeased.[11]

In the early 1930s, as the danger from Germany grew, Churchill sympathized strongly with France's fears and disapproved of the pressure upon her to disarm. By then he was out of office and a new ingredient had entered into his conception of France. 'Colour plays a great part in life', he once remarked,[12] and from the age of 40 he had become absorbed by a fresh diversion. Painting was a way of enjoying open air and intensity of hue, something he associated with holidays and good conversation of an evening and time away from politics, but pursued with unrelenting concentration. No one who sees his images of France can miss their gaiety and vivacity. This ardour for France speaks to us as clearly from the canvas as from his books and speeches. He revelled in the clear light and the limpidity of the waters; he loved the buildings and landscape, as at Carcassonne, Avignon, Mimizan, Cannes, Antibes. France and painting – the trees, the mountains, the buildings, the play of sun and shadow – became inseparable in Churchill's life and mind. There he found subjects appealing equally to his eye and his brush, with bold colours and sharp shapes and the glitter of light on water.[13] At St Georges Motel in Normandy, the château where King Henry of Navarre had slept the night before the Battle of Ivry, Churchill was at work with his French friend Paul Maze in August 1939. As they parted, Churchill remarked 'This is the last picture we shall paint in peace for a very long time.'[14]

On his way home, Churchill paused for lunch in Paris with General Georges, to whom he exclaimed 'But you are the masters'.[15] His admiration for France and his belief in her military prowess had led him astray; in which he was by no means alone. When successive blows fell in May and June 1940, he felt bewildered. Asking General Gamelin to explain what was happening, he received by way of reply a shrug and the words 'Supériorité de nombres, supériorité d'armes, supériorité de méthodes'.[16] The Prime Minister used every argument in his armoury to rally the French government. He realized that the British, their contribution on land very small by the standards of France or Germany, could not claim any deciding share in the strategy. Whatever may have been said at the time and since, Churchill and his colleagues went to the limit in 1940 in their support for France; the British army lost almost all its equipment there, the British Isles were in consequence hardly defended on land, and the Royal Air Force had suffered severely.

The order that the garrison at Calais should fight to the last man, without which far fewer British and French troops would have escaped through Dunkirk, was only the first in a series of agonizing events. Churchill pleaded earnestly with President Roosevelt in the second week of June that everything possible must be done to keep France in the fight so that she would defend each yard of her soil. The purpose was the opposite of that which has often been assumed, as the next sentence of the telegram shows: 'Hitler thus baffled of quick results will turn upon us and we are preparing ourselves to resist his fury and defend our Island … Our intention is to have a strong army fighting in France for the campaign of 1941.'[17]

To the French ministers, he stated flatly that Hitler could not win the war or mastery of the world until he had defeated Great Britain, which had not been found easy in the past and which would not perhaps be found easy now.[18] There followed in dizzying succession the offer of a declaration of union between Britain and France, with common citizenship; the fear that within a few days Britain and France might even be at war with each other; and the British insistence that the French fleet should fight at the side of Britain, or sail to the United States and be disarmed, or to a British port with reduced crews who would be repatriated. If those terms were refused, the British demanded that the French admirals should scuttle their ships, on pain of attack. Because he understood the Royal Navy's extreme reluctance to act, and fortified by secret knowledge from deciphered French communications, the Prime Minister himself gave the order to bombard the French fleet. He was determined that the French Navy should not fall into German hands, and to demonstrate that the British were resolved to fight on at any price. Long afterwards, he reflected sombrely: 'It was a terrible decision, like taking the life of one's own child to save the State.'[19]

General de Gaulle's view, at any rate in 1940, was not far different. He told the Prime Minister that Britain should make more of the fact that she stood alone as 'le champion du monde' against Hitler, and if that were accepted, all her actions would be excused; the assault at Oran would seem natural, because the fate of the world was at stake.[20] Long afterwards, Churchill confessed that once the French government had broken its agreement not to sue for a separate peace, he had never felt quite the same about France. To the end of his life, he would receive in early July of each year letters from there couched in terms of hatred.[21]

It was to him that Clemenceau said in 1918 the words which he afterwards uttered in the Chamber: 'I will fight in front of Paris; I will fight in Paris; I will fight behind Paris.' We cannot doubt that attitude and language alike sprang to Churchill's mind when he spoke in similar terms about Britain during the summer of 1940. Nor need we question his sincerity when he said in a broadcast that autumn, 'Never will I believe that the soul of France is dead. Never will I believe that her place among the greatest nations of the world has been lost for ever!'[22]

It must be confessed that Churchill's relations with General de Gaulle during the war followed a stony and downward path. What had been a warm and valued friendship in 1940 declined into disputes and spells of outright hostility. This was more than a matter of incompatible temperaments. Amongst British ministers and military men, Churchill was not solitary in believing de Gaulle to be hostile to British interests. The Foreign Secretary, Anthony Eden, generally took a more genial view, understanding that when the war at last came to its end, the interests of Britain and a wider world would require a revived France. It was, however, no simple business to decide how the British government should behave towards the Vichy regime. In the middle of the war, for example, Churchill wrote of his hope that the remainder of the French fleet might still sail to Africa, and that the British and American troops might be invited to enter French North Africa. For some time to come, the Vichy government would be the only party which could offer such gifts. The position was so anomalous and monstrous, he reflected, that very clear-cut views did not altogether cover it and there was much more in British policy towards France than to abuse Pétain and back de Gaulle. 'For thirty-five years I have been a friend of France', the Prime Minister wrote to Eden, 'and have always kept as closely in touch as possible with the French people. I therefore have a certain instinct about them upon which I rely.'[23]

When General de Gaulle was induced, under the plain threat that the British would otherwise disown him, to visit Casablanca and patch up some relationship with General Giraud, WSC found that both his advances and his threats made no difference. 'Look at him!' said Churchill after one of their interviews. 'He might be Stalin, with 200 divisions behind his words.' But when someone repeated a joking remark of Roosevelt that de Gaulle claimed to be the lineal descendant of Joan of Arc, Churchill rejoined 'France without an army is not France. de Gaulle is the spirit of that army. Perhaps the last survivor of a warrior race.' And despite all their quarrels, he had the imagination to add 'England's grievous offence in de Gaulle's eyes is that she has helped France. He cannot bear to think that she needed help. He will not relax his vigilance in guarding her honour for a single instant.'[24]

There is no denying that the events of 1943 placed a severe strain upon Churchill's fondness for France. However, he recorded at the end of May, after lunch with Generals Georges and Giraud, that he had 'recaptured some of my vanished illusions about France and her Army'.[25] The worst of the difficulties with the Free French died down over the following 12 months. American animosity towards de Gaulle was always stronger than British, and Churchill, determined not to quarrel with America on that issue, endured the embarrassments with some difficulty.[26] 'Mon Général,' said Mrs Churchill, 'you must take care not to hate your allies more than your enemies.' Her husband had urged the French Committee of National Liberation to speak with a single voice and use the utmost political discretion towards the United States.[27] Immediately before the Allied re-entry into Europe in June 1944, he told de Gaulle that the United States and Britain were two great nations willing to risk the loss of many thousands of men in an operation designed to liberate France. There followed a conversation much misunderstood in later years, the Prime Minister remarking that if the President of the United States were on one side and the French National Committee of Liberation on the other, he, Churchill, would 'almost certainly side with the President'. If de Gaulle wished the British to ask Roosevelt to give him the title deeds of France, the answer was no; but if he wished them to ask Roosevelt to agree that the Committee of National Liberation was the principal factor with which they should deal in France, the answer was yes. To this de Gaulle replied that he quite understood that in the event of disagreement between the United States and France, Great Britain would side with the United States. There followed, on the eve of the liberation of France by means of the greatest amphibious operation ever attempted, several days of squabbling, understandable when nerves were stretched taut but falling (as Churchill would have expressed it) well below the level of events. 'Cabinet 6.30. We endured the usual passionate anti-de G. harangue from P.M. On this subject, we get away from politics and diplomacy and even common sense. It's a girls' school. Roosevelt, P.M. and – it must be admitted de Gaulle – all behave like girls approaching the age of puberty.' Thus the diary for 5 June of the Permanent Under-Secretary at the Foreign Office.[28]

de Gaulle had a serene confidence in the ultimate issue because he knew that France needed him and would call for him.[29] So it proved, though with many vicissitudes. When Churchill came to Paris for Armistice Day, 1944, he was touched by a spontaneous demonstration from hundreds of thousands of French citizens.[30] He and Eden were left with the strong impression of France's desire to work with the British.[31] Friendly private relations were re-established with de Gaulle, at least for the moment. When Eden described France as a geographical necessity he meant that she must stand as a bulwark against a vengeful Germany and an immensely powerful Russia. Nor were such thoughts absent from Churchill's mind. But of course France meant far more than that to both of them. Even after a severe crisis with the French government, at the very moment of victory over Germany, we find Churchill saying 'As long as there is a kick left in my carcass I shall support France's efforts to re-establish herself. She must have a great Army; France without an Army is a cock without a comb.'[32]

Eden and Churchill alike believed that without a strong France, impoverished and battle-scarred Western Europe had little hope of revival. Churchill, no longer Prime Minister, pleaded for a partnership between France and Germany; partly, no doubt, because no one was more conscious than he of the ruin which had fallen upon the world as a consequence of Germany's bids for power, and partly for another reason. 'In this way only', he said, 'can France recover the moral leadership of Europe.'[33] That was a momentous thing to proclaim in 1946, while France was still draining the sour dregs of defeat and collaboration. And then there was the new and dominating fact: alliance with Russia had been replaced so swiftly by fear that the shape of post-war Europe assumed a dimension which the British and most others had been reluctant to recognize even as a possibility. In effect, the issue soon became not the subjugation of Germany but the containment of a Russia possessing atomic weapons and an apparent thirst for domination. That state of affairs in turn required the presence of American troops for an indefinite time, the very contingency which Roosevelt had refused to contemplate; and then the rearmament of Germany, which would have seemed inconceivable even a few years before.

On their return to office towards the end of 1951, Churchill as Prime Minister and Eden again as Foreign Secretary, they found a situation in which the proposed European Defence Community compounded their anxieties. Churchill disliked the early form of the EDC, on the grounds that it could not provide an effective fighting force. The British said that they would support the Community, but not join the European Army itself. For a variety of good reasons, they preferred the North Atlantic Treaty Organisation; and in those days Britain had large military obligations all over the world. Understandably, France wished to prevent the creation of a German national army; the government of the United States seemed bent upon confrontation with Russia; Churchill had less apocalyptic views about Russia and hoped that the EDC would enable Europe to speak to Russia from a position of strength, since German rearmament was the only thing of which the Russians were afraid. Equally, he hoped that Russia would exercise a restraining influence on Germany.[34] He recognized that 'The logic of French ideas has leaned continuously towards a European Federation', something to which he was convinced the British could not commit themselves. Meanwhile, there was no German army except the powerful one created by the Russians in the eastern zone. As he remarked to Eden, 'One thing is capital in my mind: no new engagements to France unless Germany, with a German army, is also accepted as an Ally.'[35]

The EDC had the great merit of imposing controls upon the rearmament of Germany and the production of armaments there. Nevertheless, the matter dragged interminably in the political processes of France. In December 1953, a few months after suffering a severe stroke, Churchill flew to Bermuda for a conference with the new American President, Eisenhower, and the French. Asked by the journalists how he expected to cope with so long a journey, the Prime Minister replied 'Well, I shall take a sleeping pill and either wake up in Bermuda or in heaven – unless you gentlemen have some other destination in mind for me?' By ill fortune, the French Prime Minister of those days, M. Laniel, was prostrated by illness during the conference. It was therefore chiefly to the Foreign Minister, Georges Bidault, who like Laniel had rendered most gallant service in the Resistance, that the British and Americans expressed their distress at the course of events. He had once taught the Churchills' daughter at a finishing school in Paris. When Mrs Churchill asked how she had done there, he replied 'Unfortunately I was asked to leave owing to an encounter with a young lady in a corridor.' 'Not Sarah, I hope?' She capped the Gallic gallantry of Bidault's answer – 'Non, hélas' – with a reply blending firmness and ambiguity: 'Thank goodness for that; and now you can take your mind off history, you will be able to concentrate on current affairs.'[36]

At the conference, Churchill pointed out that even with conscription there was not a complete brigade in Great Britain and begged the French to take speedy action about the Defence Community. When Bidault remarked that France was not prepared to be swamped in a new Europe and must retain an independent personality, he was talking a language the British understood well. He added pointedly that there must be no danger that the EDC would be treated by Britain and America as self-sufficient, thus relieving them of military responsibilities for the defence of Europe; German rearmament could be accepted in France and elsewhere in Europe only if there remained a full counterpoise from the British and Americans. But what was to be done, Churchill retorted, if the EDC could not be created and if President Eisenhower were right in stating that a German army could not be incorporated in NATO? If no way could be found of securing the indispensable German contribution, Europe would in effect be inviting the United States to fall back on a peripheral defence; and if the Americans withdrew from Europe, the British troops could not be kept there longer.[37] Bidault said to him, 'Do not be so unkind.' Churchill reflected afterwards: 'I did not say to him what I ought to have said: it is because of my love for France that I am unkind.'[38]

For nine months after the Bermuda conference the issue of the EDC was debated agonizingly in France. A new Prime Minister, M. Mendès-France, stated that those members of his government whom he had consulted were united on one point only, namely that they disagreed completely with everyone else.[39] Like others, Churchill uttered harsh words about the intrigues of French politics.[40] After the French Assembly decided to reject the EDC, the situation was saved on lines which largely vindicated British judgement: the government of the United States, which had been attracted by the supra-national features of the EDC and naturally hoped for a Europe strong enough to defend itself, did not withdraw; Germany came into NATO with safeguards; France, Italy and the smaller powers of Western Europe obtained what they had long sought, a promise that the British forces would be maintained on the Continent indefinitely; Chancellor Adenauer, to whom Churchill felt almost a debt of honour after the risks he had run and the patience he had shown,[41] stated that Germany wanted a strong France.[42] Here was nothing less than a transformation, and one which Churchill had done much to bring about. Indeed, it would not be fanciful to say that without the efforts which he and Eden made to find a framework into which France and Germany could fit, and which the United States and Britain could support, the containment of Russia and the breaking down of Communism would have been far more difficult to secure, and the new *entente cordiale*, between France and Germany, would scarcely have been brought to life.

Churchill's painting in France did not cease with the onset of war. On the contrary: after 1945 he went there more often than ever. He used to remark 'In politics you must have a line'; he liked his music to have a tune, his books a clear narrative, and once said to a waiter who brought a rather amorphous sweet at the end of a meal, 'Pray take away this pudding: it has no theme.'[43] In a landscape of Provence, between Aix and Arles, he took as his theme the strong vertical lines of the cypresses, the long lateral shadows which they cast, the strips of cultivation in the fields across which the shadows lie at a different angle, and the horizontal bands of country in the middle distance.[44] His fascination with water and its capacity to transmute colours and shapes remained. He chose a scene which reflected those characteristics and challenges by a way of illustration of his delightful essay 'Painting as a Pastime', and for display at the Royal Academy.[45] Over 500 pictures by Churchill survive; of these more than 200 were painted in France or Morocco. The man's zest for life and passion for France shine through.

In retirement, Churchill saw with satisfaction, sometimes tinged with apprehension, de Gaulle's return to power and reassertion of France's place in the world. He was distressed by the manner in which Britain's application to join the Common Market was rejected in 1963. When his Private Secretary observed that the President of France was most successfully seeking to prove the old maxim that no country can afford to show gratitude, Churchill replied pensively 'It would indeed be sad if so melancholy and so historically disprovable a maxim should be the epitaph on so great a man.'[46] At Churchill's funeral two years later,

General de Gaulle represented France. He wore the uniform of a *poilu*, with no medals or decorations.

On 12 November 1944, Churchill had been declared an honorary citizen of Paris, whereupon he made at the Hôtel de Ville a rousing speech in his expressive but idiosyncratic French; this he described as 'a formidable undertaking and one which will put great demands on your friendship for Great Britain.' Having paid a warm tribute to de Gaulle, the Prime Minister spoke of his determination that France must again possess the strong army necessary to re-establish a balance in Europe.[47] If that part of his oration arose from calculation and policy, his actions on the previous day had sprung from deeper wells of emotion and memory. It was understood that on 11 November, Churchill and de Gaulle would together pay homage at the tomb of the unknown soldier. The French government enquired what other engagements the Prime Minister wished to undertake? He went to the Invalides in tribute to Napoleon and then laid wreaths on the statue of Clemenceau and the tomb of Foch.

4

Rights, Wrongs and Rivalries

Britain and France in 1945

Early in 1944, Mr Duff Cooper, then British Ambassador to the French Committee of National Liberation, dined with General de Gaulle. In one of his mellower moods, the General remarked that he tried every day to imagine himself looking down on events without prejudice from the point of view of the future historian. In such moments of contemplation, it seemed to him 'that of all things the most ridiculous is that the British and French should not be on the best of terms.' The Ambassador tactfully omitted to remark that de Gaulle himself was as responsible as anyone for misunderstandings.[1]

It might indeed seem absurd that these two powers should not dwell in close alliance. After all, they had entered the war together, and though metropolitan France had been overrun, de Gaulle himself had been able with British help to fly the flag of French freedom in London and later Algiers. In the early summer of 1944, the Ambassador himself argued that while Britain should give her strong support to a new international organization after the war, that might well fail as the League had done. The alternative to international co-operation and collective security would be a policy of alliances, since the only other option, isolation, would not bear examination. Reasoning that the United States would not enter into commitments abroad, for which proposition there was plenty of evidence at the time, and reminding the Foreign Office that American interests in Europe were not the same as those of Great Britain, he judged that the most probable menace to peace after the war would come from Russia. To be sure, the British should do everything in their power to promote the friendliest of relations with Russia, but not be so imprudent as to neglect precautions should that friendship not continue. Thus the democracies of Western Europe should form close alliances based upon their geographical proximity, community of interests, shared colonial problems and inherited tradition of a distinctive civilization. To this the Foreign Secretary, Anthony Eden, replied that while he agreed with a good deal of the analysis, he dissented from the proposal about an alliance. This was partly because it would increase 'the danger (if it exists) of the Soviet Union pursuing a policy of expansion in Europe', partly because it would reinforce isolationist elements in the United States, and also because if such an alliance were rooted in the fear of an aggressive Russia, 'it would be a disastrous development, since it would lead to the division of Europe into two hostile camps with Germany in a position to throw her weight on either side.' Eden also feared that if the small powers of Europe were forced to choose between Britain and Russia, some might choose the latter.[2] Nevertheless, the Foreign Office had suggested that Britain should begin to work towards the creation of some regional system covering Western Europe, in order to make effective a general system of European security under a world organization, and acknowledged that a system of that character would also provide a reassurance against possible failure of the projected international organization.[3]

A good part of Duff Cooper's plea was based upon the proposition that Russia rather than Germany would be the enemy against which it was most necessary to provide once the war was over. Broadly speaking, that was not the view of the Foreign Secretary or the Prime Minister in the summer of 1944, or indeed for many months afterwards. At first sight, it might be supposed that as the pattern of Russian behaviour became more plain, the arguments in favour of an early and close alliance with France would be strengthened; for even if Germany were a menace to be guarded against, it was clear that for a considerable time after the war she would lie prostrate and occupied.

However, relations between Britain and France, and the prospect of an early alliance, did not turn only or chiefly on a calm measurement of the international currents. de Gaulle made enemies readily and friends seldom. Churchill, more fascinated than repelled by Stalin, was saying even at the time of their last meetings in the summer of 1945 'I like that man.' By contrast, he was convinced that the Ambassador was influenced by affectionate admiration for de Gaulle. 'You like that man,' Churchill said to Duff Cooper; 'I don't.'[4] Churchill would acknowledge de Gaulle's genius from time to time and never forgot the heroic part he had played in 1940. All the same, their relations had often been strained to breaking point, and never more so than on the eve of D-Day. The British and Americans had argued for months over the proposal to recognize the French Committee of National Liberation. Realizing that the British would have to go as far as the United States, or perhaps press President Roosevelt if the frigid relations between de Gaulle and the US government continued, Churchill declined to advance for the moment. He mistrusted the prospect of a French ministry drawn entirely from the supporters of the Committee 'whose interest in seizing the title-deeds of France is obvious'.[5] That attitude was substantially modified during September and October 1944, as de Gaulle assumed the governance of ever-larger areas of France. Eventually, and in almost comic circumstances, the French provisional administration was transmuted into a Government of Liberated France; de Gaulle welcomed Churchill and Eden graciously to a joyous Paris on 11 November 1944; the Prime Minister even said 'I felt as if I were watching a resurrection.'

The French found their guests more reserved in the matter of a Franco-British alliance, though the British did agree that France should have a zone of occupation in Germany and that France should take part in the work of the European Advisory Commission.[6] In the same conversations, de Gaulle argued that France could not regain her former power all at once and Britain would undoubtedly find herself weakened after the war by six years of effort, centrifugal forces in the Commonwealth and most of all by the rise of America and Russia, not to mention China. If Britain and France remained divided, how much influence would either wield? But if they acted together, could not they weigh heavily enough in the scales to prevent anything which they had themselves not accepted or determined? Churchill replied that in politics as in strategy it is wiser to align oneself with the stronger power than to pit oneself against him. He spoke of the immense resources of the Americans, and of his efforts to restrain Stalin 'who has an enormous appetite, but also has a great deal of common sense.' As for France, 'Don't be impatient!' Churchill exclaimed. 'Already, the doors are ajar. Soon they will be open to you ... then nothing will keep us from working together.'[7]

In his own record of this visit to Paris, Churchill remarked pregnantly to the President in Washington: 'One must always realise that before five years are out a French Army must be made to take on the main task of holding down Germany.' In another message, copied to Stalin, he confessed that when the American armies had gone home, there would be a time not many years distant when the British would have great difficulty in maintaining large forces overseas 'so contrary to our mode of life and disproportionate to our resources …'[8]

On the face of it, this consciousness of British financial and physical exhaustion, a theme which recurs constantly in WSC's conversation and correspondence in the last 12 months of the war, should have lent strength to a combination of resources with France, for precisely those reasons which de Gaulle had explained. But not for the first or last time in Anglo-French relations, a blurred understanding and the desire of each to score points at the expense of the other produced a strange, even sinister, result. Perhaps because he was disappointed with the responses of Churchill and Eden, perhaps because he wished to show that France was now an independent power again, perhaps to mark resentment at France's continued exclusion from the inner councils of the Alliance, de Gaulle betook himself to Moscow. Each side danced cautiously round the others in the diplomatic minuet. The British told Stalin that they would prefer an Anglo-French-Russian treaty of mutual assistance; de Gaulle insisted on a purely Franco-Soviet agreement; Roosevelt favoured the latter, because he feared the effects of a tripartite arrangement on the proposed international organization; and Stalin was thus able to sign with de Gaulle alone, while explaining to Churchill that he would really have liked a pact of the three.[9]

Churchill had been so afflicted by displays of ingratitude and hostility from de Gaulle that he had scant confidence in the latter's good faith. Indeed, there is no question that such lack of trust, a far more serious factor than mere dislike of personality, played a large part on both sides as matters developed during 1945. The Prime Minister feared lest de Gaulle should attempt to curry favour by stating his opposition to a supposed British desire to build up a Western bloc against Russia and then attempt to gain credit from that stance; simultaneously, Churchill was impressed by the fact that Stalin stayed away from the imbroglio in Greece, despite the obvious temptations and the opportunity to drive another wedge between Britain and the USA.[10]

And then there was the Levant. By comparison with the burning questions of the hour – the future of Germany, the slow progress of the campaign in the West, the intentions of Russia, the uncertain prospects for international co-operation – Syria and the Lebanon should have constituted scarcely more than colourful issues at the fringe. In the upshot, the crisis in the Near East did more than any other issue to ruin France's relations with Britain in the last phase of the war and the first few months of peace. Whenever discussions about an alliance looked promising, the spectre of Damascus or Beirut would wreck the prospects. There was the point of pride, of honour; the restoration of French influence in the Levant became to de Gaulle almost a touchstone of France's renascence and of his own capacity to ensure due respect for her interests.

At least from the British point of view, there were several just impediments; for example, the French themselves in 1941 had declared that Syria and Lebanon – territories formerly administered by France under mandate from the League of Nations – would become independent. The British, who had given a similar undertaking, had a substantial position there; and the French believed that General Spears, head of the British mission until December 1944, had deliberately incited Syrian and Lebanese politicians against France. Spears himself, formerly de Gaulle's admirer, had come to dislike the man heartily. Even those Frenchmen who felt genially towards Britain were convinced that Spears' hostility towards France lay beyond remedy. Nor would they credit that Spears could have followed his line for so long unless it had represented the real policy of the British government, whatever the Foreign Office might say about Britain's anxiety to compose the differences.

As events soon demonstrated, this view simplified the issues unduly. All the same, it was widely held. Duff Cooper himself had told the Prime Minister early in 1944 that he believed that there would be no peace in the Levant so long as Sir Louis and Lady Spears remained there. Several senior figures in the Foreign Office and Eden himself had pressed for Spears' removal. Having long protected Spears, a friend of many years' standing, WSC had at last been persuaded to bring him home at the end of 1944. As to high policy in the Levant, the Prime Minister believed that while independence had been promised to the people of Syria and the Lebanon, post-war France should hold there a position somewhat similar to that which Britain occupied in Iraq[11]. As the local opposition to a resumption of France's former role became clearer, the Prime Minister conceded that it could not be Britain's duty to secure single-handed any such position for France. Moreover, the very mention of Iraq raised an obvious and serious problem for the British. Nothing could have demonstrated more clearly than the war the importance of the Middle East, as a nodal point, as a source of oil, and as a base from which power could be exercised by air, land and sea throughout the Near East, the eastern Mediterranean and the deserts of North Africa. What people might learn to do against the French in the Levant, Churchill reflected, might equally be turned to account against the British later. 'We should discourage the throwing of stones since we had greenhouses of our own – acres and acres of them ...'[12]

In his instructions to Spears' successor, Eden remarked that British and French interests in the Levant were not fundamentally opposed 'so long as the French government follow a policy in accordance with their obligations and promises'.[13] Here lay the nub of the matter, for de Gaulle's view of France's obligations in the Near East accorded ill with Britain's; and Eden's observation, true enough on a reading of the larger issues at stake, broke down in the face of French policy in the next few months. As for Britain, her position resembled that of a man trying to ride two horses at once. This feat of nimbleness might be sustained for a while, but only as long as the horses ran in the same direction and at the same speed. The Ambassador in Cairo pointed out at Christmas 1944 that Britain was in fact pursuing conflicting policies: on the one side promoting Arab unity, on the other supporting Zionism in Palestine and French predominance in Syria. What he described as 'all sorts of nationalist problems' were boiling up in the Middle East and even without the millstones of the French and Zionists around their neck, the British would have quite enough to handle. This was certainly no exaggeration, and all the more reason, the Foreign Office rejoined, for an agreement between Britain and France.[14]

Stalin had said that an Anglo-French treaty would be welcome to him. The suppurating sore of the Levant meant that if all the main issues were to be embraced before a pact, and still more before an alliance – that is, an agreement which would commit the contracting parties in time of war – could be signed, then nothing could be done swiftly. Even Eden, who had consistently upheld de Gaulle's position, remarked to WSC at the end of 1944 that if the French leader declared that there could be no Anglo-French accord until everything had been settled about the Levant, he should be left to wait. Churchill agreed. He was perhaps offended that de Gaulle pitched his claims so high when France's contribution to the military stockpot remained small. Moreover,

> We must be careful not to involve ourselves in liabilities which we cannot discharge and in engagements to others for which there is no corresponding return. I do not know what our financial position will be after the war, but I am sure we shall not be able to maintain armed forces sufficient to protect all these helpless nations even if they make some show of recreating their armies.

Thus it was for de Gaulle to make his proposals. WSC's policy, in which there was at the least a difference of emphasis with the Foreign Secretary's, consisted of being helpful where he could to France – for example, over the rapid provision of arms to the growing French forces – without hurrying to the conclusion of an agreement. The Prime Minister may well have felt that the complexities of international affairs would reduce de Gaulle's claims, or even that de Gaulle might not last long in power. He certainly had no reason to anticipate in January 1945 what became the fact within seven months, that de Gaulle would still hold office in Paris after Churchill himself had lost it in London.

Reviewing the position at the turn of the year, Cooper ascribed to personal and temperamental causes de Gaulle's reluctance to take the initiative in proposing conversations. The Ambassador favoured at least the settling of all outstanding questions with France and at best the conclusion of a firm alliance. This was the time, he urged, to press ahead. Popular opinion in France expected an agreement. No foreign government was likely to object:

> France must for some time to come be largely dependent upon British assistance and must therefore be the more disposed to make an agreement favourable to Great Britain. At the same time, the popularity of the British stands so high in France that the French government would have no difficulty in recommending to their own people the terms of any such agreement. That popularity has reached a point which it would be difficult to surpass and from which in the natural course of events it is more likely to recede.

Furthermore, it was of the first importance to support the French government and nothing which Britain could do to enhance the prestige of that government, apart from the supply of raw materials, would be so valuable as the conclusion of a treaty.[15] As the Ambassador found but a few days later in the conversation with him, de Gaulle did not wish to give the appearance of desiring too keenly an Anglo-French pact, remarking that he felt confident that Britain would always come to the assistance of France in case of an attack by Germany. Unless at the end of this war France could feel completely secure against yet another invasion, there would undoubtedly grow up in France a powerful party in favour of coming to terms with Germany at all costs. The matters in dispute were only two, de Gaulle claimed. The first was the future of the Rhineland, and the other the Levant. He wanted a complete and permanent French control of the left bank of the Rhine as far north as Cologne. As for the Levant, the Ambassador said optimistically that he saw no reason why the two countries should differ there. Scanning all this, the Prime Minister noted

I hope we shall adhere to our policy of awaiting the French initiative. There can be no sort of hurry. France has nothing to give to an alliance at the present time. We should be most unwise to appear to be the suppliants. This would give de Gaulle every opportunity for misbehaviour.'[16]

The forthcoming summit conference, held in early February at Yalta, was announced by Roosevelt in the second week of January 1945. Churchill had suggested to the President some weeks earlier that France might be invited to take part in some of the discussions, and had probably been less than desolated to receive a rejection. The issue came to the surface several times in January, for the Permanent Under-Secretary at the Foreign Office, Sir Alexander Cadogan, most of his senior colleagues and Eden himself would have preferred to see France represented. At one moment, Eden conceded that the refusal by Roosevelt had settled the question. 'I do, however, think that at the forthcoming Conference,' he wrote to Churchill, 'we should try to get agreement on this for the future, and I very much hope that you would do your best to persuade the President to modify his view. I should think that you would have the support of Stalin in this.'

Probably the Foreign Secretary had come to this latter conclusion because of France's recent agreement with Russia. But the Prime Minister would not go so far, and merely undertook to listen to the arguments.[17] Eden thus returned to the charge, pointing out that the French had been admitted to the European Advisory Commission, were by agreement to occupy a zone of their own in Germany, and under the proposals for the world organization would possess a permanent seat on the Security Council:

> But we have reached the stage now when we must plan for the future, and I find it difficult to contemplate a future in which France will not be a factor of considerable importance. She must be interested in almost every European question. If we do not have her co-operation, she will be able – not at once perhaps – to make difficult the application of any solution which does not suit her.[18]

The French government naturally expressed its distaste at exclusion from the forthcoming conference, by the decisions of which France would not consider herself bound.[19]

It is hard not to discern the characteristics of a family quarrel; misfortunes of timing, occasional incivilities, misunderstandings – all played their part. However, more was at stake than that. Recognizing the force of Eden's argument about the complementary overseas interests of France and Britain, Churchill replied:

> I fear we shall have the greatest trouble with de Gaulle, who will be forever intriguing and playing off two against the third. I do not know when there will be another meeting after this, or what the conditions will be. France contributes a very small fighting stake to the pool at present. It is not French blood that is being shed to any extent in any quarter of the world. I quite appreciate that France should come in as the Fourth Power, and certainly at any moment when it is proposed to bring in China. ... Really France has enough to do this winter and spring in trying to keep body and soul together, and cannot masquerade as a Great Power for the purpose of war. She has been treated very well by being admitted so early to the E.A.C. and other allied bodies. I cannot think of anything more unpleasant and impossible than having this menacing and hostile

man in our midst, always trying to make himself a reputation in France by claiming a position far above what France occupies, and making faces at the Allies who are doing all the work.[20]

The French government had by this stage formally requested an invitation to the conference. Eden approached the Prime Minister again with the argument that the French had a strong case to be present when matters concerning the political future of Europe were discussed,

as it cannot be denied that such matters, especially those affecting the future of Germany, are of great concern to them, and that the chances of a generally agreed settlement are likely to be much greater if the French actually take part in the discussions than if they are presented with a fait accompli. In certain circumstances, too, their participation in the discussions might be useful from our point of view.

Eden proposed that the French should be invited to attend the conference whenever questions concerning the political settlement of Europe (particularly the future of Germany), or supply and shipping problems, were under debate. He feared that if a flat refusal were sent to France the position of de Gaulle's provisional government would be undermined; and the French would be encouraged to look to Russia for help and support, a tendency which the Foreign Secretary was anxious not to increase.[21]

The Prime Minister declined to move. No doubt rightly, he judged that the President, who had already set sail for Europe, would not change his previous decision that the French should be excluded. From the tone of his reply to the Foreign Secretary, Churchill felt surprised that the issue had been raised again at this late stage. He dismissed the prospect by writing simply 'I could not possibly agree to any change now. I hope you will not press it.' It is also clear that WSC was determined to cling for as long as possible to the close-knit character of the exchanges between the Big Three (or, as Sir Alexander Cadogan was soon mischievously to call them, the Big Two and a Half). Perhaps Churchill feared that to press for the inclusion of France would bring China immediately to the conference table, a prospect he had always disliked. Though he felt forebodings about Russian intentions, Churchill did not have at this stage a clear conviction that Russia would shortly replace Germany as the chief threat to Western interests. Whatever his reasons, the Prime Minister put the point with finality to the Foreign Secretary: 'The whole character of our discussions would be destroyed if de Gaulle were present, and of course he would come even though only invited on shipping and make a grievance of the rest.'[22]

The British decided to return no reply to the French request. It was already clear that the French would not be invited anyway, and efforts were made to see that M. Massigli, French Ambassador in London, understood the atmospherics. Not surprisingly, his opposite number in Paris was disappointed by the decision, reporting that the French were on the whole taking the matter fairly well, though he had no doubt it would provide de Gaulle with another grievance 'and with him grievances are an accumulative poison of which he never seems to rid his system.'[23] The French Ambassador, whom Eden esteemed, said that his government was anxious for a treaty, which would deal with the single issue of a revival of German aggression.

Ambassador and Foreign Secretary alike were agreed that it would not be necessary to reach in advance an agreement on such questions as the future treatment of Germany or the Levant, where any hopes that a new era of tranquillity would dawn after the departure of Spears had already evaporated. His successor Mr Shone rapidly reached on the crucial point a view no different in substance from Spears': that it was too late for France to reclaim a special position in the Levant, for which she had neither the political credit nor the military force. It followed that the British would be foolish to support any such position. As Shone put it 'The only thing to do was to support the Syrians.' The point was only too apparent to Churchill, who had often championed Spears against the Foreign Office; which department the Prime Minister did not always admire and suspected of being jealous towards the people in important posts who did not come from the Office's own stable. 'To meet your personal wishes and the Foreign Office prejudice against Sir Louis Spears,' Churchill minuted to Eden just before the two of them set off for Yalta, 'I have agreed to his recall ... At the same time it is not true or just to lay the burden, as some seem inclined to do, for the position in the Levant upon him. The fact that Mr Shone takes up exactly, or very nearly, the same attitude is impressive ...'[24]

Eden had already informed Massigli how stiff was the Syrian opposition to the conclusion of a treaty with France. The Foreign Secretary confessed,

1 Marrakech, 1943. WSC gave this, the only picture he painted during the war, to Roosevelt.

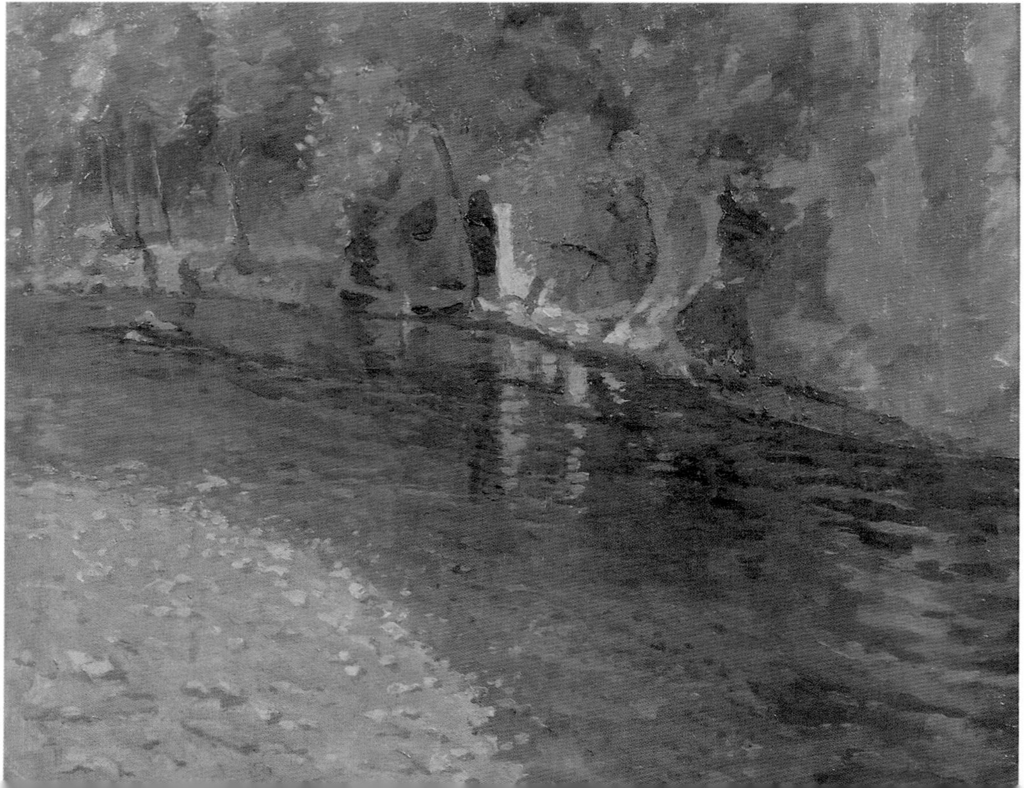

2 The Loup River, Alpes

3 A landscape in Provence, c. 1947.

4 Sailing boat in harbour at
Antibes 1920.

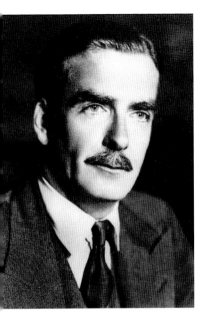

5 Anthony Eden, 1942.

6 Winston Churchill and General Charles de Gaulle, 1944.

7 General Dwight D. Eisenhower, Supreme Allied Commander, 1945.

8 Josef V. Stalin, 1945.

9 Duff Cooper, later 1st Viscount Norwich, 1940.

10 Stanislav Mikolajczyk standing in front of Polish national emblem, 1948.

11 W.L. Mackenzie King, Prime Minister of Canada, 1942.

12 Jan Christian Smuts, 1934.

even before receiving from the Prime Minister the tart minute cited above, that he had been influenced by the reports of Sir Edward Grigg (newly installed as Minister Resident in the Middle East) and Shone, who had both arrived with fresh minds. The French government would be most unwise to underrate the seriousness of this situation, which would need to be handled by a man of the highest qualities.[25]

By the end of January 1945, the main ingredients of the situation were clear. The Ambassador in Paris still hoped to see a treaty concluded promptly, but from conversations with Churchill and de Gaulle had received the impression that while both were prepared for a treaty, neither was willing to propose it.[26] Eden, casting around for practical matters about which Britain and France could collaborate, desired to offer prompt British help in building up the French Air Force, whereas the Prime Minister refused to believe there was any hurry and did not wish to give cards away in advance of a negotiation: 'We have a lot of things to settle with the French before we devote ourselves to helping them become a great Air power after the war is over';[27] and de Gaulle, though a good deal helped by Churchill and Eisenhower in the crucial matter of the battle for Strasbourg at the turn of the year, resented the domination of the Anglo-Saxons. He showed it by holding a press conference on 25 January, the tone of which the British Ambassador characterized as 'to say the least of it, ungracious … His reference to the Syrian and Lebanon question could scarcely have been more ill-tempered at a time when a certain *détente* might have been hoped for.'

This was the gathering at which de Gaulle, in advance of the conference at Yalta, announced that French forces must be installed on the Rhine from the Swiss frontier to the mouth of the river because experience had shown that unless France held that line she was foredoomed to invasion. In reply to questions about Yalta, the General replied sharply that while he had heard that there was going to be such a conference, France had not been invited. As for a treaty with Britain, the French government had not received any request to begin negotiations, but it was to be expected that the two powers would sooner or later define the terms of an alliance. The absence of a written pact, he remarked, would not prevent the two countries from waging war together as they had done for the past five years.[28] At Yalta, the British fought hard for France. While the leaders of the three great powers made their way through a devastated landscape to the sunshine and almost oppressive luxury of the Livadia Palace, de

Gaulle broadcast from a freezing and rationed Paris that France would accept only what was compatible with the aims she had set herself. Apart from the Rhine frontier, France would require not only the separation of the Ruhr from what he called 'the future German State or States' but also the independence of the peoples of Poland, Czechoslovakia, Austria and the Balkans. In the same address, he made it pointedly plain that an alliance with England was not there for the taking; it was desired by France as soon as England would consent 'to what to us is vital with regard to Germany, and as soon as we shall have eliminated between us certain vestiges of an out-dated rivalry in this or that part of the world.'[29]

At Yalta, Churchill felt as much puzzled as troubled by the Russian leader's attitude to France. 'Do you suppose Stalin reads books?' Churchill asked in private. 'He talks of France as a country without a past. Does he not know her history?' (It has emerged over the years that Stalin owned a vast library, including many works of history; he read voraciously, and possessed a working acquaintance with several languages.[30] Indeed, he had at least some command of English, a fact which British ministers meeting him may not have realized.) As Eden remarked, France was a geographical necessity. Roosevelt declared that American troops would withdraw from Europe within two years from the defeat of Germany. Officials of the Foreign Office pointed out that if the existing plans came to fruition, by the later summer of 1945 France would have a field army in Europe of 16 divisions with modern equipment, considerably more than anybody supposed the British would retain there.[31] Churchill found the Russians and Americans determined to keep France, and especially de Gaulle, out of the 'Big Three'. Indeed, both those great powers resisted British attempts to allow the French a seat on the Allied Control Commission for Germany. 'So far here we have been the only ones to speak a friendly word for France,' Churchill reported on 10 February. 'Nevertheless I am quite sure the presence of de Gaulle and his representative at this Crimean meeting would have wrecked all possible progress, already difficult enough.'[32]

In lesser matters, such as economic discussions, the building up of the French Air Force and the provision of locomotives and shipping to help the re-establishment of internal transport in France, progress was made. On the larger questions, the estrangement persisted. The American, Russian and British Ambassadors in Paris presented identical communications to the French government at the conclusion of the Yalta conference.

de Gaulle resented this treatment, and declined a somewhat tactless invitation from Roosevelt to a meeting in Algiers. Until the middle of the night M. Bidault wrestled with de Gaulle, whom he found great difficulty in calming. The British liked Bidault and admired him for his record in the war. They invited him to visit London. Receiving much confidential information from Bidault and understanding his predicament, the British Ambassador noted that while he sympathized with French resentment at not being invited to Yalta, the most foolish way of showing that resentment would be to sulk.[33] A few days later, a long-awaited French note about the Levant seemed to say nothing new and certainly promised no era of easier relations. Not given to circumlocution, Cooper said as much to Bidault, who replied that he had had a hard battle to have the note phrased as politely as it was and defined the French terms as the possession of certain bases in the Levant, safeguards for cultural interests, and a pre-eminent position for the French Ambassador.

It also transpired that France was making difficulties about the terms upon which she should be one of the inviting powers to the meeting at San Francisco, which was to create a constitution for the United Nations Organisation. Duff Cooper pointed out that this was the first occasion upon which France had been offered preferential treatment over the other powers and refusal to accept it was likely to create an impression of unwillingness to co-operate. At an earlier meeting, Bidault had told the British Ambassador that de Gaulle's temper, uncertain at the best of times, had been rendered even more tense by the fact that he was suffering from severe toothache. On this later occasion, the Ambassador remarked that though he had spoken strongly, he had done so in the interests of France and hoped that Bidault would tell General de Gaulle everything which he had said. The Foreign Minister, who had several times talked to the Ambassador of resigning, replied with understandable melancholy 'Unfortunately, I have to see the General before I go to bed.'[34]

Bidault was allowed by de Gaulle to visit London. There Eden assured him that Britain's policy was to associate France with her as far as possible; nevertheless, France could not prevent the three powers from meeting, in view of their responsibility for the conduct of the war, and he must say openly that they intended to continue such meetings for some time. In that event, Bidault rejoined, the situation for France would become impossible 'and neither he nor the French government could prevent her from joining the malcontents. This was not an official statement but it was his personal impression.' He went on to explain that while he and many of the French Cabinet had felt it their duty to urge on de Gaulle the wisdom of co-operating with the three powers, the position would become impossible if they could not show any concrete progress in the shape of close association. While France wished for a treaty with Britain, she thought it necessary first to reach general agreement in regard to the Levant and Germany; which need not take long. The rest of the conversation, it must be confessed, scarcely bore out such an optimistic conclusion. For instance, Bidault repeated that France would desire an exclusive zone in the Rhineland up to Cologne; and in respect of the Levant, the conversations which Churchill and Eden had held with the Syrian President Shukri Kuwatli on their way home from Yalta had demonstrated the strong local opposition to a treaty with France.[35]

After Yalta, Churchill proclaimed his confidence in Russia's determination to stand to her obligations, remarking in the same speech that it was not for Britain alone to defend either the independence of Syria and the Lebanon or French privilege there:

> We seek both, and we do not believe that they are incompatible. Too much must not be placed therefore upon the shoulders of Great Britain alone. We have to take note of the fact that Russia and the United States have recognised and favour Syrian and Lebanese independence, but do not favour any special position for any other foreign country.[36]

At this time of foreboding, when he still hoped that somehow the unity of the Allies might be preserved, Churchill brooded about the prospects for Europe – 'What will lie between the white snows of Russia and the white cliffs of Dover?' he wondered one evening in late February[37] – but without finding salvation in the early conclusion of an alliance with France. That the obstacles were many was conceded even by Eden, who by later March nevertheless recognized that in consequence of Russian behaviour Britain might have to recast her foreign policy.[38]

Despite efforts on the diplomatic plane, the disagreements about the terms of the invitation to the conference at San Francisco persisted. The French Council of Ministers proposed a modification which would give France the liberty of action she felt she needed, since she had not been represented at the earlier conferences and could not commit herself to agreement with proposals of which French Ministers did not approve. Although this reservation would have been acceptable to the American and British governments, the Russians refused to agree. Thereupon the French government published a statement explaining the reasons for its stance and was generally supported by the press in Paris; a turn of events regretted by the British Ambassador, for France had once more created abroad the impression of an unwillingness to co-operate. He also reported, however, that the French had been encouraged by the sympathetic manner in which their appeals for short-term assistance from Britain had been heard.[39]

It is true that a good deal had been done; the hard-pressed railways in Britain had sent to France some 850 locomotives by the end of March. Some requests, like those for coal, meat and sugar, the British could not meet. Others, for shipping and paper, they could. However, agreement about the larger issues seemed as remote as ever, and for the same underlying reason, that the Prime Minister and the War Cabinet did not know how the situation with France might develop and were unwilling to give away too much until they did know; whereas those who wished to draw nearer to France argued that only a willingness to take some risks and display goodwill in a tangible form would enable such relations to be established. In short, there was a circularity about the process, exemplified by a long series of exchanges in London about the disclosure of scientific and technical information. As the minutes of the War Cabinet put it delicately, opinion was divided on this question, some Ministers feeling that little or nothing should be disclosed to the French at this stage of the war while others pointed out that French pilots were already flying many of the British aircraft concerned, and in any case it was all too likely that full information about all British aircraft was available to the Germans.[40]

Lord Cherwell, whose incursions in the field of foreign affairs had been resented and opposed by Eden at earlier stages, advised the Prime Minister that before scientific secrets from the armed services were handed to the French, and by implication to all the other Aliies, Britain should at least wait until after the San Francisco conference or until she had a long-term arrangement with France.[41] To General Ismay Churchill minuted 'I am of course opposed to telling the French anything important at this stage'; and in that short sentence the words 'of course' tell their own tale. The reply pointed out that it was the Chiefs of Staff who wanted to be as forthcoming as possible in giving information to the French, on economic, political and strategic grounds.[42]

An official at the Foreign Office commented that the draft answer to France about the sharing of secret military information left the impression that Britain regarded the French almost as potential enemies, an attitude which must give encouragement to those elements in Washington whose influence the British had been contesting for years past. The Foreign Secretary agreed with the substance of this.[43] At last the immediate issue was patched up, with some difficulty. Meanwhile, what was to be done about the French claims in the Rhineland? Eden saw 'the strongest objections' to a French zone reaching as far north as Cologne, which he described as the natural centre of the vital Ruhr-Rhine region. The British would be in charge of the Ruhr basin. It was essential on political, administrative and economic grounds to dominate also the areas round Cologne and Aachen. Otherwise

> If the French are established in control at Cologne there is a danger that they might mismanage affairs or pursue a divergent policy in the Rhineland as they did after the last war. Any resulting disorders would have repercussions throughout the Rhine-Ruhr area, the greater part of which would remain within the British zone.

There were other objections to the proposal, which Eden asked his colleagues to reject.[44] The Chiefs of Staff agreed with him, as did the War Cabinet. A happier fate awaited a proposal by the Chancellor of the Exchequer for a financial agreement with France.[45] In respect of the Levant, the clouds showed scant sign of lifting as the day of victory in Europe drew near. Bidault seemed confident at the end of March that the difficulties were disappearing. He confessed to Cooper, however, that his difficulties lay with de Gaulle, whose resistance would inevitably be stiffened by any British intervention. The Ambassador also believed that de Gaulle was more likely to be reasonable if no pressure were placed upon him,[46] and when he saw the head of the French government on 5 April, they agreed that the two powers had no conflicting interests in the Levant. de Gaulle remarked upon the large British military presence there, observing that if the French were to give up their position at that moment it would look as if they were simply handing over to the British.[47]

In his dealings with London, Cooper had once more returned to the charge. He pointed out that Russia had now tightened her hold upon Czechoslovakia, gained an important diplomatic success in Poland, asserted dictatorial rights over Rumania and signed a treaty with France. Meanwhile, the relations of the British government with all the European powers remained as vague and indefinite as they had been 12 months before. He even feared the creation of an alliance of Western European powers independent of, and perhaps hostile to, Great Britain. If such an alliance enjoyed the approval of Russia, it would constitute a grave danger and Britain's position in the Mediterranean, in defence of which she could look for no assistance from the United States, might become untenable. This despatch received no reply.[48] Encouraged and perhaps surprised to find General de Gaulle almost friendly, Duff Cooper mentioned to him the possibility of an Anglo-French pact. Against this sentence in the record of the conversation, the Prime Minister wrote 'Why?' There was nothing, declared de Gaulle, that he desired more; but he did wish it to be something more than the Anglo-Soviet or Franco-Soviet pacts, an alliance in which all outstanding questions should be definitely settled. The later part of the same conversation indicated that this was no easier a business than it had been in the past, for de Gaulle maintained that France did indeed wish to occupy the Rhineland as far north as Cologne itself. Duff Cooper already knew that Massigli had argued against this, on the grounds that if the French attempted to occupy too much they would exhibit a weakness to the Germans. Towering over the French ministers in more senses than one, de Gaulle gave the Ambassador the impression that he was now conscious of a new menace looming up from the East against which it was more than ever necessary for the great powers of Western Europe to stand together. He favoured the world organization for one main reason, that it would commit the United States to take part in European affairs.[49]

There followed another false dawn. The head of the French Foreign Ministry, Chauvel, told the British Ambassador that he believed a comprehensive agreement could be concluded between the two countries within a week. He suggested that he might himself go to London. Duff Cooper thought Chauvel a little over-excited by the novel experience of finding de Gaulle in such a favourable mood, but believed the opportunity should not be missed. On the next day, 6 April, Bidault confirmed everything Chauvel had said.[50] Even before these telegrams were received in London, the Prime Minister's suspicions had been aroused. He questioned why the Ambassador should have mentioned the possibility of an Anglo-French pact, for he believed it had been decided that the British should not broach the matter at that time. Nor did he understand why the Ambassador should raise questions about the Levant and the Rhine:

> Why cannot we leave de Gaulle to undergo the process of realising that at present they depend on us, not we on them?
>
> All these attitudes of the Ambassador are entirely contrary to our policy as you and I have agreed it, and as it has been approved by our colleagues. Why on earth can he not remain passive and be wooed, instead of always playing into de Gaulle's hands and leaving him the giver of favours, when he has none to give? This telegram emphasises very clearly in my mind the very great difference between Mr. Duff Cooper and His Majesty's Government. Why can you not give him clear instructions that he is not to press for any engagements with France? When France comes, as she will do in due course, and stronger than she is now, all these matters can be raised and settled in an agreeable manner … I must absolutely resist any attempt for 'an all-in agreement to be done within a week'. It is a great mistake always to want to do things. Very often they will do themselves much better than anyone can do them.[51]

Eden replied in an emollient way that he had never wished to give the French 'the impression that we are suppliants or in a hurry'. He pointed out that most of the running was being made by the French and recommended that Britain should show a willingness to examine the offer:

> General de Gaulle is not a permanency, but France, we hope, will be and we want to build her up. She will be the stronger for an alliance with us and our authority with her will be the greater. For there is no doubt that the overwhelming majority of the French people also want such an alliance. As regards what the Russians may think, it is true that they may not like it; but in the light of their present behaviour I think it will do them good to see Anglo-French relations brought closer.[52]

Even those in the Foreign Office who most favoured a treaty had to concede the difficulties of making it within a week. The British had no idea what the French drafts about the Levant and the Rhineland might say. Other government departments would have to be brought in, the approval of the War Cabinet obtained, the Dominions consulted and the Russian and American governments at least informed. Neither of the two great issues, the Rhineland and the Levant, could be settled between Britain and France alone.[53]

Since the whole initiative shortly broke down, we need not dwell upon the other difficulties. Churchill remained in favour of delay until the pattern of events should be clearer, the conference at San Francisco concluded and the war in Europe over; Eden retorted that the British would commit themselves to nothing by listening to M. Chauvel.[54] When it transpired that Chauvel and Bidault had outrun their instructions, and that the former could not after all come to London because General de Gaulle had still not made up his mind about the contents of an exchange of notes with the British government concerning Germany and the Levant, the Prime Minister was confirmed in the view that 'We should leave all initiative in this subject to the French.' To Duff Cooper, he remarked that the only result of all this activity

has been what I foresaw from the beginning – that this man has another opportunity of inflicting a slight upon the western Allies and of lulling himself with the feeling that they are suitors for his favour. It is neither of interest nor of urgency to us to make a treaty at the present with the France of de Gaulle. They will come along in their own time and no-one will be more glad to extend a hand of friendship than I.[55]

Against these charges the Ambassador defended himself stoutly, rejoining that while de Gaulle was certainly not adept in the conduct of diplomacy, he had not had any intention of deliberately inflicting a slight upon the Allies.[56] A few days later, Duff Cooper told the General that the failure to accept the invitation issued to Chauvel (for Churchill had reluctantly agreed in the end to that) had caused an unfavourable impression. The head of the French government excused himself, lamely as the Ambassador thought, on the grounds that it had been necessary to bring forward the departure of Bidault for the conference at San Francisco.

He hoped the two Foreign Ministers might be able to hold discussions there. The precise borders of the French zone in Germany had still not been confirmed, and with reference to that and other military affairs de Gaulle remarked that the French were left out of everything. The Ambassador replied that this was more de Gaulle's fault than anybody's, since he repeatedly refused to come in when asked to do so. Duff Cooper reminded him of opportunities which he had let slip.[57] It is a measure of the Ambassador's quality, and of de Gaulle's, that the latter seems not to have resented such plain language.

If the Prime Minister required confirmation of the view that de Gaulle himself provided the greatest obstacle to good relations, events in the Near East were shortly to provide it. de Gaulle believed throughout, and indeed for the rest of his life, that it had been deliberate British policy to eject France from the Levant. On 30 April, he said so in terms to the British Ambassador, who was himself sympathetic to the French case.[58] What happened in May and June cannot have failed to reinforce the view that until the issues there were resolved, Britain neither could nor should make an alliance with France. An embarrassing situation in north-west Italy, where French troops were occupying territory across the frontier, had caused apprehension for some time; that issue too became acute during May. Churchill sought a settlement by diplomatic means, and reminded the Chiefs of Staff of the shameful conditions in which France had been attacked by Mussolini in 1940. Equally, the Prime Minister did his best to find a solution in the Levant, by offering to withdraw all British troops from there as soon as the French had concluded a treaty with Syria and the Lebanon. A few days later, at the moment of the German capitulation, Churchill telegraphed to de Gaulle:

> I thank you for your cordial message. Although we have had our ups and downs, I have never forgotten that day at Tours when I passed you amid the sorrowful crowd and said, in the hearing of several, "There is the man of destiny." I see you now at the head of France, representing more than any other man known to the world her will to live and her resolve to recover her greatness.[59]

Writing not long before his unexpected return to power in 1958, de Gaulle in effect swept aside all the assurances which had been given by the British during the war. He ascribed France's troubles in the Levant, then and later, to promises by Great Britain that the two states could rely on her support against France.[60] In fact, Britain had urged France not to send further and substantial reinforcements, bound to be seen in the Levant as a crude form of pressure at a time when negotiations were supposed to be under way. The French tactics went spectacularly wrong. Sporadic outbreaks of violence multiplied until a state of open warfare prevailed in several cities, including Damascus. Whatever de Gaulle may have said and thought, Churchill held his hand as long as possible. The Syrian President and others begged for British intervention. Mr Shone, in terms scarcely less apocalyptic than those which General Spears might have used, told Eden that the French had instituted nothing short of a reign of terror and were clearly determined to win a merciless war.[61] Churchill had wanted at the minimum clear support from the United States, which was not forthcoming in time. At midday on 31 May, General Paget was told to intervene.

A telegram was sent at once to Paris but did not reach de Gaulle before Eden made a statement in Parliament.[62] This was not the fault of the Embassy; nor was it deliberate British policy, as de Gaulle alleged, to inform him after the event and thus humiliate France in public. He also stated, at the time and on later occasions, that the British intervention had been wholly unnecessary since the British knew that orders had already been sent to the French Commander to cease fire. That assertion is untrue; the French Ambassador in London was not able to tell Eden of the ceasefire until after the Foreign Secretary's statement in the House of Commons, and well after the order had been given to General Paget to intervene. What is more, the shelling of Damascus was still continuing on that day, 31 May, which indicated either that the order had not been received there at the time stated by the French government, or that it had been disobeyed. According to the information reaching London, some 500 people had been killed in Damascus, an open city; another 500 seriously wounded; and a further 1,000 injured.[63]

Paget's intervention rapidly restored order, though at least one of the documents issued by the General caused fury to de Gaulle, scarcely less to Bidault, and dismay to the British Ambassador in Paris. 'They say it is worse than Fashoda', he recorded.[64]

de Gaulle observes in his memoirs that the British wished to be the only Western power in the Middle East and with that stream the frenzy of the Arab nationalists had united. He believed that the American demands in respect of the Alpine frontier with Italy, to the effect that French troops should withdraw inside the frontier of 1939 and be replaced by Allied troops in the territories thus evacuated, derived from the fact that at this moment 'England was preparing her decisive manoeuvre in the Levant. For London to inspire Washington to find a source of friction with Paris was a strategic move.' He remarks further that 'secret observers' had secured copies of the telegrams which Churchill was sending to the new President, Truman, in which the Prime Minister characterized de Gaulle as an enemy of the Allies. This passage raises an intriguing issue. Were some telegrams obtained by an agent, or were the French Intelligence Services reading at least some of the British ciphers? It seems certain that de Gaulle had access to telegrams in which Churchill's opinion of him and his policies was revealed.[65]

Whatever the truth on that score, de Gaulle was convinced that Britain's plans to dominate the Middle East were set and carried through with a passionate resolve. As for the Arabs, he adds, a political programme as subtle as costly had rendered a number of their leaders accessible to British influence; in other words, the British had bribed their way into Arab favour. Moreover, the French leader believed, Churchill calculated that in France the humiliation of events in the Levant would involve a political defeat and perhaps the fall of de Gaulle himself. The sole purpose of the delay in delivering Churchill's message of 31 May, de Gaulle avers, was to prevent him from making known in time that fighting had already stopped in Damascus. In passing, he also accused Eden of deliberately failing to receive Massigli before the House of Commons met on the afternoon of 31 May.[66]

Most of this was fantasy and distortion. A press conference on 2 June deserves no kinder description, alas; and when de Gaulle saw the British Ambassador on 4 June, he said that the French soldiers in the Levant had been ordered to stay where they were and fire on Syrian or British troops if force were used against them. In short, less than a month after the victory over Germany, Britain and France stood at the point of war; or at least they would have done if France had been capable of waging it in the Levant. Confronted with the accusation that the whole incident had been arranged by the British in order to carry out their long-planned intention to usurp the position of France in the Levant, Duff Cooper retorted that if the British wanted these disorders, why had they implored de Gaulle not to send the ships which had caused them? 'He replied rather feebly that we should have found some other excuse. We had a very unpleasant half hour' the Ambassador recorded with studious moderation. Convinced that the French still misconceived British policy in the Levant, Cooper argued in his own account that the error was due to Britain's retention of General Spears at his post for so long.[67]

That judgement has some truth, but not the whole of the truth. At his press conference, de Gaulle had suggested that all the issues arising in the Middle East, including Palestine, should be examined by the five great powers. To the British Ambassador, as their stormy interview concluded on 4 June, de Gaulle said (according to his own account) 'You have insulted France and betrayed the West. This cannot be forgotten.'[68] The luckless Bidault told Duff Cooper later that night that if the Prime Minister could say something conciliatory in the House of Commons, it would help immensely, and Churchill did his best on 5 June to minimize the difficulties without conceding too much to de Gaulle. When regrettable incidents occurred between nations as firmly attached to each other as Britain and France, he remarked, the best policy was nearly always 'the less said the better'. He denied, as Eden had already done, the charge that the whole trouble in the Levant was due to the influence of the British. He recalled his interview with the President of Syria in February; British persuasion of the Levant states to open negotiations, which they had previously been unwilling to do; the delay in receiving the French proposals; the British warning to France that the arrival of even modest reinforcements would be misunderstood. He repeated once more that the British had no ambitions in the Levant, and that they had recognized France's special position there. He reminded Parliament that de Gaulle's message in early May, saying that the French Delegate-General was returning to the Middle East to open negotiations, had made no reference to the reinforcements.

Churchill did not dwell upon the message which he had just received from the President of Syria, Kuwatli, expressing gratitude for British intervention. Transmitting the text, Shone had reported the President as saying that the French could have their schools, if any Syrians still wished to go to them, and their commercial interests, but neither the Syrian government nor the people could ever give the French any privilege in Syria after what had happened. Churchill had himself already telegraphed to General Paget 'As soon as you are master of the situation you should show full consideration to the French. We are very intimately linked with

France in Europe, and your greatest triumph will be to produce a peace without rancour.' Churchill also sent a message to Kuwatli, hoping that now the British had come to his aid the Syrians would not make the task harder by fury and exaggeration: 'The French have got to have fair treatment as well as you, and we British, who do not covet anything that you possess, expect from you that moderation and helpfulness which are due to our disinterested exertions.'[69]

What Churchill did allow himself in Parliament on 5 June was a denial that Spears had been recalled from Beirut at the request of de Gaulle or in order to please the latter. In a statement otherwise vastly more restrained than that which de Gaulle had given to the press in Paris three days earlier, the Prime Minister commented in a stinging style that Spears had been selected a long time ago for the appointment in the Lebanon

> because, among other qualifications, he wears five wound-stripes gained in his work as liaison officer between the French and British armies during the last war. He is the last person on whom General de Gaulle should cast reflections, because he personally secured General de Gaulle's escape to England from Bordeaux in his motor car and aeroplane on June 18, 1940.[70]

In his memoirs, Churchill explains that he understood de Gaulle's view and mood about a cause for which he felt passionately, and also pays tribute to the statesmanlike note which de Gaulle struck.[71] It has to be conceded this was only one of several notes to be heard at that time and later from de Gaulle's repertoire. The same is true of the minor but vexatious crisis in the Alps, where at one moment it appeared that French troops had been ordered by de Gaulle to hold their positions and if necessary fire upon the Americans and British. President Truman told de Gaulle curtly that so long as this threat remained, no more equipment or ammunition would be supplied to French forces. 'Is it not rather disagreeable', Churchill asked the President, 'for us to be addressed in these terms by General de Gaulle, whom we have reinstated in a liberated France at some expense in American blood and treasure?'[72] With an eye on the proceedings at San Francisco, where many knotted points still awaited a resolution, the President decided not to publish his first message to de Gaulle, but instead to send a further private appeal to him, couched in carefully chosen and firm language and containing the clear threat that the whole transaction would be revealed in public. Churchill thereupon telegraphed to Truman:

> I believe that the publication of your previous message would have led to the overthrow of de Gaulle, who after five long years of experience I am convinced is the worst enemy of France in her troubles. I hope you will make sure that your new letter reaches the French Foreign Secretary and other Ministers. I consider General de Gaulle one of the greatest dangers to European peace. No one has more need than Britain of French friendship, but I am sure that in the long run no understanding will be reached with General de Gaulle.[73]

de Gaulle gave way, with no excess of enthusiasm, to Truman. He had no choice, not least because the French forces depended on American fuel. A series of petty incidents followed: the Deputy Supreme Allied Commander, Air Chief Marshal Tedder, was excluded from a formal dinner when Eisenhower as Supreme Allied Commander visited Paris; the Prime Minister in London wished to let the press know this informally, but was dissuaded, probably by the argument that matters would only be exacerbated or that the British might create a suspicion that they were trying to mobilize French opinion against de Gaulle; at the celebrations in Paris on 18 July, de Gaulle did not fail to notice the small Union Jacks flying on two of the ambulances. It occurred to the British Ambassador that de Gaulle's keen eyes had 'detected this solitary reminder of the fact that France had not won the war entirely unaided'; this proved indeed to be true and, what was worse, the ambulances had been given to the French by Lady Spears and in four and a half years of war had looked after 20,000 French wounded. de Gaulle ordered the immediate closure of this unit, the British members of which were sent home within days. Although expressing the strongest indignation, M. Bidault could not prevail.[74] Meanwhile, the French authorities asked the British Ambassador to postpone a ceremony at which he would have conferred British decorations on French officers.

'I believe', the Permanent Under-Secretary of the Foreign Office wrote to Churchill on 18 June, 'French opinion to be forming its own conclusions about de Gaulle's suitability for the future and if that is so, we must be careful not to be taking a hand in discrediting him.'[75]

In private, de Gaulle told a young French friend that he was tired and disgusted, believed his work accomplished and intended to retire from politics. Duff Cooper was not at all sure that the General really meant this. His withdrawal would make it far easier to conclude an Anglo-French treaty; on the other hand, such a retreat would be bad for internal stability in France and the Communists might be the principal gainers. Cooper believed that if de Gaulle were to go at once, it would do far more harm than good.[76]

None of this reduced the arguments on a longer view for a close alliance with France. Even those who felt most warmly towards that prospect recognized that it must now await the result of the British General Election and of elections due in France that autumn. If Churchill had counted on the crisis to isolate de Gaulle from leading French circles, he was justified; so says de Gaulle himself in his memoirs, for that episode had left him with no effective support among the majority of men holding public office. Most of the French diplomats concurred only remotely with the attitude which the leader of the government had adopted. For many of those in charge of foreign affairs, good relations with England constituted a principle. The tone of French newspapers was disappointing from de Gaulle's point of view, and matters stood no better in the Consultative Assembly.[77] The Assembly had indeed passed unanimously a resolution which referred to the need for alliance with Britain.

The story for the remainder of 1945 constitutes little more than an appendix. It was always improbable that the Americans or Russians would agree to France's participation in the Potsdam conference, and de Gaulle's behaviour since Yalta made it certain that Churchill and Eden would not press for his inclusion. Cooper continued to urge the case for an alliance, acknowledging mournfully that the Prime Minister had no enthusiasm for it. But Churchill fell from office on 26 July, when the results of the General Election were at last known. The Minister Resident in the Middle East explained at length why Britain should not attempt any partnership with France in the Middle East or support French claims to predominance in the Levant.[78] Nonetheless, the Labour government in Britain was anxious to do business with France. Some progress was made about exchange of scientific information and the release to France of certain aircraft designs. Whether de Gaulle would wish to make terms with England remained in doubt. When the British Ambassador asked Bidault about this, the Foreign Minister hesitated. He remarked that there were two men inside de Gaulle, *l'homme d'esprit* and *l'homme d'humeur*. It was the latter part of de Gaulle which was responsible for all his follies; while the General knew that a treaty would be a good thing, desired by the French people and the Quai d'Orsay, it would be hard to say that he wanted it himself.[79]

The new Foreign Secretary, Ernest Bevin, looked to establish close relations between Britain and the countries on the Mediterranean and Atlantic fringes of Europe, in commercial and economic matters as in political. He desired to make a start with France, and to begin with the Levant. On the other hand, he did not wish to take active steps for a Franco-British alliance or the formation of a Western group until he had time to consider possible Russian reactions.[80] Not for the first time, the Ambassador in Paris went further than his government had intended in tackling the issue with Bidault. The latter was hopeful of concluding a satisfactory treaty within a month from mid-August.[81] Three weeks later, however, Bidault was telling the British Ambassador that there were still difficulties in the way, the chief of which remained in the Levant. After many ticklish exchanges, an agreement of sorts was reached in December. Meanwhile, a Conference of Foreign Ministers in London that autumn included Bidault, but merely demonstrated the cleavage between the Russians and the rest. Germany had in effect been split in two. As de Gaulle observes mordantly, the ministers separated after 23 days of discussion as futile for the present as they were depressing for the future.[82] For the moment, the General's position as a political leader in France remained strong, though rumours persisted of his early retirement. At a press conference on 12 October, de Gaulle declared with much truth 'When one considers how we started, what we have been through and where we stand today, we haven't done too badly.'[83]

Molotov, asked outright by Bevin whether he saw any objections to an Anglo-French treaty on similar lines to the Anglo-Soviet and Franco-Soviet agreements, said that he did not. Such a pact would have had very considerable symbolic value, after all the antagonisms of the previous year. It might indeed have enabled the two powers to align their policies in many matters and places. However, it would have required a greater measure of agreement than existed in the autumn of 1945, in respect of the Levant and of wider issues. Everything depended on the view formed of Russian intentions, and that was a more fluid matter at the time than most have been willing to concede in retrospect. Once more the Foreign

Ministers of Britain, the United States and Russia met, on this occasion in Moscow from mid-December. To the French, this seemed like another deliberate slight and exclusion. The ministers made no substantial progress and the French government announced, as on previous occasions, that the conclusions of the conference did not commit France.

de Gaulle, whose position had been weakened by the outcome of elections in the autumn of 1945, was still strong enough to remain in power if he had the will and the taste. His capacity to surprise persisted to the last. Rumours of his possible resignation had circulated for months. All the same, the British Ambassador was taken aback when, depressed by the bickerings and manoeuvrings of the politicians, de Gaulle demitted office on 20 January 1946. In respect of the Levant, de Gaulle had found once again that most of those with whom he was dealing in France did not share his view. Mistakenly, he believed that the British refused to reconsider what seemed to him unsatisfactory aspects of the agreement concerning the Levant because they realized that with a little patience they could achieve their purpose once he had left office.[84] In truth, the other pressures were too great. The British had long had more than enough to do in the Middle East and elsewhere. Whatever de Gaulle might think, they had no desire to remain lengthily in Syria and the Lebanon. Those two countries arraigned Britain and France before the United Nations; all the British and French troops had gone by the late summer of 1946. Nor was France able to secure all that she had declared indispensable in the Rhineland and Western Germany.

J.M. Keynes once remarked that a financial settlement which led Britain to bankruptcy would seem an outrageous crown and conclusion to all that had happened in the war.[85] The same judgement can scarcely be resisted in respect of France's relations with Britain. To see squabbling and quarrelsome two powers which had suffered so badly and survived so narrowly has elements of tragedy or even of black comedy. In the end, the rising fear of Russia, the process by which she replaced Germany as the major potential enemy, effected what other arguments had failed to achieve. The disappearance from power of de Gaulle, which most observers imagined to be permanent, eased the position. It would be unjust to say of him as of the Bourbons that he forgot nothing and learned nothing. All the same, he did not forgive what he took to be Britain's deliberate maltreatment of France over the Levant.

At last the British and French buried most of their differences and in 1947 signed an agreement at Dunkerque, of all appropriate places. This was largely the doing of the Ambassador and of Bevin, who bore none of Churchill's baggage of five years' intermittent disputes with de Gaulle. When the moment came to sign the treaty, the Secretary of State had disappeared. He was found in the courtyard of the hotel, raising his hands to heaven amidst the pouring rain and crying with gusto 'I love the French! I love the French!'[86]

5

Churchill, Eden and Stalin

How best to explain the phenomenon of Churchill, the man's personality and methods and moods, to a Commander in the field urged against his better judgement to undertake an early offensive, and affronted by the Prime Minister's tone and style? The Commander was General Auchinleck, the date the spring of 1942 and his correspondent in London Churchill's admiring but not uncritical servant General Ismay, the hinge and hyphen between the War Cabinet and the Chiefs of Staff:

> You cannot judge the Prime Minister by ordinary standards [Ismay wrote]; he is not in the least like anyone that you or I have ever met. He is a mass of contradictions …: either in an angelic temper or a hell of a rage: when he isn't fast asleep he's a volcano. There are no half-measures in his make-up. He is a child of nature with moods as variable as an April day.[1]

It was not only a matter of temperament. Churchill's position was different from that of any other prime minister, because for more than five years he held also the post of Minister of Defence, and in no merely formal style. As Ismay provided the link with the Chiefs of Staff on the official plane, so Churchill himself provided it on the political; and, especially in the first half of the war, military issues were more often resolved by the Defence Committee, in which he was the dominant force, than by the War Cabinet itself. The crucial importance of holding both offices was throughout apparent to him; hence his refusal to surrender the post of Minister of Defence in the dog days of February 1942.

Nowadays, Eden is sometimes treated as a figure of the second or even third rank. His reputation will revive in time, not least because of his services during the war. Of his closeness to Churchill, and willingness to argue vigorously with him, there is no doubt. The Prime Minister liked to say wryly of his Latin tags 'They are few but faithful'; the disagreements between Churchill and his lieutenant were not numerous but significant. Perhaps the most important of all lay in the difference of emphasis (to put it no higher) in their approach to de Gaulle and his place in post-war France.

In the September of 1940, when Eden was still at the War Office, Churchill expected him to become leader of the Conservative Party in due course; we must remember that this was a position which Churchill himself had not then attained. 'We shall work this war together.'[2] Less than two years later, King George VI was advised by Churchill that in the event of his death, Eden should become Prime Minister because he was the outstanding minister in the government. In his turn, the King, rightly judging that 'He is, so to speak, your Second-in-Command in many respects', argued strongly that Churchill should not let Eden go to India as Viceroy.[3] Eden too had a strong interest in military affairs, broadly defined, and a brave fighting record. This was generally a sure passport to Churchill's heart. 'You are my war machine,' the Prime Minister once exclaimed to him; 'Brookie [General Brooke], Portal, you and Dickie [Mountbatten]. I simply couldn't replace you.'[4]

In sum, Eden was closer to Churchill than any other minister who held office lengthily in the War Cabinet, far closer than Attlee or Bevin or Anderson, though not perhaps than Beaverbrook; he, however, appeared on the scene but intermittently. Churchill used to reflect that he and Eden were instinctively of one mind on a wide range of issues; if the two of them were thousands of miles apart and given the same sheaf of telegrams, they would arrive without consultation at similar conclusions nine times in ten. Eden was one of those people with whom it was 'agreeable to dine', which was less obviously true of most other members of the War Cabinet. He lived at the edge of his resources and was very quick in repartee; in some of his reactions and instincts feminine but not in the least effeminate, a splendid raconteur and linguist. It is characteristic of Churchill that until 1954, in his 80th year, he had no idea that Eden had read Oriental Languages with distinction at Oxford and could recite Persian poetry by the ream, and of Eden that he should never have paraded such accomplishments even before one with whom he had been intimately associated for the better part of two decades.[5]

London abounded in people who were on the point of waxing valiant before the Prime Minister but was less full of those who had actually steeled themselves to this feat, which did require no mean degree of courage. One of the leading Labour members of the War Cabinet said that the Prime Minister's relations with the Foreign Secretary resembled those of father and son. Nonetheless, Eden would stand up manfully to him, despite a gap in age of a generation, somewhat as Alanbrooke did in the military sphere. Occasionally, their disputes concerned broad questions of foreign policy. More often, immediate issues loomed. In the midsummer of 1942, for example, we find Eden – to whom these lengthy talks must sometimes have proved a burden, for he was preoccupied with pressing questions, and conversation was for him something to be savoured but abbreviated, a means of reaching a conclusion, whereas for Churchill it was a diversion, almost an indulgence – arguing for most of an afternoon against Churchill's desire to set off forthwith to the Middle East. Eventually Churchill succumbed – 'You mean [that I should be] like a great blue-bottle buzzing over a huge cowpat!'[6] – but not for long. He went there four weeks later, with the consequence that General Ismay's correspondent in Egypt was removed from his command.

Between 1940 and 1945, as Secretary of State for War and Foreign Secretary, Eden travelled to Ankara, Washington and Quebec twice, Athens and Moscow thrice, Cairo four times; he attended the conferences at Tehran, Yalta, San Francisco and Potsdam, and with Cordell Hull participated in the meeting of Foreign Ministers at Moscow in the autumn of 1943, when Britain and the United States came more nearly into harmony about post-war issues than at any later date. For five years Eden served on the Defence Committee; for four-and-a-half years as Foreign Secretary; and for the better part of three years as Leader of the House of Commons after Cripps' star had waned rapidly. Among ministers, only Churchill bore a heavier burden. In particular, the combination of endless hours of duty in the House of Commons, where Eden's gifts of conciliation and readiness in debate shone, and the never-ceasing, critical business of the Foreign Office proved exhausting, almost killing; in 1944, Eden confessed he was so weary that he hardly cared what happened so long as he could shed one office or the other.[7] In the event, he had to sustain both to the end.

'In wartime,' Eden wrote, 'diplomacy is strategy's twin.'[8] No Foreign Secretary could do more than a small portion of the Office's business and by temperament Eden was hesitant to delegate. That the system worked relatively well in such desperate circumstances as those of 1940–5 owed much to the Permanent Under-Secretary, Sir Alexander Cadogan. No matter what might be said about his closeness to Chamberlain, which he never made any attempt to dissemble, or his considerable responsibility for the policy which the British government had pursued in 1938 and 1939, Cadogan was esteemed by Eden from their early days together at Geneva; he was competent and unruffled, the more so perhaps because he would occasionally relieve himself by tart remarks in his diary. Churchill trusted him. 'Thank God I brought you with me', he said suddenly to Cadogan when the latter had helped a good deal with the drafting of the Atlantic Charter in the summer of 1941; and, in August 1945, 'All the work you have done in this War has been excellent.'[9] The fact that within a few weeks of returning to the Foreign Office at the end of 1940 Eden could disappear to the Middle East for nearly two months tells its own story. In that phase, the business of the Office was largely run by Cadogan in consultation with the Parliamentary Under-Secretary, R.A. Butler, and on vital questions with the Prime Minister himself.

WSC counted a number of diplomats as friends. For the Foreign Office itself he had a lesser respect, believing it so well attuned to the needs and cultures of other countries that it was institutionally inclined to give way; this opinion did not change during his last spell in office, from 1951 to 1955.[10] He took a lively interest in diplomatic appointments and deplored the tendency to move heads of mission every two or three years. From time to time he would inveigh against the flaccidity of memoranda coming from the Foreign Office – 'If you want to find a clear line, you must take alternate paragraphs; it doesn't matter where you start,' he once remarked irreverently – and would protest against interminable telegrams. His Private Secretary Mr Colville, himself from the Foreign Office, listened with some pain. Eventually he asked the Prime Minister 'Which do you dislike the more, the Treasury or the Foreign Office?' 'The War Office', Churchill answered.[11]

War, they say, is too serious a business to be left to generals, and foreign affairs during the war could not be simply a matter for the Foreign Office. Many of the normal responsibilities had vanished – for Germany, Italy, most of Western and Northern Europe, Japan, large tracts of Asia –

whereas other duties, especially with the neutrals (Russia until the summer of 1941, the United States until December 1941, Turkey, Spain, Portugal throughout) had increased notably. The financial position was often dire. Economic warfare, embracing everything from the blockade to supplies of wolfram and meat and tobacco, had obvious implications for foreign policy; but financial matters were mainly for the Treasury, and economic warfare for the Ministry with that title. The policies of the Combined Chiefs of Staff in Washington; the aspirations and recommendations of the Ministers Resident in the Middle East, the Mediterranean and West Africa, all reporting directly to the Prime Minister and War Cabinet; the tenebrous world of propaganda, overt and black; the proceedings of the Special Operations Executive; the conduct of relations with the USA, where even by September 1940 Britain had no less than nine missions reporting to departments other than the Foreign Office;[12] the war-effort and political status of India; the conduct of a foreign policy for the Commonwealth – all these activities concerned the Foreign Office directly and intimately. None lay in its direct control.

Nor were those the only constraints, for instinct and experience alike had given Churchill an unfeigned belief in the transaction of business through direct contact between heads of government. In practice, he handled personally most high-level questions with Roosevelt, and often with Stalin. To the former, he sent about 1,000 telegrams in 5 years, receiving some 800 in reply; for his first meeting with the latter in August 1942, as for his meeting with Roosevelt a year before, he took Cadogan but not Eden. On 22 June 1941, when he offered all aid to Russia, the text of his broadcast was finished so late that not even Eden had seen it.[13] Most expert opinion then thought that Germany would conquer Russia, and Churchill sometimes inclined to the same view, though not consistently. At least the German assault meant that he saw Russians fighting less for Communism than for their fatherland and homes, as did many of the Russians themselves. Not for nothing was the epic named 'The Great Patriotic War' and not for nothing did portraits of Suvarov and Kutusov, heroes of earlier wars, replace those of Marx and Engels in the Kremlin.

There had been no immediate change of policy towards the Soviet Union when Eden returned to the Foreign Office. Earlier in 1940, Sir Stafford Cripps at the Embassy in Moscow had favoured substantial concessions. This proposal was characterized as 'silly' by Cadogan, who was convinced, correctly as all the evidence available since then suggests, that Russian policy would be guided simply by a cold calculation of Russia's interest (which is not to say that such calculation was well founded):

> Russian policy will change exactly when and if they think it will suit them. And if they do think that, it won't matter whether we've kicked Maisky [the Russian Ambassador in London] in the stomach. Contrariwise, we could give Maisky the Garter and it wouldn't make a penn'orth of difference.[14]

Cripps was held sternly at arm's length in Russia; he seldom saw Molotov, let alone Stalin. Maisky behaved in London after a fashion which would scarcely have been permitted to any other diplomat, though as one of the British official historians suggests, it is by no means certain that Russian interests profited from that fact. According to a report reaching the Foreign Office in December 1940, the Ambassador had said that Russia was content to see the belligerents exhaust themselves; he was in the habit of adding all the losses together in one column.[15] Basing himself upon intercepted messages, Churchill sent a warning to Stalin in April 1941 of German intentions. This was much delayed by Cripps, to the Prime Minister's understandable anger. It was never acknowledged. The same is true of alarming information tendered by Eden to Maisky.[16]

Churchill had long loathed Communism as much as Nazism. The two creeds, he would remark, reminded him of the North and South Poles, at opposite ends of the earth but indistinguishable in essentials. Though there might be more penguins in the one and more polar bears in the other, 'all around would be snow and ice and the blast of a biting wind'. Few described more tellingly than he the horrors of a regime which terrorized and murdered its own citizens, snuffed out grace and culture, sought without cease to overturn other civilizations by stealth and propaganda. In Churchill's grimly hilarious rendering of the visit paid to Russia by George Bernard Shaw and Lady Astor, Stalin himself receives the guests with smiles of overflowing comradeship, 'pushing aside his morning's budget of death warrants.'[17]

Russia was guilty in the 1930s of far greater crimes against humanity than any yet perpetrated by Hitler. This was the power and this the man sought briefly as an ally against Germany by Churchill and others in the summer of 1939. Once Russia had made terms with Nazi Germany, partitioned Poland and attacked Finland, WSC lost no time in pointing to the military incapacity of the USSR. 'Many illusions about Soviet Russia have been dispelled in these few fierce weeks of fighting in the Arctic Circle', he said in a broadcast of 20 January 1940. 'Everyone can see how Communism rots the soul of a nation; how it makes it abject and hungry in peace, and proves it base and abominable in war.'[18] Churchill's account of Stalin's policy in the period 1939–41 condemns him in terms equally unsparing; having waited to see whether Britain would be promptly defeated, and witnessed the collapse in France of the Second Front for which they were soon to clamour, the Soviet leaders became more earnest about gaining time. Nevertheless, Stalin made massive miscalculations and displayed ignorance of what was coming to him; 'at once a callous, a crafty and an ill-informed giant.' In their failure to prepare a Balkan front, with active British aid, during the first half of 1941, in their indifference to warnings and in other ways, 'Stalin and his commissars showed themselves at this moment the most completely outwitted bunglers of the Second World War.' 'Nothing that any of us could do pierced the purblind prejudice and fixed ideas which Stalin had raised between himself and the terrible truth.'[19] All this, however, was published a decade later, when high hopes had turned to ashes.

As an ally, Russia proved herself demanding, suspicious, often insulting, but above all self-confident. The very thought of Stalin's Russia as a partner in a war for freedom and the rights of small nations presented obvious difficulties. These were apparent within a few months, for when Eden and Cadogan visited Moscow in December 1941, hearing in the quiet of the night the thud of the German guns at the fringe of the city, Stalin made demands incompatible with the Atlantic Charter. It was plain that he intended at the minimum to control the Baltic States, and to tolerate no unfriendly neighbours on the western and south-western borders of Russia. From Washington Churchill telegraphed that such terms could not be accepted. Ironically, in view of all that was to happen later, the American government expressed itself as strongly hostile to Russian wishes. But Russia was after all bearing the brunt of the war on land, and had done wonderfully well to survive the initial German onslaught. She had in a few months lost over 3 million killed, wounded or captured. These were facts to which Churchill repeatedly paid tribute in no grudging a fashion. Naturally, he sought to sustain Russian morale.

His view about Stalin's demands changed by March 1942, though the American attitude did not. It was thanks largely to Cadogan's adroitness that the immediate problems were surmounted in the Anglo-Russian Treaty of May 1942, at the price of sweeping the territorial issues under the carpet for a while; a process not without its advantages to Russia, for Stalin realized that these matters would in the end be settled by force.

Equally serious issues arose, but in a more urgent form, in the spring of 1943, when the German forces invading Russia discovered at Katyn mass graves containing the bodies of Polish officers, perhaps as many as 10,000 or even 15,000. Nothing had been heard of them since 1940. The German accusation that the Russians had murdered them was taken up by many Poles but denounced as an outrageous slander by Moscow. WSC understood both that the charge might well be true and that Russia was suffering deaths and casualties in many millions as she slowly choked the life out of the Wehrmacht. In effect, the British government buried the matter of Katyn for the moment, and indeed for many years. At the time, the sifting and gathering of evidence were undertaken by Sir Owen O'Malley, British Ambassador to the Polish Government in exile, devout Roman Catholic and more clear-eyed than most of his Foreign Office colleagues about the nature of Stalin's regime. His report left little doubt of Russian guilt. How, it was asked, could a liberal parliamentary democracy, fighting the war on issues of principle, associate itself with such a power? The Permanent Under-Secretary pointed out that on this argument Britain and Russia could not have been associated at any stage, since Russia had for years been in the habit of butchering its own citizens. O'Malley's conclusions were suppressed. So compelling was the need to remain on terms with Stalin, so heavy the burden that Russia was bearing, so unacceptable the thought that the end of the war might see the substitution of one tyranny for another, that Churchill was willing only to show the report to Roosevelt, but not to leave a copy with him. Many years after, asked by his Private Secretary about Katyn, WSC said 'I could not allow myself to believe that our allies were responsible. I put it behind me.' 'Do you regret it?' 'I regret many things.' He then indicated that what he had feared most was a separate peace between Germany and Russia, another Nazi-Soviet pact.[20]

British policy towards Russia had to be conducted, as it must still be judged, in relation to the military and financial situation. By the end of 1942, it was likely that Germany would not be able to defeat the USSR and certain that the weight of the United States within the alliance would increase enormously. Churchill, Eden and their colleagues in the British government are frequently accused of dragging their feet in respect of the so-called Second Front. The term is a misnomer, since a whole series of second fronts had been fought in the Middle East, East Africa and North Africa from 1940; the third front was being contested, and for a long time lost, in the Far East and South Asia; yet another front opened with the Anglo-American landings in North Africa towards the end of 1942; and that is to make no mention of the Battle of the Atlantic which came at least as near as the Battle of Britain to causing this country's collapse. Losses of shipping in 1942 raised the spectre of starvation and if sustained would have made the invasion of Western Europe impossible; in which event the Nazi nightmare would have lasted a very long time indeed, since it was only from a belligerent Britain that an assault upon the mainland of Europe could be launched. Seen from Russia, these other fronts doubtless looked a secondary affair; seen from Washington or London, not to mention Ottawa or Canberra, they were not.

Against all his instincts, Churchill endured Russian taunts of British cowardice. Roosevelt and Marshall, neither comprehending the problems of a cross-Channel assault against a heavily fortified France, at first desired a 'Second Front' in 1942. Stalin clamoured for the same thing. The British were heavily dependent upon the United States for money and munitions. Churchill, who had every incentive to open a successful land assault upon Germany at the earliest moment, since it was clear that each month of warfare would leave Britain (far and away the smallest of the three great Aliied powers in territory, population and natural resources) increasingly bankrupt and exhausted, had to resist such pressures for a good part of 1942 and some part of 1943. Until the late autumn of 1942, he had no solid military success at his back. All the same, he had one substantial asset, often overlooked in later years; that Britain and the Commonwealth had larger forces fighting in the field than had the USA. That position did not change until the midsummer of 1944. The enormous practical difficulties of an operation to cross the Channel were never understood by the Russians, and only with much difficulty by the government of the USA. That Stalin and Molotov and the Russian military should protest vehemently, believing that they were being deliberately left to pay most of the blood-tax, was entirely understandable. It is doubtful whether the full depths of

Russian suspicion and dislike were ever comprehended by the Embassy in Moscow, or by the senior figures in the Foreign Office. Churchill himself believed, as did almost all those around him, that his apparently warm personal relations with Stalin would enable many of the difficulties to be surmounted in the end.

There are signs in Foreign Office papers of the strains produced by such attitudes, which were not shared, for example, by O'Malley, or some of his (mainly junior) colleagues. Occasional frictions arose on Russian subjects between Churchill and Eden in the last 18 months of the war, but in general these concerned tactics rather than principles. Prime Minister and Foreign Secretary were at one in believing that substantial concessions must be made to Russia, as was done from the time of the Tehran Conference onwards. The process entailed a relentless pressure upon the Poles, which continued up to the time of Yalta and indeed beyond. Churchill hoped that Overlord would strengthen his hand. By the end of June 1944, 850,000 men had landed in France, with 150,000 vehicles and 570,000 tons of supplies. Eventually, the Allies deployed some 80 divisions (three-quarters of them American) in Western Europe. For three years Russia had borne the lion's share of the land battles; that was no longer true to the same degree and as the invasion of France got under way, the balance changed somewhat. The Russian summer offensive began at the same time. Stalin told WSC of this, and received the immediate reply 'I thank you cordially … I hope you will observe that we have never asked you a single question, because of our full confidence in you, your nation and your armies.' Four days later, Stalin telegraphed in tribute to Overlord, 'My colleagues and I cannot but admit that the history of warfare knows of no other like undertaking from the point of view of its scale, its vast conception, and its masterly execution. … History will record this deed as an achievement of the highest order.' Churchill's account remarks 'Harmony was complete.' It is pertinent to add that, by the spring of 1944, the Allies had sent to Russia more than 5,000 tanks, 4,000 lorries and ambulances and nearly 8,000 aircraft, together with raw materials and other items to the value of £80 million. The larger part of these supplies had come from Great Britain.[21] In the later stages of the war aid to Russia from the United States and Canada increased enormously.

Russian behaviour during the Warsaw rising of August and September 1944 made little difference to official British attitudes. Within a week or two, Churchill and Eden were in Moscow, where they accepted Stalin's explanations. The Prime Minister presented a photograph of himself bearing an inscription which in its first part recorded an undeniable fact and in its second an aspiration soon belied: 'From his Friend Winston S. Churchill To Marshal & Premier Stalin Who at the head of the Russian Armies & of the Soviet Government broke the main strength of the German military machine & helped us all to open paths to Peace, Justice and Freedom.'

A difference of perspective emerged within the British government at that time and onwards, but not between Churchill and Eden, or the Foreign Office and the Embassy in Moscow; rather, between the senior military figures and the politicians. Whereas the Chief of the Imperial General Staff judged that Russia would pose the great danger of the post-war period, so great a danger indeed that Germany would have to be built up to help contain her, the Prime Minister and the Foreign Secretary, like almost all the other politicians and senior diplomats, believed that the essential challenge would be the containment of Germany. Foreign Office papers did not neglect or ignore the risks, but were on the whole hopeful that Russia would wish to collaborate. By and large, the same opinion was held by the Ambassador and his colleagues in Russia. Between Churchill and Eden, there were differences of emphasis before Yalta. These related to the substance of the issues rearing up and to the means of handling them; for on this occasion there was to be no repetition of the Foreign Ministers' conference which had prepared the ground before Tehran. Early in January, we find in the Foreign Secretary's diary:

> I am much worried that the whole business will be chaotic and nothing worth while settled, Stalin being the only one of the three who has a clear view of what he wants and is a tough negotiator. P.M. is all emotion in these matters, F.D.R. vague and jealous of others.[22]

Being convinced that his private relations with Stalin were good and that they mattered, the Prime Minister was inclined to offer more to Russia than was Eden. Both desired Russian abstention in Greece as strongly as Russian entry into the war against Japan.

To the last, the British had no clear idea of the way in which the Russian government worked. Though their Ambassador in Moscow Sir

Archibald Clark Kerr saw something of Stalin and a good deal of Molotov, he could not pierce the veil, inclining to think of Stalin as a moderating influence, lurking behind whom stood 'extremist advisers'.[23] To be sure, Stalin often seemed an improvement on his Foreign Minister Molotov, not a difficult status to achieve. Doubtless the two played off each other and Stalin's reputation as the man of relative moderation derived partly from concessions which, though rarely on matters of substance, he made when Molotov had refused to yield. That the two of them in combination were formidable negotiators is incontestable. Twenty years after the war, Eden recorded that if he had to choose a team with whom to go into an international conference, Stalin would be at the top of his list.[24] After the meetings in Moscow of October 1944, Churchill observed to the War Cabinet 'Behind the horseman sits black care'; in other words there were (from a Western point of view) figures in the background more threatening and sinister than Stalin.[25] At Yalta, Stalin proved his mettle. Roosevelt was sick unto death, and Churchill, though indomitable, nearing exhaustion. Hence the judgement of Cadogan that 'He [Stalin] is a great man and shows up very impressively against the background of the other two ageing statesmen.'[26]

Asked if these conferences were of value, Clark Kerr answered without hesitation 'Stalin has got an impression of the P.M. as a broth of a boy, full of guts and determination – what Stalin calls his "desperation" and that helps.'[27] This was after Stalin in proposing Churchill's health had spoken about 1940, saying that he could think of no other instance in history where the future of the world had depended on the courage of one man. We need not assume that he was being wholly cynical. While there may be a good deal more for us to learn from Russian records as they are peeled back layer by layer, the evidence presently available suggests that whatever warm expressions were emitted at conferences, Stalin and his immediate associates continued to regard Churchill as an unreconstructed enemy of Communism. According to the Yugoslav leader Djilas, Stalin said to him in 1944:

Perhaps you think that just because we are allies of the English we have forgotten who they are and who Churchill is. There is nothing they like better than to trick their allies ... Churchill is the kind of man who will pick your pocket of a kopeck if you don't watch him. Yes, pick your pocket of a kopeck! By God, pick your pocket of a kopeck! And Roosevelt? Roosevelt is not like that. He dips in his hand only for bigger coins. But Churchill? Churchill – will do it for a kopeck.[28]

In the immediate aftermath of Yalta neither Churchill nor Eden concluded that Russia had become an enemy or a potential one. They had just heard Stalin refer to the many sins committed against Poland by Russia in the past, for which deeds she desired to make amends. The Prime Minister gave explicit assurances in Parliament, and in private to his colleagues, about Stalin's good faith. That WSC and Eden both felt fearful is incontestable; but it was not until the latter part of March 1945 that apprehension was replaced by a growing realization of Russia's determination to have her way in Poland and elsewhere. That is when we find in Eden's diary the forlorn entry 'Altogether, our foreign policy seems a sad wreck and we may have to cast about afresh',[29] while Churchill a fortnight later said of Russia, 'one might have thought one was talking to a different country.'[30] Though Roosevelt's last days had been marked by a furious protest to Stalin against Russian charges of treachery, the new President began with considerable suspicions of British policy and confessed in his memoirs, written long after the event, that in the spring of 1945 he was trying to persuade Churchill to forget power politics.[31] This cannot be accounted a promising basis for any relationship with Stalin and Molotov, as Truman himself soon discovered. For his part, Churchill remained almost pathetically grateful for signs of goodwill from Russia. Even so faithful an admirer as Colville records a fine example at the end of April:

The P.M. returned ... to find a nice telegram from Stalin, indeed the most friendly U.J. [Uncle Joe] has ever sent. This quite fascinated him and I sat beside him ... while he talked of nothing else, first of all to Brendan [Bracken] for one and a half hours and then to me for another one and a half. His vanity was astonishing and I am glad U.J. does not know what effect a few kind words, after so many harsh ones, might well have on our policy towards Russia. ... Further joy was caused by a generous message from de Gaulle. But no work was done and I felt both irritated and slightly disgusted by this exhibition of susceptibility to flattery. It was nearly 5.00 a.m. when I got to bed.[32]

A later chapter describes the investigations which Churchill commanded the Chiefs of Staff to undertake in May, under the code name Operation Unthinkable. It has in recent times been alleged that he wished to make war upon Russia almost as soon as war with Germany had finished. He did not; but he had to find out whether the West – even on the unlikely assumptions of full American support and possible later use of German troops – could conceivably resist Russia in Central Europe by conventional military force. He soon learned from the Chiefs of Staff that it could not; and there matters remained for only a couple of months, until the first successful test of the atomic bomb altered the international equation overnight, a fact demonstrated at Hiroshima and Nagasaki in early August.

Churchill's forebodings about Russia, the falling of the Iron Curtain across much of Central and Eastern Europe, the clear Russian determination to make Poland a satellite or worse – even amidst all this, he did not display any consistent hostility to the USSR. At Potsdam in July, he showed himself more forthcoming than Eden. The latter, a much more calculating negotiator, felt something akin to desperation. He said to Churchill 'I am full of admiration for Stalin's handling of you', hoping that this might move the Prime Minister. 'It did a little', says Eden in his diary.[33] It was at Potsdam that the death of Eden's elder son was confirmed, after weeks of suspense; having trained as a pilot in Canada, he had been lost in Burma on his second sortie of the day. 'Anthony and Beatrice [Eden] both came to dinner nevertheless, and dined on the balcony with Lord Moran', wrote Churchill's daughter Mary to her mother. 'I have never seen two people behave with such noble dignity.'[34] Churchill avers in his memoirs that neither he nor Eden would ever have consented to the extension of Poland's frontiers to the Western Neisse, even if that stand meant a breach with Russia. In reality, the times were too far gone for such calculations.

There was a symmetry between the events of July and August 1945 and those of six years earlier. Poland had become the test or touchstone of Russian intentions, just as it had been of German. Two generations later, what happened still arouses the deepest feelings. Much was conceded in 1938 to Germany at the pistol point in respect of Czechoslovakia and none had condemned the process more vigorously than Churchill. Much was conceded to Russia in respect of Poland and other countries between 1943 and 1945. The Prime Minister and Foreign Secretary both acknowledged the comparison. 'Shall I go down in history as an appeaser?' asked Eden. 'Poor Neville Chamberlain believed he could trust Hitler,' said Churchill privately after Yalta. 'He was wrong. But I don't think I am wrong about Stalin.'[35] Like Chamberlain in 1938, he found the alternative almost too horrible to contemplate. Both Prime Ministers had been to some degree carried along by what a later Permanent Under-Secretary at the Foreign Office called 'the dynamic of negotiation';[36] both trusted for a brief while that submissions and personal contact would lead to something constructive, even at a heavy price.

It is not fanciful to make a connection between these events and Churchill's last spell as Prime Minister from 1951 to 1955, when almost single-handedly he struggled after Stalin's death for a meeting with the Russian leaders at which he would seek to persuade them that collaboration with the West would be for everyone a more attractive course than an unrestrained race to acquire weapons far more deadly than any previously possessed. That too is a story for another chapter.

6

Epic and Tragedy

Britain and Poland, 1941–5

It was not a natural alliance, for the remoteness of Poland from Britain and the predatory behaviour of the Polish government at the time of the Munich crisis in 1938 created substantial obstacles. However, there was a more powerful force at work; the desire to show Germany that whatever might be the outcome in the short run, expansion to the east would be opposed. It would be too much to say that the invasion of Poland was the cause of World War II, and too little to say that it was merely the occasion. Much the same had been true of Belgium in 1914, but with the difference that for the British, Belgium lay near at hand and Poland did not. In September 1939, the Poles had done precisely what many had blamed Benes for not doing in 1938;[1] they had refused to knuckle under, no matter what the cost, and had forced other powers to declare themselves. But the territory of Poland provided the essential prize in the agreement between the Russian and German governments in August 1939, the Fourth Partition. The frontal assault from the west and the stab in the back from the east left Poland prostrate in a matter of weeks. What neither event extinguished was the desire of countless Poles to grapple with both enemies. Many thousands enlisted in the Allied forces and became celebrated for the almost reckless gallantry with which they fought. Within Poland, many more banded together to form the most substantial organized resistance in Europe.

With this resistance, the Special Operations Executive in London was the main point of British contact. In the utmost secrecy, SOE had been established to co-ordinate subversion and sabotage in territories held by the enemy; and half a century afterwards, nearly 400 files relating to its activities in Czechoslovakia, Hungary, the Soviet Union and Poland were released. We do not know how much documentation was destroyed after the war, nor can we assess how much of value is still withheld. Amidst all the pressures, records were not always well kept. Papers are distributed somewhat haphazardly. In the very nature of SOE's work, much went unrecorded or was destroyed after the event. All the same, we see clearly how intimate and continuous was SOE's connection with Poland. Its officers had a great deal of secret information concerning not only the state of affairs there but also the activities of Polish resistance organizations all over the world.[2] These episodic documents reveal a tale of unflinching and deliberate courage. Those nearest to the story, including many officers of SOE's Polish section, felt acutely the events of 1944 and 1945.

Some of the files are ample and contain a great deal of new material. HS4/146, for example, holds notes of an important discussion on Polish operations, dated 6 March 1944; a long memorandum entitled 'Stores Policy for Kensal' [Poland] of 29 May 1944; another concerning flights to Poland and the fighting and sabotage equipment to be carried by those aircraft, dated 7 July 1944; material about the impending rising in July; notes entitled 'Stores and General Policy for Kensal' of 4 September 1944; a plea from Lt. Col. Threlfall to the Air Officer Commanding, Balkan Air Force, arguing forcefully on 13 September 1944 that 'We cannot let the Polish Home Army down now'; numerous messages passing between SOE in London and its representatives with the Poles in Southern Italy; papers about the resignation of Mikolajczyk; and much else of the deepest interest.

We find directives from the Chiefs of Staff and the Combined Chiefs of Staff, with a confirmation that SOE should continue to act as the co-ordinating authority with the General Staffs of the Allied governments whose territories were occupied and as the body to which those governments should refer all matters relating to sabotage and the organization of resistance.[3] One file deals with use of the diplomatic bag for the transmission of propaganda and arrangements made in 1942 to despatch material by that method to Russia and the Middle East,[4] and another on a connected subject contains correspondence about pamphlets to be dropped over Poland. SOE, in this as in other matters, found it difficult to reach common ground with the Political

Warfare Executive, part of which had its origins within SOE itself before the Foreign Office became wholly responsible for that part of the war effort. The exasperated head of the Polish section wrote shortly before Christmas 1942 'PWE ... will not appreciate that why the Poles appear somewhat allergic to leaflets generally is that they consider them mere evidence of our inability to drop bombs and, in fact, of our general gutlessness.'[5] Another officer of SOE had remarked a year earlier in equally pithy style 'Pamphlets are useless in Poland; there is no need to stiffen the resistance of the people, and one bomb in any case is worth a million pamphlets.'[6]

The letters and memoranda written during the summer of 1941, in the immediate aftermath of Barbarossa, deal with deadly matters: for example, sabotage in German territory, which was intensified, and the question of sabotage against German communications in Poland itself. Further, what was to happen to all those Poles who had been deported from the eastern part of their country? Would Russia be willing to give some recognition of the old frontiers of Poland? These pregnant questions, raised by the exiled Polish government in London with the Soviet government, exercised a baleful influence for the rest of the war and long beyond.[7] The lines of potential battle were drawn from the start. A month after Barbarossa began, General Sosnkowski (a minister in the Polish government in exile, later to become C.-in-C. of the Polish Army) remarked on the serious dissensions among his colleagues concerning Russia, for even then the Soviet government refused to recognize the prewar frontiers of Poland. With justice, Sosnkowski emphasized that Poland had been the first country to oppose with force the German programme of domination and that she had now lost all in the common struggle. How could her Allies, and more especially England, expect her to make further sacrifices before the war was even over, while she was still playing her full part? Was it not beyond reason that such sacrifices should be made in favour of Russia, a power which had only just become the ally of Great Britain? It would be unthinkable to compromise now on the question of frontiers. How could it be explained to the people of Poland and the huge masses of Polish deportees in Russia that their homes might eventually be surrendered to the Russians and their Polish nationality lost? The Polish people, he said, felt an almost mystical trust in the British and their honesty of purpose; 'but were his Government to compromise on this question with the Bolsheviks, the people would attribute this to pressure on the part of the British and might suffer disillusionment which would have unfortunate reactions.'[8]

In the short run, the difficulties were smoothed over, though Sosnkowski insisted upon resigning in protest against the agreement. Of all ministers, none was better disposed to Poland than Dr Hugh Dalton, then in charge of SOE. Even he, in his letter of congratulation to the Foreign Secretary upon the patient diplomacy that had produced the treaty (which omitted all mention of frontiers), remarked 'I quite fail to understand why some prominent Poles have been so silly about it.'[9] MP, the Polish section of SOE, became a very substantial affair, first under Bickham Sweet-Escott and later under Captain Harold Perkins. In the person of General Sir Colin Gubbins, who became Operational Head (CD) of SOE in September 1943, the Poles had a warm sympathizer, acutely aware of the political and military difficulties, for Gubbins had himself been a member of the British military mission to Poland at the outbreak of the war. For obvious reasons, the documents abound in pseudonyms, some unexpected; for example, Sir Stafford Cripps appears as GAFFER. Some can be guessed with a little luck; thus we deduce that STOUT means Lt. Col. Guinness. General Sikorski becomes ACE and occasionally RUBIE; Professor Kot FELIX; Mikolajczyk QUEEN and Sosnkowski SHINE. All the same, the innocent reader finds ingenuity fully exerted when a document begins: 'Quite recently SHINE saw General ("Oh, to be in England") BABBLING (sorry, I forgot you do not do crosswords) and QUEEN saw the CIGAR MERCHANT.'[10] We must take it that BABBLING means Alan Brooke, who had by then been a Field-Marshal for some months, though a reader with a literary turn of mind might consider the claims of General Browning. Doubtless 'the CIGAR MERCHANT' signifies Churchill.

★ ★ ★ ★ ★

The Foreign Secretary, Anthony Eden, travelled to Moscow just before Christmas 1941. Though the German armies stood at the gates of the city, they might have been a thousand miles away as Stalin described Russia's post-war demands. He seemed surprised, and perhaps was genuinely so, that the British were not in a position to make an immediate and secret arrangement with him. It was already clear that if Russia dominated the settlement in Eastern Europe, she would keep the Polish territories annexed under the Ribbentrop-Molotov agreement of 1939; and if Russia did not dominate the settlement, the issue would not arise. At the same moment, MX (Colonel, later Sir Peter, Wilkinson) drew up in London a long and informative note about SOE's work with the Poles. It described Sikorski's honesty of purpose and the dependence of the British on personal contacts with the Poles 'since ... we are in no position to issue orders and have to resort to persuasion'. The paper estimated the size of the Secret Army in Poland at about 120,000, though no more than 35,000 were armed. Col. Wilkinson explained why the Polish government was unwilling for the moment to order an intensification of the Secret Army's activity: there would be little value at the Peace Conference if a premature and forlorn rising were attempted; since the political party which controlled the Secret Army at the end of the war would be in an impregnable position, the Polish government in London was determined to retain control of that weapon to the last and use it at the moment of maximum advantage; in the first two years of the war over 50,000 Polish civilians had been executed by the Germans, and many thousands more murdered, for acts of resistance:

We must therefore accept that the Poles will not allow their Secret Army, either in Poland or abroad, to be exploited by us until the time is ripe for a general revolt. All we can do is to see that, in the intervening period, sufficient preparations are made both by us and by the Poles themselves to ensure that, when the time comes, they can make full use of their potential manpower. This depends mainly on the improvement of our air communications over which we are having so much difficulty at present.

Finally, in dealing with the leaders of these organisations here in London we should do well to remember always that we shall gain more from our patience than from force.[11]

Desultory negotiations in the next few months produced no resolution of the issues raised by Stalin. The British wished to exclude any discussion of the Russo-Polish frontier from their projected treaty with Russia, for the latter's demands could scarcely be reconciled with Britain's obligations to Poland or with the Atlantic Charter, agreed between Roosevelt and Churchill in August 1941, and promptly endorsed by Russia. More in hope than confidence, the Foreign Office substituted something of much vaguer character, leaving out frontier claims and proposing an agreement which would be directed against a German resurgence in the post-war world; a proposal characterized by Molotov, the Russian Foreign Minister who was in London for the negotiations, as an empty declaration which Russia did not need. In contradicting that view and ordering him to sign, Stalin defined Russian policy with candour:

> It [the draft treaty] lacks the question of the security of frontiers, but this is not bad perhaps, for this gives us a free hand. The question of frontiers, or to be more exact, of the guarantees for the security of our frontiers at one or other section of our country, will be decided by force ...[12]

Given the military position then prevailing, these brute questions could be pushed aside for the time being. It was established by June 1942 that SOE was the British authority with which the Poles should deal in all matters affecting sabotage and the organization of resistance, as well as the activities of patriot forces in occupied territories. Well and good; but whereas the Poles maintained that the potential worth of the Secret Army justified the allocation of a considerable force of aircraft, the Allies were always short of long-range planes. Regular liaison with Poland was one thing; the allocation of sufficient aircraft to support a general rising was something different and the Chiefs ruled in the summer of 1942 that they could not think this a practical possibility in the foreseeable future. Many delicate matters would normally have been subject to discussion between the Polish and the British foreign offices; they included projects which involved the use of diplomatic or other official British cover, the granting of special visas, facilities for ciphers. Sometimes the Polish authorities preferred not to consult their own Foreign Office but rather to use SOE as a direct channel to the British government.[13]

These divisions amidst Polish *émigré* opinion were carefully studied within SOE. One of its senior officers explained to his colleagues in the spring of 1943 why General Sikorski had been compelled to make a definite and public stand against what most Poles considered to be Russian aggression:

> It cannot be too strongly emphasised that to the average Pole irrespective of social class or education, Soviet domination would

be no smaller a calamity than has been German domination. The Poles will fight as fanatically against one as against the other, and it is Sikorski's duty to act in accordance with this imperative. British politicians are often unable to understand or sympathise with [the] methods or principles of Polish policy, and there is hardly a government in the world which has not at one time or another accused the Poles of being irresponsible or romantic.

This detailed survey concluded that Russia could not require territory in Eastern Poland for colonization, or for industrial or strategic reasons; if the Russians insisted on the annexation of parts of Eastern Poland, that could serve only the purpose of extending Soviet domination over the whole of Europe eventually and over Central Europe immediately. The Poles might be wrong sometimes, Major Truszkowski conceded, but not all the time and it should not be assumed without question that their claims were invariably fantastic when they happened to conflict with those of Russia:

It is to the interests of the Western Democracies to make every effort that the Polish thesis receives sympathetic consideration and that the Poles shall be protected as far as possible against aggression from the East. Unless this is done the whole set up of resistance to Germany in Axis-occupied countries, built up with much labour and expense during the past few years, will be seriously jeopardised.

A good deal of this analysis was open to dispute, as another official pointed out:

I believe, as I think you do, that fear of Germany is and will be the key to the Russians' attitude and that the unfertile Eastern provinces of Poland which they look like claiming would be used by them entirely as a strategic bulwark and not as part of a scheme for domination or aggression.[14]

The same document expresses the British government's conviction, as against Stalin's, that resistance in Poland should turn upon co-ordinated sabotage and guerrilla operations under central control, which could be exercised only by Sikorski. The fact that the Poles depended very largely on British facilities for carrying out their operations gave the British what the memorandum describes as 'a very close insight into the nature of these activities, and we could assure the Russians from first-hand knowledge that the Poles were in fact making an all-out effort.'[15] The British government had become seriously concerned by statements in Russian newspapers and broadcasts alleging a fundamental difference of policy between London and Moscow in respect of the organization of resistance in Poland. The Foreign Office duly the supplied the Russians with information about the activities of the underground movement there, which was operating under direct orders from London: everything from damage to locomotives to derailment of trains, destruction of bridges, petrol dumps set on fire, assassination of Gestapo chiefs and agents.[16] 'The Polish resistance movement is certainly the most effective and best controlled of all such Allied movements and it is in our view important that it should not be sacrificed to Soviet short-term designs or become a pawn in Polish-Soviet political dispute', Eden added for the guidance of the British Embassy in Moscow.[17]

This was not the only occasion upon which such explanations were tendered. None ever produced a lasting effect. To the occasional and no doubt inevitable mistrust between the Foreign Office and SOE was added a new dimension. Officers in the Polish Section noted with anxiety and indignation a growing tendency to measure Polish affairs against the yardstick of Russian reaction. Its head referred to

the very clever Russian propaganda which as perhaps S.O.E. and the Poles alone know, is in so many instances totally untrue. We know that Katyn [the massacre of Polish officers by the Russians in 1940] took place; we know that the Polish army could not fight on the Eastern Front [in 1939] because it had neither boots nor food; we know that the formation of the Free Poles in Russia has been forced upon the Poles in that country as their only means of obtaining bread and a cover against the ravages of the Russian winter; but these facts are known neither publicly nor officially ...

Unless we wish to be a party to one of the greatest injustices of history, I consider it necessary that some clear-cut policy should be laid down by the British Government with regard to Poland and their Secret Army, and that the Russian Government should be so informed.[18]

Until this stage, in the summer of 1943, General Sikorski had combined the posts of C.-in-C. of the Polish Army and Prime Minister. He was killed when his aircraft crashed in July, being succeeded in the former office by Sosnkowski and in the latter by Mikolajczyk. The loss of Sikorski dealt a hard blow to the hopes of the British government that some tolerable arrangement might be made between Poland and Russia. It was promptly alleged by the Germans that Sikorski had been murdered on the orders of Churchill. Echoes of this preposterous charge are occasionally heard even now.

Whereas Moscow might see the Partisans in Yugoslavia as at least potential coadjutors, the Polish resistance could hardly be viewed in a similar light. The Russians had treated Polish *émigrés* and prisoners of war with notable cruelty; Russia made no secret of her designs on territory held by Poland until 1939; Russia and Germany had collaborated in the partition. As one officer of the SOE expressed it to another, 'The man who has already been robbed by his neighbour cannot be expected to go to him and tell him exactly where he has hidden the rest of his silver.'[19] But this was something which the Red Army, as the military balance of the war changed in the next few months, intended to find out for itself. For their part, the British had often assured Poland that they would not recognize territorial changes effected there since August 1939. The government of the USA, lacking Britain's obligations to Poland, had taken a strong line against recognition of changes brought about by force. Nevertheless, the British government wished the Poles to accept a boundary that would entail substantial loss of territory in the east, but with extensive compensation in the west. In return, Russia would demonstrate her goodwill by resuming relations with Poland and co-operating to find a solution to the problems concerning the Polish resistance, the position of Poles in the USSR and other matters. In all this, as the Tehran Conference showed towards the end of 1943, there was a large element of wishful thinking.[20]

A gulf had opened between Britain's commitments to Poland and her ability to fulfil them. Knowing this all too well, the British devoted themselves to a search for a solution which the Russians would accept and the Poles tolerate; and as the Foreign Secretary was aware, this was not simply a question of adjusting frontiers, even on a massive scale. At Tehran, Churchill defined Britain's desire as a strong and independent Poland, friendly to Russia. In effect, he had accepted most of the Russian case. Before the Conference convened, Eden had told the War Cabinet candidly of Polish fears that what was at stake was

> not so much the frontiers as the future existence of Poland. Their anxieties are (1) that Russia's long-term aim is to set up a puppet Government in Warsaw and turn Poland into a Soviet republic, (2) that disorders would be provoked on the entry of Soviet forces, (3) that it will then be impossible to maintain the present instructions of the Polish Government restraining the Polish population from taking action against the Russians, and (4) that all the leading resistance elements in Poland will be disposed of by the Soviet forces of occupation.

The Foreign Secretary then set out the assurances which the Russians would have to give 'in return for our undertaking to impose on the Poles a frontier settlement on the above lines'. The word 'impose' is revealing, as is his open admission that the Poles had the precedent of Munich keenly in mind. He accepted that it was 'essential for our own good name as well as to satisfy the Poles' that such a settlement should differ from Munich in that the Poles would receive adequate compensation in the west and 'an effective instead of an ineffective guarantee of their future security from the Western Powers as well as from Russia.'[21]

★ ★ ★ ★ ★

How the Western Powers could provide any effective guarantee of Poland's future security was not explained. It was a conception which could be realized only if harmony prevailed after the war between the three major allies. Russia had broken off all relations with the Polish government in London after the Poles had in April 1943 demanded an investigation into the allegations about Katyn. At Tehran, seven months later, Stalin had not scrupled to blame Poland for that request. He alleged, moreover, that the Polish government-in-exile and its adherents had collaborated with the Germans and killed 'Partisans'. Churchill and Eden urged the

Poles to accept with enthusiasm the Soviet offer of a frontier based on the so-called Curzon line; this would leave Lwow (a city with a special significance for many Poles) in the hands of Russia, though Poland would receive large tracts to the west. To the Russians, Eden handed a Polish memorandum refuting the charge that the Underground Movement co-operated with the Germans and attacked Soviet Partisans. Indeed, the Poles said that they wished to co-ordinate the Underground Army's action with the general strategic plans of the Allies, including Russia. No response was received. Seven weeks later, Churchill put forward to Stalin proposals for a settlement between Poland and Russia, suggesting that military co-operation between those two powers might precede the formal resumption of diplomatic relations. Stalin refused to contemplate such a settlement. Nor did the British Ambassador in Moscow fare any better a month later when he asked what instructions the Russians had issued to their forces concerning co-operation with the Polish Underground Movement. Again, no answer came.[22]

The Poles had always retained control of their own wireless and ciphers for communication between Britain and Poland. Occasional suggestions that the British should have copies of the ciphers, so that assurances could be given to the Russians that the Polish government was not fostering anti-Russian or pro-German activities in Poland, were strongly resisted by SOE.[23] Sir Alexander Cadogan, to his credit, believed that it would be out of the question to ask the Poles for all their ciphers, which would be an insulting demand to address to a loyal ally. He also doubted whether, even if the British had the ciphers, Stalin would be willing to accept Britain's word or anybody else's about the good faith of the Polish Underground Movement.[24] Like other organs of the British government, SOE had reliable information that collaboration at local levels between commanders of the Polish Secret Army and units of the Red Army had already been witnessed in Eastern Poland. However, Molotov denied that any such collaboration existed. There seemed no hope of any effective co-ordination at high levels; even personal letters from Churchill to Stalin had availed nothing. Nor had the efforts of the Chiefs of Staff, the Director of Military Intelligence remarking in the spring of 1944 that he received little information from the Russians.[25] The British cast around, but normally without useful result, for ways of bringing the Poles and the Russians into closer harmony.[26]

As the Russian forces moved nearer to areas inhabited by Poles, the arguments for action by the Secret Army gained strength. It would be able to assist operations on the Eastern Front; the Army would by an uprising justify its existence, whereas if it waited for much longer the Russian advance would mean that it had not acted effectively; the Russians might be persuaded that the Polish government, in ordering action by the Army, was endeavouring to co-operate. Many months before the Warsaw uprising, SOE had enquired of the General Officer Commanding in Poland what plans he had for operations to be carried out with the material then available to him, and what might be done by way of larger-scale activity based both upon local resources in Poland and material sent from the West?[27]

Nevertheless, the Chiefs of Staff concluded in early June 1944, as the Allied invasion of Normandy was being launched, that they were too distant from the scene to take responsibility for calling upon the Poles to rise against the Germans, which could be done effectively only in agreement with the Russians. This situation persisted until the last days of July, when the Russians were drawing very near to Warsaw. Stalin told Churchill brusquely that 'the so-called Underground Organisation directed by the Polish Government in London had proved ephemeral and devoid of influence.'[28] Just as the gallant and long-suffering Mikolajczyk was setting off for conversations in Moscow, the Russian government cut the ground from beneath his feet by announcing recognition of the Council of Liberation as the only government to be tolerated in Poland; which Council in its turn immediately denounced the Polish government in London and those who took their orders from it. When Mikolajczyk told Molotov on 31 July that before leaving London he had discussed with General Tabor a rising in the Polish capital, Molotov made no reply but remarked 'Our troops are 10 kilometres from Warsaw.' At a later meeting, when Mikolajczyk pressed desperately for help, Stalin said that he had counted on entering Warsaw on 6 August, but had not succeeded because of the strength of the German reinforcements. According to the Polish records, Stalin confirmed in this same conversation of 9 August that everything possible would be done by the Russian government to send help.[29]

The British had known that the uprising might occur at any moment. General Bor-Komorowski, commanding the Secret Army in Poland, had reported on 21 July that with the further advance of the Red Army and the breaking down of the German defence the battle for Warsaw would soon begin, and with it the uprising. He had decided to carry on fighting against the Germans independently of the political situation and only in relation to the situation at the front, and to ignore hostile acts, including arrests and the disarming of Secret Army units, already carried out by the Russians. General Tabor, himself brought out of Poland in April and now bearing a particular responsibility for the Home Army, had pointed out to Gubbins on 29 July 1944, that the OC intended

> to use [these] considerable forces of the Polish Secret Army in Warsaw to liberate the capital. He expects assistance from the Allies. In putting forward the demands of the OC Secret Army, General Tabor emphasised the absolute need for immediate assistance, stressing that this is a matter of days or even hours.

Well might General Gubbins, whose own sympathies were not in doubt, remind his Polish comrade that the decisions of the Combined Chiefs of Staff had not changed; and that most of the demands just put forward (they included the recognition of the Polish Secret Army as part of the Allied fighting forces, the immediate despatch of an Allied military mission to Warsaw, the bombing of airfields around the capital, the sending of the first Polish Parachute Brigade to Poland) were inseparable from political issues, which depended for decision on the Prime Minister and the War Cabinet.[30]

There is little point in speculating now upon the mixture of motives which determined the nature and timing of the Warsaw rising. It had not been co-ordinated with the Russian General Staff, nor could it easily have been since the Russian government had no diplomatic relations with the Polish government in London. The GOC of the Home Army in Poland knew that the Russians were at the edge of Praga, the eastern outpost of Warsaw. He and his comrades were not alone in failing to foresee the fierceness of the German reaction to the Russian advance, with four panzer divisions brought up swiftly and four further divisions concentrated against the Polish uprising. No doubt the Polish patriots wished to liberate their own capital, to have a Polish administration in place before the Russians took over the city and to hasten the downfall of Germany. Their action, and the indescribable bravery with which it was pursued for the next two months, raised issues of morality and loyalty.

Lord Selborne, now the Minister responsible for the activities of SOE, immediately pointed out to Churchill that Britain's relations with the Polish Secret Army had been similar to those with the French Secret Army, and of the two the Polish was certainly the better organized and more competent:

> A fresh instance of their efficiency has just occurred. The aerodrome in Poland from which the parts of the German secret rocket were brought back last week by S.O.E. was seized and held by a Brigade of the Polish Secret Army for the purpose of this operation. Up to that morning the aerodrome had been in use by the Germans.[31]

Whatever might have been said to Mikolajczyk in Moscow, the Russians would neither help Warsaw directly nor, as events unfolded over the next few weeks, allow the British and Americans to do so through the use of aerodromes in Russian-held territory. What could be done by flights from the United Kingdom and Italy was limited by the long distances, the weather, the strength of the German anti-aircraft defences round Warsaw and other operational factors. Understandably, General Wilson and Air Marshal Slessor in the Mediterranean had concluded within days that what was being urged upon them was 'just not an operation of war and in our view, we should exert pressure on the Russians who are in a much better position to know exactly what is going on in Warsaw, what is required and where it is required.'[32] Neither they nor anyone else then understood how impossible it would prove to exert any effective pressure upon the Russians. Meanwhile, Stalin returned another of his truculent replies to Churchill as messages arrived from Poland reminding the British of their obligations. This is one of them, received in London on 7 August:

> We begin the sixth day of the battle of Warsaw.
> The Germans are introducing into the fight technical means we do not possess – armour, artillery, flame throwers. That is their advantage; we dominate them by the morale of our troops. I state solemnly that Warsaw in fighting does not receive assistance from the Allies in the same way as Poland did not receive it in 1939.
> Our alliance with Great Britain has resulted only in bringing her our assistance in 1940 in repelling the German attack against the

British Isles, in fighting in Norway, in Africa, in Italy and on the Western front.

We request you to state this fact before the British in an official démarche; it should remain as a document.

We do not ask for equipment – we demand its immediate despatch ...[33]

Thereupon the Foreign Secretary wrote to the Prime Minister:

It occurred to us, as of course it has to the Poles themselves, that the Russians may be delaying the occupation of Warsaw in order that the Germans should liquidate a large number of Polish patriots during the present rising in that city who might later on be troublesome to the Russians. I have enquired of the War Office whether there is any military reason for the Russian delay in the capture of Warsaw and I am told that the Germans are making great efforts to hold this nodal point in their communications and that they have surrounded and annihilated a Russian armed force which was advancing on that city.

This, if true, does put Stalin in a slightly better light, although it is odd that he did not say so in his message to you.

Churchill minuted merely 'I agree.'[34]

The Polish Prime Minister and Foreign Minister believed on their return to London that the prospects of a settlement had been improved by their visit to Moscow. It is not altogether easy at this distance of time to understand why; and Mikolajczyk did say immediately that it was essential for the Soviet Government to assist the Poles fighting in Warsaw. 'If no help were forthcoming from the Soviet side it would irremediably harm Russo-Polish relations.' Stalin had repeated to them that he wished to see a democratic and independent Poland, and that he attached importance to Poland's retention of her alliances with the United Kingdom and France and her friendly relations with the USA. Both Stalin and Mikolajczyk had been anxious to avoid a deadlock at that stage over the frontier questions, and Stalin had offered Poland East Prussia (excluding the district around Konigsberg), upper Silesia, the whole of lower Silesia and some territory on the west bank of the Oder.[35]

Eden sent another telegram to Moscow, asking the Ambassador to impress on the Russians the very serious view taken in London of their attitude and 'our deep anxiety regarding the probable effect not only upon Polish-Soviet but also upon future Anglo-Soviet relations.' He pointed out that the Russian government had hitherto condemned the inactivity of the Polish underground movement. What was to be made of the constant exhortations of the Soviet press and wireless to the Polish population to rise and attack the Germans? Especially in view of the undertakings just given by Stalin to Mikolajczyk, the complete absence of Russian assistance would be 'misinterpreted and seriously prejudice future Polish-Soviet relations. Nor can we see any justification whatever for the Soviet government's decision to refuse the necessary facilities required by our American allies to make their contribution to relieve Warsaw.'

The Foreign Secretary also dwelt on the effect of the Russian attitude upon the position of Mikolajczyk and therefore on the prospect of an eventual solution of the Polish problems. After all, Mikolajczyk had come back from Moscow

> with a determination to base his future policy upon faith in Soviet good intentions and was prepared to go very far with his colleagues in London to bring about a solution in the sense desired by the Soviet government.
>
> His main trump card in playing his difficult hand was Marshal Stalin's undertaking to send help to Warsaw. ... If the present Soviet attitude is maintained I fear M. Mikolajczyk's personal position will be fatally harmed ...
>
> Important sections of British Parliamentary and public opinion of all political parties are already showing grave anxiety over the Warsaw situation and apparent Soviet inaction. We have hitherto done our best to present the facts in the most favourable possible light ...[36]

However, Vyshinski (the Vice-Commissar for Foreign Affairs in Moscow) had already told the American Ambassador that the insurrection had been 'purely the work of adventurers and the Soviet government cannot lend its hand to it.' He turned down not only the request that American aircraft dropping supplies in Poland should be allowed to land in Russia, but also the proposal for an operation by the Russian forces. In vain did the British and American Ambassadors point out that if this became known, 'hostile voices would be raised and colour would be lent to the false story that the Red Army were holding back from Warsaw for reasons of policy.' To this suggestion Vyshinski retorted that even now the Soviet Union and the Red Army were being slandered and that it was impossible to put a limit on that kind of meanness; in this connection he mentioned the Vatican, the Polish press and British and American newspapers. When the British Ambassador remarked that Stalin had told Mikolajczyk he would help, whereas Vyshinski now condemned the rising, the latter pretended not to understand the point.[37] Two days later, Stalin stated that the actions in Warsaw constituted a reckless adventure from which the Soviet High Command dissociated itself entirely.[38] According to a message which reached London on the next day, Russian aircraft dropped leaflets in Warsaw describing the rising as the work of an irresponsible clique in London and encouraging the population to cease resistance.[39]

At least one high officer of SOE believed that in their anxiety to help General Bor in Warsaw, Polish officers in London had sent all manner of promises and were now blaming the British in order to cover themselves.[40] The situation during August was somewhat confused by direct approaches made by the Poles in London to the Air Ministry, almost certainly because of misunderstanding about the role of SOE.[41] Meanwhile, appeals from Warsaw reached London without cease. 'The soldiers and the population look hopelessly at the skies expecting help from the Allies' read one of them. 'On the background of smoke they see only German aircraft. They are surprised, feel deeply depressed and begin to revile.' Forwarding this to the Prime Minister, Lord Selborne appealed for extra help.[42] Later in the month, the War Cabinet received through Eden messages from Sergeant J. Ward of the RAF, who had for three years worked in the Polish Underground Army. These were at once sober and piteous. 'There are thousands of civilian wounded men, women and children suffering from the most horrible burns and in some cases from shrapnel and bullet wounds.' 'On the outskirts of the city are huge concentration camps full of women and children living in the open air without food or help of any kind. They are dying of hunger and disease under the most terrible conditions. The Germans show no mercy to these helpless people.'[43] Although the British press was told roundly by Churchill's confidant Brendan Bracken, Minister of Information, that it was 'a foul lie' to assert that the Polish government in London had foolishly given orders for a premature rising in Warsaw, the same minister doubted whether the newspapers would believe what the Polish government's propagandists said about Warsaw's agony; and the people whom he termed 'Uncle Joe's newspaper friends' would be spurred on to attack the Poles.[44]

According to the Air Ministry's information, 161 aircraft had flown missions to Warsaw during August. Eighty had dropped their precious cargoes successfully, in or near Warsaw and in other parts of Poland; 27 had been lost. The strengthened anti-aircraft defences in and around Warsaw ruled out low flying for the proposed American operations; it would be necessary to drop the supplies from 10,000 feet, which meant that the large bulk of such stores would probably not land in Polish-held areas; and since the American aircraft did not have the range to make a return flight to Britain, they would require authorization to land in Russian territory. It is depressing but necessary to record that the Allied planes were regularly shot at by the Russians as well as the Germans. No British aircraft could make the return journey from Britain to Warsaw without additional petrol tanks, to fit which would reduce substantially the number of containers carried, though Lancasters could just manage the flight from Britain to Warsaw and onwards to a landing in Italy.[45]

Before the end of August, Roosevelt had declined to join WSC in a strong message to Stalin, which he thought would not prove 'advantageous to the long-range general war prospect.' Long afterwards, Churchill recorded that though the Cabinet had met together on many unpleasant affairs, he did not remember any occasion when such deep anger had been shown by all the members as on the evening of 4 September. He would have liked to say to the Russians 'We are sending our aeroplanes to land in your territory, after delivering supplies to Warsaw. If you do not treat them properly all convoys [to the northern ports of Russia] will be stopped from this moment by us.' In fact, he did not propose this drastic step, though he concedes that it might have been effective: 'The reader of these pages in after-years must realise that everyone always has to keep in mind the fortunes of millions of men fighting in a world-wide struggle, and that terrible and even humbling submissions must at times be made to the general aim.'[46]

To a further appeal sent after the Cabinet's meeting, the Russian reply brought little comfort. Nor did it answer the telling point that up to the moment of the Warsaw rising, Soviet propaganda had been calling on the Poles to take up arms. On 9 September, Molotov rehearsed all the military difficulties but did say at last that if the British and Americans were convinced that the dropping of weapons and food would be effective, the Soviet command would be prepared to organize that jointly with the British and Americans. Such aid would, however, have to be rendered in accordance with pre-arranged plans. He again refused to accept any responsibility for what he too called the Warsaw adventure. Indeed, he put the blame upon the British, for failing to ensure that the Soviet command was warned of the rising in good time. There followed sentences of the most blatant cynicism. That Churchill and his colleagues were prepared to endure such taunts is eloquent of their urgent desire to stay on friendly terms with the Russians: 'Why did the British Government not find it necessary to warn the Soviet Government of this? Was it not', asked the Foreign Minister of the government which had itself ordered the execution of the Polish officers, 'a repetition of what happened in April 1943 when Polish Émigré Government, in the absence of resistance on the part of the British Government, came out with their slanderous statement hostile to the USSR about Katyn?'[47]

The British Ambassador in Moscow commented in his optimistic way that while the Russians were still not 'grown up enough to come clean when they know that they have made a bad mistake', the whole thing gave him fresh hopes for a settlement with Poland.[48] To Eden the apparent change of heart in Moscow seemed a triumph for Britain's persistence;[49] the Russian forces did give some assistance to Warsaw in September but too late to make any serious difference. Churchill told Parliament on 26 September that when Russian operational plans permitted and direct contact had been established with the Polish Commander-in-Chief in Warsaw, the Soviet armies had sent supplies to the Polish forces and provided them with air cover and anti-aircraft support. A few days later, after the resistance had come to its end, the Prime Minister paid a tribute to the heroic conduct of the Poles under inconceivable conditions of hardship, but remarked again: 'Despite all the efforts of the Soviet Army, the strong German positions on the Vistula could not be taken, and relief could not come in time.'[50]

Warsaw had held out for 62 days. That the Germans should have reasserted their control there constituted a military defeat. For the Polish resistance, the events of August and September constituted a most serious but not mortal blow, even though General Bor himself had been captured, some members of his headquarters staff killed and others taken prisoner. Scattering elsewhere in Poland, the remainder fought on. A great part of the city had been ruined in the fighting, and after 2 October the Germans destroyed much of the rest. Many civilians were deported to Germany, while the Gestapo hunted down the remaining members of the Home Army.[51] 'This is the stark truth', stated one of the last broadcasts received from Warsaw,

> We were treated worse than Hitler's satellites, worse than Italy, Roumania, Finland. May God, Who is just, pass judgement on the terrible injustice suffered by the Polish nation, and may He punish accordingly all those who are guilty. ... Immortal is the nation that can muster such universal heroism. For those who have died have conquered, and those who live on will fight on, will conquer and again bear witness that Poland lives when the Poles live.[52]

Churchill's Private Secretary describes the Russian actions simply as 'one of the vilest double-crosses in history', and contends that the tragedy in Warsaw convinced Churchill that an enduring Russian danger had now to be faced. The Prime Minister later said that this treacherous episode had finally revealed to him the chasm which divided the Western from the Soviet code of honour.[53] Perhaps so; all the same, the records of the time leave a different impression.

As Eden had foreseen, the position of Mikolajczyk was undermined by Russia's behaviour. The Prime Minister and Foreign Secretary alike urged him to stand firm among his colleagues, and could see no hope of making progress with the Russians so long as General Sosnkowski remained in office. For his part, Mikolajczyk said he would have to resign if Sosnkowski were not dismissed. Eden pressed on the Polish President Rackiewicz the argument that a position in which a C.-in-C. with independent authority pursued a different policy from that of the Polish government must be remedied. Sosnkowski's dismissal was announced on 28 September.[54]

★ ★ ★ ★ ★

Hardly had the tragedy in Warsaw drawn to its conclusion than Churchill and Eden took off for Moscow. Stalin took pains to give the Prime Minister a colourable explanation; evidence now available suggests that it was at least partially true. In conversation after an ample dinner at the British Embassy on 11 October he explained that the failure to relieve Warsaw had not been due to any lack of effort by the Red Army, but rather to German strength and the difficulties of the terrain. He could not admit this failure before the world. Exactly the same situation had arisen at Kiev, which in the end had been liberated only by an out-flanking movement. Whatever may have been felt by the War Cabinet, the Prime Minister said that he accepted this view absolutely and assured Stalin that no serious persons in the United Kingdom had credited reports that failure had been deliberate. Criticism had only referred to the apparent unwillingness of the Soviet government to send aircraft. Mr Harriman, acting as an observer on Roosevelt's behalf, said the same was true of people in America. Perhaps hoping for some gesture of reciprocity, Churchill and Eden tried to impress upon Stalin how essential it was that the Polish question should 'now be settled on a basis which would seem reasonable to the British people.' Later that evening, Eden argued with the Russian Foreign Minister that Mikolajczyk should not return to London but form a new government and then proceed to Lublin. Mikolajczyk, countered Molotov, had on his previous visit to Moscow given the impression of being willing but weak.[55]

Whatever his sympathy for the Poles, WSC was confident that he and Eden had reached more intimate terms with the Russians than ever before. The Prime Minister apparently credited a remark of Stalin that he and Molotov were the only two in the inner circle of Russian policy in favour of dealing 'softly' with Poland, was convinced by Stalin's expressions of personal esteem and believed that the Russian leader had to pay attention to strong pressures from the Communist party and the military.[56] Mikolajczyk had meanwhile been summoned to Moscow, under the threat that if he declined to come the British government would wash its hands of any further responsibility towards the Polish government in London. The Polish records of Churchill's conversations with him in Moscow that October make painful reading. Of the substance there can unhappily be no doubt. Churchill admitted at the time that he had been 'pretty rough with Mikolajczyk. He was obstinate and I lost my temper.' Nine years later, when he was again Prime Minister but recovering from a stroke, Mikolajczyk's account of the meetings in Moscow was read to WSC, and then at his request repeated. 'Does he exaggerate?' asked Lord Moran. Churchill replied 'You see we were both very angry.'[57]

The British had encouraged themselves and others to believe in a Russia which did not exist. The Atlantic Charter, the solemn pledges that territories should be transferred only with the consent of the peoples involved, the earnest belief that a world of free elections and democratic government would be the fruit of victory – all this was integral to the war effort of Britain, the United States and many other powers. To Russia, it was not. For those who lived at a distance, there might even be an element of irony, mingled with hope, in conceiving of Stalin's Russia as a pillar of international order or an upholder of individual rights. The point is perfectly caught in the reaction of the Permanent Under-Secretary of the Foreign Office, Sir Alexander Cadogan, after he had read a despatch in the summer of 1943 which showed the overwhelming probability that the Russians had been responsible for the murders at Katyn:

> I pointed out that, years before Katyn, the Soviet Government made a habit of butchering their own citizens by the 10,000's, and if we could fling ourselves into their arms in 1941, I don't know that Katyn makes our position more delicate. The blood of Russians cries as loud to Heaven as that of Poles. But it is very nasty. How can Poles ever live amicably alongside Russians, and how can we discuss with Russians execution of German 'war criminals', when we have condoned this?[58]

How indeed? On the plane of morality, there could be no convincing answer to those questions. On the plane of practicality, which dictated that the British, the Americans and the Russians must somehow fight the war together, there could be and was an answer; but it was one which lasted only as long as those powers needed each other for the common purpose. However little the British or Americans cared to avow it, the acceptance of Russia's demands in respect of Poland had become not a matter of morality or common sense, but of bowing to Russia's military presence and Stalin's will of steel. The facts of geography and distribution of the races fitted ill with the imperatives of politics and strategy. It could scarcely be denied, if the wishes of the populations were to be the guiding principle, that Poland should have Wilno, Bialystok and Lwow. By contrast, it was not at all clear that Poland should have, say, East Prussia or the German part of Pomerania.

Eden concedes that Churchill used 'every method of argument and menace on the frontier question' with the Polish ministers.[59] Indeed, WSC asked Mikolajczyk to recognize that Britain was supporting the Russian attitude towards Poland's eastern frontier 'not because Soviet Russia is strong but because she is right and because a solution on this basis provides the best guarantee for future of Poland which His Majesty's Government are anxious to see prosperous'. When on a later occasion Mikolajczyk stated that he and his colleagues could not deprive themselves of Polish territory or agree to join the Lublin Committee, Churchill threatened to wash his hands of them. 'Because of quarrels between Poles we are not going to wreck the peace of Europe. In your obstinacy you do not see what is at stake. It is not in friendship that we shall part. We shall tell the world how unreasonable you are. You will start another war in which 25 million lives will be lost. But you don't care.'

When – modestly enough, we may think – Mikolajczyk asked 'Would it not be possible to proclaim that the three Great Powers have decided on the frontiers of Poland without our presence?', he received the reply 'We will be sick and tired of you if you go on arguing.' Later that afternoon, Churchill spoke to Mikolajczyk still more vehemently and woundingly: 'You do not care about the future of Europe, you have only your own miserable interests in mind ... In this war what is your contribution to the Allied effort? ... You may withdraw your divisions if you like. You are absolutely incapable of facing facts. Never in my life have I seen such people ... You hate the Russians.' And on yet another occasion: 'You only deserve to be in your Pripet marshes.'[60]

In judging what was said and done about Poland in these days, it is right to remember all the other great issues then fermenting and the supreme importance attached to Stalin's promise, repeated at Moscow, that after the defeat of Germany Russia would enter the war against Japan. We must trust that there was more than an element of diplomatic tact in Churchill's letters to Stalin after this visit. One of them referred to 'our very pleasant talks together' and stated that 'my hopes for the future alliance of our peoples never stood so high'; and another that the memorable meeting in Moscow had shown 'that there are no matters which cannot be adjusted between us when we meet together in frank and intimate discussion.'[61]

Warsaw had been crushed. All the same, the flame of Polish resistance still burned, and General Tabor pleaded for the resumption of flights from Britain, in addition to the effort being made from Southern Italy; not on a large scale, but as a supplement. The Prime Minister had urged Lord Selborne to do everything he could to support the Polish Home Army in the western part of the country. When the Secretary of State for Air refused the proposal, Selborne argued the case again:

I only ask that, on the very few nights when it is possible to fly from this country to Poland, this shall be done within the limits of existing resources. I urge this for reason of politics and morale rather than those of strategy. I am sure that you will agree that we political chiefs must weigh the technical advice we get from our experts against these considerations sometimes. Poland put her shirt on Britain in 1939. Have we not a debt to repay?[62]

In his correspondence with WSC, Selborne drew pointed attention to the paucity of help being made available for the Polish Home Army; since the end of September only eight successful sorties had been made to Poland from Italy, dropping a mere ten tons of supplies. Russian permission had already been asked to fly over Hungary for these purposes, and had been peremptorily refused. General Tabor argued vehemently that the Poles most required money and medicines. 'However impractical Polish politicians may be,' the Minister wrote to Churchill, 'their Services have fought with us with the utmost gallantry on many fronts, and I fear that if we do not make more strenuous efforts to help them even at some loss to ourselves, the Polish people will feel not without cause that we have let them down.'[63]

This was the situation at the moment of Mikolajczyk's long-heralded, and by the British deeply regretted, resignation at the end of November. Thereupon flights to Poland were suspended for a time. Little could be done unless Stalin would withdraw the ban on flights over Russian-held territory; but given the character of the new Polish administration in London (and, we may add, given the way in which the Russians had chosen for many months past to interpret Polish affairs) it might well, as Eden expressed it at the time, have caused 'misunderstanding of our attitude in Russian minds if we were to choose this particular moment to approach them with proposals for maintaining our assistance to the Polish Underground Movement.'

He nevertheless wished that Polish crews should be allowed to resume operations to Poland by the longer and more dangerous route from Italy over German-held territory. Lord Selborne supported this, as did Churchill.[64] The Russian advance to Budapest had placed the Red Army in control of areas which Allied aircraft needed to traverse on their journeys to Poland from Southern Italy. For most of the month of November, the Allied air forces continued to seek permission to fly behind Russian lines on the way to targets in Poland, the only alternative being to run the gauntlet of the German night fighter defences between Vienna and Cracow. The Russian general staff eventually declined, stating that by far the greater part of the supplies sent to Poland fell into the hands of the Germans or of the 'so-called partisans' fighting against the Red Army. The Chief of the Air Staff wrote to Churchill 'If it is politically necessary that we should continue to supply the Poles by air, I suggest that we ought to try to get this absurd decision reversed.'[65]

By that stage Russian policy had become impossible to reconcile with the most cautious interpretations of those 'very pleasant' conversations held in Moscow less than two months before. Stalin in a message to Churchill referred to 'terrorists encouraged by the Polish émigrés' who 'kill our people in Poland and carry on a criminal fight against the Soviet troops which are liberating Poland.' There followed a statement from the Russians that in proposing a line running from north to south down Eastern Germany which should not be crossed by Allied bombers, they had it in mind to prevent aircraft from reaching Poland. The Foreign Secretary understood the issue – 'The Russians have clearly shown their desire to prevent us sending further assistance to the Polish Underground Movement' – but confessed his uncertainty about the best method of handling such a situation. Only if Churchill approached Stalin would there be any hope of sustaining a reasonably effective support to the Poles, and even that method seemed unlikely to succeed; indeed, it might only prejudice the bombing of German oil refineries in Silesia, because the Russians could readily prevent that by maintaining a stiff attitude about over-flying. The military advantages of sending supplies to Poland were small, the political and moral aspects another matter. To abandon the Polish Underground Army might well arouse serious discontent among the large Polish forces serving elsewhere with the Allies; there would be considerable criticism when it became known that the British had suspended help to Poland and acquiesced without question in the Soviet attitude. Yet if they resumed flights from Italy via the longer route, or direct flights from Britain, they would be sending supplies to Poland in direct opposition to the views of Stalin and the Russian High Command.[66]

Stalin in a message of 8 December had condemned Mikolajczyk's 'negative role'. As for the Polish ministerial changes in London, they were to him

> not of serious interest. That is still the same process of marking time by people who have lost touch with the national soil and have no contact with the Polish people. At the same time the Polish Committee of National Liberation has achieved notable successes in strengthening its national democratic organisations on Polish territory, in the practical carrying out of land reform for the benefit of the peasants and in broadening the organisation of its Polish forces, and it exercises great authority among the Polish population.

> I think that now our task consists in backing up the Polish National Committee at Lublin and all those who are willing and able to work with them.[67]

To Parliament on 15 December 1944, Churchill admitted the words he had spoken on his return from Moscow – 'The most urgent and burning question was of course that of Poland, and here again I speak words of hope, of hope reinforced by confidence' – no longer held true to the same degree. He regretted that Mikolajczyk had not been able to return promptly in early November after the 'very friendly conversations which had passed between the Polish leader and Stalin'. He lamented the resignations of Mikolajczyk and a number of other Polish ministers. He confessed that the solutions so long recommended by Britain would entail the 'disentanglement of populations', with several millions of people affected, and the complete expulsion of the Germans from the area to be acquired by Poland in the west and the north. 'For expulsion is the method which, so far as we have been able to see, will be the most satisfactory and lasting. There will be no mixture of populations to cause endless trouble ... A clean sweep will be made.' As for the future,

> We have never weakened in any way in our resolve that Poland shall be restored and stand erect as a sovereign, independent nation, free to model her social institutions or any other institutions in any way her people choose, provided, I must say, that these are not on Fascist lines, and provided that Poland stands loyally as a barrier and friend of Russia against German aggression from the west.[68]

* * * * *

The melancholy coda needs no lengthy description. The Lublin Committee, regarded by the British as mere creatures of Moscow, became the provisional government of Poland. At last, British observer parties had gone into the western part of the country and the Polish armed forces continued to fight doughtily on the Western Front, in Italy and elsewhere.[69] At Yalta, Stalin affirmed that the advance of the Red Army and the liberation of Poland had completely changed the mood of the people there. It was promised that the provisional government would be reorganized on a broader democratic basis, and that free and unfettered elections would soon be held. The assurances given by Stalin and Molotov were belied within weeks. By mid-March, Churchill was telegraphing to Roosevelt about 'a great failure and an utter breakdown of what was settled at Yalta.'[70] Leading representatives of the Polish Underground were tricked into attending a meeting, spirited away from Poland to Russia and eventually admitted in early May to be 'undergoing investigation in Moscow'.

After a trial of the usual kind, most were sentenced in June, Stalin paying no more heed to Churchill's remonstrances than he did to the British attempts at Potsdam to restrict Poland's frontier to the Eastern Neisse. So much for the effective guarantees from the Western Powers as well as Russia; so much for the free elections and enlarged government of the new democratic Poland. Though Mikolajczyk and others had accepted the loss of the eastern provinces, Poland had been in truth little more consulted than Czechoslovakia in 1938 over the detachment of the Sudetenland. Unlike Czechoslovakia, Poland had received substantial compensation, but only at the price of extensive violations of the Atlantic Charter and the Allies' own professions.

What was done in 1945, as in 1938, was largely dictated by geography and military strength. Both transactions were more than merely opportunist, for in each case those who bore the responsibility in Britain believed that the prospect of harmony between the great powers, or even an armed truce, must be preferred to unavailing defence of other principles. 'I do not suppose,' said WSC to his daughter Sarah during the fateful conference at Yalta, 'that at any moment in history has the agony of the world been so great or so widespread. Tonight the sun goes down on more suffering than ever before in the world.'[71] Whatever may have been claimed later, Britain did not during the war, or even at Potsdam, base her policy upon a firm conviction of Russian ill-faith. There was a genuine admiration, not least on Churchill's part, for Stalin and his supposed moderation and prudence. There was a profound irritation with the Poles for adhering to a different view, or for their passion for the retention of Lwow. How could they be so unreasonable, so obstinate, so unpractical?

Thus the British and Americans and others were led into courses which could then and can now be defended on the ground that necessity knows no law. We may well concede that there was little choice, that the statesmen were grappling with immense imponderables. Humbling submissions were indeed called for; the suppression of the near-certainty about the events at Katyn, for example, with everything such knowledge signified. While recognizing the pressures under which Churchill and the War Cabinet worked, we are not called upon to admire everything that was said and done in respect of Poland. The least required by the facts is a thankful acknowledgement of Polish valour throughout the war and of the unquenchable spirit with which Poland bore her tribulations then and afterwards, tribulations not easily understood on this side of the English Channel. A test of Polish opinion after the collapse of the Russian empire showed that, despite years of unrelenting denigration, those who rose up against their oppressors are regarded not as the glorious defeated but as patriots who fell for their homeland's independence, even though that was not recovered for two generations.[72]

7

The Bitter Fruit of Victory

Churchill and an Unthinkable Operation, 1945

When the documents about Operation Unthinkable were released in London, the newspaper which first gave extensive coverage to them carried the headline 'Churchill's plan for Third World War against Stalin' and explained that he had in May 1945 ordered 'his War Cabinet to draw up contingency plans for an offensive against Stalin that would lead to the "elimination of Russia"…'[1]

Reverberations were heard from every part of the world, often in scandalized tones. Some believed that the Prime Minister had sought a war with Russia but was deterred by military advice; many took the very notion of such a war as proof of Churchill's entrenched hostility towards Russia. Some mistakenly imagined, as *The Daily Telegraph* had done, that the matter preoccupied the War Cabinet. Many assumed that this subject had previously been enveloped in secrecy. However, we have only to turn to the diaries of the Chief of the Imperial General Staff, published half a century ago, to find the following entry:

> *May 24th [1945]* This evening I went carefully through the Planners' Report on the possibility of taking on Russia should trouble arise in our future discussions with her. We were instructed to carry out this investigation. The idea is of course fantastic and the chances of success quite impossible. There is no doubt that from now onwards Russia is all powerful in Europe.[2]

That the alliance with Russia had been a troubled one from the beginning is well attested. It could hardly have been otherwise, since Russia had been at least a friendly neutral towards Germany until June 1941, had supplied the German war machine with essential raw materials, partitioned Poland, attacked Finland and annexed the Baltic States. Once Barbarossa began, and after Pearl Harbour a little less than six months later, the position was transformed. Britain and the Commonwealth no longer stood alone against Germany; the latent strength of the United States began to make itself felt; the new theatres of war embraced South and South-East Asia, the Far East, Australasia, the whole Pacific; and Russia bore on land, though not at sea or in the air, a far heavier burden than any other partner in the coalition, with a loss of life running into many millions. For roughly two years, from the summer of 1941 until the successful conclusion of the North African campaign, frictions and misunderstandings abounded but were (as Churchill would have expressed it) drowned in the cannonade. Once the tide of the war had begun to turn, the issue of Russia's post-war relations with the West attracted the attention of the planners in London. The sensitivities were all too obvious.

When in the autumn of 1943 the Chiefs of Staff Committee accepted a proposal that a paper on this subject should be prepared, it was laid down that the enquiry must be conducted with the greatest secrecy and on the basis 'that it remained the policy of HMG to foster and maintain the friendliest possible relations with the USSR'. More than seven months passed before the first version was produced; it was submitted to the Chiefs of Staff and partly rewritten during the month of May 1944, and returned in a revised version on 6 June, the day upon which Operation Overlord was launched.[3] At that time, no one knew how quickly the war might end. Many good judges believed that it would be over before Christmas. So it might have been, if the attempt on Hitler's life in July had succeeded, or if the Allies had been able to break out more swiftly and decisively from their bridgehead in Normandy; in which event the political situation in Europe after the war would have been markedly different, with the Red Army far to the east of the line which it eventually reached.

Given the possibility that the European war might finish within a few weeks, and the near-certainty that it would be won within a twelvemonth, a tension developed in the Post-Hostilities Planning Sub-Committee. The representatives of the armed services believed that Britain must take account of the possibility, however remote, of Russia as an eventual enemy; whereas the chairman of the Sub-Committee, that rising star of the Foreign Office Mr Gladwyn Jebb, felt certain that his department would not accept such a hypothesis, on the grounds that it would be politically dangerous and not in accordance with the facts.[4] A draft paper had pointed out that apart from a resurgent Germany or Japan, only two nations could for the foreseeable future constitute a serious threat to the British Commonwealth: the USSR and the USA. 'It is quite clear that it is not within the power of the British Commonwealth to support a war against the Soviet Union unaided by either the United States or Allies on the Continent of Europe.' The next sentence of the same paper indicates the balancing and theoretical nature of such studies, for it reads:

Neither is it conceivable that the British Commonwealth could go to war against the United States unless at least supported by the Soviet Union and assisted by the other European States. It would therefore appear to be idle for us to plan on the assumption that the British Commonwealth stands alone.

The Post-Hostilities Staff argued that on balance relations with Russia were rather more liable to deteriorate than those with the United States, and that a serious threat against Britain from Russia would amount also to one against the USA. It was probable that in the long run America would be prepared to fight to maintain the existence of the United Kingdom, although that assumption could not be absolutely relied upon. The policy of the British government at the time assumed a tripartite alliance for the post-war period between the Commonwealth, the United States and the Soviet Union, and to plan on that basis, or at any rate to assume a fairly close association between the three great powers 'would accordingly seem to be the most reasonable course.' As the authors of the paper pointed out, Russia might at some stage break away from this alliance and become a potential or even an actual enemy; but they saw no evidence of a Russian desire to dominate the world. The Chiefs of Staff in the middle of June 1944 approved a version which stated that 'The British Commonwealth should maintain adequate naval and air strength to secure our vital interests vis-à-vis Russia.'[5]

In these assessments, no attempt had been made to deal with the possibility that Russia might try to extend her influence over Western

Europe and thus dominate that continent, or Asia through the development of Siberia. The Vice-Chiefs of Staff mentioned as vital strategic interests, which might be threatened by Russia, the supply of oil from the Middle East; Mediterranean communications; sea communications (if Russia were to become after the war a naval and air power of the first rank); and the concentrated industrial areas of the British Isles (if Russia built up a large strategic bomber force). The Vice-Chiefs concluded, with the authority of the Chiefs of Staff themselves, that the best means of avoiding friction would be 'a real endeavour to secure the full and friendly participation of the U.S.S.R. in any system of world security.' It followed that Britain should not oppose reasonable demands of the USSR where these did not conflict with the crucial strategic interests of the United Kingdom itself. Russia in exchange would be expected 'not to oppose our claims in areas vital to us.' It was rather uneasily acknowledged that the weakness of Europe after the war would leave a vacuum which Russia, if she wished, might fill and this was the context in which it was stated that the Commonwealth should maintain adequate naval and air strength to secure its interests. At the head of the document stood a note in capital letters: THIS PAPER IS A STAFF STUDY. IT IS PURELY EXPLORATORY, HAS NO MINISTERIAL AUTHORITY AND IS NOT INTENDED TO BE THE BASIS OF ANY EXECUTIVE ACTION.[6]

By the end of July 1944, with the Allied armies strongly established in France, we find the Chief of the Imperial General Staff discussing with the Secretary of State for War the crucial question: should Germany be dismembered or gradually converted into an ally to meet the Russian danger? The CIGS felt no doubt on the point. Germany to his mind was no longer the dominating power in Europe; Russia was, and with her vast resources could not fail to become the main threat in 15 years' time:

Therefore foster Germany, gradually build her up, and bring her into a Federation of Western Europe. Unfortunately this must all be done under the cloak of a holy alliance between England, Russia and America. Not an easy policy, and one requiring a super Foreign Secretary![7]

In justice to Field-Marshal Brooke, let us acknowledge at once that his prescription was close to the policy followed by Labour and Conservative governments alike after 1945, whereas in 1944 the view of the Foreign Office remained that provided the British Commonwealth and the United States gave reasonable consideration to Russian views and showed themselves determined to prevent any menace to Russia from Germany or Japan, the USSR would welcome a lengthy spell of peaceful relations. The grounds given were convincing enough: that Russia would need a prolonged period for her rehabilitation and internal development, during which time she would not be likely to risk the interruption of a major war. All this depended, however, upon Russia's being satisfied with the measures taken to render Germany and Japan innocuous; and if she were not thus satisfied, she might well become an intensely disruptive force within Europe and beyond its boundaries. The Foreign Office had predicted 'with some confidence' that for at least five years after the end of the war Russia would constitute no menace to Britain's strategic interests. 'So far as can be judged at present,' one of the Foreign Office papers remarked, perhaps with a certain sly humour, 'she is most unlikely to be troubled by internal disorders.' The Joint Intelligence Sub-Committee, the purpose of which was to gather intelligence from a wide range of sources and over which a senior representative of the Foreign Office presided, had seen no occasion to disagree with those opinions; nor did that Committee change its view when it produced an assessment in late August 1944. As it nevertheless pointed out, Russia would possess the capacity to wage war against the British Commonwealth. The area in which friction could most easily arise would be the Middle East, particularly in Persia and Iraq. If Russia struck in those two countries, she would be in a position to threaten seriously British communications through the Mediterranean to India and the Far East.[8] Time and again we notice the assumption that 'the British Commonwealth' constituted, if not a unit, at least an association of states which would act together in vital matters.

As Germany's defeat drew near, the politicians and the military alike had to reconsider their assumptions about Russia's attitude. Certainly there was nothing consoling in the Russian government's behaviour during the Warsaw uprising, though that was a matter which Churchill and Eden put firmly behind them. The Prime Minister evidently believed that there was no point in pursuing such disputes when greater issues – including Britain's capacity to secure reasonable treatment for Poland itself – were at stake. Stalin denied most earnestly that Russia wished to convert the world to Communism. 'We could not, if we wanted,' he said to Churchill. 'We Russians are not as clever as you think; we're simple, rather stupid. No one in Europe can be persuaded that England is either simple or stupid.'[9] This was the visit during which Stalin and Churchill reached the 'percentages agreement'; it dealt with spheres of influence in the Balkans, was intended to apply only while the war raged, and gave Britain the predominant voice in Greece. WSC was impressed in the coming months by the fact that in respect of Greece Stalin stood by their bargain. In London, the Chiefs of Staff had considered the threat to British security if Russia became aggressive; a meeting held in the Foreign Office in October 1944 had come only to the conclusion that until directions were given by the War Cabinet, no firm assumptions could be made about Russia in documents dealing with the post-war period. The Chiefs of Staff were told to restrict to the narrowest possible limits any papers in which the hypothesis of Russia as a possible enemy was mentioned.[10]

The British Ambassador in Moscow, Sir Archibald Clark Kerr, normally at least fair and perhaps more than fair to the Russian government, remarked that the latter had since 1941 shown no jealousy of Britain's strength as a great power. Indeed, Russian propaganda had abandoned almost all criticism of Britain on the charge of Imperialist designs. He believed that so long as Britain pursued an anti-German policy in collaboration with Russia, that attitude would persist. The Russians would claim to organize an orbit of power in the regions adjacent to their borders, and would leave the British at liberty to pursue a similar policy along the Atlantic and Mediterranean seaboards.[11]

When the Joint Intelligence Sub-Committee rendered another assessment just before Christmas 1944, it confessed that the British had little evidence to show what view Russia took of her own strategic interests or what policy she intended to pursue after the war. Russia would at that stage present a phenomenon new in modern history: a land empire containing within its own frontiers a large and rapidly growing population, possessing nearly all the raw materials essential to a war economy and with an industry capable of sustaining armies larger than those of any other power in Europe. The Sub-Committee pointed to Russia's immense advantages in depth of defence and dispersal of economically important targets, issues which the war in Europe since 1939 had thrown into sharp relief; and even the exceptions – the oilfields of the Caucasus, the industry and minerals of the Ukraine, the industrial areas of Moscow and Leningrad – were far less vulnerable to attack than the corresponding areas of any other country in Europe.

Nonetheless, the Sub-Committee felt confident that Russia would at least try out a policy of collaboration after the war with America and Britain. She would regard Finland, Poland, Czechoslovakia, Hungary, Rumania, Bulgaria and to a lesser extent Yugoslavia as forming a protective screen, and would wish to dominate the Black Sea and control Northern Persia. If the other great powers were prepared to accept Russia's dominance in those areas and follow a policy designed to prevent a revival of German and Japanese military strength, Russia would have achieved

> the greatest possible measure of security and could not hope to increase it by further territorial expansion. Nor is it easy to see what else Russia could under such conditions hope to gain from a policy of aggression … Russia's relations with the British Empire and the United States will depend very largely on the ability of each side to convince the other of the sincerity of its desire for collaboration.[12]

From the Embassy in Moscow, Mr Jock Balfour, Clark Kerr's deputy, reminded the Foreign Office in January 1945 that Russia looked upon South-East Europe, no less than upon Poland, as a zone in which it was to her peculiar interest to see there was no renewal of the German drive towards the East; self-confidence in the Soviet Union had been immeasurably increased by victory; but he took Stalin to be a shrewd realist who had no wish to overreach the limits within which he could prudently exercise autocratic power.[13] On this latter and crucial point the Prime Minister held a similar view.

Under the Anglo-Soviet Treaty of 1942, it had been agreed that the two governments would furnish each other with information about weapons. The agreement had never been entirely fulfilled by the British, chiefly because of the difficulty of obtaining the assent of the Americans to the disclosure of information in which the United States was interested. Nonetheless, the British and Americans had done far more than the Russians, who in most cases had failed to reply to repeated requests for information. The situation at the time of the Yalta Conference was that, since the summer of 1941, the British had disclosed about 300 major items, many of them of the first importance (such as radar), whereas the Russians had given practically no information of value. Hence the dismaying, almost farcical, fact that British information about important items of Russian equipment was based upon German publications.[14] It would not be difficult to multiply such instances, or to demonstrate the apprehensions of the Prime Minister. Yet the British delegation came home convinced that they had secured the best terms obtainable for Poland and, more generally, convinced of Russia's good faith. On the evidence presently available to us, it was the events of late February and March 1945 that brought about a reversal in the opinions of Prime Minister and Foreign Secretary alike and, no doubt, of other ministers and officials. It rapidly became apparent that Russia's insistence upon a glacis or rampart of friendly states all round her western borders would preclude the free and unfettered elections to which, especially in Poland, all parties had pledged themselves at Yalta.

We can now read many of the documents which passed daily to the Prime Minister from the Government Code and Cypher School through the head of the Secret Intelligence Service. On the face of it, these papers do not contain anything of sufficient importance to warrant the instructions which Churchill was soon to give for the consideration of Operation Unthinkable. Most of the deciphered texts are concerned with military matters (troop movements, reinforcements, lorry traffic). There are also intercepted diplomatic messages. For example, the Japanese Ambassador in Berlin summarized several conversations which he held with the German Foreign Minister in the second half of March, when Ribbentrop remarked that it would be very difficult with things as they were to separate Russia from Britain and America and to conclude a separate peace with the USSR. Some military success on the Eastern Front was essential before this could be done and apparently Hitler was confident that he would be able to secure such a change in the position. Ribbentrop said also that it would be a long time before Britain and America again disposed of such enormous forces and the idea of destroying the USSR might 'quite well spring from American desires for world domination or from British anxiety to prevent the bolshevisation of the British Empire'.

Believing that even Russia had little hope of standing out against the British and American navies and air forces, Germany's Foreign Minister clutched at the hope that Moscow would welcome the idea of making friends with Germany and Japan in order to stand up to Britain and America. Indeed, he apparently contemplated a journey thither for direct negotiation with Stalin, on the lines of the visit which had produced the Nazi-Soviet Pact of August 1939. Most of this belonged in the realms of fantasy and, as we shall see, the notion that the British and Americans could destroy the USSR 'now at one blow' was utterly removed from the opinions the British themselves entertained.[15]

From their clandestine sources, the Western Allies also knew that Ribbentrop had instructed the German Minister in Dublin (and by implication German representatives in other capitals) to argue that since Germany was about to be overrun by the Red Army, the West should ally with Germany, the only power able to stop the Communists' conquest of Europe. If the Allies should refuse this last chance, Germany would find the means of reaching an understanding, at their expense, with Russia. We should note in passing, though the point is incidental to the main theme of this chapter, that the British turned down an American proposal to pass this information to the Russians. The head of the Secret Intelligence Service had pointed out that the source could not be effectively disguised and that any leakage would be disastrous 'at a moment when I have every hope of reconstructing the system used by the Germans for the bulk of their diplomatic communications, to which we have never before had access.' Churchill agreed wholeheartedly.[16]

Nor do we find anything in the papers of the War Cabinet which would provide an immediate and clear occasion of instructions to consider the possibility of war with Russia. In February and March 1945, ministers received lengthy papers about Yalta, with glowing reports about Stalin and the Red Army. There followed documents on Poland, prisoners of war, Rumania, Czechoslovakia, Bulgaria and preparations for the conference to be held at San Francisco, in all of which growing friction with the Russians is discernible. Churchill's alarm about Russian behaviour was manifest. In the diary of the Foreign Secretary for 23 March, we find remarks at once candid and bleak, which give a measure of Britain's previous reliance upon good relations with Moscow.[17] Eden also wondered whether there were any means other than a public statement that could force the Russians to choose between mending their ways and the loss of Anglo-American friendship. He believed this was the only method by which 'we can hope to attain anything approaching a fair deal for the Poles.'[18]

The events of the next week or two made it plain that 'a fair deal for the Poles', at least as conceived by the British, could not be secured thus. Early in April, Churchill learned from Roosevelt that Stalin had in effect accused the Western Powers of deliberate treachery, in the shape of secret negotiations with the Germans to make peace in the West while the fighting went on in the East. Even Roosevelt, who had generally been more sanguine than Churchill about Russia, reacted furiously; or rather, someone else reacted furiously in his name. It seems clear that the British did not realize at the time how gravely ill the President was, or that his telegrams were mostly being written by others. The Prime Minister also sent a powerful blast in the direction of Moscow. His Private Secretary Mr Colville wonders in his account whether the Germans had persuaded the Russians that something sinister was afoot.[19] This is not implausible. As we have seen, the intercepts show that Ribbentrop had thought of making contact with the Russians if the West would not enter into an arrangement with Germany, and from that aspiration to the planting of false information on Russia would not have required a large step. There followed the spiriting away of Polish leaders who had been invited to Moscow. It was clear that in Yugoslavia Tito was looking almost entirely to Russia. The Western Powers therefore faced, admittedly on a smaller scale, an issue in Southern Europe comparable with that which they were facing in Central Europe: should they side with a recent enemy, Italy, in order to oppose Tito over Trieste?[20]

At San Francisco, Eden handed to Molotov a memorandum which referred to the profound and disturbing cumulative effect of Soviet actions. He gave examples. The Russian reply brushed aside most of the complaints and refused in a grand manner to accept the 'obviously one-sided and disproportionate pretensions expressed in this memorandum ignoring as they do the actual facts and responsibility of the British side for the majority of the instances referred to, as well as the constant endeavour of the Soviet organs to meet the legitimate wishes of the British side.'[21]

Meanwhile, Molotov had at last admitted to the 'arrest' of 16 leaders of the Polish underground. In vain did Eden protest that the British knew that these Poles had been good patriots all through the period of German occupation, who desired close relations with Russia.[22] What was the British government to make of such behaviour? In Moscow, the former Russian Ambassador in London, M. Maisky, asserted that what was happening amounted to no more than a few ripples on the surface and spoke of the need to treat Russians with circumspection, to which the British Ambassador in Moscow replied robustly that 'We have been at pains to be circumspect, frank and honest, and all we had got was a series of affronts.' Was it a matter, as the Russian Ambassador in Stockholm Madame Kollontay indiscreetly suggested to her old friend Clark Kerr, of Russian immaturity? She remarked that the Russians were as naive, clumsy and blundering as the English had been in the age of Cromwell; they were children and must be treated accordingly; their present unruliness would pass; and meanwhile the British must practise patience and more patience. Clark Kerr added by way of comment, 'The truth is that the Russians are in a hurry to be great, and that is uncomfortable.'[23] Was Stalin now obliged, as Sir Orme Sargent of the Foreign Office wondered in early May, to handle the Russian Generals more cautiously than before and might the hardening of the Soviet attitude towards the British derive from the influence of these victorious warriors?[24]

But suppose such diagnoses were mistaken, or even delusive? That was the risk which the Prime Minister and others in London had to weigh. Eden rejoined

We have shown great consideration and forbearance and have made ample allowances for the peculiarities of Russian mentality ... We have been shocked, recently, to have had evidence of the morbid suspicion with which the Soviet Government attributes to us the most sinister and disgraceful motives ... M. Maisky really must not ask us to extend our understanding and tolerance to cover, e.g., Soviet Government's attitude on Poland and Roumania, which he knows as well as I do that the Prime Minister and I cannot possibly commend to Parliament.[25]

Ten days later, Churchill sent to President Truman, whom he had never met, the celebrated telegram expressing his deep forebodings about the Russian misinterpretation of the Yalta decisions (as he politely termed what had happened since February), and the effect of the melting away of the Allied armies in the near future. Unwittingly taking the phrase from Dr Goebbels, of all people, Churchill wrote that an Iron Curtain was drawn down upon the Russian front.

The papers relating to Operation Unthinkable do not show with the usual clarity who was giving instructions to whom, or when. Even to contemplate such a subject would require an order from the Prime Minister, and we must assume that he acted at the very latest by the middle of May, immediately after the German surrender, since the documents could scarcely have been prepared in less than a week. It was probably in this interval that Churchill, exhausted in body but not in mind and spirit, confronting the most painful fact that the events of 1940 seemed scarcely more perilous than those now threatening, told the Russian Ambassador in London in no uncertain terms of his anxieties and dissatisfaction. Churchill made a conversational tour of those capitals of Eastern and Central Europe from which Russia's Western Allies were excluded; Berlin, Warsaw, Prague, Vienna. When Poland was touched upon, M. Gousev (who took but a slight part in the conversation, a fact which may not have been due entirely to his limited command of English) said something about lines of communication and the Red Army. The Prime Minister recognized the point but remarked that the fighting was now over and a new situation had arisen. How were the Russians facing it? By dropping an iron screen across Europe from Lübeck to Trieste. 'All we knew was that puppet governments were being set up about which we were not consulted and at which we were not allowed to peep.' He reminded Gousev that the Allied armies had checked their advance on Prague out of deference to Russian susceptibilities, but had been rewarded only by being refused admission to the town where Dr Benes was trembling for the future of his country, while M. Masaryk was making a moaning noise in San Francisco. All this, Churchill went on,

was incomprehensible and intolerable. The Prime Minister and His Majesty's Government objected in the strongest terms to being treated as if they were of no account in the after-war world. They felt that they still counted for something and they refused to be pushed about. Their determination not to see this happen had moved them to postpone the demobilisation of the Royal Air Force. They were resolved to enter upon discussions about the future of Europe with all the strength they had. They were perfectly willing to meet the Russians and to talk in the friendliest way ... it must be on terms of equality, but the Russians seemed to wish to close down upon every place they had occupied and to shut if off from the rest of the world. This could not be allowed. Why could

not the Russians content themselves with the Curzon Line and let
us have a look at what was happening West of it?

Sir A. Clark Kerr noticed that M. Gousev listened 'with a strained
expression on his large face.' This we may well believe. The British
Ambassador could not judge how much Gousev had absorbed of the
Prime Minister's discourse, but thought it must have been sufficient
for him to inform his government that Churchill was very irritated,
concerned about what was happening, and determined to resist.[26] A
few days later, Gousev informed the Foreign Secretary with some
force that fears about Anglo-Russian relations were groundless, and of
his surprise at the terms in which the Prime Minister had spoken to
him. Eden thereupon made it plain that he entirely shared Churchill's
sentiments.[27]

We must take it that the grievances rehearsed to M. Gousev constitute
the main reason for which the Joint Planning Staff had been asked to
examine what was termed from the start Operation 'Unthinkable'. The
final version of the report is dated 22 May 1945. It is not clear whether
earlier drafts had been produced. What is certain is that it had been
prepared in deep secrecy ('the normal staffs in the Service Ministries have
not been consulted'); perhaps inessential parts of the files were destroyed
at the time or later. What we have is a paper of six typed pages, to which
were added some twenty pages by way of four appendices ('Appreciation
of Campaign in Europe', 'Russian Strengths and Dispositions', 'Allied
Strengths and Dispositions' and 'German Reactions'), and four maps
('Russian Strengths and Dispositions', 'Allied Strengths and Dispositions',
'The Campaign in North East Europe' and 'Vulnerable Points of Russian
Lines of Communication').

The first paragraph of the report remarks that 'as instructed',
presumably by General Ismay on Churchill's behalf, the Joint Planning
Staff had been guided by certain assumptions: that the undertaking had
the full support of public opinion in the British Empire and the United
States and consequently the morale of British and American troops
continued to be high; Britain and the USA would have full assistance
from the Polish Armed Forces and could count upon the use of German
manpower and what remained of Germany's industrial capacity; no weight
was given to assistance from the forces of other Western Powers, though
bases and other facilities in their territories would be made available; the

hostilities would begin on 1 July 1945, until which date redeployment and release schemes would continue.

We should pause to weigh these assumptions. On all we know of public opinion and war weariness in Britain and the United States alike, it is most unlikely that short of flagrant Russian aggression, such an operation would carry 'the full support of public opinion.' Beneath this assumption lay a still more daring one, that whatever the state of public opinion, the United States would be prepared to fight in such a cause. That would have been contrary to everything Roosevelt had said, for he had always looked to the early withdrawal of the American forces from Europe and Truman had then done nothing to contradict those assertions. To judge that the British and Americans could 'count upon the use of German manpower and what remains of German industrial capacity' also called for a considerable leap of the imagination. There followed a still more startling assumption; namely that 'Russia allies herself with Japan'. After all, Stalin had repeatedly promised, most recently at Yalta, that Russia would enter the war against Japan soon after Germany was defeated. In the event, Russia remained in her state of neutrality with Japan until the last, and declared war only after the first of the atom bombs had been dropped. For Stalin to have allied himself with the Emperor of Japan would have required flagrant and cynical reversals; but then, the same had been true of the Nazi-Soviet pact in 1939.

The object of the Operation would be to impose upon Russia the will of the United States and the British Empire, which in this document and many others was treated as if it were a single entity. As the Prime Minister and others knew only too well, it was not. There, then, lies another optimistic assumption; for the notion that troops from Canada to South Africa, Australia to New Zealand, Barbados to India, would fight against Russia in Central Europe contains at the least much that is questionable. The paper went on to remark that 'Even though "the will" of these two countries' (i.e. the USA and the British Empire, where we notice again the assumption that the British Empire was a unit) might be defined as 'no more than a square deal for Poland', that would not necessarily limit the military commitment. The Russians might or might not be induced to submit, at least for the time being, by a quick military success on the part of the West; and if the Russians wanted total war, they were in a position to wage it.

In other words, only by winning such a war could the West achieve its stated object with certainty and lasting results. The Staff considered that hypothesis and the alternative that because a quick success might suffice to gain the political object, a continuing commitment need not be of concern. Leaving aside the chances of a revolution in Russia and the collapse of the regime, the elimination of the USSR in such a war could be achieved only by occupation of so much of the country that it would not be able to sustain further resistance, or such a decisive defeat as to render it impossible for Russia to continue the war; or, presumably, by both events. The paper pointed out that although in 1942 the Germans had reached the area of Moscow, the Volga and the Caucasus, Russia had nevertheless been able to continue fighting; it was scarcely conceivable that the Allies could penetrate as far or as quickly as the Germans in 1942, a penetration which had produced no decisive result.

The annexes to this report examined in detail the balance of strength in Central Europe. There, Russia enjoyed a superiority on land of approximately three to one. That fact made it most unlikely that the Allies could achieve complete and decisive victory in the area. Allied organization might be better, equipment slightly better, and morale higher, but the Russians had proved themselves formidable opponents of Germany; they had competent commanders, adequate equipment and an organization which had stood the test. To achieve a decisive defeat of Russia in a total war would require the massive mobilization of manpower. Unsurprisingly, the authors concluded that while they could not forecast the result of such a war, they could say with certainty that to win it would take 'a very long time.'

As for the possibility of a rapid victory, even an early success on the part of the West might not cause Russia to submit; in other words, the West might still be committed to a total war. It would be impossible to limit hostilities to one particular area and therefore necessary to think of a worldwide struggle. Even a quick success would not of itself bring a lasting result, because the military power of Russia would not be broken and it would be open to her to resume the war whenever she thought fit.

With this somewhat unpromising preamble, the paper remarked that there would be no threat from Russian strategic bombers or submarines comparable to the earlier German threat; but there would be the Red Army, the main strength of which was concentrated in Central Europe. That army might well overrun Turkey in Europe. South-East Europe, including Greece, 'would immediately become barred to our influence and commerce.' In Persia and Iraq, an extremely dangerous situation would arise. It appeared to the planners almost certain that Russia would take the offensive there in view of the oil resources to be gained and the extreme importance of those areas to the Western Powers. Since there were some 11 Russian divisions available against an Allied force of 3 Indian brigade groups, it was difficult to see how the region could be defended. If Russia and Japan allied, Japanese forces would be freed to reinforce the home islands or resume the offensive in China.

However, the principal theatre would undoubtedly be Central Europe. Allied air superiority would be offset to some extent by the fact that the strategic bomber force would in the earlier stages have to be based in England. The only means of securing a quick success would be a land campaign making full use of air superiority both in tactical support and in attacks on the Russian lines of communication. The main effort of the land offensive would have to lie in North-East Europe. A force of some 47 divisions, including 14 armoured divisions, could be made available for offensive operations on the assumptions already described. Against this the Russians would be able to produce a force equivalent to 170 divisions, of which 30 would be armoured. The Allies would therefore face odds of the order of two to one against them in armour, and nearly four to one in infantry. As the report remarks, without exaggeration, 'the above odds would clearly render the launching of an offensive a hazardous undertaking.'

The main armoured fighting would probably develop east of the Oder-Neisse Line. On the outcome the campaign would probably depend. If the result were favourable

We might reach the general line Danzig-Breslau. Any advance beyond this, however, would increase the length of the front to be held during winter and increase the danger resulting from the salient formed by Bohemia and Moravia, from which the Russians would be under no necessity to withdraw. Unless, therefore, we have won the victory we require west of the line Danzig-Breslau it appears likely that we shall, in fact, be committed to a total war.

The success of a land campaign, therefore, would depend upon the result of the fighting west of the above line before winter conditions set in. There is no inherent strength in our strategic position and, in fact, we should be staking everything upon one great battle, in which we should be facing very heavy odds.

We conclude that: -

(a) If we are to embark on war with Russia, we must be prepared to be committed to a total war, which will be both long and costly.
(b) Our numerical inferiority on land renders it extremely doubtful whether we could achieve a limited and quick success, even if the political appreciation considered that this would suffice to gain our political object.

One of the appendices dealt with the possibility of German assistance and estimated that 10 German divisions might be reformed and re-equipped in the early stages. They could not, however, be available by 1 July. These possible allies had not been included in the calculations.

Even this lengthy summary cannot do justice to all the material in these papers. From a strictly British point of view, there were some hopeful aspects; for example, that the Royal Navy, even without the help of the United States, was entirely adequate to deal with Russian naval strength, or that when aluminium from Allied sources was denied to Russia and the Allies inflicted heavy losses, Russian production of aircraft would be 'totally inadequate to meet the demands'. Against such assertions, there had to be placed the overwhelming facts of Russia's strength and proved record in the war. As the report pointed out, the Red Army had developed a capable and experienced high command, was extremely tough, lived and moved on a lighter scale of maintenance than any Western army, and employed bold tactics based largely on a disregard for losses.

The Chiefs of Staff, meeting on 31 May, were convinced that the idea of such a war against Russia was indeed unthinkable. In notes written years later, Brooke recalled that Churchill had come to the Chiefs of Staff expressing anxiety at seeing the Russian bear sprawled all over Europe, phraseology which would again suggest that this enquiry had originated from a general fear rather than a particular incident; and the Chiefs of Staff had concluded that 'the best we could hope for was to drive the Russians back to about the same line the Germans had reached. And then what? Were we to remain mobilized indefinitely to hold them there?'[28]

The Chiefs of Staff put the bare facts to Churchill on 8 June, by which time the election campaign was well under way. They estimated that because Russian divisions were not comparable in establishment with Allied divisions, the enemy forces would amount to a total of 264 divisions (including 26 armoured divisions) as against the Allies' 103 divisions (including 23 armoured divisions). In short, there were significant differences in the proportions as estimated by the Chiefs of Staff on the one hand, and the Joint Planning Staff on the other. As for air strength, the Allies would have a little over 6,000 tactical aircraft and some 2,500 strategic aircraft; the comparable figures on the Russian side would be nearly 12,000 and 960. The dominance in numbers of Russian aircraft would, the Chiefs of Staff stated, for a time be offset by the vastly superior handling and efficiency of the Allied air forces, especially the strategic air forces. After some while, however, the lack of replacement aircraft and air crews would seriously impair the West's strength in the air. The situation on land made it clear that the Allies would not be in a position to take the offensive with a view to achieving a rapid success. Since Russian and Allied land forces were in contact on a long line stretching from the Baltic to the Mediterranean, there was no chance of avoiding land operations:

> Our view is ... that once hostilities began, it would be beyond our power to win a quick but limited success and we should be committed to a protracted war against heavy odds. Those odds, moreover, would become fanciful if the Americans grew weary and indifferent and began to be drawn away by the magnet of the Pacific War.[29]

Major-General Hollis, Ismay's deputy, drafted a reply which on 10 June the Prime Minister adopted in its entirety except for one important change at the end. In effect, it abandoned the notion of an assault, and pointed out that if the Americans withdrew to their zone in Germany and moved the bulk of their forces back to the USA or to the Pacific, the Russians would have the power to advance to the North Sea and the Atlantic. How then could Britain be defended, assuming that France and the Low Countries were powerless to resist a Russian advance to the sea? What naval, air and land forces would be required? The retention of the code word 'Unthinkable' would cause the Staff to realize that 'this remains a precautionary study of what, I hope, is still a purely hypothetical contingency.' Instead of the last four words, General Hollis' draft had suggested 'a highly improbable event.'[30]

On the next day, the Prime Minister gave to the Chiefs of Staff what Brooke's diary describes as a long and very gloomy review of the situation in Europe. The Russians were all-powerful there; they could march across the rest of Europe and drive the British back into their island; and the Americans were returning home. The quicker they went home, Churchill said, the sooner they would be required in Europe again. 'He finished up by saying that never in his life had he been more worried by the European situation than he was at present.'[31]

When the Joint Planners examined on behalf of the Chiefs of Staff the Prime Minister's minute of 10 June, they concluded that the Russians would not be able to develop any immediate threat to Britain's sea communications comparable to that which had been posed by Germany; it would take Russia years to develop a submarine fleet or a maritime airforce capable of producing a decisive threat; Russia would be greatly handicapped by lack of experience in planning an invasion either by sea or by air; the assessment ruled out a decisive invasion of the UK by airborne operations alone. Allied retention of bridgeheads on the Continent would offer Russia a compact target, their defence would impose a continuous drain and their retention would bring no operational advantage. To defend the island and attack targets in Europe would require the full support of the United States. That prospect, needless to say, raised the question of the Japanese war. The document concluded:

> It is only by the use of rockets and other new weapons that the Russians could develop any serious threat to the security of this country in the initial stages. Invasion or a serious attack upon our sea communications could only be undertaken after ... preparation which must last some years.[32]

By the time those words were written, the Prime Minister was painting in the south of France, whence he travelled directly to the Conference at Potsdam. It is noticeable that the preserved texts of this report of 11 July, and the still more important initial paper about Operation Unthinkable of 22 May, are both marked 'No. 15'. It is likely that a copy or summary found its way to Stalin. Had any such suggestion been put to Churchill or Ismay, it would doubtless have been dismissed out of hand, elaborate precautions having been taken to ensure the secrecy of the whole enquiry. As Ismay remarked in one of his notes to Churchill, the Chiefs of Staff felt 'that the less was put on paper on this subject, the better.'[33]

All the same, we now know what was not apparent to the Prime Minister, that a great deal of most secret information reached Russia because of penetration of the British public service by communist agents and sympathizers; and we must assume that they were prone to supply material which fitted with their own preconceptions. Churchill's celebrated description of the way in which Stalin received from Truman the news about the successful testing of the atomic bomb does not suggest that the Prime Minister, writing long after the war, was aware even of a possibility that Stalin might have known the essential facts in advance.[34] No less an authority than Professor John Erickson suggested that the assessments connected with Operation Unthinkable may account for the decisive change in Russia's military dispositions which occurred at the end of June 1945.[35] In other words, it is credible that there was at work a self-fulfilling, indeed self-reinforcing, process: because Russia was so powerful and her attitude so menacing, the Prime Minister felt bound to discover whether the British and Americans had any serious chance of opposing her by military force; and if Stalin knew that such an enquiry had been undertaken, his own convictions of Western enmity would certainly have been strengthened.

At Potsdam, Churchill remarked to Eden that Russian policy was now one of aggrandizement.[36] All the same, the Prime Minister did not adopt an attitude of hostility to all Russian demands. According to Eden, whose impression is supported from other sources, Churchill had again fallen under the spell of Stalin. The Prime Minister favoured Russia's claim to a substantial portion of the captured German fleet, and to at least one warm-water port. Stalin denied any intention that Russia would roll on westwards.

As the Chiefs of Staff and the Joint Planning Staff had shown, Russia's strength in conventional forces outstripped anything which the British and Americans could bring to bear. When the planners wrote their memoranda, they did not know about the atomic enterprise, any more than Truman or Churchill knew whether the first trial would succeed. The American and British governments had assumed that an intense and bloody campaign in the Far East, perhaps lasting as long as 18 months, would follow the defeat of Germany. But as the pregnant conversation between Truman and Stalin had indicated, and as the devastation of Hiroshima and Nagasaki showed within a few days, the new weapon upset all those careful calculations about the numbers of divisions and submarines and aircraft. Here was something which might well transform not only the nature of warfare but relations between the great powers, for a weapon of unimaginable potency could now be delivered from bases lying at a great distance from the target and practically invulnerable; moreover, delivered with devastating effect, if necessary without declaration of war. Whereas it had taken years of relentless pounding to ruin the cities and industry of Germany, destruction over a vast area could now be achieved at a stroke. The point was immediately apparent to Churchill who, as Alanbrooke's diary recounts, told the Chiefs of Staff on 23 July that

> we now had something in our hands which would redress the balance with the Russians! The secret of this explosive, and the power to use it, would completely alter the diplomatic equilibrium which was adrift since the defeat of Germany! Now we had a new value which redressed our position (pushing his chin out and scowling), now we could say that if you insist on doing this or that, well we can just blot out Moscow, then Stalingrad, then Kiev, then Kuibyshev, Karkhov, Sebastopol etc. etc. And now where are the Russians!!![37]

Two days after that colloquy, Churchill left Potsdam for London. Twenty-four hours later, he resigned as Prime Minister on learning of the Labour Party's overwhelming victory in the General Election. Attlee and Bevin, the new Prime Minister and Foreign Secretary, found themselves possessed of no more cards in negotiation than Churchill and Eden. They were, for a while, more hopeful than their predecessors about Russia and the post-war situation. When Churchill uttered at Fulton, Missouri, in March 1946, truths which could hardly be denied by any serious observer, but which were accompanied by expressions of admiration for Stalin and the valiant Russian people, the British and American governments alike refused to endorse his speech.

There is a twist to this tale, for the file relating to Operation Unthinkable does not close in the summer of 1945. It comes to life again in August 1946, by which time the Chiefs of Staff in the United States judged that matters in Europe had reached a critical stage. If a war began with Russia, they believed that the British and American forces should withdraw from their zones of occupation in Germany to a bridgehead, the course which the planners had not recommended in the summer of 1945. Air cover and air striking forces would be available from bases in the United Kingdom; from the bridgehead in the Low Countries there would be short lines of communication with Britain. Messages were exchanged in profound secrecy during the autumn of 1946. Field-Marshal Montgomery, by then Chief of the Imperial General Staff, held conversations with Mackenzie King, Prime Minister of Canada, President Truman and General Eisenhower. By the end of that year, the British and American planners had agreed, as had the Chiefs of Staff in London, that in the event of Russian aggression, the best course would be to withdraw the British and American forces into the area of Zeebrugge and Dunkirk.[38]

These exchanges remind us that Operation Unthinkable was not merely or even largely the result of Churchill's hostility towards Russia, or of fevered imagination as the coalition crumbled into disarray in 1945 with the disappearance of the only factor which had held it together. Given the scale of demobilization by the Americans and the British by the end of 1946, the disparity between their and the Russians' conventional forces was greater than when the planners had reported in the early summer of 1945, but with the difference that the Americans now had the atomic bomb (the secrets of which they refused after the war to share with the British), and the Russians had not. Even now, we do not know whether Russia was deterred from westward expansion by the knowledge that the other side possessed the bomb. What is clear is that within a few years, a vast reversal of British, American and European opinion was brought about by Russian policy and above all by Stalin. Churchill made this point with force in November 1954, near the end of his last spell as Prime Minister, in the context of the policy – which would have seemed unthinkable even a few years before – of rearming Germany within NATO. The speech created uproar, for Churchill added that when the Germans were surrendering in their hundreds of thousands in 1945, he had told Montgomery to collect German arms so that they could easily be issued again to the German soldiers with whom the British would have to work if the Soviet advance continued. (Let us note in passing that on 10 November 1918, he had said something similar to the War Cabinet: 'We might have to build up the German army, as it was important to get Germany on its legs again for fear of the spread of Bolshevism.')[39]

There ensued an intense search for the text of this message. There is a probability, but not a certainty, that it was never sent. On the other hand, as Churchill's published history of the war had already shown, he telegraphed to Eisenhower on 9 May 1945 that he hoped the policy of destroying German weapons and other equipment would not be adopted. Normally, his memory was Napoleonic in its range and accuracy. The Prime Minister apologized to Parliament for his failure to observe the rule he had so often inculcated, 'Always verify your quotations.' No trouble would have arisen with the Soviets in the summer of 1945, he added, unless they had continued their advance to a point at which they caused the outbreak of a new war between Russia and the Western Allies; and to prevent such a disaster it might have been helpful to warn the Russians that 'we should certainly in that case rearm the German prisoners in our hands who all together, including those in Italy, numbered 2.5 million.'

Enquiry was naturally made of Montgomery. He in his turn consulted the two colleagues who had in 1945 been the heads of his Operations and Intelligence staffs, and then informed Churchill that the message had come 'on a very secret link: which you sometimes used, to me. I remember that too. Messages sent on that link had to be destroyed *at once*, when read. You can therefore take it that the message was destroyed.'[40]

Whether Montgomery and his colleagues were accurate in every particular, almost ten years after the event, is beside the point. It is plain that ultra-secret communications went to him and others, the texts of which were immediately burned by the recipient. In respect of Operation Unthinkable, we may yet have a good deal to learn from Russian sources; and we do well to remind ourselves that files apparently complete are not necessarily so.

8

The Solitary Pilgrimage

Churchill and the Russians, 1951–5*

At earlier banquets, you have been addressed by people who could speak of Churchill from intimate knowledge acquired at first hand: his daughter and grandson; Sir John Colville, Sir David Hunt, Sir Anthony Montague Browne and Professor R.V. Jones. Lacking their qualifications, I have tried to move away from the beaten track of the war to a theme which is of more than merely historical significance even now, namely the substance and style of the West's attitude to Russia in the early 1950s. You may perhaps wonder, 'Was that last phase not the period of Churchill's sad decline, and was not the notion of friendly or even tolerable relations with Russia, with Stalin or Malenkov or Khrushchev, a mere figment of his imagination? Was there not on the other side of the Iron Curtain an implacable enemy, deaf and blind to reason, and if that were true, then there was nothing more to say and nothing to do but prepare for war?'

As Churchill had to ask himself every day on returning to office in the autumn of 1951, were those assumptions (so deadly in their implications) ones which could be relied upon? With the stakes far higher than ever because of atomic weaponry, must not every effort be made to contain the alarming cost and reduce these risks? Would not this prospect of endless antagonism, and perhaps eventual conflict, provide the most unfitting sequel to the heroic efforts of the war itself? If the peoples of the world, and nowhere more than in vulnerable Britain, were to confront such a future, must not every nerve be strained to prove there was no

---

* This is an edited version of a speech delivered by the author to the Churchill Society for the Advancement of Parliamentary Democracy, Toronto.

alternative? These lines of thought, and the sustained effort to build up the armed strength of the West, provide the spinal cord of what I shall say tonight. You will respond, 'Have we not heard some of these questions before: what are the enemy's intentions, what can we afford for defence, must we not go the last inch to preserve the peace?' Yes, you have. They are the questions over which Chamberlain and his colleagues agonized in 1938.

Whatever the books, the newspapers or indeed the Russians may claim, Churchill was no unrelenting foe of the Soviet Union. During the war he had suppressed many of his fears, even after the uprising in Warsaw, even at the Yalta Conference in February 1945, even at Potsdam. He had gone bail in the Cabinet and in Parliament for Russia's trustworthiness,[1] partly out of confidence in Stalin's intentions and perhaps also because he was old enough to remember the Russia of earlier days, ally of Britain in World War I. To the Prime Ministers of the Commonwealth, Churchill had proclaimed in 1944 his confidence that the spirit of freedom in the world would prevail in the end over the brutish regimentation of the new Russia and had declined to consider the possibility of a confrontation between Russia and the English-speaking peoples.[2] Soon that was more than a possibility. It had become a grim fact. In his celebrated speech at Fulton in March 1946, Churchill spoke words of solemn warning but added what is less often noticed, 'We welcome Russia to her rightful place among the leading nations of the world', and that he did not believe Russia desired war. Rather, she desired the fruits of war without war itself, and only military strength, he judged, would compel Russia to respect Western rights.[3] In Moscow, Churchill was at once accused of initiating a war of words. When the British Ambassador pointed out that WSC was now a private individual, Stalin retorted that he was Leader of the Opposition. Nevertheless, rejoined Sir Maurice Peterson, the British government was not responsible for Churchill's activities. Dictator and Ambassador argued the point for a while. Then Stalin raised his arms and dropped them: 'If he is indeed a private individual, all I can say is that we have no private individuals like him in this country',[4] an assertion which the Ambassador had no need to contest.

Part of my purpose tonight is to convey some flavour of Sir Winston's personality and presence. No British politician of the twentieth century made so much of, and depended so consistently upon, words. He loved nothing more than to waylay the unexpected adjective or phrase. He lived handsomely by his pen. He did not lack self-belief. As a young man he remarked brightly 'We are all worms, but I do believe that I am a glow-worm.'[5] When Churchill toured this country with his young son in 1929, Randolph was so incautious as to remark that it was terrible to see beautiful Alberta being grubbed up by uncultured folk who would make piles of money but have no idea how to spend it; only to be told by his father, without a moment's pause, 'Cultured people are merely the glittering scum which floats upon the deep river of production.'[6]

Churchill had courage of a rare kind, physical, mental and moral, not the courage of the man who does not apprehend danger but that of the man who measures the risks and does not quail. Acknowledging these qualities and achievements, let us not flinch from the question: where should his reputation stand, nearly 60 years after he left office? To put the case for the prosecution in the baldest terms: the British Empire, which he vowed to defend, was liquidated in short order after the war; and the balance of power in Europe, which it was Britain's interest to uphold, was overturned by the triumph of Russia. More vehement critics avow that Britain should not have given the guarantee to Poland or declared war in 1939. Then Hitler, so the theory runs, would have attacked an unprepared Stalin in 1940. The result might have been the elimination of Bolshevism in Russia and China, no Cold War, no Korea, no Vietnam, limitless prospects; instead of six years of bloodletting there might perhaps have been six months of war between Germany and Russia, ending with the one dead and the other crippled. How remote it all sounds, especially to young people! But to recreate the mood and perils of times past is a principal purpose of history, which 'with its flickering lamp stumbles along the trail of the past, trying to reconstruct its scenes, to revive its echoes, and kindle with pale gleams the passion of former days', words which I appropriate from Churchill's moving and poetical tribute to Chamberlain.[7]

It was with a sense of fulfilled romance, feeling that he had reversed the defeat of 1945 though by the slimmest of margins, that Churchill returned to 10 Downing Street in 1951 a few weeks short of his 77th birthday. Deciding at once to visit Washington and Ottawa, he invited Canada's Secretary of State for External Affairs, Lester Pearson, to lunch at Chequers on 9 December. By a happy chance Pearson left a record which lacks nothing in vivacity. He observes that Churchill looked old and tired, 'at least until the luncheon got well under way, when he revived and became his normal, sparkling and dramatic self under the influence, not of my company, I suspect, but of his own natural reaction to an audience, assisted somewhat by champagne, burgundy, port and quantities of brandy. I did my best,' says Pearson, who was a generation younger than his host, 'to keep up with him, in this latter respect at least, but when he suggested after lunch that we now have a Scotch and soda, I gave up.' Churchill said that he felt the most dangerous period with Russia would come in the next year or two as the West grew stronger, and while he thought that Russia would not provoke a war, she might easily blunder into one through miscalculation. His purpose was to convince the Russians that he was willing to take up the relationship where it had been left off in 1945.[8]

I cannot resist a reference to the matter of 'Rule, Britannia', which loomed over Churchill's visit to Ottawa. With displeasure he had learned of the Canadian government's decision that 'Rule, Britannia' should no longer be played on ceremonial occasions by the bands of the Royal Canadian Navy or the RCAF. He commanded the new Secretary of State for Commonwealth Relations, General Ismay, to complain to the Prime Minister of Canada. Mr St Laurent replied politely that the decision could not be reversed. To a renewed protest St Laurent made the same response. Who, Churchill muttered in high displeasure, were these republican upstarts in Ottawa? He would not go there. He would come home directly from Washington.

Eventually Mrs Churchill put a stop to the performance by remarking that she had it in mind, should he continue in this vein, to close down Chartwell and move to a flat by the sea in Brighton. Though the threat was not intended to be taken literally, it had the effect of bringing her husband to order. He disembarked somewhat grumpily from the sleeper at the old station in Ottawa opposite the Château Laurier. The band of the RCAF stood smartly on the platform. It struck up 'Rule, Britannia'. Churchill, so 'unEnglish' in so many ways, with none of the stiff upper lip and reserve, wept. Thereafter, says Sir John Colville, 'nobody ever dared to utter even the mildest criticism of Monsieur St. Laurent or of Canada.'[9]

The records of the conversations between Churchill, Eden, Ismay, Lord Cherwell and their Canadian colleagues in Ottawa indicate what we must make the effort of imagination to recall across a gap of two generations: that this was a time of the deepest apprehension. The very headings in the documents – atomic weapons and their development (upon which subject the British shared the most secret information always with Canada); policy towards the Soviet Union; the Far East and the Korean War; the Middle East; the Atlantic Command (where Churchill had pleaded with the American government to allow the command in the eastern part of the Atlantic to remain in British hands, because that was for us a matter of life and death as it had so nearly been in 1942 and 1943 and the floor of that sea was strewn white with the bones of Englishmen); the reorganization of NATO – tell their own tale.[10]

Amidst all this, Churchill judged that the central element of Soviet policy was not the desire to dominate, but fear; and that for the moment the Russian government feared the friendship of the West more than its enmity. He desired to stand that on its head, so that Russia would fear the growing strength of the West, and thus its enmity more than its friendship. He acknowledged that agreements with Russia could be reached only through strength.[11] A deterrent factor, he told the Canadian Cabinet, was that war would be extremely unpleasant for both sides, for both would suffer what they dreaded most at the outset; Europe would be overrun by the Russians and the USSR would be blasted by atomic weapons in all its vital points. It seemed certain that at best there would have to be a prolonged period of Cold War. That, however, would be much better than catastrophe.[12]

To be Prime Minister from 1940 was one thing; to be Prime Minister in 1951 and after something quite other. In the first instance, there had been no serious party warfare, the government had all the parliamentary battalions, there was nobody else in the War Cabinet of Churchill's stature. In the second, everything had altered. The government scarcely possessed a working majority, the colleagues in the Cabinet had to have much more of their own way, relationships with the United States were far different because Britain was now plainly the junior partner. To these new circumstances Churchill was sensitive. His anxiety in office as in Opposition was to discuss the issues candidly with Russia. In the sinister twilight of the gods which preceded Stalin's death, marked by the arrest of his doctors and the accusation that they were engaged in a Jewish conspiracy against him, little could be done.

With the new President of the United States Churchill dwelt on terms of friendship, even affection, from the war. Eisenhower held strong religious convictions, as Churchill did not, and apocalyptic views about the nature of Communism. Churchill pressed him time and again over the next two and a quarter years. 'I have the feeling', he telegraphed to Washington immediately after Stalin died in March 1953,

> that we might both of us together or separately be called to account if no attempt were made to turn over a leaf so that a new page would be started with something more coherent on it than a series of casual and dangerous incidents at the many points of contact between the two divisions of the world.[13]

Two months later, he told Eisenhower that he would like to address Molotov in this style:

> Naturally I do not imagine that we could settle any of the grave issues which overhang the immediate future of the world but I have the feeling that it might be helpful if our intercourse proceeded with the help of friendly acquaintance and goodwill instead of impersonal diplomacy and propaganda.[14]

When the President expressed fear lest Churchill's going on his own to Moscow might seem to give too great a hostage to fortune, he received the reply

> I am not afraid of the 'solitary pilgrimage' if I am sure in my heart that it may help forward the cause of peace, and even at the worst can only do harm to my reputation. I am fully alive to the impersonal and machine-made foundation of Soviet policy, although under a veneer of civilities and hospitalities. I have a strong belief that the Soviet self-interest will be their guide. My hope is that it is their self-interest which will bring about an easier state of affairs.[15]

This was the phase in which, because of Anthony Eden's serious illness, Churchill had taken charge of the Foreign Office. He boldly announced in public, as in the telegrams just cited, his desire for a parley at the summit, a meeting of the heads of government, not a series of encounters at lower levels. To cope with the business of the Premiership and of the

Foreign Office imposed at his great age an intolerable strain. Three powers, Britain, the United States and France, were due to meet at Bermuda in late June 1953; partly so that the French could be pressed to come to a conclusion about the European Defence Community, uncertainty about which over-hung the whole of Western policy, and partly so that Churchill could try to persuade the President that an approach should be made to Russia. One evening towards the end of that month the newly knighted Sir Winston was entertaining the Italian Prime Minister at 10 Downing Street and did what he seldom did, made a speech without a script; a delightful disquisition about the influence which Italy had exercised upon the civilization of Europe, and how the Roman legions crossing the Alps bore with them something greater than they knew.

As he sat at the table afterwards he suffered a severe stroke, which within a day or two deprived him of the use of his left side. For a while his speech was affected. His doctor, Lord Moran, thought that the Prime Minister was about to die.[16] The Prime Minister thought rather differently. The meeting at Bermuda had to be put off. It was announced that Sir Winston must take a period of complete rest from his arduous duties.

There were in that summer some encouraging signs: an apparent effort on the part of the new leaders in Russia to minimize frictions, and the end of the fighting in Korea. There remained, however, the prime issue of the rearmament of Germany, which had to be accommodated within the framework of Western European defence or of NATO. This Churchill was determined to achieve somehow. In the period of convalescence, during which he rehabilitated himself by supreme exertions, he mused on change and fortune. On 30 June, he said to his doctor 'I'm finished, but only a week ago I had big plans. My influence everywhere had never been greater ... Of course I knew that I was taking risks by my advances to the Russians. I might have taken a big toss'; and a month later, 'Before I lead the British people into another and more bloody war, I want to satisfy my conscience and my honour that the Russians are not just play-acting. I believe they do mean something. I believe that there has been a change of heart.' In another conversation – you will gather why Foreign Offices and Ministries of Defence all over the Western alliance were alarmed by Churchill – he set out what he would have said in Russia if allowed to get there: 'I would have met them more than half-way. It might have meant a real U.N.O., with Russia working with the rest for the good of Europe'; and because he could see what the arms race meant, not only its colossal cost but the lamentable fact that what man has once invented he cannot disinvent, he added

> We would have promised them [the Russians] that no more atomic bombs would be made, no more research into their manufacture. Those bombs already made would be locked away. They would have had at their disposal much of the money now spent on armaments to provide better conditions for the Russian people.[17]

Asked what was the point of all this, he replied with spirit that he wished to see the leisured classes of his youth give place to the leisured masses of tomorrow, observing pointedly that if the State Department and the Foreign Office had their way unchecked, the world would be consigned to years of hatred and hostility.[18]

When eventually he was well enough to reach Bermuda at the end of 1953, what should he encounter, on suggesting that there might be a new look in Soviet foreign policy, but a short and violent diatribe from Eisenhower, who described Russia as a woman of the streets; whether her dress was new or the old one patched up, it was the same whore underneath, and America intended to drive her off her present beat and into the back streets. Churchill expressed a slightly pained amazement at this attitude and urged a dual policy combining military and political strength with gestures of friendship.[19]

It was WSC's practice to scan all the main newspapers, sometimes to the discomfiture of ministers who did not feel the same impulse. Asked whether this was a proper use of his time, he retorted 'I get far more out of them than out of the official muck.' In February 1954, Mr Colville, then Joint Principal Private Secretary, came into Churchill's bedroom one morning and found him reading *The Manchester Guardian*. Alone among the British newspapers of that day it reported a speech delivered in the United States by the chairman of the Joint Congressional Committee on Atomic Energy, who had described the explosion of the first hydrogen bomb. Sir Winston then told Colville, with what the latter termed a mixture of triumph and indignation, that he had just rung up the Foreign Secretary, the Secretary of the Cabinet and all three Chiefs of Staff. None had the slightest idea of what had happened; yet he believed that 'we were now almost as far from the atom bomb as the atom bomb itself had been from the bow and arrow'. This tremendous event, Churchill foresaw, would change the history of mankind because it would make wars of the old kind – that is, prolonged conflict between the major powers – obsolete. The immediate effect must be to alter Britain's strategic thinking, and perhaps to make easier a rapprochement with the Soviet Union; and even though that result was delayed for many years, the Prime Minister was to my mind right. It was lucky, he remarked to Colville, that at least one person in Whitehall read the newspapers.[20]

After meetings in Washington four months later, oppressed by the futility and cost of a renewed arms race, Churchill said that he would redouble his efforts to seek an easement of ten years, during which 'our riches and ingenuity could be diverted to ends more fruitful than the production of catastrophic weapons.'[21] With enormous relief he detected in Eisenhower a change of heart, the crossing of a gulf. The President seemed to have made up his mind that it was not the mission of the United States, for the moment anyway, to destroy Bolshevism by force but somehow to live side by side in peace.[22] 'Although we don't consider [in Britain] that we are surpassed by anyone in our resolute hatred of Communism,' said Churchill to the press in Ottawa, 'we do not exclude the possibility of having to live together for a number of years and side by side ... I don't see why we should in any way depart from the idea that you may have to live with all sorts of people in this wicked world ...' The Russians, he thought, might

> very likely be content to have a good time, instead of another phase of torture and slaughter such as they've gone through. They haven't had much of a good time, the people of Russia, with whom I have no quarrel – never had, always great sympathy – but I assure you if the capitalist democracies had to go through the sort of life they have to lead, there would be lots to talk about at the general elections which would occur. They have a very hard life in Russia; and I was trying to explain to our American friends, why shouldn't they have the kind of fun the democracies everywhere are expecting, now that the primal needs for food are being met?[23]

In their different fashions, Mr Pearson, Sir Anthony Eden, Mr Dulles and President Eisenhower were all hostile to the notion that Churchill might go to Moscow or Bern or Stockholm to negotiate with Stalin's successors.

They feared he was too frail. As Pearson expressed it, the Russians would probably press him hard and do their best to break him down; 'he is really not physically and mentally strong enough to stand a serious discussion with the Communists.'[24] But Lord Moran, who accompanied him on this visit to Washington and Ottawa, saw that the only thing now left to Churchill on the eve of his 80th birthday, his one consuming purpose, was to hold off the threat of war until it was no longer worthwhile for anybody to break the peace; and that in the Prime Minister's heart lay a great fear. He dreaded another war because he believed England could not survive it, there in the front line with those US Air Force bases from which the bombing of Russia would have to be launched. It seemed to Moran that his patient held with an almost religious intensity the belief that he alone could save the world from a war which would put an end to civilized life.

'Time is short', Churchill kept saying. He had not forgotten the taunt at the election of 1951 that he was a warmonger, which had apparently hurt him more than we might guess. He wanted to show that he was as distinguished a peace-maker as war-maker; and even Lord Moran, apt to put not altogether pleasant complexions upon his patient's motives, conceded that it was not simply a question of Churchill's thinking of himself or craving personal distinction. An idea that stirred his imagination could still drive the frail frame to surprising exertions, and the Prime Minister well knew that the longing for peace represented the deepest feelings of the country. WSC said he would like once again to speak for England as he had done in the trough of war, if that would avert another conflict. What is more, we may be sure that as a seasoned politician he was by no means oblivious of the parliamentary aspects. Here was he, a Conservative Prime Minister acknowledged to have been a great leader in wartime, who now sought earnestly a stretching of the hand of friendship towards Russia. As the Deputy Leader of the Labour Party observed ruefully in August 1954, 'You have to move pretty fast if you are going to keep to the left of Churchill nowadays.'[25]

It was not only in relation to the United States that Churchill saw Britain, and Canada too, as a mediator, interpreter and link. He wished West Germany rearmed so that the defence of Europe should be stronger. He intended thereby to give the Russians something to think about, but also that the Russians should give the Germans pause. In other words he hoped that the one power would curb the other, as in fact happened for a long time. He trusted that the British would in turn be able to use their growing influence and military strength to relieve both the Germans and the Russians of the anxiety which each might feel about the other. These convictions he sustained to the end. One last great speech was delivered a month before his eventual resignation. Force and science, he cried, hitherto the servants of man, threatened to become his master. The Cold War he described as something which 'we all detest but have to endure.' The Soviets and their satellites had an immense superiority in so-called conventional forces, and to devise a balanced and phased disarmament would constitute the best kind of defence. He drew, as always, a distinction between the Communists and Russia, and expressed his strong admiration for the Russian people, their bravery, their many gifts, their kindly nature. It might well be 'that we shall by a process of sublime irony have reached a stage in this story where safety will be the sturdy child of terror, and survival the twin brother of annihilation.'

He had been asked what he would tell the Russians if the meeting should ever take place. His replies in public were the same as in private, which is a measure of the man's integrity. Here we learn clearly what line Churchill would have taken:

As one might say to them, 'Although you might kill millions of our peoples, and cause widespread havoc by a surprise attack, we could, within a few hours of this outrage, certainly deliver several, indeed many times the weight of nuclear material which you have used, and continue retaliation on that same scale.' 'We have', we could say, 'already hundreds of bases of attack from all angles and have made an intricate study of suitable targets.' Thus, it seems to me with some experience of wartime talks, you might go to dinner and have a friendly evening. I should not be afraid to talk things over as far as they can be. This, and the hard facts, would make the deterrent effective.

These were the considerations which led Churchill to believe that the Soviets would be ill-advised to embark on major aggression within three or four years. But what of the period after that? The hydrogen bomb would then be available to both sides and, as he remarked, it would be folly to suppose that if war broke out, such weapons would not be used.

The interlude must be put to good use. All deterrents would improve and gain authority in the coming years. Indeed, the deterrent might then reap its final reward:

> The day may dawn when fair play, love for one's fellow men, respect for justice and freedom, will enable tormented generations to march forth serene and triumphant from the hideous epoch in which we have to dwell. Meanwhile, never flinch, never weary, never despair.[26]

As Churchill explained to Parliament a few days later, he would regard it as an act of insanity to drive the German people into the hands of the Kremlin and thus tilt into Communist tyranny the destiny of mankind. The only safe policy, much as he desired peaceful co-existence with Russia, was peace through strength; and without unity there would be no strength. 'Weakness makes no appeal to Moscow ... The sooner we can get our united ratification [of the Paris agreements for European defence] settled, the sooner the top-level Four-Power Conference may come ...'[27]

Churchill had clung on against the odds, to see whether even a marginal improvement of temper and understanding could be achieved between Russia and the West. Neither American nor Russian tactics had helped what he was trying to do. If the agonized discussions about European defence had come to a conclusion two years earlier, or even nine months earlier, matters might indeed have been put to the test. As it was, the Russian government showed little anxiety to meet him.

Sir Winston Churchill left office for good in April 1955, being succeeded by Eden. There had been unpleasant episodes in the preceding months with his Cabinet colleagues. Despite the sharpness of their disagreements, marring for a while a friendship of many years, Churchill said benignly 'I only want to help Anthony. I have no scrap of anger, jealousy or spite.'[28] He had perhaps not comprehended that Eden's opposition to the summit meeting stemmed largely from doubt about Churchill's own fitness to conduct the talks. The agreements relating to European defence were promptly ratified, and the long-delayed conference with the Russian leaders followed at once. As Churchill remarked, 'How much more attractive a top-level meeting seems when one has reached the top!'[29] Mr Macmillan, who took part in that encounter as Foreign Secretary, remarks frankly in his memoirs that Churchill had done a last service by realizing that the Soviet monolith would itself begin to undergo changes inseparable from growth and the lapse of time; the retiring Prime Minister had set Western statesmen on a path which they subsequently pursued, not only of peaceful co-existence but of something like genuine *détente*.[30] That was written in 1968, and published in the following year. Neither Macmillan nor anyone else could then foresee the tremendous exertions, the bitter hostility and the unimaginable expense of the next 20 years and more.

In the fine eulogy of Neville Chamberlain from which I quoted earlier, Churchill reflected that history has her changing perspectives: in one generation men seem to have been right, in the next to have been mistaken; the only guide to a man is his conscience, the only shield to his memory the rectitude and sincerity of his actions, and 'with this shield, however the fates may play, we march always in the ranks of honour.'[31] Even those well disposed to Churchill often conceive of him as dwelling unduly in the past. In the essentials, that seems to me the reverse of the truth. Does not his desire to tide over the worst of the animosities, to speak from a position of sufficient strength to convince the Russian leaders that nothing but disaster would fall upon humanity if either side tried conclusions in the new age of nuclear warfare, have a ring of good sense and sobriety and long views? Is not what Churchill was aiming at very much what has happened in Russia and Eastern Europe in the last 20 years, and do we not all breathe more easily in consequence? Were Sir Winston amongst us tonight, he would warn against imagining that because Communist regimes around the world have collapsed, all danger has vanished. With his long historical perspectives, he would also tell us that changes on this scale have never occurred, save as the direct result of a great war, since the early phases of the French Revolution. The year 1989 should stand as prominently in the history books as 1789. If peace does not sit untroubled in her vineyard even now, hope may properly triumph over fear. As for Churchill's conviction that applied science stood ready to pour untold riches into the hands of people in every part of the world if only hatred could be contained and colossal waste upon armaments prevented, his longing for the days when millions could know a broader and fuller life and taste at last something of the prosperity hitherto reserved for the few, do not those attitudes carry a resonance which crosses the generations?

His purpose in this final phase of his political life was to contribute to a durable peace if such could be secured and to ensure the best preparations if the worst should befall. If the effort involved him in criticism or even ridicule, that was a risk he was prepared and able to run. By the words 'I am expendable', he meant that he was an old man, soon to retire, who did not mind being thought feeble or receiving a rebuff from the Russians. Let us pay our tribute to that cast of mind, central to the health of the parliamentary democracy which your Society fosters, a system of government requiring the leadership not of compulsion but of faith, character and persuasion; and one which has to show, as another prime minister pointed out before the war, that democracy can be as efficient as any dictatorship.[32]

If you avow to yourselves 'What we have heard tonight does not fit the accepted picture' you will be quite right; for what we find is not someone consumed by blind hatred of Russia or even of Communism, but cautious and balancing; not someone indifferent to the lives of the millions, but a man who had the opening of opportunities to them at the forefront of his mind as the prize of wise management of international affairs; not somebody bent upon squaring up to the enemy without thought or reason, but one who longed to see whether by parley it might be possible to avoid nuclear warfare. A civilian with profound military knowledge, far from dwelling on the tactics or weaponry of his own ardent youth, he understood the horrors of the new armaments and correctly discerned from the start that the only way to achieve security in so troublous a world was to possess indestructible means of retaliation. Here was not the man forever opposed to appeasement but the devoted disciple of easement; not the mere slave of the United States, as the Russians in their disobliging way would call the British from time to time, but someone who made it clear that he might go his own way to a meeting with Russia if Eisenhower and Dulles felt they could not follow the path with him. Here was also the stern, unbending foe of Nazism who stood out within a few years of the war's end for the rearmament of Germany; the statesman who knew that the fruits of the free spirit of man do not grow in the garden of tyranny and who felt by powerful instinct that the Communist regimes would in the end, if contained and opposed, collapse because of their denial of liberty and the exercise of conscience. When President Yeltsin addressed the Houses of Parliament in London after the collapse of the Russian Empire, he said that Churchill had been entirely right to treat Stalin's Russia as an aggressive force which had to be put into quarantine.

Let us conclude of Churchill, as was well remarked of Einstein, that he possessed the authentic magic which transcends logic and distinguishes the genius from the mass of lesser men with greater talent. Some sense of that must reach out to every part of the world, for Churchill Societies flourish in unexpected places. Why? Perhaps because of his capacity simultaneously to grasp the essence of an issue and to range round its periphery, to put complicated matters in their wider context and so to elevate the plane of discussion that his hearers were almost compelled to rise to the level of events and see themselves as part of an enterprise not only beneficent but noble? Let us take by way of example his conception of Canada's role in the affairs of the world, conveyed as he ended the last great speech that he delivered in this country:

> We have surmounted all the perils and endured all the agonies of the past. We shall provide against and thus prevail over the dangers and problems of the future, if we will withhold no sacrifice, grudge no toil, seek no sordid gain, fear no foe. All will be well. We have, I believe, within us the life-strength and guiding light by which the tormented world around us may find a harbour of safety, after a storm-beaten voyage.
>
> A magnificent future awaits Canada. When I first came here after the Boer War these mighty lands had but 5 million inhabitants. Now there are 14 million. When my grandchildren come here there may well be 30 million. Upon the whole surface of the globe there is no more spacious and splendid domain open to the activity and genius of free men, with one hand clasping in enduring friendship the United States, and the other spread across the ocean both to Britain and to France. You have a sacred mission to discharge. That you will be worthy of it I do not doubt. God bless you all.[33]

As the guests dispersed that night from the Château Laurier, a journalist asked a former prime minister of Canada for his impression of Churchill's speech. Mr Meighen replied in terms which might fittingly lodge themselves in the consciousness of Societies like ours: 'I bow in humility before the majesty of his life's performance.'[34]

9

'Historians Are Dangerous'

Churchill, Chamberlain and Some Others[*]

*Historians are dangerous and capable of turning everything topsy-turvy.
They have to be watched.*

(Khrushchev, 1956)[1]

'I wish I were as sure as anything in this world as Tom Macaulay is of
everything.' Thus spoke a statesman (in the world-weary form of Lord
Melbourne) about a historian – and no ordinary historian, for it was
the one whose assaults upon the character of the Duke of Marlborough
Mr Winston Churchill set out to avenge in the 1930s. It would be more
satisfying, and in general more accurate, if such a remark had been made
by a historian about a man of affairs. Yet we in our profession should
feel a meed of sympathy for the politicians, who have their legitimate
grievances. We subject their policies, private lives and personalities to
unrelenting scrutiny. Their failings are exposed to stinging criticism,
sometimes proffered by people whose own capacity to manage great affairs
is not obvious. Nor does the grave bring immunity. Thus in the preamble
to the war against Iraq in 2003 the Leader of the Liberal Democrats, Mr
Kennedy, suddenly found himself dubbed 'Chamberlain Charlie', while
Mr Blair characterized Neville Chamberlain as 'a good man who made
the wrong decision.' In other words, Britain should have fought in 1938 at
the latest. Justifying the impending war against the dictator in Baghdad,
the Prime Minister stated that Britain and the world would face a living

---

[*] This is an expanded version of an address given by the author to a conference of
historians at the University of Birmingham.

nightmare if they appeased him as they had appeased Hitler. There must be no retreat, as there had been before 1939:

> The lesson we learned then was that, if confronted by a threat, we back away because we assume that our good and peaceful intentions are matched by those threatening us, the threat only grows and at a later time has to be confronted again, but in a far more deadly and dangerous form.[2]

This line of argument assumes that there are sufficient similarities between the events of the 1930s and those of 2003 to justify the drawing of direct analogies and thus of prescriptions for policy. It reflects a cast of mind which looks directly to history for lessons, justifications, even consolations. Professional historians should not deplore such habits. After all, what intelligent man or woman does not brood upon experience, direct and vicarious? Who does not, in weighing the consequences of a course of action, search for parallels? 'History', whether sound or false, will always be looked to by those who bear the heaviest responsibilities. No one exemplifies this habit more powerfully than Churchill, who lived near the eye of the storm and wrote of his experiences with a persuasive power which no other leader of the twentieth century has matched. If war – as Briand remarked to Lloyd George – is much too serious a business to be left to military men, history is much too pervasive to remain the sole preserve of historians.

★ ★ ★ ★ ★

> *To know what to surrender, and what to hold firm, and indeed to recognise the situation of critical choice when it arises, is an art requiring such resources of experience, wisdom and insight, that I cannot envy those public men of whatever party who may at any moment be called upon to make decisions, and who may in due course be censured by posterity, either as fanatics or as opportunists.*
>
> (T.S. Eliot)[3]

When is it justifiable to wage preventive war? Even in dealing with a hostile and contemptuous dictator, can no point of contact be found, nothing which, if the immediate crisis is contained, can be built upon?

May the menace be countered by deterrence and if so how is that force best exerted? What if the consequences of going to war are likely to be its extension into many other fields, and an orgy of death and destruction? What if the fate of civilization itself may hang upon the outcome? The language may sound apocalyptic. Nevertheless, those are issues which Chamberlain had to confront in 1938 and 1939, as did Churchill during the war and again in his last spell as Prime Minister. President Bush and Mr Blair were no strangers to such calculations, although the danger posed by Iraq, or even by terrorism in all its international manifestations, does not begin to compare with the perils so narrowly surmounted two generations ago.

Once upon a time, it all looked so simple. The economic problems of the 1930s would have been mitigated, perhaps resolved, if only benighted politicians had listened to Keynes; the League would have checked the Japanese onslaught upon East Asia if only Sir John Simon had welcomed the proposals of Mr Stimson; collective security would have contained Hitler and Mussolini if only the powers – but essentially the British – had behaved more boldly in the Abyssinian crisis or over the Rhineland. To come more precisely to the gravamen of the charges against Chamberlain, he should either have given a British guarantee to Czechoslovakia in 1938 or stood apart from the brewing crisis. This was one of the principal themes of Churchill's speech in the Munich debate; he could not conceive, he argued, a worse result for Czechoslovakia if the British had disinterested themselves publicly.[4] In the first volume of the six which he devoted to World War II, the arguments are reinforced: had the British stood firm, the French would have done likewise; a conspiracy among the German generals might well have overthrown Hitler; Russia would probably have come to the aid of Czechoslovakia in an effective way; the Czech defences would have held if France had marched against Germany; the Czech army was so formidable that Germany would have been highly vulnerable in the West; Germany gained more than her opponents by the year's delay; and to extend the argument into the following year, if only the British had been more forthcoming in their dealings with Russia, a powerful military alliance would have been formed. As Churchill himself expressed it, had Chamberlain said to Stalin 'Let us three band together and break Hitler's neck', history might have taken a different course, or at any rate it could not have taken a worse.[5] In sum, Beneš should have refused to be bullied; rather, he should have behaved as the Poles did in 1939.

Only timely action and bold, self-confident statesmanship were needed to avert catastrophe, Churchill told the Congress of the United States in the aftermath of Pearl Harbour: 'Five or six years ago it would have been easy, without shedding a drop of blood, for the United States and Britain to have insisted on fulfilment of the disarmament clauses of the treaties which Germany signed after the Great War ...'[6] A day or two later, he remarked to Parliament in Ottawa: 'We did not make this war. We did not seek it. We did all we could to avoid it. We did too much to avoid it. We went so far at times in trying to avoid it as to be almost destroyed by it when it broke upon us.'[7] In the Preface to *The Gathering Storm*, the point is put yet more baldly: 'There never was a war easier to stop than that which has just wrecked what was left of the world from the previous struggle.'[8]

We nowadays know a great deal more about these events than any minister or government could have done at the time. It would be a proper exercise of historical judgement to say that while the actions of 1936, 1938 and 1939 were understandable, given the information available to those in power, we see that those decisions were mistaken. But most German historians, with every reason to espouse the opposite view, do not suggest that a military or civilian coup against Hitler was likely to succeed in 1938; in other words, the British and French governments were right not to stake everything on that prospect. There is no likelihood that a different handling of President Roosevelt's initiative in January 1938 would have led to an effective American intervention in Europe; not that such an outcome was ever probable, for even the fall of France and the imminent peril of Britain in the summer of 1940 provoked nothing of the kind and the United States' spending upon defence remained modest to a degree. Whatever the French might have stated as their official policy, it is hard to imagine a robust French onslaught against Western Germany in October 1938. There is no reason to suppose that any Russian intervention could have been effective in that year. It is possible, but scarcely more, that the internal divisions in Czechoslovakia would not have hobbled the fighting capacity of the Czech Army, and that the Germans would not have been able to turn the established Czech positions by moving in from the freshly conquered Austria. It is certainly true that Germany rearmed rapidly in the year between Munich and the outbreak of war, and equally true that the British did likewise; by the summer of 1939, British aircraft production equalled that of Germany, though there were still long arrears to retrieve, and by the summer of 1940 Britain had Spitfires and Hurricanes in squadron service, the radar chain and Enigma, none of which advantages it possessed in 1938 or 1939. No one could have refused more firmly than Stalin to say *tout court* in May 1939, 'We shall band together and break Hitler's neck'; for excellent reasons, he wished to know the terms in detail first.

The fact is that no country – not France, not Britain, not Russia – wished to fight Germany, the strongest single power in Europe. You will recall Roderick Spode, impressively muscular founder of the Saviours of Britain, a Fascist band of the 1930s known as the Black Shorts because the entire supply of black shirts had run out before the organization was formed. 'Stop saying "Oh, yes" you miserable worm,' snarls Spode at Bertie Wooster, 'and listen to me.' Many chaps, Wooster reflects, might have resented Spode's tone. 'I did myself, as a matter of fact. But you know how it is. There are some fellows you are right on your toes to tick off when they call you a miserable worm, others not quite so much.'[9]

At least to my mind, it is not clear that Czechoslovakia would have been well served in 1938 by a British public declaration of detachment. The evidence strongly suggests that Hitler – though whether this was a rational calculation is quite a different matter – desired a war against Czechoslovakia and would not have scrupled to launch it. That is what Chamberlain concluded at the time and in later years Hitler repeatedly lamented that the British Prime Minister's persistence and the Czech government's agonized decision to cede the Sudetenland had deprived him of the war he sought.

It is common to read, even now, that Chamberlain pursued a foreign policy of his own, regardless of the judgement of the Foreign Secretary or indeed of the Foreign Office. That is in substance untrue. It was the unenviable task of the Permanent Under-Secretary to consider the currents of opinion, within the Office and among British diplomats abroad, and then to submit his advice. A similar duty, though we know relatively little of what was said and done, fell upon the head of the Secret Intelligence Service, MI6; but it chances, no doubt by a fault in the process of weeding, that the views tendered to the Prime Minister by MI6 in the middle of September 1938 have long been available for scrutiny, and that the policy of the British government followed closely MI6's recommendations.[10] On the broader plane, the Permanent Under-Secretary of the Foreign Office, Sir Alexander Cadogan, carried much weight both with his immediate master, Lord Halifax, and with the Prime Minister. In no first-class issue did the government act against Cadogan's advice, and he was often the initiator of foreign policy. It was he who remarked that while Chamberlain was not in the least a gullible or obstinate old man, he had perhaps insufficient cynicism.[11] We may say the same, though not necessarily as a criticism, of Churchill too. He liked to work on the principle that you should believe well of people unless you have very strong reason to conclude otherwise.

This is not to avow that the decisions taken in 1938 were necessarily the right ones. Upon that subject there is room for ample and legitimate disagreement. But it is to say that there has been no revelation of recent years which would demonstrate beyond doubt that the decisions of 1938 were wrong, given the scale of the issues. This latter point is no formal quibble. To provide a yardstick, let us think of the war in the Gulf of 1991, or of the invasion of Iraq a dozen years later. Grave as those acts were, comparisons with 1938 lie beside the mark. In recent times, overwhelming military power has resided with the United States and its allies. In 1938, the West enjoyed no such advantage; Germany might have defeated France and besieged Britain, as in 1940. That was why pre-war Germany mattered more, as a potential enemy, than Japan or Italy or indeed Russia. Germany might stab the British Empire to its heart. The other enemies, strong and dangerous as they were, could strike only at the limbs. From such wounds recovery might be – and in the event proved to be – possible.

Let me turn to another aspect. It is a mistake to see the agreement reached at Munich, and the Anglo-German declaration signed immediately afterwards, merely as pieces of paper extorted at a time of crisis. They were that, to be sure; but they were more, the embodiments of a process going back many years. If it is sometimes hard enough to establish what happened, even with the mass of documentation available to us for the 1930s, it is still harder to weigh motives and practical possibilities. At the least, historians must re-examine evidence and test long-established assumptions and fashionable opinions; not because there is special merit in arriving at views contrary to those held by the majority but because patient reassessment is of the essence of our discipline. It is a matter not only of the facts, but also of the temper of the times and the climate of opinion, the effect of which – as Churchill acknowledged – is overwhelming. As he remarked in his valediction of

Chamberlain, 'When the perspective of time has lengthened, all stands in a different setting. There is a new proportion. There is another scale of values.'[12]

Nor is it only a question of judging events as recorded in weighty monographs, or in materials selected by conscientious editors. To take a single example, I do not know of any collection of documents or a general work which reflects in its true proportions the attention devoted in Britain to the Spanish Civil War in all its manifestations. To traverse files of old newspapers is not always an enlivening business, and often they are difficult of access. Not everyone cares to spend months reading Hansard, but even a look at the index tells part of the story. There were many then, and are some now, to whom the Spanish Civil War presented an issue of principle as stark as Munich. Cold print conveys at least some impression of the fury vented upon ministers who were at worst accused of being secret supporters of Fascism and Nazism, or at best of neglecting a clear opportunity to defeat the forces of evil upon the plains of Spain. Such presumptions have a great deal to do with the attitudes taken up towards Chamberlain, Hoare, Simon, R.A. Butler and others. Neither at the time nor in retrospect did Churchill have any sympathy with these criticisms. He judged that with everything else it had on its hands, the British government was right to keep out of Spain. As for the forces of the far left, increasingly dominant in the government of Spain, he remarks 'Naturally I was not in favour of the Communists. How could I be when if I had been a Spaniard, they would have murdered me and my family and friends?'[13]

I mentioned the need to establish scales of measurement. Let us remember, then, the magnitude of the economic disaster of the 1930s. Not since the establishment of modern systems of commerce and exchange had anything of the kind occurred: the failure of banks, soaring unemployment, the ruin of whole industries, the collapse of international trade, the fall of prices (and thus of purchasing power) which increased the burden of debt, reduced revenues and on all scores made it harder for Britain to honour financial commitments abroad, contracted in very different circumstances. Negotiations with Germany over reparations and with the USA over the British debt were soon to be strongly influenced by this factor. It is easy in retrospect to dismiss the crisis of 1931 and after as exaggerated and misunderstood. At the time, it seemed so to precious few. The hopes of the 1920s, of what was called a 'return to normalcy', vanished. The old expression 'as safe as the Bank of England' rang hollow. Although belief in Free Trade had quasi-religious overtones in the Liberal and Labour parties, and also with Churchill, the former, and somewhat doubtfully Conservative, Chancellor of the Exchequer, even he felt obliged to refashion his views in the cataclysm of 1931 and 1932.

It has been the custom for many years to deride the National Government: for the ardent protectionists, of whom that omniscient Birmingham M.P. Leo Amery was the most fervent spokesman, it did too little for Imperial Preference; for some, most of them exercising a high degree of hindsight, it did too little about rearmament; for others, it did too little about disarmament. Churchill himself, who could not stand Ramsay MacDonald, believed that the National Government had destroyed the normal robustness of British politics by leaving only the merest rump of Opposition. It is generally assumed that the National Government was merely a Conservative administration in another guise, the diaphanous drapery of National Labour and National Liberal insufficient to disguise its essential character.

It would be pointless to deny that there is some force in each of these allegations. I said a little earlier, however, that old assumptions and assertions should be constantly tested. It seems to me that none of the views just summarized contains the whole truth.

The National Government set itself to reach agreements which would bind up the wounds of the past, or put an end to obvious anomalies, thus to stave off some of the emerging threats. In that light, for example, we should see the Lausanne Conference of 1932, in which the Labour Prime Minister MacDonald, the Liberal President of the Board of Trade Runciman and the Conservative (and convinced protectionist) Chamberlain played the principal roles. Does not Churchill himself tell us that the economic clauses of the 1919 settlement were 'malignant and silly to an extent that made them obviously futile', and condemn as insane, complicated idiocy the arrangement of the 1920s under which loans to Germany far outstripped the reparations she paid?[14] Ministers well realized in the summer of 1932 that Germany would not continue these payments on more than a token scale. They also understood the degree to which successive German governments, as the Weimar regime crumbled, were corroded by the accusation that in complying with the terms of Versailles they were undermining their country's status and prospects. To bring France, and Italy and other powers into the agreement required skill and nerve, as did the task of persuading the United States government that Britain could not honour her debts indefinitely if she were not to receive the larger amounts due to her. For this prolonged default, the word itself being studiously avoided, a large levy was exacted; the Johnson Act of 1934 forbade American loans to countries which had not repaid their debts, and the currents running in favour of a strict neutrality, entirely understandable from the American point of view but highly damaging from a British, were strengthened.

Chamberlain moved directly from Lausanne to the Ottawa Conference. In Canada, he was the main ministerial mover, along with Baldwin (who, Churchill wrote well after the war with pained disapproval, not only had 'a manufacturer's ingrained approval of protection' but also felt 'that the times were too far gone for any robust assertion of British Imperial greatness'[15]), a lifelong Labour man in the person of J.H. Thomas, then Secretary of State for the Dominions, and the former Free Trader Walter Runciman. The situation disclosed at Ottawa was alarming. Afterwards, Chamberlain told his colleagues how thin the cement of Empire had worn. Let us leave for another day a discussion of the economic merits of the Ottawa agreements. Not enough has been made of their political significance. They played their part, as did careful attention to the Dominions by Baldwin, Chamberlain and other ministers, in bringing about one of the more important and least-noticed facts of the twentieth century, that the entire Commonwealth (with the exception of semi-detached Eire) fought from 1939 to 1945 and that its contribution to victory was indispensable.

The National Government attempted, you will doubtless say with small prospect of success, to apply the same processes of argument and negotiation to the long-drawn agony of the Disarmament Conference at Geneva. It had some hopes, in the event frustrated by Roosevelt's cavalier brushing-aside of the recommendations of his own delegation in London, of the World Economic Conference. It negotiated the Naval Treaty of 1935 with Germany, on the principle that Germany's protestations had better be put to the test, and that the alternative was an unlimited German rearmament at sea. This treaty was essentially the work of the Admiralty and the Foreign Office. Of course it could not be reconciled with the provisions of Versailles. Rather, it had to be reconciled with something pressing and intractable: the determination of Germany to rearm, with or without permission, and the evident unwillingness of others to thwart her.

No minister grasped more clearly than Chamberlain the essential fact of Britain's international position in the 1930s: that the country had not the resources in money or men to fight three front-rank powers – or if you insist that Fascist Italy was not a front-rank power, then let us say two and a half front-rank powers, though Italy's ability to threaten crucial and ill-defended parts of the British Imperial structure magnified her significance as an enemy – in theatres scattered all over the world. That this was the crux of the matter was not understood by many at the time or later. Whole works of a generation ago would discuss Britain's policy towards Hitler's Germany without serious mention of the Mediterranean or the Middle East or South-East Asia or the Pacific. Churchill himself had been dismissive in the 1920s of the supposed threat from Japan. Thus he had justified many of his stringent curbs upon the budget of the Royal Navy. He does not appear to have viewed Japan with any great alarm, even when her assault upon China turned into a full-scale war after 1931.

You see the nature of the dilemma. It was not only that the theatres of war might be spread across the globe; it was that if Britain became involved in a long war, for example in the Far East, the temptation to Italy in the Mediterranean or the Near East or North Africa, or to Germany in Scandinavia or Western Europe or the Atlantic, might become irresistible. In other words, there was every possibility that war with one power would eventually entail war with two or three, as in the end it did. Chamberlain apprehended this only too well as bad turned to worse during that decade. It was in its nature a prospect which could not be discussed in public by ministers, but it does provide the context in which we should place the attempts which he supported between 1934 and 1936 to make terms with Japan in the field of economics as well as of foreign policy.

This search for agreement, with its several motives, is perhaps seen most plainly of all in respect of India. I hope not to offend your sensibilities by coming to the defence of the National Government again. Here was far and away the most pregnant Imperial issue for that generation. The policy embraced by the Government of India Act, 1935, could hardly have been carried into law without the broad range of opinions represented in the coalition. As it was, a substantial section of the Conservative forces in Parliament, and a more substantial section of the party outside Parliament, opposed the bill. At the head of those forces stood Churchill. Some have suggested that he was wilfully or unworthily excluded from the National Government formed in 1931. In reality, he had excluded himself by leaving the Committee of Business, which we should nowadays call the Shadow Cabinet, on this issue in January of that year.

The merits of the Government of India Act provide too large a subject to embark upon here. It seems to me that a policy along those broad lines was necessary, not least because the British had to show that India would be able, and at no remote date, to take her place on terms of equality with the Dominions. Incidentally, it is unjust to dismiss Churchill's views about India as merely reactionary or anachronistic. There was solid substance in many of the fears which he expressed. He pursued his campaign in a style which often caused offence and, as he well knew, made it impossible for him to be a member of the government until the Indian question was resolved in one way or the other. Almost worse, Churchill was doing as his father had done before him, attempting to use the structures and machine of the party against the leaders of the party itself. It is scarcely possible to convey now a sense of the place which India, and more generally Imperial affairs, occupied in the British politics of those days. As with the Spanish Civil War, only a prolonged immersion in the newspapers, literature and debates will furnish some of the flavour.

I might take other examples of the search for agreement and attempt to meet grievances, especially those of resurgent Germany: the visit which Sir John Simon and Anthony Eden paid to Hitler in 1935; the effort to ascertain Germany's demands after the coup in the Rhineland a year later; the conversations between Halifax and the German leaders in November 1937, and the earnest quest for the outlines of a possible settlement which followed. Within the Foreign Office, the chief protagonist of that policy had been Cadogan. 'German demands, like mushrooms, *grow in the dark*', he wrote after the Anschluss, recommending that yet another attempt be made to elicit a statement of Germany's terms.[16]

The British government knew that it might be impossible to meet those claims, and in that light we should see the negotiations with Italy. Here too the prospects were doubtful. Had the British possessed in the spring of 1938 a substantial army, and the strength in the air achieved by the summer of 1939 or still better the summer of 1940, the outlook would have been transformed. To achieve any such state of affairs would have required rearmament on a very large scale from 1933 or 1934, and to indulge in counter-factual history is a risky business. Still, we must permit the habit from time to time if we aspire to distribute praise and blame among statesmen. In theory, it would have been open to the USA, Britain, France, Italy and perhaps some lesser powers to prevent by force Germany's rearmament from 1933. At the time, whatever he may later have believed, not even Churchill thought that feasible. When Germany re-entered the Rhineland zone in 1936, a prompt French riposte, with what could have been no more than token British support, might have inflicted at least a check on Hitler. The French Foreign Minister, Flandin, said to Chamberlain that if a firm front were maintained by France and England, Germany would yield without war. 'We cannot accept this as a reliable estimate of a mad dictator's reactions', Chamberlain commented crisply in his diary.[17] Whether even token British support could have been offered is highly debatable and, unbelievable as it may seem, the French government had no coherent plan for a swift military retort even though the contingency had been foreseen for many years. By 1938, however, the circumstances were far more perilous.

To have undertaken heavy rearmament – as distinct from the modest measures actually introduced – by 1934 would have required large borrowing and increased taxation. Such a programme could not have been carried out so early, on the evidence then available, without the demise of the National Government. It was not until after the end of the Disarmament Conference, the open announcement of Germany's rearmament, Hitler's brazen claim to have reached parity with the Royal Air Force in March 1935, the obvious Italian preparations for an assault on Abyssinia, that the position changed out of recognition. Chamberlain would have liked to fight the General Election of 1935 openly on the question of substantial and early rearmament; Baldwin preferred something less clear-cut, but even the most casual reader of a newspaper during the election campaign could have had no doubt about the difference between the National Government, which said that rearmament must go ahead on a much larger scale than heretofore, and the two main Opposition parties, which denied that anything of the kind was necessary.

It is, I think, plain that serious British rearmament ought to have begun at least a year earlier than it did; but I cannot persuade myself that it would have been possible. Even a purely Conservative administration could scarcely have embarked on such a course without calling a general election. Whether such an election could have been won in, say, 1933 or 1934 upon such a programme must remain distinctly doubtful. As Baldwin remarked in a speech persistently and in some cases deliberately misrepresented,

> Supposing I had gone to the country [at the end of 1933 or in 1934] and said that Germany was rearming and that we must rearm, does anybody think that this pacific democracy would have rallied to that cry at that moment? I cannot think of anything which would have made the loss of the election from my point of view more certain.

Reflecting in old age upon that period, he said simply 'It was a nightmare.'[18]

Given Mussolini's behaviour in Abyssinia and Spain, to negotiate with him in 1937 or 1938 was evidently a course fraught with risk. To go to war with Italy at no late date, however, without bending every effort to avoid a catastrophe, was to Chamberlain's mind unthinkable on moral and practical grounds; and not only to his mind, since the opening of negotiations was supported by almost every senior figure in the Foreign Office and after exhaustive debate by every member of the Cabinet save one, that devoted Chancellor of this University Anthony Eden. Quite apart from the general imperative to avoid war, there was the practical consideration that Italian neutrality would be of high value to the British and French if they were at odds with Germany, and still more to the British if they were grappling with Germany and Japan simultaneously. The editor of *Ciano's Diplomatic Papers*, later to edit *Punch*, represents Chamberlain as believing without qualification that it was 'possible to win over Mussolini with kind words and complaisant actions'. The Duce, we are told, was looking only for indications of some counter-force to the German pressure which would shortly reach the Brenner Pass. As a matter of fact, the German forces had reached the Brenner Pass before the negotiations began in earnest. Mussolini was met, we are informed, with the 'maundering goodwill of a Mayor of Birmingham addressing a Rotary lunch.'[19] By an effort of self-restraint, I forbear to comment on the merits of these judgements, pausing only to remark upon their ineffable metropolitan condescension. It is a solace to all of us in the Midlands, you will agree, to realize that no Lord Mayor of London would stray into the most fleeting expression of maundering goodwill.

Let us notice here one other attempt, fiercely criticized by Churchill, to assuage grievances. I refer to the Anglo-Irish Agreement of 1938, of peculiar interest in this context because so much of it depended upon a reading of history, ancient and modern. The Irish, Chamberlain reflected, have a terrible memory for grievances. That devoted Labour man Malcolm MacDonald, supple, personable, imaginative, frank, who became as fond of Chamberlain as Chamberlain of him – perhaps to the surprise of both – discovered in 1936 that the latter was willing to support proposals to reduce the frictions between Britain and Eire. On the British side, the Agreement of April 1938, patiently pursued over many months, owed most to MacDonald and after him to Chamberlain. The Prime Minister made a sincere and sustained effort to understand Irish claims. He refused to haggle over small matters, in the interests of a wider settlement. He accepted the view of the Chiefs of Staff that whatever might be said in theory, it would in practice be impossible for the British to hold the Irish ports by force as enclaves in a hostile country.[20] He hoped that the hostility might turn in the end to something more helpful to both sides; no unworthy aspiration, and one not entirely belied in the event, for Ireland's neutrality during the war proved more benevolent than it might have been.

★ ★ ★ ★ ★

The past is a foreign country: they do things differently there.
(L.P. Hartley, *The Go-Between*)

When he became Prime Minister at the end of May 1937, Chamberlain knew that it might prove impossible to avert war. He said so in terms to a private meeting of the government's Parliamentary supporters.[21] To the House of Commons and the world at large, he remarked at the height of one of the innumerable crises over Spain:

I have read that in the high mountains there are sometimes conditions ... when an incautious move or even a sudden loud exclamation may start an avalanche. That is just the condition in which we are finding ourselves today. I believe, although the snow may be perilously poised, it has not yet begun to move, and if we can all exercise caution, patience and self-restraint, we may yet be able to save the peace of Europe.[22]

In the same speech, Chamberlain observed that there was 'not a country or a government that wants to see a European war', an assertion made in the context of intervention in Spain but with a much wider connotation. This sense of impending earthquake, of civilization treading upon a crumbling crust, was constantly present in the minds of British ministers who held office in the 1930s. It connected indissolubly with a strong sense of duty to ensure that the tragedy of the first war was not allowed to repeat itself; or, when that seemed too high an ambition, at least to make sure that every expedient had been explored before war was declared again, for a new war was expected to spread over most of the world – as the first war had not done – and to prove even more devastating. The general sense that sophisticated science would render war more destructive than ever was by no means misplaced.

I have argued that it is a mistake to think of the policy pursued by Chamberlain and his colleagues, even when the pace was increasingly dictated by the dictators, as simply one of hapless concession. Chamberlain told the House of Commons after the Anschluss in March 1938 that Britain might well find herself involved in war at an early date, but refused to give a commitment to Czechoslovakia in advance. As Eden had often done, in company with plenty of ministers between the wars, he warned once more – of course with a reading of history in mind, a judgement on the experiences of the decade before 1914 – against the dangers of dividing Europe into two armed and exclusive camps. At the Town Hall of this city, in the middle of April 1938, Chamberlain spoke of rearmament and air raid precautions and the urgent need to do everything possible to preserve the peace. The heart of the oration deserves quotation:

To me the very idea that the hard-won savings of our people, which ought to be devoted to the alleviation of suffering, to the opening out of institutions and recreations, to the care of the old, to the development of the minds and the bodies of the young – the thought that these savings should have to be dissipated upon

253

the construction of weapons of war is hateful and damnable. Yet I cannot shut my eyes to the fact that under the present conditions of the world we have no alternative but to go on with it, because it is the very breath of our British being, our freedom itself, that is at stake.

Do not let us not forget that this freedom has come down to us from the past, bought for us at a price. If we wish to keep it we must pay the interest on that price in each succeeding generation ...Whatever differences there may be between us and other nations ... do not forget that we are all members of the human race and subject to the like passions and affections and fears and desires. There must be something in common between us if only we can find it, and perhaps by our very aloofness from the rest of Europe, we may have some special part to play as conciliator and mediator. An ancient historian once wrote of the Greeks that they had made gentle the life of the world. I do not know whether in these modern days it is possible for any nation to emulate the example of the Greeks, but I can imagine no nobler ambition for an English statesman than to win the same tribute for his own country.[23]

In respect of Germany, the most formidable of the potential enemies, three interlinked questions arose. How should Britain (and France, where the policies could be harmonized) treat Germany, the whole political entity? How should they deal with the German polity, including the Wehrmacht? Most important of all, what was to be done about Hitler? It might well prove that by comparison with that last, the other two questions scarcely counted. These were the imponderables which Chamberlain and his colleagues tried to assess. Was it possible, for example, by fair treatment of grievances, to deprive the German government and its leader of support for rash and extreme courses? That did not seem an entirely fanciful prospect at the time of the unplanned, to Hitler unwelcome, but unmistakable demonstrations in Chamberlain's support when he went to Germany in 1938. If Hitler was 'the child of the rage and grief of a mighty empire and race that had suffered overwhelming defeat', might those injuries be diminished? Or would he let loose another war 'in which civilization will inevitably succumb'? Both possibilities still stood open, wrote Churchill in 1935.[24] Was Hitler a gambler, a supreme actor and stage-manager, capable of threatening open war, as he did to Chamberlain at their meetings in September 1938, of piling tension on tension, but nevertheless calculating and rational? In other words, was he susceptible to deterrence? Could he not see that if a great war were unleashed, the very forces which he affected to fear and despise most, Russia and Communism, would profit? Might he be persuaded by a mixture of concession and firmness to see that he could have, indeed already possessed, a substantial measure of power in central Europe where the British had neither the intention nor the strength to resist him?

Whether to risk a bluff was discussed between British and French ministers after the Anschluss and before the 'May crisis' of 1938. Chamberlain remarked that he thought a time might come when a gamble upon the issue of peace and war could be contemplated with less anxiety than at present.[25] The record shows that he was oppressed by the military prospects as they then stood, and by the horrible consequences for many millions should war break out. In the summer of 1938, the Prime Minister read with attention Professor Temperley's book on the foreign policy of George Canning, who had repeatedly laid down that statesmen should not utter threats in international affairs unless willing and able to carry them out. Chamberlain, who relished the company of the young, invited one of his daughter's friends to stay at Chequers in the first week of August 1938. She said to him, 'Mr Chamberlain, you know that in all these years I have never asked you about anything political. But do you mind if I do, just once?' 'No, of course I don't mind. Ask me anything you like.' 'There are all these terrible stories in the newspapers. What is Hitler really like?' 'He is mad, and especially dangerous because unpredictable.'[26]

Thus we return to the question of preventive war and the level at which the threshold of proof needs to be set, remembering that its height must vary according to the scale of risk. We find Chamberlain writing in the second week of September 1938, with Canning much in mind, 'I fully realise that, if eventually things go wrong and the aggression takes place, there will be many, including Winston, who will say that the British government must bear the responsibility, and that if only they had had the courage to tell Hitler now that, if he used force, we should at once declare war, that would have stopped him. By that time it will be impossible to prove the contrary, but I am satisfied that we should be wrong to allow the most vital decision that any country could take, the decision as to peace or war, to pass out of our hands into those of the ruler of another country, and a lunatic at that.'[27]

Hitler stated in solemn terms that the Sudetenland would constitute the last of his territorial demands. He might well be lying, as many suspected. Could his potential opponents be so sure of it that they could justify going to war? The mounting tally of Hitler's threats, the chorus of hatred against Czechoslovakia, his apparent indifference to the prospect of a war, did in the end cause Britain to inform him on the morning of 27 September that if he persisted in all his demands, France would fight and Britain would support her. Hitler's blustering reaction demonstrates that he understood the message plainly enough. It is often asserted that the Führer simply imposed his will upon a gullible Chamberlain, a fawning Mussolini and a tremulous Daladier. In reality, matters were not quite so neat. Hitler was soon to lament that he had denied himself the chance to crush Czechoslovakia. To adapt a phrase which became notorious 18 months later, Hitler felt that he had missed the bus.

In the Parliamentary debate after Munich, Chamberlain said that he felt convinced that by his actions he had averted war, in which he was almost certainly correct, and that he was equally sure he was right to do so. He was convinced that public opinion would not have supported a war to prevent the Sudeten Germans from joining the Reich, and made a powerful retort to Churchill's argument that the British might well have washed their hands of the whole issue much earlier in the summer. The belief that war was inevitable he characterized as a bleak and barren policy: 'Does the experience of the Great War and the years that followed it give us reasonable hope that if some new war started that would end war, any more than the last one did? No.'

As for the words 'peace in our time', which in an echo of Disraeli he had used on his return from Munich, Chamberlain asked Honourable Members not to read into a phrase used at a moment 'of some emotion, after a long and exhausting day, after I had driven through miles of enthusiastic, cheering people' more than the words were intended to convey:

> I do indeed believe that we may yet secure peace for our time, but I never meant to suggest that we should do that by disarmament ... Our past experience has shown us only too clearly that weakness in armed strength means weakness in diplomacy, and that if we want

to secure a lasting peace. ... diplomacy cannot be effective until the consciousness exists, not here alone, but elsewhere, that behind the diplomacy is the strength to give effect to it.'[28]

* * * * *

In matters where shades of feeling are involved, it is not always easy for the historian to be as definite as he could wish. He wants to keep the record straight, and yet he cannot take any one particular moment of time, pin it down to the scrutiny of Posterity and say 'This was the moment when Lord Emsworth for the first time found himself wishing that his guest would tumble out of an upper window and break his neck.'

(P.G. Wodehouse)[29]

The very words 'Munich' and 'appeasement' have come to signify something shameful, a purblind refusal to face unpleasant facts, a failure to recognize that danger redoubles when not confronted, a timid surrender to brute force; still worse, surrender at the expense of a third party. In the face of threatened aggression, it was always possible to say in 1938 'We must strain every sinew for peace but if all fails, we must not take up arms; that is simply to compound the crime.' As Churchill remarks, 'Everyone respects the Quakers. Still, it is not on these terms that Ministers assume their responsibilities of guiding States.'[30] It was equally possible to make a stand of principle in the opposite sense by saying 'Germany's claims are outrageous, her methods shocking, her leadership corrupt, even crazy. We must therefore as a matter of honour stand and fight, no matter what the consequences.' That is, I believe, not an unfair summary of the position of Duff Cooper and Churchill, which commands respect; but it is vital to remember that they believed Britain and France would win a war fought on those issues and at that time. There was a moment at which Cadogan, when it seemed likely that some of Hitler's more outrageous demands would be accepted, confided to his diary 'I *know* we and they [the French] are in no condition to fight: but I'd rather be beat than dishonoured.'[31]

My purpose is not to contend that the policy followed during the 1930s by the British government was right, for its stated goal was to preserve the peace and by peace Chamberlain and his colleagues meant something more than the mere absence of war. Rather, I am trying to suggest, especially if we are to seek direct connections between the events of 1938 and those of 2003, that we should not accept without deep reflection any version of the past, no matter how securely established it may appear. My theme is uncertainty. Clausewitz writes of the fog of war. The fog of peace in 1938 and 1939 was scarcely less dense. Ministers and Chiefs of Staff and civil servants must often make policy in a hurry, take decisions on inadequate information, grapple with vast unknowns in times of high tension. We should not be surprised to find them less confident about the motives, intentions and characters of those with whom they deal than we like to feel many years afterwards. If we accept that Hitler did not have a timetable and sequence of aggressions carefully planned, so that even the most punctilious reading of *Mein Kampf* (with its expressions of Hitler's strong desire for good relations or even an alliance with Britain) would not have shown which crises would come in which order, perhaps we shall understand the hesitations and fumblings the better. Chamberlain was highly disciplined in his concentration, his appetite for facts, his capacity to use the official machine, his control of emotions; even in those agonizing months of August and September 1938 he retained his steely composure. Churchill was by temperament quite the opposite. Perhaps that helps to explain why the two of them made so formidable a combination after September 1939. Referring somewhat spaciously to the long serious of miscalculations and misjudgements of men and facts on which Chamberlain based himself, Churchill adds 'The motives which inspired him have never been impugned, and the course he followed required the highest degree of moral courage.'[32]

In the broadcast he made on the evening of 27 September 1938, when the issue trembled in the balance, Chamberlain had said that if he were convinced that any nation had made up its mind to dominate the world by fear of its force, he would feel it that it must be resisted:

> Under such a domination, life for people who believe in liberty would not be worth living; but war is a fearful thing, and we must be very clear, before we embark on it, that it is really the great issues that are at stake, and that the call to risk everything in their defence, when all the consequences are weighed, is irresistible.[33]

Those were essentially the grounds upon which Britain and France went to war a year later. They had become convinced that Germany did intend to dominate the world, or at any rate a large part of it, by fear of its force.

Deterrence, incidentally, was an issue not only for the Germans but also for the British. This country was not deterred in 1939 by a prudential balancing of forces, some nicely calculated less or more. That was even truer after the fall of France in June 1940.

After March 1939, when Hitler had clearly broken his own undertakings and thrown overboard the argument that he was claiming for Germany only those people who were rightfully part of the Fatherland, the uncertainties were much reduced. The military position remained perilous, since the threat from Japan was far greater than it had been in 1938. Indeed, Britain and Japan came almost to the point of war in July 1939. It is right to add, since even now books and articles abound with references to inadequate and belated rearmament, that the government was spending upon arms sums which, whether measured absolutely or as a proportion of national income, vastly exceeded the amounts spent by any previous British administration in peacetime; in 1939, more than 20 per cent of the gross domestic product was consumed by the needs of defence, and by the following year the figure had risen to almost 50 per cent. Chamberlain's government had the melancholy distinction of being the first in British history to introduce conscription, against powerful opposition in Parliament from the Labour and Liberal parties, in peacetime; or rather in the period of armed truce which prevailed between March and September 1939.

During that summer, the British tried to steer between weakness and provocation. The very notion that Hitler could be provoked if he did not wish to be has been much derided. Nonetheless, ministers dealing with a man whom Chamberlain described as a paranoiac possessing terrible weapons had to be concerned with that aspect. The events of 1914 cast their long, black shadow. It was arranged that a vast British fleet should exercise in the Channel and the North Sea, so as to emphasize that land power was not the only ingredient of armed strength and to remind Hitler of what he had himself proclaimed in *Mein Kampf*, the strangling effect of British sea power. (Nor was it Hitler alone who indulged in a *kampf*; when war became inevitable, Chamberlain said to the Cabinet 'The event against which we have fought so long and so earnestly has come upon us.') Once the news broke of what seemed the unnatural, almost inconceivable, alliance between Russia and Germany – though less unnatural when we remember the similarities between the systems, and the considerable admiration which Stalin seems to have felt for

Hitler – Chamberlain reminded the latter of the events of 1914. It had often been stated that if the British attitude had been made clear then, the Great War might have been prevented. On this occasion, the Prime Minister wrote, the British government was resolved that there should be no such tragic misunderstanding.[34] In other words, whatever had been arranged in Moscow, Britain and France would declare war if Germany invaded Poland. They would not patch up a peace if Germany overran that country. The war would be fought out on several fronts. So it was. Hitler had given proof of his lust for violence, being neither appeased nor deterred. What he got was not the kind of war he had anticipated, however. The British and French governments, even had they been sure beyond all question that Germany intended war, could not be certain of the timing; and they had to convince their own peoples, together with many in the wider world, that there was now no alternative.

* * * * *

History resembles but never repeats itself.

(Dean Inge)

Necessity knows no law and circumstances sometimes upset old certainties. If conscious only of established readings of the past, we read with surprise of Churchill's remark at the end of May, 1940, that if Hitler were prepared to make peace on the terms of restoration of the German colonies and overlordship of Central Europe, he would be prepared to consider the matter, though he believed it quite unlikely that Hitler would make any such offer. Equally, the new Prime Minister told his predecessor that if he could get out of the jam with Italy by sacrificing Gibraltar and Malta and some African colonies, he would jump at the chance. Neither thought the prospect probable. Both remarks were made at a time of bewilderment and disaster as France reeled to defeat and before the deliverance at Dunkirk. The essential fact is that under Churchill's inspired leadership the War Cabinet, Parliament and country determined to fight to the last in Europe, and soon in the Mediterranean and Middle East. In the Far East, temporization and concession followed. The decision to close the Burma Road at Japan's behest later that year was indeed an act of appeasement in the damaging sense, which is not in the least to say it was unjustifiable. Small wonder that Chamberlain observed in his diary, 'I was relieved and gratified to find that Winston, with the responsibilities of the P. M. on his shoulders, was firmly against the bold line.'[35] By contrast, the minister and official most closely identified with appeasement, Halifax and Cadogan, were both opposed to this temporary surrender.

Churchill said repeatedly that a declaration of war by Japan in 1941 could not be reconciled with reason. As he observed, 'However sincerely we try to put ourselves in another person's position, we cannot allow for processes of the human mind and imagination to which reason offers no key.'[36] Exactly so, and with some justice Chamberlain might have written much the same thing about Germany. We readily understand why Churchill and the War Cabinet repeatedly suppressed their anger and fear over Moscow's behaviour in the latter part of the war, for Russia's sacrifices were enormous, Stalin and his associates inscrutable. It was of supreme importance to keep Russia's goodwill and bring her into the war against Japan as soon as possible. We find WSC bullying the Polish leader in a way which went well beyond any treatment meted out by Chamberlain's government to the Czechs. Churchill believed, needed and longed to believe, in Stalin's goodwill and in the warmth of their personal relations. He in respect of Poland, as Chamberlain of Czechoslovakia, had to face the fact that the country would not be reconstituted within its old boundaries. He supported the ethnic cleansing of Germans, several millions in number, in the areas to be acquired by Poland and in the Sudetenland. In public and in private, he was far more favourably disposed towards Stalin and Russia than ever Chamberlain had been to Hitler. Like his predecessor, Churchill knew what would be the consequences of open discord between the great powers, and flinched from the prospect unless every alternative had been tried. He said in the strict privacy of the War Cabinet immediately on returning from Yalta that he was quite sure Stalin meant well to the world and to Poland. Conscious of the comparison with Chamberlain and 1938, he remarked to his colleagues 'I don't think I am wrong about Stalin.'[37]

Churchill's statement that he felt bound to proclaim his confidence in Stalin's good faith in the hope of procuring it[38] makes it sound as if his strong declarations were more a matter of calculation than of conviction. It is doubtful – to put the matter no higher – that the written record will support that view. Even if it were true, it is worthwhile to remember how severely Chamberlain has been arraigned for a similar line of thought in respect of Germany and Italy. Parliament was asked to approve of the Yalta settlement on the grounds of its rightness. A few independent souls refused to vote for this proposition. One of them said, 'When the Prime Minister says he accepts this as an act of justice, I must take a fundamentally opposite view. We have, dozens of times in our history, accepted this kind of arrangement as a fact of power. I accept it as a fact of power, but I cannot be asked to underwrite it as an act of justice.'[39] The speaker was Lord Dunglass, later to be Foreign Secretary and Prime Minister, and formerly Chamberlain's devoted Parliamentary Private Secretary.

Let us then recur to the question, 'Is it wrong, regardless of circumstances, for great powers to make peace at the expense of a weaker country?' In other words, is there a principle which can always be applied? If there is, we must condemn much that was done at the expense of Poland and other countries in 1945 but be careful about the terms of condemnation. It is usual to be told that Roosevelt and Churchill 'gave away' large tracts of Eastern and Central Europe. Actually, Russia seized them, as Germany had done in 1938 and 1939. In the latter instance Chamberlain, and in the former Churchill, found themselves driven to policies they would by far have preferred to avoid. If it is always wrong to give way to threats, that puts an end to the debate. But it is scarcely conceivable that statesmen responsible for decisions involving – as they thought – the outbreak of war and the ruin of civilization, a war, moreover, to be fought with weapons largely unknown, where the consequences of going to war too early might easily be a swift defeat, could decide matters by so simple a criterion.

★ ★ ★ ★ ★

That pilot of the state
Who sets no hand to the best policy,
But remains tongue-tied through some terror, seems
Vilest of men.

(Sophocles)

The proper memory for a politician is one that knows what to remember
and what to forget.

(John Morley, *The Life of Richard Cobden*)

Churchill combined the roles of statesman and historian with unmatched effectiveness. No single work has done more than *The Gathering Storm* to shape the general conception of the 1930s. In its pages Baldwin was harshly condemned. Baldwin's son, defending his father's reputation 50 years ago against a solid wall of hostile opinion, lighted upon some interesting quotations. Here are three of them:

Nothing less than the deeds of Germany would have converted the British nation to war. To act in advance of those deeds would have led to an exposure of division worse than the guarded attitude which we maintained, which brought our country into the war united.

A British threat to intervene, if unwarranted by national authority, could only have convinced Germany that we were impotent and out of it.

To threaten war upon Germany would have been repudiated by Cabinet, Parliament, and People ... The cannon gained by its first salvo ... a verdict for which all the statesmen and soldiers of the British Empire would have pleaded in vain.

Had such passages come from a manuscript in Baldwin's handwriting, the son declared, the historians would have sprung on the cheap excuses, the timorous withholding of expenditure vital for the security of the state, the dread of provoking Germany.[40] As it happened, these and similar statements were taken from Churchill's own account of the origins of World War I. Even those who admitted the impeachment would have felt minded to reply, 'But at least Churchill had learned the lesson thoroughly, whereas Baldwin and Chamberlain had not.' Perhaps matters are not quite so clear-cut.

Stalin once remarked to Anthony Eden, 'That was the trouble with Hitler. He didn't know where to stop.'[41] But did Stalin himself, and his successors, know where to stop? Judgements upon the affairs of the 1930s often dominated the policy of the two succeeding decades. Until we know more of the Russian records, we cannot judge how real was the prospect that Russia might have moved across Western Europe in 1947 or 1948, or whether Russia might later have used atomic and nuclear weapons against the West. What we do know is that Churchill in his last phase as Prime Minister sought early discussions with Stalin's successors, and with a bold agenda. It would have included, for example, the abandonment of all further research on nuclear weapons, and it would also have entailed 'appeasement', in the shape of acceptance of Russian control of East Germany, Poland, Czechoslovakia, Hungary and the Baltic States, not to mention other regions. Let it be conceded at once that deadly as the perils had been in 1939, nuclear weapons raised the scale of risk immensely. On the other hand, there was only one serious military threat to face, as against three before the war; and by a still more startling contrast, the large bulk of the money, armaments and manpower would be supplied, for any war against Russia, by the United States.

'We must not go further on the path to war unless we are sure there is no other path to peace.' That was said, one might surmise, by Chamberlain before or after Munich; it is actually a remark of Churchill's in 1953 as he pondered what to do about Russia. 'For the old aphorism, "force is no remedy", I would substitute "the fear of force is the only remedy".' Strong Churchillian doctrine, you will think; except that those words come from Chamberlain's diary in the summer of 1934, and demonstrate, as does much else, that there was no gulf of ideology between him and Churchill in the realm of international affairs. 'Our hopeful assumptions were soon to be falsified. Still, they were the only ones possible at the time.'[42] A very large claim, you may judge, no doubt advanced by Chamberlain in a bid for self-exculpation after Munich, or perhaps after Prague? Not a bit of it; that is Churchill writing long after the war about Yalta, and you will notice that in stating that no other assumptions were possible at the time, he goes well beyond anything Chamberlain said about Germany or Munich.

When Churchill wrote that he would not fear a solitary pilgrimage to Russia if it would help forward the cause of peace, regardless of the possible harm to his reputation,[43] and hoped that Russia's self-interest would bring an easier state of affairs, he may well have reflected on the events of 1938; after all, Chamberlain entertained similar hopes, and was resolved to run similar risks, with Germany. What was the degree of certainty required before the world was plunged into another wilderness of sorrow and destruction? The British government in 1938 set the threshold of proof high. Churchill did not behave very differently towards

Russia in the 1950s and for that, it seems to me, we have solid reason to be thankful.

To the press at Ottawa in the summer of 1954 Churchill freely conceded that he was trying to have it both ways: to build up fighting strength and simultaneously to hold out a hand to Russia. Both parts of the policy were indispensable. 'Peace through strength means that you will keep a friendly alternative before the eyes of your principal opponents.' He acknowledged with candour that peaceful coexistence entailed living side by side with 'people whose system you think produces great evils, very great abuses, a hideous state of society based upon profound fallacies', but asked his hearers to recognize the argument about the scale of risk:

> If you had to choose between living side by side with them, and perhaps bringing about the destruction of the human race by trying to reform them, there might be a lot to be said for letting reforms stand over for the time being ...[44]

Requested to comment upon accusations that Britain was pursuing towards Russia the same policy of appeasement that Chamberlain had followed towards Germany in 1938, the Prime Minister countered adroitly that he and Eden, of all ministers, could afford to treat with contempt

> the idea that we are animated by a spirit of appeasement, not in the sense of reducing tension, but in seeking to avoid doing our duty ... As for the idea of shirking the other alternative of doing one's duty and facing the consequences, I do feel that that is best treated with the contempt which it deserves. I won't elaborate on that because, as you know, contempt is not contempt if you have to take any trouble expressing it. It's got to be quite involuntary, and if possible unconscious.[45]

You observe how nimbly this is put. He says, or at any rate plainly implies, that appeasement is highly desirable if directed to 'reducing tension', which is what Chamberlain and his colleagues intended. Appeasement in a worse sense was defined by Churchill on this occasion as 'seeking to avoid doing our duty' and whatever other criticisms of Chamberlain's administration may be just, that is not. It is hardly necessary to add that Churchill was careful in his last years of office not to recommend 'appeasement'; rather, he spoke of 'easement'. By the latter term, he meant very much what Chamberlain had meant by the former.

After the war, Churchill would sometimes remark 'I think it will be convenient to leave these contentious matters to history, especially as I propose to write that history myself.' He was being mildly mischievous, for in his volumes on the second war as in those on the first he claims no more than to make a contribution to the record which would have to be written from a wide variety of sources, when far more facts were known and passions had cooled. Only then could history with its flickering lamp stumble along the trail of the past. Field-Marshal Smuts, it is said, remonstrated with Churchill: 'Oh, Winston, why? Why did you have to do that? You, more than anybody in the world, could have written as no one else could have written, the true history of the war', only to receive the characteristic retort, 'These [books] are *my* story. If someone else likes to write *his* story, let him.'[46]

* * * * *

Whether you like it or not, history is on our side. We will bury you.
(Khrushchev, at a reception for Western
Ambassadors in Moscow, 1956)

In the bleak midwinter of 1940, two scientists working in this University produced the paper which paved the way in terms of theoretical physics for the making of the atomic bomb. One was an Austrian, the other a German; both were Jews admitted to this country under the policy which brought about the greatest enrichment and revitalization of our academic life known in the twentieth century. The decision of the British and French governments to go to war with Germany in 1939 represented perhaps the last occasion upon which the great powers could as a rational act challenge each other to an outright contest on the battlefield, whereas the easement which Churchill sought at the end of his political life sprang from his conviction that the powers would destroy themselves, and much of the rest of the world, if they followed that example.

Does the document which those two scientists composed here more than 60 years ago prove that nuclear physics is the most dangerous subject in the curriculum? Let us consider this quotation from a celebrated autobiography of the twentieth century, describing the author's history teacher:

> The old gentleman, whose manner was as kind as it was firm, not only knew how to keep us spellbound, but actually carried us away with the splendour of his eloquence. I am still a little moved when I remember the grey-haired man whose fiery description made us forget the present and who evoked plain historical facts out of the fog of the centuries and turned them into living reality. Often we would sit there enraptured in enthusiasm and there were even times when we were on the verge of tears.
>
> Our happiness was the greater in as much as the teacher not only knew how to throw light on the past by utilising the present, but also how to draw conclusions from the past and apply them to the present. More than anyone else he showed understanding for all the daily problems which held us breathless at the time. He was the teacher who made history my favourite subject.

Touching, is it not? Encouraging to our profession? Something to remember with a glow, perhaps, when you settle down to the correction of that heap of essays or the marking of scripts? So it might seem, until we remember that the boy held spellbound was Hitler and that the autobiography from which I have quoted is *Mein Kampf*.[47]

In the spring of 1999, as in 2003, 'appeasement' was routinely denounced as if the choices of 60 years before had been easy ones. For example, we were told that ethnic cleansing must be opposed by overwhelming force, even at enormous cost, on grounds of the principle involved. Very well; that is at least a clear policy, which if indeed a matter of principle would have required intervention in Sudan, Rwanda, Tibet and elsewhere. There are very strong reasons for opposing the spread of weapons of mass destruction. In extreme circumstances, that policy may require outright attack on states which possess such weapons; but before we embrace it as a matter of principle, let us remind ourselves that Israel, India and Pakistan are among the possessors of such weapons.

Standing alongside the Mayor of New York a few days after the attack on the World Trade Center, the British Prime Minister recalled the time of the blitz and demonstrated the perils of reliance upon simple versions of the past:

> My father's generation knew what it was like. They know what it is like to suffer this type of tragedy and attack. There was one country and one people that stood by us at that time. That country was America and those people were the American people.[48]

At least let us admire those last two sentences for their compression.

Not long after World War I, the Classical Association elected to meet in Cambridge. A.E. Housman, Kennedy Professor of Latin, the most redoubtable classical scholar of his day, found himself dragooned into giving an address. He groaned, for the meeting fell in early August. That fact perhaps lent additional vigour to his concluding admonition. To be a textual critic, he remarked, requires aptitude for thinking and willingness to think. It also calls for other qualities, but those are supplements and cannot be substitutes: 'Knowledge is good, method is good, but one thing beyond all others is necessary; and that is to have a head, not a pumpkin, on your shoulders, and brains, not pudding, in your head.'[49]

I am far from possessing the authority, and if by some miracle I acquired it I should not have the hardihood, to pronounce in that wise. My more modest purpose has been to suggest that those who write the history of modern times have a plain duty, and one with profound effects. Let us take it for granted that such historians have heads, not pumpkins, on their shoulders, and brains rather than pudding between the ears. Their obligation is to ascertain the facts as accurately as possible, without pretending that everything can be discovered and set down as in a catalogue; to exercise their imaginative faculties in harness with critical instincts; not to be deterred by the weight, however heavy, of received opinion; and to persuade those who make policy that they should listen. J.M. Keynes remarked that practical men, supposing themselves exempt from any intellectual influences, are usually the slaves of some defunct economist.[50] Ministers and civil servants, even prime ministers, do not conceive of themselves as being detached from intellectual influences.

The more alert are aware of history, and no doubt believe that the history upon which they rely is sound. That theirs is a more difficult condition to influence increases the responsibilities of all who pursue this most dangerous and exhilarating of subjects.

Notes

Details of most works cited are to be found in the Select Bibliography. For Churchill's *The Second World War*, 6 vols, I have used the most widely available edition, issued by The Reprint Society (London, 1950–6). 'TNA' denotes The National Archives, London, (formerly The Public Record Office) and 'LAC' Libraries and Archives, Canada. British official documents – for example, papers from Cab. 63 or FO 371 or Prem. 3 – are to be found in TNA unless otherwise indicated.

1. Churchill Up and Churchill Down

1   J. Connell, *Auchinleck*, p. 473.
2   M. Soames, *Winston Churchill: His Life as a Painter*, p. 20, citing her father's *Painting as a Pastime*.
3   M. Soames, *Clementine Churchill*, p. 77–8.
4   Lady Juliet Duff in *The Sunday Times*, 31 January 1965.
5   M. Gilbert, *'Never Despair': Winston S. Churchill 1945–1965*, pp. 364–72.
6   C. de Gaulle, *Mémoires de Guerre: L'Appel 1940–1942* (Paris, 1954), p. 5.
7   W.S. Churchill, *My Early Life*, p. 109.
8   Lord Curzon, *Modern Parliamentary Eloquence* (Oxford, 1913), pp. 37–9, 47–8.
9   *The Toronto Daily Star*, 12 August 1929, in D.N. Dilks, *"The Great Dominion"*, p. 50; hereafter cited as Dilks.
10   Lord Moran, *Winston Churchill: The Struggle for Survival 1940–1965*, p. 429; hereafter cited as Moran.
11   W.S. Churchill, *My Early Life*, p. 27.
12   Ibid., p. 17.
13   Ibid., p. 111.
14   Ibid., pp. 107–9.
15   B.E.C. Dugdale, *Arthur James Balfour*, vol. 2 (1936), p. 337.
16   W.S. Churchill, *Great Contemporaries*, p. 3.
17   *Ottawa Evening Journal*, 28 December 1900, cited in Dilks, pp. 17–18.
18   Moran, p. 368; W.S. Churchill, *The Second World War*, vol. 4, p. 665.
19   Lady Soames, Foreword to Dilks, pp. xii–xiii.
20   Moran, p. 598.
21   W.S. Churchill, *My Early Life*, pp. 4–5; Moran, p. 369. I am grateful to Mr Christopher Fildes, whose researches reveal that Iroquois, winner of the Derby in 1881, was almost certainly the horse in question; it was the first American-bred horse to win, though trained at Newmarket.
22   Dilks, pp. 23, 28.

23 W.S. Churchill, *Great Contemporaries*, p. 121.

24 Ibid., p. 142.

25 L.S. Amery, *My Political Life*, vol. 2, p. 510.

26 E. David (ed.), *Inside Asquith's Cabinet: From the Diaries of Charles Hobhouse*, pp. 118, 121, 140, 192, 206, 231.

27 R.S. Churchill, *Winston S. Churchill*, vol. 2, pp. 704–5.

28 R.W. Thompson, *Churchill and Morton*, p. 78.

29 M. and E. Brock (eds.), *H.H. Asquith: Letters to Venetia Stanley* (1982), pp. 263, 266–7.

30 W.S. Churchill, *Thoughts and Adventures*, pp. 6–7.

31 M. Soames, *Speaking for Themselves*, p. 96.

32 M. Pottle (ed.), *Champion Redoubtable*, p. 25.

33 M. Soames, *Clementine Churchill*, pp. 155, 205.

34 Lord Beaverbrook, *The Decline and Fall of Lloyd George*, pp. 295, 139.

35 Mackenzie King's diary, 4 October 1922, cited in Dilks, p. 37.

36 I owe this version to Mr Harold Macmillan, later Earl of Stockton.

37 T. Jones, *Whitehall Diary* (1969), vol. 2, p. 103.

38 D.N. Dilks, *Neville Chamberlain*, vol. 1 (1984), pp. 441.

39 M. Gilbert, *Winston S. Churchill*, vol. 5, pp. 296–7.

40 P. Williamson (ed.), *The Modernisation of Conservative Politics: The Diaries and Letters of William Bridgeman, 1904–1935* (1988), p. 234.

41 D.N. Dilks, *Neville Chamberlain*, p. 515; M. Soames (ed.), *Speaking for Themselves*, p. 328; M. Soames, *Clementine Churchill*, p. 281.

42 Dilks, p. 71.

43 W.S. Churchill, *Great Contemporaries*, p. 229.

44 M. Gilbert, *Winston S. Churchill*, vol. 5, pp. 675–6.

45 Dilks, pp. 116–24.

46 Neville Chamberlain to his sister, 13 December 1936, and Chamberlain's diary, 2 December (University of Birmingham); Moran, p. 370.

47 J.R. Colville, *Footprints in Time*, pp. 202–3.

48 Moran, p. 744.

49 A. Montague Browne, *Long Sunset*, p. 225.

50 F.W. Deakin, *Churchill the Historian*, p. 1.

51 Churchill to Professor L.B. Namier, 18 February 1934; CHAR8/484A, Churchill College, Cambridge.

52 M. Gilbert, *Winston S. Churchill*, vol. 5, p. 287.

53 S. Churchill, *Keep on Dancing*, p. 12.

54 R.S. Churchill, 'Evelyn Waugh: Letters (and Post-cards) to Randolph Churchill', *Encounter*, vol. xxxi, no.1, p. 18.

55 F.W. Deakin, *Churchill the Historian*, pp. 14–15; for the version which W.S.C. eventually decided to publish, in 1956, see *A History of the English-Speaking Peoples*, vol. 1, p. 90.

56 M. Soames, *Clementine Churchill*, p. 142.

57 Entry of 12 June 1939; MG 26 J 13, LAC.

58 W.S. Churchill, *The Second World War*, vol. 1, p. 332.

59 Churchill to Chamberlain, 22 September 1939; NC7/9/53, Chamberlain papers, University of Birmingham.

60 D.N. Dilks, 'The Twilight War and the Fall of France: Chamberlain and Churchill in 1940', in Dilks (ed.), *Retreat from Power*, vol. 2 (1981), p. 53.

61 Ibid., pp. 53–5.

62 W.S. Churchill, *The Second World War*, vol. 1, p. 527; K.G. Feiling, *The Life of Neville Chamberlain* (1946), p. 442.

63 W.S. Churchill, *The Second World War*, vol. 1, p. 532.
64 Moran, p. 324.
65 M.H. Macmillan, *Tides of Fortune* (1969), p. 42–3.
66 Dilks, p. 355.
67 I owe this revealing remark to the 3rd Earl Baldwin, son of the former Prime Minister.
68 D.N. Dilks (ed.), *The Diaries of Sir Alexander Cadogan*, p. 284; hereafter cited as Cadogan.
69 Mackenzie King's diary, 29 April 1940; C. Schroeder, *He Was My Chief* (2009), p. 55.
70 Moran, p. 324.
71 Lord Strang, *Home and Abroad* (1956), p. 70.
72 *The Memoirs of General the Lord Ismay*, pp. 113–14.
73 F. Field (ed.), *Attlee's Great Contemporaries* (2009), pp. 157–9.
74 A. Bryant, *The Turn of the Tide* (1957), pp. 42–3.
75 I owe this to the late Viscount Boyd, who as a junior minister was present. He recollected that both WSC and the secretary kept straight faces.
76 Moran, p. 184.
77 M. Soames, *Clementine Churchill*, p. 325.
78 J.R. Colville, *The Fringes of Power*, p. 280.
79 J.R. Colville, *Footprints in Time*, p. 118.
80 J.R. Colville in J.W. Wheeler-Bennett (ed.), *Action This Day*, pp. 68–9, and *The Fringes of Power*, p. 394; M. Soames, *Clementine Churchill*, p. 255.
81 R.V. Jones, 'Winston Leonard Spencer Churchill', in *Biographical Memoirs of the Royal Society 1966*, p. 72. For other examples of WSC's interest in applied science, see the same appreciation and R.V. Jones, *Most Secret War*.
82 Ismay (note 72), p. 346.
83 J.R. Colville, *The Fringes of Power*, p. 196; C. Richardson, *From Churchill's Secret Circle to the B.B.C.*, p. 177; D. Hart-Davis (ed.), *King's Counsellor* (2006), p. 372, hereafter cited as Hart-Davis.
84 C. Eade (ed.), *The War Speeches of the Rt.Hon. Winston S. Churchill*, vol. 1, pp. 279–80; hereafter cited as Eade.
85 Ibid., p. 201.
86 D. Hunt, *On the Spot*, p. 40.
87 Eade, vol. 3, pp. 128–31. For a Russian perspective, see 'Barbarossa and the Soviet Leadership: A Recollection', by S.A. Mikoyan (son of Stalin's close colleague A.I. Mikoyan) in J. Erickson and D.N. Dilks (eds.), *Barbarossa: The Axis and the Allies* (Edinburgh, 1994), pp. 130–3.
88 Richardson (note 83), pp. 68–9.
89 W.S. Churchill, *The Second World War*, vol. 3, p. 460; Churchill to Eden, M.588/3, 19 September 1943, Cab.101/243.
90 Moran, p. 17.
91 C. Bridge (ed.), *A Delicate Mission: The Washington Diaries of R.G. Casey, 1940–42* (Canberra, 2008), pp. 214–15.
92 Moran, p. 20.
93 Eade, vol. 2, pp. 236–7.
94 Hart-Davis, p. 210.
95 M. MacDonald, *Titans and Others*, p. 109.
96 Ibid., p. 104.
97 WSC spoke on several occasions to his literary assistant Denis Kelly of his gratitude for Attlee's loyalty during the war; see Kelly's unpublished memoir, DEKE 2, p. 24, Churchill College, Cambridge.

98   Earl of Avon, *The Reckoning*, Foreword.
99   *The Memoirs of Lord Chandos*, p. 171.
100 I owe the first example to Sir Alexander Cadogan; notes by Charles Eade of a luncheon with Churchill, 24 July 1941, EADE 4/1, Churchill College, Cambridge.
101 Hart-Davis, p. 143.
102 W.S. Churchill, *My Early Life*, p. 113.
103 R.S. Churchill (ed.), *Europe Unite*, p. 337; M. Soames, *A Daughter's Tale*, p. 260.
104 N. Nicolson (ed.), *Harold Nicolson: Diaries and Letters 1939–45* (1967), p. 238.
105 Eade, vol. 1, pp. 402–7.
106 Parl. Deb., 5th ser., H. of C., vol. 387, col. 1598, 23 March 1943.
107 Mackenzie King's diary, 12 August 1943, cited in Dilks, p. 265.
108 M. Soames, *A Daughter's Tale*, p. 283.
109 Ibid., pp. 290–1.
110 Hart-Davis, p. 233.
111 A. Danchev and D. Todman (eds.), *War Diaries 1939–45: Field Marshal Lord Alanbrooke*, p. 566; Earl of Avon, *The Reckoning*, pp. 461–2.
112 Minute by Churchill, 13 December 1941, to Amery and the Secretary of the Cabinet, M1103/1, Cab.101/241.
113 J. Barnes and D. Nicholson (eds.), *The Empire at Bay*, p. 779.
114 Ibid., pp. 822, 832.
115 W.S. Churchill, *The Second World War*, vol. 4. p. 175.
116 Hart-Davis, p. 143.
117 Barnes and Nicholson (note 113), p. 836.
118 Ibid., pp. 992–4.
119 Ibid., pp. 1018–19; Cadogan, p. 678.
120 Ibid., pp. 688–9, 693; Avon (note 111), p. 497.
121 Cadogan, p. 697; J.R. Colville, *The Fringes of Power*, pp. 554–5.
122 W.S. Churchill, *The Second World War*, vol. 6, p. 471; J.R. Colville, *The Fringes of Power*, p. 599.
123 M. Gilbert, *Road to Victory* (vol. 7 of the official biography), pp. 1350–1; Avon, op. cit., p. 534.
124 Eade, vol. 2, pp. 425–37.
125 M. Gilbert, *'Never Despair'* (vol. 8 of the official biography), pp. 19–20, 27.
126 R.W. Thompson, *Churchill and Morton*, p. 99.
127 Eade, vol. 3, p. 497.
128 Avon, op. cit., pp. 553, 550.
129 British Broadcasting Corporation, *A Selection from the Broadcasts Given in Memory of Sir Winston Churchill* (1965), p. 60.
130 Hart-Davis, p. 138.
131 For a telling comparison of the British and American systems see Richardson, op. cit., pp. 95–7.
132 Mackenzie King's diary, 12 September 1944.
133 Ismay to Brooke, 25 June 1946, Ismay papers IV – ALA-1D, King's College, London; Ismay, *Memoirs*, p. 163.
134 Moran, p. 324.
135 M. Soames, *Winston Churchill: His Life as a Painter*, p. 144.
136 Eade, vol. 3, p. 522.
137 Ibid., p. 523.
138 Moran, p. 374.
139 I owe this to Mr Harold Macmillan (later Earl of Stockton), who was present.

140 Hart-Davis, p. 406.
141 Record by C. Eade of a conversation with WSC, 16 March 1954, EADE 2/1, Churchill College, Cambridge; Moran, p. 701; R. Hart-Davis (ed.), *The Lyttelton Hart-Davis Letters*, vol. 6 (1984), p. 168; Lord Fraser of Kilmorack, who was present as a young official at the Conservative Central Office, to the author; Lord Soames in P. Midgley (ed.), *The Heroic Memory*, p. 231.
142 Moran, p. 357.
143 *The Globe and Mail*, Toronto, 15 January 1952.
144 Sir A. Douglas-Home (later Lord Home) in *The Heroic Memory* (note 141), p. 70.
145 P. Catterall (ed.), *The Macmillan Diaries: The Cabinet Years*, p. 232.
146 C. Haste (ed.), *Clarissa Eden: A Memoir: From Churchill to Eden*, pp. 147, 149.
147 Moran, p. 473.
148 Colville to Beaverbrook, 25 June 1953, Beaverbrook papers Bbk C/89, House of Lords Library.
149 Moran, p. 445. The remark about the film is recorded in Denis Kelly's unpublished memoir, DEKE 2, chap. 6., p. 17, Churchill College, Cambridge.
150 M.H. Macmillan, *Tides of Fortune*, p. 582; A. Montague Browne, *Long Sunset*, pp. 114, 145; Cadogan, p. 794.
151 V. Bonham Carter in J. Marchant (ed.), *Winston Spencer Churchill*, p. 155.
152 Moran, p. 682.
153 A. Montague Browne, *Long Sunset*, p. 302.

2. Great Britain, the Commonwealth and the Wider World, 1939–45

1   C. Eade (ed.), *The War Speeches of the Rt. Hon. Winston S. Churchill*, vol. 3 (2nd edn, 1964), p. 121.
2   The Earl of Avon, *The Reckoning*, pp. 86–8.
3   Churchill to the UK High Commissioners in New Zealand and Australia, 16 June 1940, Prem 4/43B/1.
4   W.S. Churchill, *The Second World War*, vol. 2 (1951), pp. 20–3. Other sources place the total of US deaths at 350,000 or more.
5   Ibid.
6   These figures are based on tables printed in *Whittaker's Yearbook 1947* and Central Statistical Office, 'Casualties in the Armed Forces of the British Empire', Cab 139/56.
7   W.K. Hancock and M.M. Gowing, *British War Economy* (HMSO, 1949), pp. 368–9.
8   'Report for the Month of December, 1942, for the Dominions, India, Burma and the Colonies and Main Mandated Territories', WP (43) 40, 25 January 1943, Cab 66/33.
9   P. Barua, 'Strategies and Doctrines of Imperial Defence: Britain and India, 1919–45', *The Journal of Imperial and Commonwealth History*, vol. 25, no. 2 (1997).
10 Churchill, op. cit., p. 20.
11 Churchill, op. cit., vol. 3 (1952), p. 477.
12 F.W. Perry, *The Commonwealth Armies* (Manchester University Press, 1988) p. 227.
13 For this information I am indebted to Air Commodore J.W. Frost.
14 Despatch from Sir G. Campbell, Ottawa, to Eden, Dominions Office, 19 December 1940, enclosed in Eden to Chamberlain, 16 January 1940, Prem 1/397; Avon, op. cit., p. 70. The other main partners in what became the British Commonwealth Joint Air Training Plan were Australia and New Zealand. For an enthusiastic account of the Scheme's progress, and changed attitudes in Canada, see a memorandum from Capt. Harold Balfour to the S.

of S. for Air, 10 September 1940, enclosed in Sinclair to Churchill, 17 September 1940, Prem 3/24/5.

15 Hancock and Gowing, op. cit., p. 375. Cf. a memorandum by Kingsley Wood, then Chancellor of the Exchequer, 'Financial Arrangements between the United Kingdom and Canada', WP (42) 14, 7 January 1942, Cab 66/20.

16 UK High Commissioner in Canada to Dominions Office, 27 May 1941, annexed to a memorandum by Lord Cranborne, 4 June 1941, 'Meeting of Dominion Prime Ministers', WP (41) 121, Cab 66/16.

17 Churchill to the Governor-General of Canada, Lord Athlone, 12 September 1941, Prem 4/44/10.

18 The text of this speech was circulated to the Cabinet by Churchill on 20 September 1941; WP (41) 228, Cab 66/19.

19 Churchill to the Prime Ministers of Australia and New Zealand, 11 August 1940, Prem 4/43B/1.

20 Menzies to Churchill, 29 September 1940; Churchill to Menzies, 2 October 1940; Menzies to Churchill, 4 October 1940, Prem 4/43B/1.

21 Governor General of New Zealand, embodying a message from Fraser to Churchill, 4 December 1940; Dominions Office to the High Commissioner in New Zealand, embodying a message from Churchill to Fraser, 14 December 1940, Prem 4/43B/2.

22 Minute by Cranborne to Churchill, 23 December 1940, and reply, 25 December 1940, Prem 4/43B/1.

23 Churchill to Minister of State, Cairo (Lyttelton), T.592, 18 September 1941, Prem 3/63/2. For examples of bitter criticism of the events in Greece and Crete, see a despatch from R.R. Sedgwick, Acting UK High Commissioner in Canberra, 14 July 1941, annexed to a memorandum by Cranborne, 'The Political Situation in the Commonwealth of Australia', 21 August 1941, WP (41) 198, Cab 66/18. For a vivid account of Menzies' activities and thoughts, see D. Day, *Menzies and Churchill at War*.

24 Churchill to Fraser, T.201/2, 8 February 1942, Prem 3/63/10; Churchill to Curtin, T.1072, 27 December 1941, Prem 3/394/2.

25 Churchill to Smuts, T.794, 8 November 1941, Prem 3/476/3.

26 Churchill, op. cit., vol. 4 (1953), pp. 178–9, 185–7.

27 Lord Harlech to Churchill, 2 October 1941, Prem 4/44/1.

28 Avon, op. cit., pp. 350–1; the telling phrase 'so rammed with life' comes from Shakespeare's contemporary Ben Jonson.

29 H.F. Batterbee to the Dominions Office, embodied in a memorandum by Cranborne to the War Cabinet, 5 February 1942, WP (42) 67, Cab. 66/21.

30 Smuts to Churchill, 20 January 1942, Prem 4/44/1.

31 Curtin to Churchill, 24 January 1942, circulated to the War Cabinet on the same day; WP (42) 34, Cab 66/21.

32 Memorandum by Cranborne, 'Co-operation with the Dominion Governments', WP (42) 30, 21 January 1942, Cab 66/21.

33 Ibid.

34 Note by Sir E.E. Bridges, 'Relations with Australia', covering a memorandum from Cranborne to Churchill and telegrams from Sir R. Cross (Canberra), 22 January 1942, Cab 66/21. Cf. D. Day, *The Great Betrayal* (Melbourne, 1988).

35 Memorandum by Cranborne, 'Lease-Lend Agreement', 21 January 1942, WP (42) 32, Cab 66/21.

Notes

36 Note by E.E. Bridges, 'Relations with Australia', 22 January 1942; see note 34.

37 Churchill to Cripps, T. 477/2, 27 March 1942, Prem 3/142/2.

38 Cripps to Churchill, enclosed in a telegram from Karachi to the War Office, T. 563/2, 13 April 1942, Prem 3/142/2.

39 Memorandum by Attlee to Churchill, c. 16 April 1942 and Churchill's reply, same date, Prem 3/142/2.

40 Wavell to CIGS, 1 May 1942, Part 2, Prem 3/232/8.

41 Minutes of a meeting with Dominion representatives held at the White House, Washington, 20 May 1943, Prem 3/443/2.

42 Churchill, op. cit., vol. 4, p. 316.

43 Lord Harlech to Attlee, 6 July 1942, Prem 3/391/9.

44 Minute by Churchill, 18 November 1942, Prem 3/63/10.

45 R. Usborne, *After Hours with P.G. Wodehouse* (New York, 1991), p. 12; D.M. Davin's article on Freyberg in *The Dictionary of National Biography 1961–1970* (Oxford, 1981), pp. 401–5; Churchill to Fraser, 6 December 1942, T.1666/2, Prem 3/63/10.

46 Curtin to Churchill, 30 November 1942, T.1620/2, Prem 3/63/10.

47 UK High Commissioner in New Zealand to Dominions Office, 10 December 1942, No. 501, Prem 3/63/10.

48 Minutes of a meeting with Dominion representatives, 20 May 1943, Prem 3/443/2. For material supplied to Dr Evatt during his mission to London, in the summer of 1943, and for a discussion of papers to be withheld, see DO 35/1462, especially Bridges to Cadogan, 22 June 1943, and Gladwyn Jebb to Bridges, 25 June 1943.

49 Attlee to Churchill, Concrete No. 201, 14 August 1943, DO 35/1843.

50 For documents concerning the proposed meeting and its postponement see DO 35/1472.

51 MacDonald to the Dominions Office, 17 July 1943, and Churchill to Mackenzie King, same date, T.1048/3, Prem 3/83/2.

52 Despatch from MacDonald to Attlee, 6 August 1043, No. 441, Prem 3/83/2.

53 Note by Bridges, 'Anglo-Canadian Discussions at Quebec', 25 August 1943, WP (43) 380, Cab 66/40.

54 Bruce to Churchill, 19 October 1943, and Churchill's reply of 21 October 1943; Churchill to Bruce, 3 November 1943, and Bruce's reply, 8 November 1943, DO 35/1468.

55 M. Pottle (ed.), *Champion Redoubtable*, pp. 312–13.

56 Memorandum by Attlee, 'The Relation of the British Commonwealth to the Post War International Organisation', 15 June 1943, WP (43) 244, Cab 66/37.

57 Memorandum by Attlee, 29 January 1943, 'The United Nations Plan', and annexes, 28 January 1943, WP (43), Cab 63/33.

58 Circular letter from Eden to British representatives overseas, 11 December 1943, FO 371/50373. Cf. the record of a 'Discussion on the Status and Representation of the Members of the British Commonwealth in the International Sphere', 1 April 1943, DO 35/1838; see especially the remarks of the Canadian High Commissioner in the UK, Vincent Massey, at p. 3.

59 Memorandum by Cadogan, Foreign Office Circular No. 14, 31 May 1943, FO 371/50373.

60 For the file of replies to the Foreign Office's request for suggestions from British representatives abroad, see FO 371/42674, especially the minutes by J.D. Campbell, 22 March 1944, and Sir Basil Newton, 17 April 1944. See also Eden to all British representatives abroad, 3 October 1944, in the same file.

61 For the text of Halifax' speech of 24 January, see DO 35/1204, WC 75/9; MacDonald to Dominions Office, 27 January 1944, annexed to a memorandum by Cranborne, 'Lord Halifax' speech in Toronto', 29 January 1944, WP (44) 67, Cab 66/46; Churchill to Cranborne, M 53/4, DO 35/1204, WC 75/9; High Commission, Ottawa, to Dominions Office, 1 February 1944, in the same file.

62 MacDonald to Cranborne, 12 February 1944, DO 35/1204, WC 75/9.

63 Memorandum by MacDonald, 'Canada and Imperial Co-operation', forwarded under cover of a letter to Cranborne, 8 April 1944, DO 35/1489.

64 Letter from Bevin to Cranborne, 1 February 1944, and DPM (44), second meeting, 20 February 1944, DO 35/1474.

65 For an interesting commentary on the system practised in Washington, see S. Holmes (British Embassy, Washington) to Sir J. Stephenson (Dominions Office), 24 April 1944, DO 35/1204, WC 75/23.

66 Memorandum by Cranborne, 'Co-operation in the British Commonwealth', 18 April 1944, WP (44) 210, Cab 66/49.

67 J.W. Holmes, The Shaping of Peace, vol. 1 (Toronto, 1979), pp. 149–50; King's statement was drafted by Holmes.

68 Sir R. Cross to Cranborne, 13 April and 1 July 1944, PRO DO 35/1476.

69 Observations by Curtin at the meeting of Prime Ministers of 3 May 1944, PMM (44) 2, DO 35/1630; memorandum of 5 May 1944, circulated by request of Fraser to the Prime Ministers, PMM (44) 10, 16 May 1944, DO 35/1631; minutes of a staff conference held in the Prime Minister's Map Room, 26 May 1944, COS (44) 46(0), Prem 3/6318.

70 Memorandum by the Vice-Chiefs of Staff, 30 March 1944, 'The Co-ordination of Defence Policy Within the British Commonwealth in Relation to a World System of Security', COS (44) 58, 31 March 1944, DO 35/1474.

71 Avon, op. cit., p. 442.

72 Meetings of Prime Ministers, 4 and 5 May 1944, and memorandum by Sir Firoz Khan Noon, 12 May 1944, PMM (44), fourth and fifth meetings, Prem 4/42/5.

73 Meetings of 1, 2, 3, and 5 May, ibid.

74 Smuts to Churchill, embodied in Acting High Commissioner in Pretoria to Dominions Office, 29 September 1944, Prem 3/391/9.

75 Curtin to Churchill, 12 August 1944, JOHCU No. 81, DO 35/1630.

76 Memorandum by Lord Keynes, 12 June 1944, annexed to a memorandum by Sir. J. Anderson, Chancellor of the Exchequer, 1 July 1944 WP (44) 360, Cab 66/52.

77 'Report for the Month of April 1945, for the Dominions, India, Burma and the Colonies and Mandated Territories', 22 May 1945, Cab 66/65.

78 Draft telegram from Churchill to Fraser, T.204/5, 22 February 1945, Prem 3/356/4.

79 Minutes of the 'British Commonwealth Meeting', 6 April 1945, BCM 9(45), fourth meeting, DO 35/1479.

80 Avon, op. cit. p. 534.

81 United Kingdom Delegation, San Francisco, to Foreign Office, embodying a message from Smuts to Churchill, 14 May 1945, Prem 3/495/3.

82 Meeting of Dominion Prime Ministers, 1 May 1944, PMM (44), second meeting, Prem 4/42/5.

3. An Affair of the Heart

1   M. Soames, *Speaking For Themselves*, pp. 443–4. For Churchill's description of Joan of Arc's martyrdom, see *A History of the English-Speaking Peoples*, vol. 2, pp. 329–30.

2   Lord Moran, *Winston Churchill: The Struggle for Survival*, p. 546.

3   M. Soames, op. cit., p. 116.

4   M. Gilbert, *In Search of Churchill*, p. 86.

5   M. Soames, op. cit., p. 206. Cf. W.S. Churchill, *Thoughts and Adventures*, pp. 120–32.

6   W.S. Churchill, *Great Contemporaries*, p. 148.

7   W.S. Churchill, *A History of the English-Speaking Peoples*, vol. 4, p. 221.

8   W.S. Churchill, *Great Contemporaries*, p. 239.

9   Ibid., pp. 143–4.

10 Ibid., pp. 236–7.

11 Note by Churchill of his conversation with the President of the French Republic, 11 January 1925, circulated to the Cabinet on 5 February 1925, FO 371/10727.

12 Moran, op. cit., p. 321.

13 For examples, see D. Coombs, *Sir Winston Churchill's Life Through His Paintings*, pp. 139 (Riviera), 77 (Var), 74–5 and 144–5 (South of France), 42 and 59 (Mimizan), 146 (Avignon), 147–9 (Carcassonne).

14 *Painting as a Pastime: Winston Churchill – His Life as a Painter* (Sotheby's, London, 1998), p. 26.

15 W.S. Churchill, *The Second World War*, vol. 1, pp. 323–4.

16 J.R. Colville, *The Fringes of Power*, p. 261.

17 W.F. Kimball, *Churchill and Roosevelt: The Complete Correspondence*, vol. 1, p. 43.

18 Ibid., p. 44.

19 A. Montague Browne, *Long Sunset*, p. 160; F.W. Deakin, *Churchill The Historian*, pp. 17–18; Moran, op. cit., p. 259.

20 Colville, op. cit., p. 311.

21 Montague Browne, op. cit., p. 160.

22 C. Eade (ed.), *The War Speeches of the Rt. Hon. Winston S. Churchill*, vol. 1 (1967), p. 282.

23 Churchill to Eden, 14 June 1942, M. 248/2, Cab. 120/524.

24 Moran, op. cit., p. 81.

25 M. Soames, op. cit., p. 484.

26 See, for example, a note by Churchill for the War Cabinet, 'United States Policy towards France', 13 July 1943, Cab. 121/398.

27 M. Soames, *Clementine Churchill*, p. 387; record of a conversation between Churchill and M. Viénot, representative of the French Committee of National Liberation, 27 September 1943, Cab. 121/398.

28 Record of a conversation between Churchill and General de Gaulle, 4 June 1944, Cab. 121/399.

29 Duff Cooper (Algiers) to the Foreign Office, 16 May 1944, Cab. 121/399.

30 Churchill to Stalin, Prime Minister's Personal Telegram, T. 2127/4, 16 November 1944, Cab. 20/524.

31 Minutes of the War Cabinet, 13 November 1944, WM (44), 149th conclusions, minute 3, confidential annex, Cab. 121/399.

32 Moran, op. cit., p. 259.

33 M. Gilbert, *'Never Despair': Winston S. Churchill 1945–1965*, pp. 265–6.

34 Moran, op. cit., p. 431.

35 Minute by Churchill to Eden, 3 November 1953, M. 317/53, and annexed memorandum, Prem. 11/618.
36 Montague Browne, op. cit., pp. 156–7; S. Churchill, *Keep on Dancing*, p. 9.
37 Bermuda conference, BC (P) (53), second and third meetings, 5 and 6 December 1953, Prem. 11/618.
38 Moran, op. cit., pp. 506–7.
39 Memorandum by Sir I. Kirkpatrick to Churchill, 6 August 1954, Prem. 11/618, ff. 223–4.
40 Moran, op. cit., p. 574.
41 Churchill to J.F. Dulles, 19 August 1954, T. 587/54, Prem. 11/618.
42 Moran, op. cit., p. 602.
43 M.H. Macmillan, *Winds of Change, 1914–1939* (1966), p. 29.
44 D. Coombs, op. cit., fig. 460, p. 219.
45 Ibid., fig. 349, p. 174; for examples painted after the war, see pp. 176–7, 212–13.
46 Montague Browne, op. cit., p. 269.
47 Eade, op. cit., vol. 3, pp. 268–70.

4. Rights, Wrongs and Rivalries

1   Duff Cooper, *Old Men Forget*, p. 320.
2   These arguments are conveniently summarized in Duff Cooper to Bevin, 19 March 1946, FO 371/59952.
3   The stages of this discussion are traced in a paper by the Reconstruction Department of the Foreign Office, 10 July 1945, 'The "Western Group" and Franco-British Treaty'; this was prepared as a brief for the United Kingdom delegation at the Potsdam Conference. FO 371/219069.
4   Cooper, op. cit., p. 315.
5   W.S. Churchill, *The Second World War*, vol. 6, p. 208.
6   C. de Gaulle, *War Memoirs* (English edn, 1960), vol. 3, pp. 53–5.
7   Ibid., pp. 55–7.
8   Churchill, op. cit., p. 213.
9   Churchill, op. cit., pp. 218–19.
10 Churchill, op. cit., p. 566.
11 Churchill, op. cit., p. 550.
12 A.B. Gaunson, *The Anglo-French Clash in Lebanon and Syria, 1940–45* (1987), p. 147.
13 Ibid., pp. 166–7.
14 Ibid., pp. 164–5.
15 Cooper to Eden, 29 December 1944, Prem. 3/173/1.
16 Minute by Churchill to Eden, 5 February 1945, on Cooper to Eden, 6 January 1945, Prem. 3/1173/1.
17 Minute by Eden to Churchill, 12 January 1945, and Churchill's manuscript note on the same document, same date, Prem. 3/185/4.
18 Minute from Eden to Churchill, 16 January 1945, Prem. 3/185/4.
19 Cooper to Foreign Office, 15 January 1945, Prem. 3/185/4; for the text of the French Government's memorandum, 15 January 1945, see FO371/49154.
20 Churchill to Eden, 19 January 1945, Prem. 3/185/4; the particular secrecy which Churchill attached to this assessment is evidenced by the note at the heading of the paper 'Not for official circulation'.

Notes

21 Eden to Churchill, 23 January 1945, Prem. 3/185/4.
22 Churchill to Eden, 25 January 1945, Prem. 3/185/4.
23 Cadogan to Cooper, 27 January 1945 and reply 29 January 1945, FO 371/49154.
24 Gaunson, op. cit., pp. 169–70.
25 Eden to Cooper, 23 January 1945, FO 371/49066.
26 Cooper to O.C. Harvey, Foreign Office, 22 January 1945, FO 371/49154.
27 Eden to Churchill, 22 January 1945, and reply, 27 January 1945, Prem. 3/180/5.
28 Cooper to Eden, 28 January 1945, FO 371/49071.
29 For the text of de Gaulle's broadcast see *The Times*, 6 February 1945, in FO 371/49154.
30 S. Sebag-Montefiore, *Stalin: The Court of the Red Tsar* (2003), pp. 83, 86–8. I am grateful to Professor O.A. Rzheveshky for information concerning Stalin's library.
31 Minutes by J.G. Ward, G. Jebb, F.R. Hoyer Millar and others, 17–21 February 1945, on Churchill's minute M3/5 of 5 February 1945, FO 371/49066; for an expression of dismay at the American attitude towards France, see R.K. Law (Minister of State, Foreign Office) and O.G. Sargent from the Foreign Office to Eden at Yalta, 9 February 1945, Prem. 3/185/2.
32 Churchill to Attlee for the War Cabinet, 10 February 1945, Prem. 3/185/4.
33 Cooper to the Foreign Office, 19 February 1945, FO 371/49066.
34 Cooper to the Foreign Office, 24 February 1945, 371/49066; cf. Cooper to the Foreign Office, 19 February 1945, same file.
35 Record of conversations with M. Bidault at Binderton (Eden's country home), 25 February 1945, Prem. 3/182/8.
36 Churchill, op. cit., p. 450.
37 J.R. Colville, *The Fringes of Power*, p. 563.
38 The Earl of Avon, *The Reckoning*, p. 525.
39 Cooper to Foreign Office, 10 March 1945, situation report no. 11, FO 371/49073.
40 Minutes of the War Cabinet, 12 March 1945, W.M. (45) 29th conclusions, Prem. 4/34/9.
41 Colville, op. cit. p. 550; minute by Lord Cherwell to the Prime Minister, 12 March 1945, Prem. 4/34/9; the paper upon which Lord Cherwell was commenting, WP (45) 153, of 9 March 1945, is in the same file.
42 Minute by Churchill to Ismay, D71/5, 12 March 1945; and Ismay's reply, same date, Prem. 4/34/9.
43 Minute by Eden, 17 March 1945, on minutes by R.L. Speaight of 15 and 16 March 1945, FO 371/49180.
44 Memorandum by Eden for the War Cabinet, 17 March 1945, WP (45) 172, Cab. 66/63.
45 Memorandum by Sir John Anderson for the War Cabinet, WP (45) 169, 16 March 1945, and 33rd conclusions of the War Cabinet, WM 33 (45), 19 March 1945, Cab. 65/49.
46 Cooper to the Foreign Office, 29, 30 and 31 March, FO 371/45562, cited by K.E. Evans, '"The Apple of Discord": The Impact of the Levant on Anglo-French Relations during 1943' (University of Leeds, unpublished Ph.D. thesis, 1990), p. 625.
47 Ibid., p. 626.
48 It is summarized in Cooper to Bevin, 19 March 1946, FO 371/59952.
49 Cooper to the Foreign Office, 5 April 1945, Prem. 3/173/3.
50 Cooper to the Foreign Office, telegrams Nos. 565 and 569, 6 April 1945, FO 371/49067.
51 Churchill to Eden, 6 April 1945, Prem. 3/173/3.
52 Minute by Eden to Churchill, 7 April 1945, Prem. 3/173/3.
53 Minute by O.C. Harvey, Foreign Office, 7 April 1945, FO 371/49067.

54 Minute by Churchill to Eden, 8 April 1945, and reply, same date, Prem. 3/173/3.

55 Cooper to the Foreign Office, 18 April 1945, Churchill to Eden, 19 April, and Churchill to Cooper, 20 April, Prem. 3/173/3.

56 Cooper to Churchill, 22 April 1945, Prem. 3/173/3.

57 Cooper to Churchill, 28 April 1945, Prem. 3/173/3.

58 J.J. Norwich, *The Duff Cooper Diaries*, p. 363.

59 Churchill to de Gaulle, 9 May 1945, FO 371/49067.

60 de Gaulle, op. cit., pp. 185–7.

61 Gaunson, op. cit., p. 174.

62 Cooper to Foreign Office, 31 May 1945, cited by K.E. Evans, op. cit., p. 633.

63 These figures were given in Churchill's speech to Parliament on 5 June 1945, C. Eade (ed.), *The War Speeches of Winston S. Churchill*, vol. 3, p. 461.

64 J.J. Norwich, op. cit., p. 371. In 1898, a small French expeditionary force had been compelled by the British to leave Fashoda, on the White Nile; this event was felt as a humiliation and caused the resignation of the French Premier.

65 de Gaulle, op. cit., pp. 180–1.

66 de Gaulle, op. cit., pp. 189–90.

67 Cooper, op. cit., pp. 354–5; cf. J.J. Norwich, op. cit., pp. 371–2.

68 de Gaulle, op. cit., p. 192.

69 Eade (ed.) op. cit., pp. 458–60; Churchill, op. cit., pp. 452–3.

70 Eade, op. cit., pp. 462–3. The issue about the aeroplane has been much disputed; see Max (Lord) Egremont, *Under Two Flags* (1977), pp. 191–2. The material points are that Churchill firmly believed what he said, and that Spears did play a substantial part in securing de Gaulle's departure.

71 Churchill, op. cit., p. 452.

72 Churchill to Truman, 4 June 1945, Prem. 3/275/7.

73 Churchill to Truman, 7 June 1945, Prem. 3/275/7; it seems clear that this telegram is one of those to which, by whatever means, de Gaulle gained access. Cf. de Gaulle, op. cit., pp. 180–1.

74 Cooper to O.C. Harvey, Foreign Office, 21 June 1945, FO 371/49068.

75 Cadogan to Churchill, 18 June 1945, FO 371/49068.

76 Cooper to O.C. Harvey, 28 June 1945, FO 371/49068.

77 de Gaulle, op. cit., pp. 193–4.

78 Memorandum by Sir E. Grigg, CP (45) 55, 2 July 1945, Prem. 3/296/10.

79 J.J. Norwich, op. cit., p. 384.

80 Record of a meeting held by Bevin in the Foreign Office, 13 August 1945, FO 371/219069.

81 Cooper to Foreign Office, 14 August 1945, FO 371/219060.

82 de Gaulle, op. cit., pp. 213–14.

83 Cooper to Bevin, 16 October 1945, FO 371/49077.

84 de Gaulle, op. cit., pp. 277–8.

85 D. LePan, *Bright Glass of Memory* (Toronto, 1979), p. 87.

86 I owe this cameo to the late Sir Peter Tennant, who was present.

Notes

5. Churchill, Eden and Stalin

1   J. Connell, *Auchinleck*, pp. 472–3.

2   Earl of Avon, *The Reckoning*, p. 146.

3   J.W. Wheeler-Bennett, *King George VI*, pp. 544, 700–1.

4   Avon, op. cit., p. 404. Eden's account of his childhood and career in the Army, written just before his death, is revealing: *Another World* (1976).

5   Lord Moran, *Winston Churchill: The Struggle for Survival 1940–1965* (1966), p. 579.

6   Avon, op. cit., pp. 332–3.

7   Ibid., p. 449.

8   Ibid., Foreword.

9   D.N. Dilks (ed.), *The Diaries of Sir Alexander Cadogan*, pp. 401, 774; hereafter cited as Cadogan.

10   A. Montague Browne, *Long Sunset*, p. 132.

11   J.R. Colville in J.W. Wheeler-Bennett (ed.), *Action This Day* (1968), p. 78.

12   E.L. Woodward, *British Foreign Policy in the Second World War*, vol. 1 (1970), p. xxv.

13   J.R. Colville, *The Fringes of Power*, p. 405.

14   Cadogan, p. 321.

15   Woodward, op. cit., pp. xxix, 487–500.

16   The main documents are conveniently collected in 'Prime Minister's Warning To M. Stalin About The German Danger, April 1941', Prem. 3/403. There are numerous additional papers in FO 954/24.

17   R.M. Langworth (ed.), *Churchill by Himself*, p. 384; W.S. Churchill, *Great Comtemporaries*, pp. 38–9.

18   C. Eade (ed.), *The War Speeches of the Rt. Hon. Winston S. Churchill*, vol. 1, p. 137.

19   W.S. Churchill, *The Second World War*, vol. 2, p. 458, and vol. 3, pp. 286, 297. Cf. D. Volkongonov, *Stalin: Triumph and Tragedy* (1991), pp. 393–414.

20   Cadogan, p. 537; A. Montague Browne, op. cit., p. 158.

21   W.S. Churchill, *The Second World War*, vol. 6, p. 23; Eade, op. cit., vol. 3, pp. 128–31; G.C. Herring, *Aid to Russia 1941–1946* (1973).

22   Avon, op. cit., p. 504.

23   Sir A. Clark Kerr (Moscow) to the Foreign Office, No. 567, 29 February 1944, Prem. 3/355/9.

24   Avon, op. cit., p. 514.

25   W.S. Churchill, *The Second World War*, vol. 6, p. 203.

26   Cadogan, pp. 708–9.

27   Moran, op. cit., p. 227.

28   M. Djilas, *Conversations with Stalin* (1963), p. 61.

29   Avon, op. cit., p. 525.

30   Minutes of a meeting with Commonwealth representatives, 6 April 1945, BCM 9(45), 4th meeting, DO 35/1479.

31   Woodward, op. cit., p. xliii.

32   J.R. Colville, *The Fringes of Power*, p. 593.

33   Avon, op. cit., p. 545.

34   M. Soames, *A Daughter's Tale*, p. 352.

35   Cadogan, p. 716.

36   Lord Strang, 'War and Foreign Policy: 1939–1945', in D.N. Dilks (ed.), *Retreat From Power*, vol. 2 (1981), p. 87.

6. Epic and Tragedy

1 Amongst these was Churchill; see *The Second World War*, vol. 5, p. 353.
2 For a survey of the files, and a list of those relating to Poland, see L. Atherton, *SOE in Eastern Europe* (Public Record Office, London), pp. 2, 4, 15–23. Much valuable, not to say poignant, material may be found in J. Garlinski, *Poland, SOE and the Allies* (1969) and *The Survival of Love: Memoirs of a Resistance Officer* (1991).
3 HS4/152.
4 M to AD/1, 26 June 1942, HS4/166.
5 M to CD, 14 December 1942, HS4/170; 'CD' was the Operational Head of SOE.
6 M to CD, 31 December 1941, HS4/136. For an example of tensions over the control of secret communications between Britain and Poland, see M to CD, 8 July 1941 HS4/136.
7 See file HS4/323, including notes from G.J. [Gladwyn Jebb] to CD, 24 June 1941; CD to CEO, 25 June 1941; G.J. to Air Commodore Dixon of the Air Ministry, 28 June 1941.
8 Unsigned memorandum, 'Discussion with General Sosnkowski on his position in view of Soviet-Polish Relations', a document bearing conflicting dates of 23 July and 29 July 1941 HS4/136.
9 Dalton to Eden, 31 July 1941, HS4/323.
10 MP to MP1, 4 June 1944, HS4/146. There is a useful list of some of the code names in file HS4/142; for others, see L. Atherton, op. cit., pp. 36–41.
11 Memorandum by MX, 'Note on SOE's Work with the Poles', 24 December 1941 HS4/136.
12 O. Rzheshevsky, 'The Grand Alliance. New Documents and Commentaries', in *1945 Consequences and Sequels of the Second World War* (Bulletin du Comité international d'histoire de la Deuxième Guerre mondiale, nos. 27/28, Paris, 1995), p. 26.
13 The initial at the bottom of this letter is illegible; the paper was addressed to M and dated 26 July 1942, HS4/147.
14 Memorandum by R.T. (Major R. Truszkowski), 17 March 1943, HS4/323; AD/S to SO 3 April 1943, ibid.
15 For a good example, see the paper entitled 'Co-ordination of Anglo-Soviet Resistance Policy', the marginal note from CD to SO, and SO's comment, 1 June 1943, HS4/323.
16 Foreign Office to the British Embassy in Moscow, telegrams nos. 690 and 691 of 12 June 1943, HS4/149.
17 Foreign Office to the British Embassy in Moscow, telegram no. 692 of 12 June 1943 ibid.
18 MP to V/CD, 13 August 1943, HS4/144; cf. the attached memorandum by MPX, of 11 August 1943.
19 D/P to AD/O, 11 August 1943, HS4/144.
20 See memoranda by Eden for the War Cabinet, 'Western Frontiers of the USSR' and 'Resistance in Poland', both dated 5 October 1943, WP (43) 438 and 439, FO 1079/11.
21 Memorandum by Eden, 'Possible Lines of a Polish-Soviet Settlement', WO (43) 528 22 November 1943, FO 1079/11.
22 These developments are conveniently summarized in a paper prepared by the Central Department of the Foreign Office, 30 September 1944, C13186/761/G, Prem. 3/352/11.
23 For a good example, see MP to D/Plans, 15 January 1944, and a memorandum from the Foreign Office of 8 January 1944, HS4/144.
24 K/POL to CD, HS4/138.

25 MP to C/D, MP/PD/5975, 23 May 1944, HS4/138; compare the record of a conversation with Mikolajczyk, 24 May, reported in a memorandum of CD to AD/H, 27 May 1944, ibid.

26 For a good example see MP to A/CD, MP/INT/6111, 26 June 1944, HS4/138, which explores the prospects of providing intelligence to the Russians, derived from the Secret Army of Poland, in respect of events behind the German Eastern Front.

27 Memorandum entitled 'Operations by the Polish Secret Army', unsigned but marked 'Top Secret SOE/99', 5 April 1944, HS4/323.

28 These developments are conveniently summarized in a paper prepared by the Central Department of the Foreign Office, 30 September 1944, C 13186/761/G, Prem. 3/352/11.

29 Memorandum entitled 'Conversations between the Soviet Government and the Polish Prime Minister in Moscow', Central Department of the Foreign Office, 30 August 1944, C 11639/8/G, Prem. 3/352/12.

30 Record, translated from the Polish, no. 6131/Tjn./44, 29 July 1944, of the meeting between Major-General C.McV. Gubbins and Major-General S. Tabor, 29 July 1944, HS4/156. Cf. P. Wilkinson and J. Bright Astley, *Gubbins and SOE* (1993), pp. 204–5. 'Tabor' was a name used by General Stanislav Tatar. For a vivid modern account see N. Davies, *Rising '44: The Battle for Warsaw* (2003); and more generally on the fate of the states unfortunate enough to lie between Nazi Germany and the USSR, T. Snyder, *Bloodlands* (2010).

31 A memorandum unsigned, but from Selborne, to Churchill, 1 August 1944, HS4/156.

32 For a statement of the reasons, see General Wilson and Air Marshal Slessor to the Chiefs of Staff, 4 August 1944, HS4/156.

33 Cited in the memorandum 'Negotiations between Polish GHQ and Chiefs of Staff during Warsaw Rising', HS4/157; cf. 'Special Operations to Warsaw', enclosed in Major Morgan to Lt. Col. Threlfall, 12 August 1944, ibid.

34 Minute by Eden to Churchill, 8 August 1944, and Churchill's manuscript note, 10 August, PM 44/580, Prem. 3/352/12. For a summary of Polish requests and British responses in the first ten days of the crisis, see the unsigned paper 'Negotiations between Polish G.H.Q. and Chiefs of Staff during the Warsaw Rising', 10 August 1944, HS4/317.

35 Foreign Office to British Embassy, Moscow, 16 August 1944, recording Eden's conversation with the Polish Prime Minister and Minister for Foreign Affairs on 14 August HS4/157.

36 Eden to British Embassy, Moscow, 16 August 1944, HS4/157; cf. minutes of the meeting of the War Cabinet, 16 August WM (44) 107th Conclusions, Prem. 3/352/12.

37 Sir A. Clark Kerr, Moscow, to the Foreign Office, 15 August 1944, HS4/157.

38 Churchill to Roosevelt enclosing the text of a telegram from Stalin, 18 August 1944, Prem. 3/352/12.

39 Foreign Office to Churchill, 20 August 1944, CLASP no. 138, Prem. 3/352/12.

40 MP to CD, 17 August 1944, HS4/157. For a detailed description of some of the operational difficulties experienced by the air forces in Italy, see Lt. Col. Threlfall to Lt. Col. Hancza, 17 August 1944, ibid.

41 MP to CD, 30 August 1944, HS4/158.

42 Selborne to Churchill, forwarded to Churchill on 11 August 1944, HS4/156.

43 Memorandum by Eden for the War Cabinet, 'Situation in Warsaw', WP (44) 461, 22 August 1944, FO 371/39494.

44 Bracken to Churchill, 24 August 1944, FO 371/39494.

45 Minutes of a meeting held at the Air Ministry on 31 August 1944, HS4/156; D. Dodds-Parker, *Setting Europe Ablaze* (1983), p. 184.

46 W.S. Churchill, *The Second World War*, vol. 6 (1956), pp. 125–6.

47 Eden to Churchill, repeating the telegram of the previous day from Moscow, CORDITE No. 89, 10 September 1944, Prem. 3/352/12.

48 Eden to Churchill, repeating a telegram from Moscow, CORDITE No. 91, 10 September 1944, Prem. 3/352/12.

49 Eden to Churchill, CORDITE No. 180, 13 September 1944, Prem. 3/352/12.

50 C. Eade (ed.), *The War Speeches of the Rt. Hon. Winston S. Churchill*, vol. 3, pp. 239–40.

51 For a graphic account of events during the Warsaw uprising, see the report by 2nd Lt. Adam Truszkowski, forwarded to the Foreign Office on 18 June 1945, by Major M.J.T. Pickles, HS4/211; and for an account of special operations to Poland from the Mediterranean theatre, see the memorandum by Lt. Col. H.M. Threlfall, 30 May 1945, with appendices, in HS4/184.

52 Churchill, op. cit., vol. 6, p. 128.

53 J.R. Colville in J.W. Wheeler-Bennett, *Action This Day* (1968), pp. 91–2.

54 For action taken by the British to support Mikolajczyk and prevent his resignation, see the memorandum by the Central Department of the Foreign Office, 30 September 1944, C 13186/761/G, Prem. 3/352/11.

55 Eden to Sir Orme Sargent, Foreign Office, 12 October 1944, Prem. 3/352/11. For evidence that the Russian forces were in need of rest, and not in a position to take Warsaw in August 1944, see S. Sebag Montefiore, *Stalin: The Court of the Red Tsar* (2003), p. 421, and the documents published in 2011 by the Russian Academy of Sciences, Moscow, vol. 1, pp. 381–4. Cf. R. Service, *Stalin* (2004), pp. 470–2.

56 Churchill, op. cit., vol. 6, pp. 202–6.

57 Lord Moran, *Winston Churchill: The Struggle for Survival, 1940–1965*, pp. 198–200.

58 D.N. Dilks (ed.), *The Diaries of Sir Alexander Cadogan*, p. 537.

59 Earl of Avon, *The Reckoning*, p. 486.

60 M. Gilbert, *Road to Victory: Winston S. Churchill 1941–1945*, pp. 1008–9, 1012–16, 1019–20.

61 Gilbert, loc. cit., pp. 1031, 1035.

62 Lord Selborne to Sir Archibald Sinclair, 22 November 1944, HS4/156; cf. Selborne to Sinclair and the reply, 30 October and 14 November 1944, ibid.

63 Lord Selborne to Churchill, 24 November 1944, HS4/156.

64 Eden to Churchill, 4 December 1944, and Churchill's minute on the same document undated, HS4/156; cf. Selborne to the Prime Minister, 8 December 1944, ibid.

65 Sir Charles Portal to Churchill, 23 November 1944, Prem. 3/352/11.

66 Eden to Churchill, 13 December 1944, HS4/156.

67 Stalin to Churchill, 8 December 1944, HS4/318.

68 For the text of this speech see C. Eade (ed.), op. cit., pp. 310–20.

69 For much interesting material about the conditions in Poland at the end of 1944, see the report on the British Observer mission to German-occupied Poland by Col. D.T. Hudson and others, 26 December 1944, HS4/249.

70 W.S. Churchill, op. cit., vol. 6, p. 349.

71 S. Churchill, *Keep on Dancing*, p. 76.

72 T. Szarota, 'Vivre l'histoire ou l'"histoire vivante": la Seconde Guerre mondiale dans l'esprit des Polonais cinquante ans après', in *1945: Consequences and Sequels of the Second World War* (Bulletin du Comité international d'histoire de la Deuxième Guerre mondiale, nos. 27/28, Paris, 1995), p. 305.

Notes

7. The Bitter Fruit of Victory

1   *The Daily Telegraph*, Thursday, 1 October 1998, pp. 1, 8–9.

2   A. Bryant, *Triumph in the West* (1959), pp. 469–70.

3   The papers are collected in Cab. 121/64; see in particular extracts from the minutes of the Chiefs of Staff, 224th meeting, 23 September 1943; the report of 1 May 1944, PHP (43) 1 (0); minutes of the Chiefs of Staff, 172nd meeting, 24 May 1944; and the revised version of the paper, 6 June 1944, PHP (44) 132 (0) Final.

4   A.T. Cornwall-Jones to the Vice-Chiefs of Staff, 13 June 1944, Cab. 121/64.

5   Draft paper, 'Basic Assumptions for Staff Studies and Post-War Strategical Problems', attached to A.T. Cornwall-Jones to the Vice Chiefs of Staff, 13 June 1944 (see note 4); minutes of the Chiefs of Staff Committee, 195th meeting, 15 June 1944, Cab. 121/46, circulated as C.O.S. (44) 527 (0) PHP, 15 June 1944, Cab. 121/64.

6   C.O.S. (44/527) (0) (PHP), 15 June 1944, circulated to the War Cabinet together with an annex, 'The Effect of Soviet Policy on British Strategic Interests', and an appendix summarizing the treaty engagements of the Soviet Union with foreign countries; the latter paper was prepared in the Foreign Office and dated 28 March 1944, all in Cab. 121/64.

7   A. Danchev and D. Todman (eds.), *War Diaries 1939–45: Field Marshal Lord Alanbrooke*, p. 575. The three officers who produced the report went on to follow distinguished careers as Admiral Sir Guy Grantham, Maj.-Gen. Sir Geoffrey Thompson and Air Chief Marshal Sir Walter Dawson.

8   Report by the Joint Intelligence Sub-Committee, 'Russian Capabilities in Relation to the Strategic Interests of the British Commonwealth', 22 August 1944, J.I.C. (44) 366 (0) Final, Cab. 121/64.

9   Lord Moran, *Winston Churchill: The Struggle for Survival, 1940–1965* , p. 202.

10 Extract from the minutes of the meeting held on 4 October 1944 in the Foreign Secretary's room, 'The Study of Post-war Problems and the Dismemberment of Germany', Cab. 121/64.

11 Sir A. Clark Kerr to Eden, 19 November 1944, No. 772, enclosing a 'Memorandum Respecting Observations on the Attitude of the Soviet Government towards Possible Formation of a Group of Western European Democracies'; this paper was circulated by Eden to the Cabinet, Prem. 3/396/14.

12 Report of the Joint Intelligence Sub-Committee, 'Russia's Strategic Interests and Intentions from the Point of View of Her Security', J.I.C. (44) 467 (0), 18 December 1944, Cab. 119/129.

13 Extract from a letter dated 16 January 1945 from Mr J. Balfour (Moscow) to Mr C. Warner, Head of the Northern Department of the Foreign Office, circulated to the War Cabinet under cover of a note, 'Soviet Foreign Policy', by Eden, 12 March 1945, W.P. (45) 156, Cab. 121/64.

14 Foreign Office to Sir A. Cadogan at Yalta, Fleece no. 128, 4 February 1945, Prem. 3/396/14.

15 These reports are contained in a series of files, HW1; the report from the Japanese Ambassador in Berlin to the Minister of Foreign Affairs in Tokyo, summarizing talks with Ribbentrop between 17 and 28 March 1945, is in file HW1/3678.

16 'C' to Churchill, C/8727, 2 March 1945; Churchill's manuscript note, addressed to the Foreign Secretary, on the same document, 8 March 1945, HW 1/3562; for Ribbentrop's message to the German Legation in Dublin, 16 February 1945, see HW 1/3539; Foreign Office to British Embassy, Washington, 10 March 1945, no. 2310, HW 1/3562.

17 Earl of Avon, *The Reckoning*, pp. 525–6.

18 Ibid.

19 J.R. Colville, *The Fringes of Power* (1985), p. 582.

20 Ibid., p. 591.

21 Eden (San Francisco) to the Foreign Office, 4 May 1945, No. 133; and 14 May 1945, No. 290, Cab. 121/64.

22 Avon, op. cit., p. 536.

23 Clark Kerr to the Foreign Office, 6 April 1945, No. 1137, Cab. 121/64.

24 Sargent to Churchill, 2 May 1945, PM/OS/45/60, Prem. 3/396/14.

25 Eden to Clark Kerr, 8 April 1945, No. 1721, Cab. 121/64.

26 Record by Clark Kerr of a discussion between the Prime Minister and the Soviet Ambassador at 10 Downing Street on 18 May 1945, Prem. 3/396/12.

27 Memorandum by Clark Kerr, 25 May 1945, recording a conversation of 23 May, Prem. 3/396/14.

28 For the report of the Joint Planning Staff, 'Operation "Unthinkable"', 22 May 1945 (signed by G. Grantham, G.S. Thompson and W.L. Dawson), see Cab. 120/691; Danchev and Todd (eds.), op. cit., p. 694.

29 Memorandum by the Chiefs of Staff to Churchill, 8 June 1945, enclosed with Ismay to Churchill, same date, Cab. 120/691.

30 Churchill to Ismay for the Chiefs of Staff Committee, 10 June 1945,Cab. 120/691.

31 Danchev and Todman (eds.), op. cit., p. 697.

32 Report by the Joint Planning Staff, 'Operation Unthinkable', 11 July 1945, Cab. 120/691.

33 Ismay to Churchill, 8 June 1945, Cab. 120/691.

34 M. Gilbert, *'Never Despair': Winston S. Churchill 1945–1965*, pp. 99–100.

35 'Churchill's Plan for Third World War against Stalin', *The Daily Telegraph*, 1 October 1998, p. 1.

36 Eden to Churchill, P.M./45/2.P, 17 July 1945, Prem. 3/396/14; cf. Eden, op. cit., p. 545.

37 Danchev and Todman (eds.), op. cit., p. 709.

38 The papers are in Cab. 120/691; see, for example, Joint Staff Mission, Washington, to Cabinet Office, embodying a message from Field-Marshal Wilson to General Ismay, 30 August 1946, FMW 271; and Ministry of Defence to Joint Staff Mission, Washington, DEF. 96, embodying a message from General Hollis to Field-Marshal Wilson, 16 January 1947, Cab. 120/691.

39 D. Carlton, *Churchill and the Soviet Union*, p. 5.

40 Numerous papers are preserved on this subject in Prem. 11/915, including extracts from *The Times* of 24 and 25 November 1954; from Hansard, 25 November; note to Churchill from DK (Denis Kelly), 27 November 1954; Churchill's statement in Parliament on 1 December 1954; Montgomery to Churchill, 6 December 1954, enclosing a copy of Montgomery to CIGS, 14 June 1945. A memorandum to Churchill from Denis Kelly, 6 December 1954, shows that between 30 March and 26 July 1945, Churchill sent or received 883 telegrams.

8. The Solitary Pilgrimage

1 For example, see Churchill's speech of 27 February 1945, Parl. Deb., H. of C., 5th ser., vol. 408, cols. 1267–95.

2 Meetings of Commonwealth Prime Ministers, 1–5 May 1944, Prem. 4/42/5.

3 M. Gilbert, *'Never Despair': Winston S. Churchill 1945–1965* (1988), pp. 200-3.

Notes

4   M. Peterson, *Both Sides of the Curtain* (1950), p. 258.

5   M. Pottle (ed.), *Champion Redoubtable: The Diaries and Letters of Violet Bonham Carter 1914–1945*, p. 239.

6   M. Gilbert, *Winston S. Churchill*, vol. 5, 1922–39 (1976), p. 343.

7   C. Eade (ed.), *The War Speeches of the Rt. Hon. Winston S. Churchill*, vol. 1, p. 299.

8   Memorandum by Pearson, 'Discussions with Mr. Churchill', 9 December 1951, papers of L.B. Pearson, pre-1958 series, Britain-Canada Relations 1950–7, MG26 NI, vol. 19, LAC.

9   J.R. Colville, *Footprints in Time* (1976), pp. 132–3.

10 Secretary of State for External Affairs, Ottawa, to Canadian Ambassadors and High Commissioners, 'Mr. Churchill's discussions in Ottawa', 21 January 1952, file no. 50274-40, LAC.

11 Canadian Ambassador in Washington to Secretary of State for External Affairs, Ottawa, 9 January 1952, file no. 50274-40, LAC.

12 Secretary of State for External Affairs, Ottawa, to Canadian Ambassador and High Commissioners, 21 January 1952; see note 10.

13 Churchill to Eisenhower, Prime Minister's Personal Telegram no. T.62/53, 10 March 1953, Prem 11/422, PRO.

14 Churchill to Eisenhower, 3 May 1953, Prem 11/421.

15 Eisenhower to Churchill, embodied in a telegram from British Embassy, Washington, to Foreign Office No. 973, 5 May 1953, and reply, 6 May, embodied in a telegram from Foreign Office to Washington no. 2019, 7 May 1953, Prem 11/421.

16 J.R. Colville, *The Fringes of Power*, p. 668.

17 Lord Moran, *Winston Churchill: The Struggle for Survival*, pp. 416, 446, 428.

18 J.R. Colville in J.W. Wheeler-Bennett (ed.), *Action This Day*, pp. 132–3.

19 J.R. Colville, *The Fringes of Power*, p. 683; cf. Colville in *Action This Day*, pp. 134–5.

20 A. Montague Browne, *Long Sunset*, p. 114; Colville, *Action This Day*, p. 122.

21 Ibid., p. 135.

22 Moran, op. cit., p. 572.

23 D.N. Dilks, *"The Great Dominion"*, pp. 422–5.

24 L.B. Pearson to Norman A. Robertson, Canadian High Commissioner in the UK, 7 July 1954, MG 26 NI, vol. 19, LAC.

25 Moran, op. cit., pp. 562–3; I owe the anecdote about Mr Morrison to the late Viscount Boyd, who was then Secretary of State for the Colonies.

26 Parl. Deb., H. of C., 5th ser., vol. 537, cols. 1893–905.

27 Parl. Deb., H. of C., 5th ser., vol. 538, cols. 964–5.

28 Moran, op. cit., p. 655.

29 M.H. Macmillan, *Tides of Fortune, 1945–1955*, p. 587.

30 Ibid., p. 559.

31 See note 7.

32 S. Baldwin, *Service of our Lives* (1937), p. 160.

33 The text of Churchill's speech is printed as an annex to the despatch of the British High Commissioner in Ottawa to the Secretary of State for Commonwealth Relations, 25 January 1952, FO 371/97593.

34 *Winnipeg Free Press*, 'Mr. Churchill's Speech', 15 January 1952.

9. 'Historians Are Dangerous'

1   Cited by M. Ferro, *The Use and Abuse of History* (2003), p. 14.
2   *The Guardian*, 28 February 2003; *The Times*, 1 March 2003. Mr Blair's *A Journey* (2010), pp. 207–9, gives a sympathetic account of Chamberlain but condemns him for believing that 'fascism' could be contained, whereas he should have judged that it must be eradicated. No distinction is drawn between 'fascism' and Nazism, or between Germany and Italy. Nor are the issues of resources and timing addressed.
3   *The Literature of Politics* (Conservative Political Centre, London, 1955), pp. 16–17.
4   Parl. Deb., H. of C., 5th ser., vol. 339, col. 361.
5   Churchill, *The Second World War*, vol. 1, p. 298.
6   C. Eade, *The War Speeches of the Rt. Hon. Winston S. Churchill*, vol. 2, p. 154.
7   D.N. Dilks, *"The Great Dominion"*, p. 199.
8   Churchill, op. cit, p. x.
9   P.G. Wodehouse, *The Code of the Woosters* (Penguin edn., London, 1953), p. 85.
10   D.N. Dilks, 'Flashes of Intelligence', in C. Andrew and D.N. Dilks (eds.) *The Missing Dimension* (1984), pp. 118–22.
11   D.N. Dilks (ed.), *The Diaries of Sir Alexander Cadogan*, p. 132; hereafter cited as Cadogan.
12   C. Eade (ed.), op. cit., vol. 1, p. 29.
13   Churchill, op. cit., p. 183.
14   Churchill, op. cit., pp. 24–6.
15   Ibid., pp. 35–6, 44.
16   Cadogan, p. 73.
17   K.G. Feiling, *The Life of Neville Chamberlain*, p. 279.
18   G.M. Young, *Stanley Baldwin*, p. 177.
19   M. Muggeridge (ed.), *Ciano's Diplomatic Papers* (1948), p. xix.
20   For an account of Chamberlain's role, see M. MacDonald, *Titans and Others* (1972), pp. 58–84.
21   I owe this to the late Lord Home, who as Chamberlain's Parliamentary Private Secretary attended the meeting.
22   N. Chamberlain, *In Search of Peace* (1938), p. 29; speech of 25 June 1937.
23   Ibid., pp. 176–7.
24   Churchill, *Great Contemporaries* (1939 edn., repr. by Odhams Press, 1947), p. 203.
25   *Documents on British Foreign Policy*, ser. 3, vol. 1 (London, 1948), p. 225.
26   Chamberlain's guest was the late Miss Hermione Hammond, who told me on 16 June 2003 that she made note of the conversation there and then.
27   K.G. Feiling, op. cit, p. 360.
28   Parl. Deb., H. of C., 5th ser., vol. 339, cols. 545–51.
29   P.G. Wodehouse, *Blandings Castle* (1935), p. 99.
30   Churchill, op. cit., p. 265.
31   Cadogan, p. 104.
32   Churchill, op. cit., vol. 1, p. 270.
33   N. Chamberlain, *In Search of Peace*, p. 276.
34   E.L. Woodward, *British Foreign Policy in the Second World War* (1970), vol. 1, p. 1; *Documents on British Foreign Policy*, ser. 3, vol. 7, pp. 127–8.
35   Minutes of the War Cabinet, 26 and 27 May 1940, Cab. 65/13; Neville Chamberlain's diary, 26 May 1940, and Chamberlain to his sister, 14 July 1940 (Chamberlain papers, University of Birmingham).

36 Churchill, op. cit., vol. 3 (1952), p. 474.

37 This is noted in manuscript on the entry of 23 February 1945, in the diary of Dr Hugh Dalton (British Library of Economic and Political Science, University of London).

38 Churchill, op. cit., vol. 6, p. 328.

39 Parl. Deb., H. of C., 5th ser., vol. 408, col. 1306.

40 A.W. Baldwin, *My Father: The True Story* (1955), p. 286.

41 Sir Anthony Eden (later Earl of Avon) told me this in 1960.

42 J.R. Colville, *The Fringes of Power*, p. 675; K.G. Feiling, op. cit., p. 252; Churchill, op. cit., vol. 6, p. 329.

43 Churchill to Eisenhower, 6 May 1953, Prem. 11/421.

44 D.N. Dilks, *"The Great Dominion"*, pp. 424, 422.

45 Ibid., p. 425.

46 Lord Tedder, *With Prejudice*, Preface. For an illuminating examination of Churchill's six volumes on World War II, see D. Reynolds, *In Command of History*.

47 B. Rees (ed.), *Robert Birley: History and Idealism* (1990), pp. 236–7.

48 *The Daily Telegraph*, 21 September 2001.

49 C. Ricks (ed.), *A. E. Housman: Collected Poems and Selected Prose* (Harmondsworth, 1988), p. 339.

50 J.M. Keynes, *The General Theory of Employment, Interest and Money* (1973 edn.), p. 383.

Select Bibliography

In the English language alone, many hundreds of books have been written about Churchill, not to mention thousands of articles. I have excluded the latter as being generally too detailed for a work of this kind; the more important aspects brought out in articles are often subsumed in the volumes noted below. Significant works about Churchill are regularly reviewed in *Finest Hour*, the journal of the Churchill Centre (info@winstonchurchill.org).

To make a selection amidst such riches is no easy task. A number of works published in Churchill's lifetime or soon after his death are included, for they often contain direct testimony from those who knew him well – for example, the tributes published in 1965 by the BBC and *The Observer*. The place of publication is London unless otherwise stated. Normally the date given is that of the first edition but where a revised edition incorporates significant changes or new material, I have occasionally inserted the latter date.

This list concentrates on the final phases of Churchill's career, from 1939 to 1955. Several of the works cited contain full records of Sir Winston's own writings, and comprehensive bibliographies.

The Official Biography

Churchill, R.S., *Winston S. Churchill*, vols 1–2 (1966, 1967).
Gilbert, M., *Winston S. Churchill*, vols 3–8 (1971–88).

Companion volumes: 16 have so far been published, covering the years 1874 to 1941; the first 5 were edited by Randolph S. Churchill and the remainder by Sir Martin Gilbert.

Works by Sir Winston Churchill

Lord Randolph Churchill (2 vols, 1906).
The World Crisis, 1911–1918 (6 vols, 1923–31).
My Early Life (1930).
Thoughts and Adventures (1932).
Great Contemporaries (rev. edn, 1939).
Marlborough: His Life and Times (4 vols, 1933–8).
The Second World War (6 vols, 1948–54).
A History of the English-Speaking Peoples (4 vols, 1956–8).
Winston S. Churchill: His Complete Speeches 1897–1963 (ed. R.R. James, 8 vols, 1974).

The Collected Works of Sir Winston Churchill (34 vols, 1974–6).
The Collected Essays of Sir Winston Churchill (ed. M. Wolff, 1976).

Documentary Sources, Works of Reference, Compendia

The official histories of World War II published over many years under the aegis of the Cabinet Office in London contain countless references to Churchill. The most important works in this context are those of the Grand Strategy series (6 vols, 1956–76) but they lack the important, sometimes all-important, dimension of signals interception and other activities of the intelligence services. The volumes appearing in more recent times under the title *British Intelligence in the Second World War* (F.H. Hinsley and others, 4 vols, 1977–90) and *Strategic Deception* (M.E. Howard, 1990) therefore form an essential supplement. The author of the official history of British foreign policy during World War II (E.L. Woodward, 5 vols, 1970–6) gracefully acknowledges his own indebtedness to Sir Winston Churchill's memoirs. Unfortunately, it was decided long ago not to publish volumes of documents covering Britain's foreign policy during the war. A good deal of original material can, however, be retrieved from *Foreign Relations of the United States*, with several volumes to cover each year, and from the official biography.

Barnes, A.J.L., and Nicholson, D. (eds.), *The Leo Amery Diaries 1896–1955* (2 vols, 1980, 1988).
Boyle, P. (ed.), *The Churchill-Eisenhower Correspondence, 1953–55* (Chapel Hill, 1990).
Catterall, P. (ed.), *The Macmillan Diaries: The Cabinet Years 1950-1957* (2003).
Churchill, R.S., and Gernsheim, H. (eds.), *Churchill: His Life in Photographs* (1955).
Churchill, W.S. (ed.), *'Never Give In!' The Best of Winston Churchill's Speeches* (2003).
Cohen, R. (ed.), *Bibliography of the Writings of Sir Winston Churchill* (3 vols, 2006).
Colville, J.R., *The Fringes of Power: Downing Street Diaries, 1939–1945* (1985).
Coombs, D., with Churchill, M., *Sir Winston Churchill's Life Through His Paintings* (2003).
Coote, C. (ed.), *Sir Winston Churchill: A Self-Portrait Constructed from His Own Sayings and Writings* (1954).
Danchev, A. and Todman, D. (eds.), *War Diaries 1939–45: Field Marshal Lord Alanbrooke* (2001).
David, E. (ed.), *Inside Asquith's Cabinet: from the Diaries of Charles Hobhouse* (1977).
Dilks, D.N. (ed.), *The Diaries of Sir Alexander Cadogan* (1971).
Eade, C. (ed.), *The War Speeches of the Rt. Hon. Winston S. Churchill* (3 vols, 1952).
Gilbert, M. (ed.), *Winston Churchill and Emery Reves: Correspondence 1937–1964* (Austin, Texas, 1997).
Hall, D., *The Book of Churchilliana* (2002).
Hart-Davis, D. (ed.), *King's Counsellor: Abdication and War – The Diary of Sir Alan Lascelles* (2006).
Harvey, J. (ed.), *The Diplomatic Diaries of Oliver Harvey 1937–1940* (1970).
———, *The War Diaries of Oliver Harvey 1941–1945* (1978).
Hunter, I. (ed.), *Winston and Archie: The Letters of Sir Archibald Sinclair and Winston S. Churchill, 1915–1960* (2005).
James, R.R. (ed.), *Chips: The Diaries of Sir Henry Channon* (1967).
Kimball, W.F. (ed.), *Roosevelt and Churchill: The Complete Correspondence* (3 vols, Princeton, 1984).
Lamb, S. (ed.), *The Wisdom of Winston Churchill* (2010).

Langworth, R.M. (ed.), *Churchill by Himself* (2008).

——, *Churchill's Wit* (2009).

——, *The Patriot's Churchill: An Inspiring Collection of Churchill's Finest Words* (2010).

Macmillan, M.H., *War Diaries: the Mediterranean, 1943–1945* (1984).

Martin, J.M., *Downing Street: The War Years* (1991).

Midgley, P. (ed.), *The Heroic Memory: The Memorial Addresses to the Rt. Hon. Sir Winston Churchill Society, Edmonton, Alberta, 1965–1989* (Edmonton, 2004).

Muller, J.W. (ed.), *Churchill's 'Iron Curtain' Speech Fifty Years Later* (1999).

Norwich, J.J., *The Duff Cooper Diaries 1915–1951* (2005).

Paterson, M., *Winston Churchill: Personal Accounts of the Great Leader at War* (Newton Abbot, 2005).

Pottle, M. (ed.), *Lantern Slides: The Diaries and Letters of Violet Bonham Carter, 1904–1914* (1996).

——, *Champion Redoutable: The Diaries and Letters of Violet Bonham Carter, 1914–1945* (1998).

——, *Daring to Hope: The Diaries and Letters of Violet Bonham Carter, 1946–1969* (2000).

Richardson, S., *The Secret History of World War II: The Ultra-Secret Letters and Cables of Roosevelt, Stalin and Churchill* (1987).

Sand, G.W. (ed.), *Defending the West: The Truman-Churchill Correspondence 1945–1960* (2004).

Soames, M., *A Churchill Family Album* (1982).

——, *Winston Churchill: His Life as a Painter* (1990).

——, *Speaking for Themselves: The Personal Letters of Winston and Clementine Churchill* (1998).

Stansky, P. (ed.), *Churchill: A Profile* (1973).

Woods, F. (ed.), *Young Winston's Wars: the Original Despatches of W.S. Churchill War Correspondent 1897–1900* (1972).

——, *Winston Churchill War Correspondent 1895–1900* (1992).

——, *Artillery of Words: The Writings of Sir Winston Churchill* (1992).

Wrigley, C., *Winston Churchill: A Biographical Companion* (Oxford, 2002).

Zoller, C.J., *Annotated Bibliography of Works about Sir Winston S. Churchill* (2002).

Personal Testimony: Evidence from Those Who Knew Churchill Well

Amery, L.C.M.S., *My Political Life* (3 vols, 1953–5).

Ashley, M., *Churchill as Historian* (1968).

Avon, the Earl of, *The Eden Memoirs: Full Circle* (1960).

——, *The Reckoning* (1965).

Beaverbrook, Lord, *Politicians and the War* (2 vols, 1928, 1931).

——, *Men and Power* (1956).

Bonham Carter, V., *Winston Churchill as I Knew Him* (1965).

British Broadcasting Corporation, *A Selection from the Broadcasts Given in Memory of Winston Churchill, K.G., O.M., C.H.* (1965).

Browne, A. Montague, *Long Sunset: Memoirs of Winston Churchill's Last Private Secretary* (1995).

Butler, Lord, *The Art of the Possible* (1971).

Chandos, Lord, *The Memoirs of Lord Chandos* (1962).

Churchill, J., *A Crowded Canvas* (1961).

Churchill, S., *A Thread in the Tapestry* (1967).

——, *Keep on Dancing: An Autobiography* (1981).

Colville, J.R., *Footprints in Time* (1971).

———, *The Churchillians* (1981).

Cooper, A. Duff, *Old Men Forget* (1953).

Deakin, F.W.D., *Churchill the Historian* (Zurich, 1970).

de Gaulle, C., *War Memoirs* (English trans., 5 vols inc. documents, 1955–60).

Eade, C., *Churchill by His Contemporaries* (1953).

Graebner, W., *My Dear Mister Churchill* (1965).

Grigg, P.J., *Prejudice and Judgment* (1948).

Harriman, W.A., and Abel, E., *Special Envoy to Churchill and Stalin* (1975).

Haste, C. (ed.), *Clarissa Eden: A Memoir: From Churchill to Eden* (2007).

Hunt, D., *On the Spot* (1975).

Ismay, Lord, *The Memoirs of General the Lord Ismay* (1960).

Jones, R.V., 'Winston Leonard Spencer Churchill 1874–1965', in *Biographical Memoirs of Fellows of the Royal Society 1966*.

Jones, R.V., *Most Secret War* (1978).

Marchant, J. (ed.), *Winston Spencer Churchill: Servant of Crown and Commonwealth* (1954).

MacDonald, M., *Titans and Others* (1972).

Marsh, E., *A Number of People* (1939).

McGowan, N., *My Years with Churchill* (1958).

Macmillan, M.H., *The Blast of War* (1965).

———, *Tides of Fortune* (1969).

Menzies, R.G., *Afternoon Light* (1967).

Moran, Lord, *Winston Churchill: The Struggle for Survival* (1966).

Nel, E., *Mr. Churchill's Secretary* (1958).

Sherwood, R.E., *The White House Papers of Harry L. Hopkins* (2 vols, 1948, 1949).

Soames, M., *Clementine Churchill* (rev. edn, 2002).

———, *A Daughter's Tale* (2011).

Spears, E.L., *Assignment to Catastrophe* (2 vols, 1954).

Tedder, Lord, *With Prejudice* (1967).

The Observer, London, *Churchill by his Contemporaries* (1965).

Thompson, W., *Assignment Churchill* (1956).

Wheeler-Bennett, J.W. (ed.), *Action This Day* (1968).

Biographies, Critical Studies, Monographs

I have included in this section a number of studies strongly – in some cases vehemently – critical of Churchill. No stranger to controversy, he took pains to make out the best case for himself and did not expect to be exempt from the stern scrutiny of later generations.

Addison, P., *Churchill on the Home Front 1900–1955* (1992).

———, *Churchill: The Unexpected Hero* (Oxford, 2005).

Alkon, P.K, *Winston Churchill's Imagination* (Lewisburg, Pennsylvania, 2006).

Alldritt, K., *Churchill the Writer* (1992).

———, *The Greatest of Friends: Franklin D. Roosevelt and Winston Churchill 1941–1945* (1995).

Alter, P., *Winston Churchill: Leben und Überleben* (Stuttgart, 2006).

Ball, S., *Winston Churchill* (2003).

Bardens, D.C., *Churchill in Parliament* (1967).

Barker, E., *Churchill and Eden at War* (1978).

Barnes, A.J.L., and Middlemas, K., *Baldwin* (1969).

Batty, P., *Hoodwinking Churchill: Tito's Great Confidence Trick* (2011).

Bédarida, F., *Churchill* (Paris, 1999).

Best, G., *Winston Churchill* (2000).

——, *Churchill and War* (2005).

Berlin, I., *Mr. Churchill in 1940* (1949).

Birkenhead, the Earl of, *Churchill 1874–1922* (1989).

Blake, R., and Louis, W.R. (eds.), *Churchill* (Oxford, 1983).

Brendon, P., *Winston Churchill* (2001).

Bryant, A., *The Turn of the Tide* (1957).

——, *Triumph in the West* (1959).

Buchanan, P.J., *Churchill, Hitler and the Unnecessary War* (New York, 2008).

Buczacki, S., *Churchill and Chartwell* (2007).

Bullock, A., *Ernest Bevin* (vol. 2, 1967).

Callahan, R., *Churchill and His Generals* (Lawrence, Kansas, 2007).

Cannadine, D., and Quinault, R. (eds.), *Winston Churchill in the Twenty-First Century* (Cambridge, 2004).

Carlton, D., *Churchill and the Soviet Union* (Manchester, 2000).

Catherwood, C., *Winston Churchill: The Flawed Genius of World War II* (Berkeley, California, 2009).

Charmley, J., *Churchill: The End of Glory* (1993).

——, *The Grand Alliance: the Anglo-American Special Relationship* (1995).

Connell, J., *Auchinleck* (1959).

Day, D., *Menzies and Churchill at War* (rev. edn, 2001).

D'Este, C., *Warlord: A Life of Winston Churchill at War, 1874–1945* (2009).

Dilks, D.N., *"The Great Dominion": Winston Churchill in Canada 1900–1954* (Toronto, 2005).

Edmonds, R., *The Big Three: Churchill, Roosevelt and Stalin in Peace and War* (1991).

Feiling, K.G., *The Life of Neville Chamberlain* (1946).

Feis, H., *Churchill, Roosevelt, Stalin* (Oxford, 1957).

Folly, M.H., *Churchill, Whitehall and the Soviet Union* (Basingstoke, 2000).

Freudenberg, G., *Churchill and Australia* (Sydney, 2008).

Gilbert, M., *Churchill: A Life* (1991).

——, *In Search of Churchill* (1994).

——, *Churchill and America* (2005).

——, *Churchill and the Jews* (2007).

Gretton, P., *Former Naval Person* (1968).

Haffner, S., *Churchill, eine Biographie* (Munich, 2001).

Harris, K., *Attlee* (rev. edn, 1995).

Hastings, M., *Finest Years: Churchill as Warlord 1940–45* (2009).

Holmes, R., *In the Footsteps of Churchill* (2005).

Irving, D., *Churchill's War* (2 vols, 1987, 2001).

Jablonsky, D., *Churchill, The Great Game and Total War* (1991).

Jackson, A., *Churchill* (2011).

James, R.R., *Churchill, A Study in Failure* (1970).

Jenkins, R., *Churchill: A Biography* (2001).

Jenkins, S.C., *Winston Churchill – an Oxfordshire Hussar* (Witney, 2009).

Johnson, P., *Churchill* (2009).

Keegan, J., *Churchill* (2002).

—— (ed.), *Churchill's Generals* (1991).

Kennedy, J., *The Business of War* (1957).

Kersaudy, F., *Winston Churchill: Le pouvoir de l'imagination* (Paris, rev. edn, 2009).

——, *Churchill and de Gaulle* (rev. edn, 1990).

Kimball, W.F., *Forged in War: Churchill, Roosevelt and the Second World War* (1997).

Kinvig, C., *Churchill's Crusade: The British Invasion of Russia* (2006).

Knight, N., *Churchill: The Greatest Briton Unmasked* (2008).

Krockow, C., *Churchill* (rev. edn, Munich, 2001).

Lamb, R., *Churchill as War Leader* (1991).

Lash, J.P., *Roosevelt and Churchill, 1939–1941* (New York, 1976).

Larres, K., *Churchill's Cold War: The Politics of Personal Diplomacy* (2002).

Lavery, B., *Churchill Goes to War: Winston's Wartime Journeys* (2007).

Lawlor, S., *Churchill and the Politics of War 1940–1941* (Cambridge, 1994).

Leaming, B., *Churchill Defiant: Fighting on 1945–1955* (2010).

Lee, C. and Lee, J., *Winston and Jack: The Churchill Brothers* (2007).

——, *The Churchills: A Family Portrait* (2009).

L'Etang, H., *Fit to Lead?* (1980).

Lewin, R., *Churchill as Warlord* (1973).

Lovell, M.S., *The Churchills* (2011).

Lukacs, J., *Five Days in London* (1999).

——, *Churchill* (2002).

Macrae, C.S., *Winston Churchill's Toyshop* (Stroud, Gloucestershire, 2010).

Manchester, W., *The Last Lion* (2 vols, 1983, 1988).

Marder. A., *Winston Is Back: Churchill at the Admiralty 1939–1940* (1972).

McGinty, S., *Churchill's Cigar* (2007).

Meacham, J., *Franklin and Winston: An Intimate Portrait of an Epic Friendship* (New York, 2003).

Parker, R.A.C. (ed.), *Winston Churchill: Studies in Statesmanship* (1995).

Pearson, J., *The Private Lives of Winston Churchill* (1991).

Pelling H., *Churchill's Peacetime Ministry 1951–1955* (1997).

——, *Winston Churchill* (rev. edn, 1999).

Plokhy, S.M., *Yalta: The Price of Peace* (2010).

Ponting, C., *Winston Churchill* (1994).

Ramsden, J., *Man of the Century: Winston Churchill and His Legend Since 1945* (2002).

Reynolds, D., *In Command of History: Churchill Fighting and Writing the Second World War* (2004).

Rhys-Jones, G., *Churchill and the Norway Campaign, 1940* (Barnsley, 2008).

Richardson, C., *From Churchill's Secret Circle to the B.B.C.: the Biography of Lieutenant General Sir Ian Jacob* (1991).

Roberts, A., *Hitler and Churchill* (2003).

——, *Masters and Commanders* (2008).

——, *The Storm of War: A New History of the Second World War* (2009).

Robbins, K.G., *Churchill* (1992).

Rose, N., *Churchill: An Unruly Life* (1994).

Roskill, S., *Churchill and the Admirals* (1977).

Rowse, A.L., *The Later Churchills* (1958).

Russell, D.S., *Winston Churchill Soldier* (2005).

Sandys, C., *From Winston with Love and Kisses: The Young Churchill* (1994).

———, *Chasing Churchill: The Travels of Winston Churchill* (2003).

———, *Churchill Wanted – Dead or Alive* (2005).

Sainsbury, K., *Churchill and Roosevelt at War* (1994).

Schofield, V., *Wavell: Soldier and Statesman* (2006).

Sebba, A., *Jennie Churchill* (2007).

Seldon, A., *Churchill's Indian Summer: The Conservative Government, 1951–1955* (1981).

Stafford, D., *Churchill and Secret Service* (2000).

Stelzer, C., *Dinner with Churchill* (2011).

Stewart, G., *Burying Caesar: Churchill, Chamberlain and the Battle for the Tory Party* (1999).

Strawson, J., *Churchill and Hitler* (1997).

Smith, C., *England's Last War Against France: Fighting Vichy 1940–1942* (2009).

Taylor, A.J.P., et al., *Churchill: Four Faces and the Man* (1969).

Theakston, K., *Winston Churchill and the British Constitution* (2004).

Thompson, K.W., *Winston Churchill's World View* (Baton Rouge, Louisiana, 1983).

Thompson, R.W., *The Yankee Marlborough* (1963).

———, *Churchill and Morton* (1976).

Tilden, P., *True Remembrances of an Architect* (1954).

Toye, R., *Lloyd George and Churchill: Rivals for Greatness* (2007).

———, *Churchill's Empire: The World that Made Him and the World He Made* (2010).

Wheeler-Bennett, J.W., *King George VI: His Life and Reign* (1958).

Wilson, T., *Churchill and the Prof* (1995).

Young, J.W. (ed.), *The Foreign Policy of Churchill's Peacetime Administration 1951–1955* (Leicester, 1988).

Young, J.W., *Winston Churchill's Last Campaign: Britain and the Cold War 1951–1955* (Oxford, 1996).

Young, K., *Churchill and Beaverbrook* (1966).

Index

Index